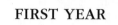

FIRST YEAR

LATIN

ROBERT J. HENLE, S.J.

LOYOLAPRESS.

CHICAGO

LOYOLA PRESS.
3441 N. Ashland Avenue
Chicago, Illinois 60657
(800) 621-1008
www.loyolapress.com

© 1958
Copyright 1945

Library of Congress Catalog Card Number: 58-10998

ISBN 13: 978-0-8294-1026-6
ISBN 10: 0-8294-1026-0

Printed in the United States of America.
19 20 21 22 TS 28 27 26 25 24

The book of exercises and readings here presented under the title FIRST YEAR LATIN is part of a complete and integrated four-year high-school Latin course and is to be used in conjunction with a companion volume, LATIN GRAMMAR, of the same series. In addition, workbooks to accompany FIRST YEAR LATIN and SECOND YEAR LATIN are available.

General intellectual values—not factual nor utilitarian—constitute the ultimate aim of this four-year course. The goals of linguistic training and humanistic insight are to be attained through mastery of the language itself and through the study of selected classics. The dominating objective of FIRST YEAR LATIN is a thorough mastery of forms, basic syntax, and vocabulary, as well as ability to read and translate simple sentences.

A few points of variance with many Latin series now in use might be noted. The author does not accept the principle that mastery should be subordinated to the presentation, especially in first year, of material interesting in itself and possessed of some utilitarian value. For a complete discussion of teaching for mastery the instructor should refer to the manual for the Henle Latin Series (first and second years). Such mastery implies habitual knowledge, lasting abilities, accuracy, sureness, and facility in use.

It is rather common practice in Latin textbooks to set down a limited vocabulary for mastery, but to employ many more words in the reading material. FIRST YEAR LATIN limits its vocabulary for use largely to its vocabulary for mastery, and this vocabulary, incidentally, is drawn largely from the Caesar readings that will be taken in second year.

The formal rather than the functional or direct method is favored in the learning of forms; that is, the paradigms are to be thoroughly memorized and then worked into active mastery by immediate and abundant exercise. The textbook provides generous exercises for private study and for class work, and the matter of one section is repeated in subsequent sections so that there is constant review. It is the teacher's responsibility to assign exercises that fit the needs of his particular class. Only those exercises marked "Essential" are required of all pupils.

It is common knowledge that first-year classes vary considerably in ability. Sufficient material to challenge the abilities of superior pupils is therefore included. Not every class, however, can be expected to complete the forty-two lessons in FIRST YEAR LATIN. Since this textbook is part of a four-year series, adequate provision has been made for classes that cover fewer lessons.

In all cases it is essential that pupils learn to the point of mastery the matter contained in Units One-Seven, or the first twenty-six lessons, in FIRST YEAR LATIN. The textbook for second year has been so constructed that, in addition to reviewing the essentials of first year, SECOND YEAR LATIN explains both new matter and topics that were introduced in Units Eight-Fourteen of FIRST YEAR LATIN. It is believed that all classes, no matter what their rate of learning may be, will find in this textbook a sufficient amount of matter to challenge their abilities and to prepare them adequately for the second year of Latin.

The LATIN PROGRESS TESTS (for first year and second year) may be used either as workbooks or for testing the mastery of pupils. They are objective, require little time, and are excellent for diagnosis and motivation.

The author gladly acknowledges his obligation to Mr. Henry A. Schaefer for the illustration on page 252; to Acme Newspictures, Incorporated, for the illustrations on pages 172 and 384; to G. Bell and Sons for the illustrations on pages 67 and 89; to The Bettmann Archive for the illustrations on pages 18, 26, 45, 106, 130, 152, 273, 379, 410, and 443; to *Compton's Source Materials* for the illustration on page 186, and to *Compton's Pictured Encyclopedia* for the illustration on page 189; to Ewing Galloway for the illustration on page 3; to International News Photos for the illustration on page 291; to the *Jesuit Bulletin* for the illustration on page 12; to Keystone View Company for the illustrations on pages 347 and 408; to the *Messenger of the Sacred Heart* for the illustration on page 299; to the *New World* for the facsimile of the signature of Pope Pius XII on page 20; to RKO Radio Pictures, Incorporated, for the illustration on page 110; to Underwood and Underwood for the illustration on page 406.

The improvements made in the 1958 printing of Latin Grammar, First Year Latin, and Second Year Latin will not be found to prevent the use of these books and earlier printings in the same classroom.

CONTENTS

ix

UNIT TWO

UNIT THREE

UNIT SIX

UNIT SEVEN

UNIT EIGHT

xiv

INTRODUCTION

To the Student

You are now beginning the study of Latin and you will continue it for two or more years. You want to make a success of it just as you do when you take up golf or bridge or build an airplane or work on a job. If you make a success of it, you will come to like Latin and to enjoy reading the great books written in that language. Besides, Latin will give you many things. It will teach you how to work intelligently and systematically; it will teach you what language—man's most wonderful and useful invention—is; it will teach you to speak and write better. You will develop habits of concentration and correct thinking and many other habits which you will be able to appreciate only after you have acquired them.

You have perhaps heard that Latin is hard. We have tried to apply in this book the old Roman principle of war: *Divide et impera*—"Divide and conquer." We have presented Latin in a series of easy steps. If you study each step day by day, Latin will become easier and you will get to like it. But you MUST study right from the beginning. Your knowledge of Latin is just like a building. If you don't put down the foundation strongly and firmly, it will be very hard to keep the third story where it belongs.

Your success in Latin will depend on three things: (1) You must study each day's lesson carefully right from the start. (2) You must learn to review for yourself so you won't forget what you have already learned. A good method is to write out a series of questions on each lesson and go over these each night at home before beginning your new lesson. Don't just *look* at the answers or *read* them. Make yourself *recite* the answers and then check them in the book. Gradually, you will have so much to review that you won't be able to go over it all each day. Then do it by turns, one section today and another tomorrow. But whenever

1

you find you cannot answer one of your questions, mark it down and review it specially every day for a week or so. If you do this regularly, you will soon find that Latin gets easier, and when you come to the examination, you won't have a lot to learn and you won't have to worry a bit. You will find hints on studying vocabulary on page 8 of this book. (3) You must do the exercises carefully. Don't try to get help on an exercise until you are really stuck. YOU LEARN BY WORKING OUT THE EXERCISES FOR YOURSELF, just as you learn to swim by blundering about in the water, not by watching someone else set a world's record in the pool. THE MORE EXERCISES YOU DO, THE MORE QUICKLY YOU WILL MASTER LATIN, AND THE EASIER IT WILL BE LATER ON. If you really want to learn, you will read and translate more Latin than your teacher assigns.

When your exercises are corrected, be sure to UNDERSTAND the corrections. Always try to learn WHY a thing is right or wrong. This is the way to develop your mind and to get a firm grasp on what you are learning. In class, too, be sure to understand explanations; when you don't understand, ask questions.

When you study at home, go some place where you will not be disturbed by other people or distracted by the radio. You simply waste time by studying without paying close attention to what you are doing. You will learn MORE in LESS time if you really concentrate on your work. You have an exercise to do. When you sit down to do it, DO IT. Don't fiddle with your papers, don't look out the window. That exercise is a job to be done and you are the one to do it—NOW. In this way you will learn how to concentrate, and the power of concentration is VITAL to any success. Great lawyers, doctors, engineers, and all successful men need and have the power to concentrate.

UNIT ONE

INTRODUCTION

To the right is a picture of a Roman soldier.

1. *He* is stationed in Gaul.[1]

2. *His* commander in chief is Caesar.

3. Caesar once praised *him* for his bravery in fighting against the Gauls.

If you look over these sentences, you will notice that the italicized words all MEAN the Roman soldier. However, they are all spelled in different ways—*he, his, him.* Why is this? Because in each sentence they have a DIFFERENT WORK to do, and the spelling is changed to show what work the words do.

In the first sentence *he* is the SUBJECT, the person about whom we are speaking. *He* is in the nominative case and has the spelling which is the sign of the SUBJECT.

In the second sentence *his* modifies *commander in chief* and tells us to whom the commander in chief belongs. *His* thus answers the question: Whose? We call this form, *his,* the possessive case because it expresses the possessor, the person to whom something belongs (e. g., *his* book, *his* house, *his* soul).

In the third sentence *him* is the object of the verb *praised;*

---

[1] Gaul was the ancient Roman name for that part of Europe which includes France, Belgium, Switzerland, and Germany west of the Rhine. See map, page 30. Northern Italy between the Alps and the river Po was called "Hither Gaul." Julius Caesar, the great Roman general (100-44 B. C.), brought most of Gaul under Roman control during the Gallic War (58-51 B. C.).

the action is done to *him*. This is the objective case, the case of the object.

If we were teaching a foreigner English and wanted to give him help in selecting the correct form of *he* for each sentence, we might line up all the different forms like this:

CASE	FORM	USE
Nominative	he	as subject
Possessive	his	to express the possessor
Objective	him	as object

This is called the DECLENSION of *he*. We have DECLINED the word *he*; that is, we have given in a simple, orderly way all its different spellings and uses.

Examine the declension of *he*. You will notice that one part of the word is the same in all forms: *h-*. This is called the STEM, the part which, in declension, REMAINS THE SAME. The last part of the word changes: *-e, -is, -im*; these letters are called the ENDINGS. They show what case the word is and what work it does in the sentence, whether it expresses the subject, the possessor, or the object.

If we were talking about TWO OR MORE soldiers, we would have to say *they, their, them*. This would be the PLURAL, which shows that the word means MORE THAN ONE. (When the word means a SINGLE ONE, it is SINGULAR. Thus *he* is singular.)

Our complete declension, in singular and plural, would look like this:

	CASE	FORM	USE
Singular	Nominative	h-e	as subject
	Possessive	h-is	to express the possessor
	Objective	h-im	as object
Plural	Nominative	th-ey	as subject
	Possessive	th-eir	to express the possessor
	Objective	th-em	as object

Our friend the foreigner would now have a guide to help him

choose the right word for any sentence. He would avoid saying such silly things as "Him is stationed in Gaul."

In English our nouns change very little in declension. We have only three cases, and even in these three our nouns have only slight changes in spelling. Not all nouns have the same endings. Some, like *son, dog, star,* form their plural by adding *-s: sons, dogs, stars;* some add *-es: brushes, glasses, boxes;* others make no change at all, like *sheep, deer, trout.* This would be very confusing to our foreigner. We could group all English nouns in classes for him with a model for each class; thus:

		FIRST DECLENSION	SECOND DECLENSION
	Nominative	son	brush
S.	Possessive	son-'s	brush-'s
	Objective	son	brush
	Nominative	son-s	brush-es
P.	Possessive	son-s'	brush-es
	Objective	son-s	brush-es

We could then tell him that all words like *son* form their cases with the endings of *son;* and so for the other groups.

Now this is just what is done in Latin, to make it easier for us foreigners to learn. All Latin nouns are divided into five main groups called declensions, and in these groups we have a model which shows us the proper endings to use. All we have to find out about a new noun is this: What declension does it belong to? This we can tell from the Latin case called the GENITIVE. The GENITIVE SINGULAR always tells to what declension a noun belongs. And therefore always be sure to learn the genitive singular.

LESSON 1: THE FIRST DECLENSION

1. THE DECLENSION OF *TERRA*

Open your GRAMMAR to No. 31. Here you see the declension of
TERRA. Terra is a model for all Latin nouns that belong to
the first declension. Look at the GENITIVE SINGULAR. It
ends in **-ae.**

> **ALL NOUNS WHOSE GENITIVE ENDS IN -*AE* ARE
> IN THE FIRST DECLENSION.**

The STEM of any noun is found by dropping the ending of
the Genitive Singular. Thus, genitive: **TERR-AE;** STEM:
TERR-.

A noun of the first declension is then declined by adding to
the STEM the ENDINGS shown for **TERRA.**

You notice that the first five forms are all singular; the rest
are plural—look at the MEANINGS.

There are five cases in each number. Study the MEANINGS
given for the cases; the USES we shall study very gradually so
they will not be too hard for you.

ASSIGNMENT: Memorize the declension of **terra** (GRAM-
MAR, No. 31).

Before you begin to study the vocabulary on page 7 your teacher
will explain the rules for quantity and accent given in the GRAM-
MAR, Nos. 9-13. Learn these rules and see whether you can tell
where the accent belongs in each of the words in the vocabulary.

Whenever nouns are given in vocabularies, both the nominative and genitive are printed. Be sure to learn the GENITIVE,
because it tells you to what declension the noun belongs. Can
you tell why all the words in the list are like **terra**?

6

VOCABULARY

terra, terrae	*earth* *land*
porta, portae	*gate*
Marīa, Marīae	*Mary*
nauta, nautae	*sailor*
victōria, victōriae	*victory*
silva, silvae	*forest*
glōria, glōriae	*fame* *glory*

RELATED ENGLISH WORDS

The following phrases contain English words related to some of the Latin words in the vocabulary: a *nautical* dictionary; a *sylvan* scene; the *portals* of the palace; rough *terrain*. Can you tell to which words they are related?

PORTA

HOW TO MAKE VOCABULARY STUDY EASY

1. Read the words after your teacher, being very careful to pronounce them just as your teacher does.
2. Look carefully at the genitive and the meanings; study them for a few minutes.
3. Place a piece of paper over the English and try to recite the English meanings. Don't look until you have really tried to remember them! Then do the same with the Latin. BE SURE TO LEARN EVERYTHING THAT IS GIVEN IN THE VO-CABULARY.
4. Repeat this several times before class.
5. Every day review some vocabulary before starting on your new lesson. If you learn each vocabulary very carefully and keep reviewing it, Latin will be easy. You will have *VICTŌRIA* over Latin and will gain the *GLŌRIA* which belongs to a good student.

EXERCISE 1

Decline the words in the vocabulary. Remember they are all like **TERRA**. Therefore:

1. Find the STEM by dropping the -ae of the genitive singular, thus: **glōri-ae**; stem: **glōri-**;
2. Add the ENDINGS of **terra**, thus: **glōri-a, glōri-ae, glōri-ae**, *etc.*

EXERCISE 2
[Essential]

Tell what cases these forms are and give the meanings:

1. terram	8. nautārum	15. porta
2. silvās	9. terrae	16. silvīs
3. portārum	10. victōria	17. victōriā
4. glōriam	11. nautae	18. terra
5. portās	12. victōriam	19. portīs
6. silvam	13. glōriae	20. nautīs
7. victōriae	14. Marīae	21. portā

22. Marīa	26. Marīam	30. silvā
23. terrārum	27. silvae	31. silvārum
24. terrā	28. terrīs	32. nauta
25. silva	29. glōria	33. portae

EXERCISE 3

1. How can you tell the difference between the nominative and ablative singular of the first declension?
2. How can you find the stem of a Latin noun?
3. How can you tell to what declension a noun belongs?

2. RULES FOR GENDER

In English gender is very simple. Nouns naming men or male animals are MASCULINE, as *John, man, sailor* (sailors are usually men), *bull, lion.* Nouns naming women and female animals are FEMININE, as *Mary, woman, waitress, cow, lioness.* Nouns naming things are NEUTER, as *book, lake, beauty, soul.*

BUT IN LATIN nouns naming things are sometimes masculine, sometimes feminine, sometimes neuter. Thus, **terra, ae,** is FEMININE although *land* is a THING and is NEUTER in English.

ASSIGNMENT: Learn the rules for the gender of nouns in the first declension, GRAMMAR, Nos. 32 and 33.

EXERCISE 4

Explain the gender of the words in the vocabulary on page 7.

3. USE OF VERBS

In Latin the pronouns *(I, we, you, he, she, it, they)*, when used as subjects of a verb, are not ordinarily expressed separately. THEY ARE CONTAINED IN THE *ENDING* OF THE VERB. Thus: ōrat means *he, she,* or *it prays. He, she,* or *it* is contained in the ending **-at.** Ōrant means *they pray. They* is contained in the ending **-ant.** The ending **-at** contains THREE

English pronouns. How can you tell which one to use? When we have been talking about a woman, and then say ōrat, translate *she prays.* If we have been talking about a man, then ōrat means *he prays.*

Use *he, she,* or *it* according to the person or thing of which the sentence speaks. (When you can't tell to whom the sentence refers, use *he.*)

Ōrat. *He prays.*
Ōrant. *They pray.*
Mariam vident. Ōrat.
They see Mary. She is praying.

When a NOUN is used as the subject, the pronoun is NOT translated in English.

Nautae ōrant. *The sailors pray.*

MARIA ORAT.

Maria ōrat. *Mary prays.*

Notice that in these sentences the subjects, **nautae** and **Maria,** are in the NOMINATIVE case.

RULE: THE <u>SUBJECT</u> OF A FINITE VERB IS IN THE <u>NOMINATIVE</u> CASE.

Notice that when the subject is singular—**Maria**—the singular *(he, she, it)* form of the verb, ōrat, is used; when the subject is plural—**nautae**—the plural *(they)* form of the verb, ōrant, is used.

RULE: A FINITE VERB AGREES WITH ITS SUBJECT IN NUMBER (AND PERSON).

HOW TO DIAGRAM A LATIN SENTENCE

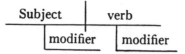

Note that the subject and verb are separated by a straight line carried below the horizontal line. Thus:

Nautae nōn ōrant.   Ōrat *(subject not expressed)*.

Nautae	ōrant
	nōn

( ) | ōrat

VOCABULARY

ōrat	*he, she, it prays*
ōrant	*they pray*
videt	*he, she, it sees*
vident	*they see*
nōn, *adverb*	*not*

RELATED ENGLISH WORDS

A *non*stop flight. The priest then read the *orations*.

EXERCISE 5
[Essential]
1. Say in English;
2. Diagram Sentences 1, 4, and 10:

1. Marīa ōrat. 2. Nautae ōrant. 3. Nauta ōrat. 4. Nautae nōn ōrant. *(Note.* When the sentence contains *not* we use the helping verb *do* in English. Thus: The sailors *do* not pray.) 5. Vident. 6. Nauta videt. 7. Marīa videt. 8. Videt. 9. Nautae nōn vident. 10. Nōn ōrat.

READING NO. 1

LATIN STILL LIVES!

THE LANGUAGE OF PRAYER

As the light of the sun moves westward it falls upon chapels and cathedrals, hospitals and camps, where in endless repetition the Sacrifice of the Mass is being offered to God. At every moment, somewhere in the world, a priest stands at the foot of an altar and says, in Latin, "Introībō ad altāre Deī," "I shall go in to the altar of God." Latin is the prayerful voice of the Roman Rite, of tens of millions of Catholics. In the universal offering of the Mass, the prophecy of the Old Testament is fulfilled: "From the rising of the sun to the going down thereof, my name is great among the gentiles."

THE LANGUAGE OF PAPAL TEACHING

When a priest in Chungking receives an official document from Rome, he finds it is written in Latin. From Rome Latin carries the decisions and instructions of the Pope to the whole world, to the bishops of Brazil, to Chicago and South Africa, to Zanzibar and England. Latin, as the official language of the head of Christendom, is today a living and universal force.

4. THE ACCUSATIVE CASE

The sailors praise Mary.

Nautae <u>Mariam</u> laudant.

In this sentence *Mary* is the DIRECT OBJECT of the verb *praise*. In English *Mary* is in the OBJECTIVE CASE. In Latin the objective case is called the ACCUSATIVE CASE.

RULE: THE DIRECT OBJECT OF A TRANSITIVE VERB IS IN THE ACCUSATIVE CASE.

HOW TO DIAGRAM A SENTENCE CONTAINING A DIRECT OBJECT

Nautae	laudant	Mariam

Note that the verb and the direct object are separated by a straight line that is *not* carried below the horizontal line.

We can tell the direct object in the model sentence by the ACCUSATIVE ENDING -AM. The verb usually, as in the model on page 13, is put LAST in the sentence.

> RULE: THE VERB USUALLY STANDS <u>LAST</u> IN THE SENTENCE.

VOCABULARY

laudat	*he, she, it praises*
laudant	*they praise*
prōvincia, ae	*province*

RELATED ENGLISH WORDS

A *laudatory* speech; a *provincial* dialect.

EXERCISE 6

1. Say in English;
2. Diagram Sentences 1, 3, 6, and 9:

1. Nautae terram laudant.   2. Nautae prōvinciam vident.
3. Marīa silvās laudat.   4. Nauta silvās videt.   5. Nauta portam videt.   6. Prōvinciam nōn laudant.   7. Nautae Marīam laudant.
8. Victōriam laudant.   9. Nautae glōriam laudant.   10. Marīam laudat.   11. Prōvinciam videt.

Note the position of **nōn**, an adverb modifying the verb **laudant,** in Exercise 6, Sentence 6.

RULE: ADVERBS USUALLY STAND <u>IMMEDIATELY</u> <u>BEFORE</u> THE WORD THEY MODIFY.

EXERCISE 7
[Essential]
Say in Latin:

1. They praise Mary. 2. The sailors see the province. 3. The sailors praise glory. 4. He sees the gate. 5. The sailor does not praise the province. 6. They praise the forest. 7. He sees the sailors. 8. She praises the victory. 9. They see the gate. 10. Mary does not praise the sailors. 11. The sailors see land.

TALKING LATIN NO. 1

When a Roman met *one* person and wished to say "Hello," he said "Salvē!"

When he met *two* or *more* persons, he said "Salvēte!"

Say "Salvē!" to your teacher tomorrow. That will show him you can *talk Latin already.*

SALVE   SALVETE

5. THE GENITIVE CASE

Mary's glory, **glōria Marīae**
The glory of the province, **glōria prōvinciae**
The sailors' victory, **victōria nautārum**

In these phrases the Latin genitive (underlined) translates the English possessive and the English *of*-phrases.

> RULE: THE POSSESSIVE CASE AND MANY ENG-
> LISH *OF*-PHRASES ARE TRANSLATED
> BY THE GENITIVE.

EXERCISE 8
[Essential]
Say in English:

1. glōria prōvinciae
2. victōria nautae
3. glōria Marīae
4. glōria nautae
5. silva prōvinciae
6. victōria nautārum
7. porta prōvinciae

EXERCISE 9
Say in Latin:

1. the sailor's victory
2. Mary's victory
3. the gate of the province
4. Mary's fame
5. the sailors' victory
6. the forest of the province

LESSON 2: THE SECOND DECLENSION

We are now ready to study the second group of Latin nouns—the SECOND DECLENSION. If you look at the vocabulary below, you will see that the nouns all have -ī in the genitive.

ALL NOUNS WHOSE GENITIVE SINGULAR ENDS IN -ī BELONG TO THE SECOND DECLENSION.

HOWEVER, SOME NOUNS OF THE SECOND DECLENSION HAVE -*US* IN THE NOMINATIVE, SOME HAVE -*UM*. Those nouns of the second declension whose nominative ends in -us are declined like **servus, servī** and are generally MASCULINE. Those whose nominative ends in -um are declined like **bellum, bellī** and are always NEUTER.

ASSIGNMENT: Learn the rules for gender in the GRAMMAR, Nos. 35 and 38.

1. THE DECLENSION OF *SERVUS*

VOCABULARY

servus, servī	*slave* / *servant*
fīlius, fīliī	*son*
Deus, Deī	*God*
amīcus, amīcī	*friend*
Chrīstus, Chrīstī	*Christ*
Chrīstiānus, Chrīstiānī	*Christian*
et, *conjunction*	*and*

RELATED ENGLISH WORDS

A *servile* spirit; *amicable* relations; with *filial* affection.

17

SERVI

ASSIGNMENT: Memorize the declension of **servus**, GRAM-MAR, No. 34.

EXERCISE 10

Decline all the nouns in the vocabulary (but decline **Deus** only in the singular). Remember:

1. Find the stem by dropping the ending of the genitive singular, -ī;

2. Add the endings of **serv-us, serv-ī,** *etc.*

EXERCISE 11

1. Tell what forms these are;
2. Give the English meaning:

1. Deus	3. fīliīs	5. amīcus
2. servōs	4. Chrīstum	6. Deum

7. amīcīs	15. fīlium	23. Chrīstiānōrum
8. servus	16. amīcī	24. fīliōs
9. Chrīstiānī	17. servō	25. Chrīstus
10. amīcōs	18. fīlius	26. servum
11. servōrum	19. Deō	27. Deī
12. amīcum	20. servīs	28. Chrīstō
13. fīliō	21. amīcōrum	29. amīcō
14. servī	22. fīliī	30. fīliōrum

EXERCISE 12
Translate:

1. glōria Deī
2. amīcus servī
3. amīcus Deī
4. victōria Deī
5. glōria Chrīstī

6. glōria Marīae
7. victōria Chrīstiānōrum
8. servus Deī
9. amīcus Chrīstī
10. Fīlius Deī

EXERCISE 13
[Essential]

1. Translate;
2. Diagram Sentences 2, 3, and 10:

1. Chrīstiānī ōrant.
2. Amīcī Deī Chrīstiānōs laudant.
3. Chrīstiānī Fīlium Deī laudant.
4. Chrīstiānī Marīam laudant.
5. Nautae servōs nōn vident.
6. Servī Chrīstiānōs laudant.
7. Chrīstiānī servōs Deī laudant.
8. Glōriam Deī vident.
9. Chrīstiānī Chrīstum laudant.
10. Marīa et Chrīstus amīcōs Deī laudant.
11. Deus terram et silvās videt. Nautās et servōs et Chrīstiānōs videt.
12. Chrīstiānī Fīlium Marīae laudant.

EXERCISE 14
[Essential]
Translate into Latin:

1. Christians praise the Son of Mary. 2. Mary sees the Son of God. 3. Christians praise the victory of Christ. 4. Mary praises God. 5. God praises the glory of Christ. 6. Christ praises the friends of Mary. 7. The servants of Mary praise Christ. 8. The friends of God praise Mary. 9. The sailors do not praise the victory of the slaves. 10. Mary sees the glory of God and the victory of Christ. 11. God sees the earth; He sees the forests.

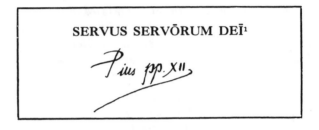

SERVUS SERVŌRUM DEĪ[1]

2. THE DECLENSION OF *BELLUM*

bellum, bellī, *war*

This word has **-ī** in the genitive. Therefore it is in the second declension. But its nominative ends in **-um.**

> ALL WORDS OF THE SECOND DECLENSION WHOSE NOMINATIVE ENDS IN *-UM* ARE NEUTER AND ARE DECLINED LIKE *BELLUM.*

ASSIGNMENT: Learn the declension of **bellum,** GRAMMAR, No. 37. Note that it is like **servus** except in three cases.

---

[1] Popes end their letters thus because Christ said: "Whoever wishes to be first among you shall be your slave" (Matthew 20:27).

HINT: IN <u>ALL NEUTER</u> NOUNS AND ADJECTIVES
THE ACCUSATIVE IS ALWAYS LIKE
THE NOMINATIVE.

VOCABULARY

bellum, bellī	*war*
caelum, caelī[1]	$\begin{cases} sky \\ heaven \end{cases}$
rēgnum, rēgnī	$\begin{cases} kingdom \\ royal\ power \end{cases}$
praemium, praemiī	*reward*
perīculum, perīculī	*danger*
imperium, imperiī	$\begin{cases} command \\ power \\ empire \end{cases}$

RELATED ENGLISH WORDS

A *belligerent* nation. An *interregnum*. A *premium* was offered.
His *Imperial* Majesty.

EXERCISE 15
1. Tell what forms these are;
2. Translate:

1. caelō
2. perīculōrum
3. perīculīs

4. imperiō
5. bellīs
6. perīculī

7. praemiīs
8. rēgnī
9. imperium

10. bella
11. rēgnō
12. praemia

EXERCISE 16
Translate:

1. rēgnum Chrīstī
2. perīculum servōrum
3. imperium Deī
4. praemia Chrīstiānī

5. porta Caelī
6. praemium Marīae
7. perīculum amīcī
8. victōria Chrīstī

---

[1] When Caelum is used to mean the Christian heaven the *c* will be capitalized.

EXERCISE 17
[Essential]
Translate; underline the direct objects:

1. Amīcī Deī rēgnum Chrīstī laudant. 2. Marīa praemium et victōriam Chrīstī videt. 3. Nautae caelum et terram vident. 4. Deus perīcula Chrīstiānōrum videt. 5. Deus bella nōn laudat. 6. Servī Chrīstī imperium Chrīstī laudant. 7. Marīa glōriam rēgnī Chrīstī videt. 8. Fīlius Deī praemia Marīae laudat. 9. Nautae perīcula bellī nōn laudant.

EXERCISE 18
REVIEW

1. Explain the gender of: (a) nauta, (b) porta, (c) rēgnum, (d) Chrīstus, (e) Marīa, (f) praemium.
2. Mark the accents on the words in Number 1 and give the rule for each.
3. What is the position of adverbs in Latin? Of verbs?
4. How can you tell the difference between the nominative and ablative singular in the first declension?

3. THE INDIRECT OBJECT

Chrīstus glōriam Deō dedit.
Christ gave glory to God.
Christ gave God glory.

In these sentences *to God* and *God* are INDIRECT OBJECTS. (*Glory* is the DIRECT object.) The indirect object expresses the person (less frequently the thing) TO OR FOR WHOM something is said, told, given, entrusted, *etc.*

RULE: THE INDIRECT OBJECT IS PUT IN THE DATIVE CASE.

HOW TO DIAGRAM SENTENCES CONTAINING AN INDIRECT OBJECT

Chrīstus	dedit	glōriam

                                                        Deō

VOCABULARY

dedit	*he, she, it gave*
dedērunt	*they gave*
gladius, ī	*sword*
sed, *conjunction*	*but*

RELATED ENGLISH WORD

The *gladiator* fought bravely.

EXERCISE 19
[Essential]
1. Translate;
2. Diagram Sentences 3, 5, and 9:

Warning. One Latin sentence has no indirect object. Can you find that sentence?

1. Chrīstus Deō glōriam dedit. 2. Servīs gladiōs nōn dedērunt sed nautīs gladiōs dedērunt. 3. Nautae amīcīs victōriam dedērunt. 4. Deus amīcīs Marīae praemia dedit. 5. Deus Fīliō rēgnum dedit. 6. Chrīstiānī glōriam Marīae et Fīliō Marīae dedērunt. 7. Deus Chrīstō terram dedit. 8. Nautae glōriam bellī laudant sed perīcula bellī nōn laudant. 9. Prōvinciam amīcō dedit. 10. Deus glōriam et victōriam Chrīstiānīs dedit. 11. Amīcō gladium dedit.

EXERCISE 20
[Essential]
Translate:

1. God gave a kingdom to Christ. 2. He gave a sword to the friend but not to the slave. 3. The Christians gave glory to God.

4. They did not give the province to the slaves. 5. The Son of God gave heaven to the Christians. 6. Sailors do not praise the dangers of war but they praise victory and the rewards of war. 7. God gave a kingdom and an empire to Christ. 8. The sailors see the sky.

EXERCISE 21

REVIEW

Complete these sentences and translate:

1. Chrīstiān............ ōrat. 2. Chrīstiānī ōr............ 3. Marīa De............ vid............ 4. Nautae terr............ vid............ 5. Servus Chrīstī Cael............ laud............ 6. Amīcī Deī Chrīst............ laud............ 7. Chrīstus De............ vid............ 8. De............ terrās vid............ 9. Fīlius Deī Deum laud............ 10. Marīa glōri............ Deō dedit. 11. Servīs gladi............ nōn dedit. 12. Chrīstiānī rēgn............ et imperi............ Chrīstī laudant.

4. USE OF PREPOSITIONS

Cum amīcō, *with a friend*

Cum is a preposition. It governs the word **amīcō**. (With *what?* With a *friend.*) Amīcō is in the ablative case.

IN LATIN SOME PREPOSITIONS ARE FOLLOWED BY THE ABLATIVE CASE, SOME BY THE ACCUSATIVE CASE.

Post bellum, *after the war*

Bellum is in the ACCUSATIVE case because the preposition **post** takes the accusative.

In prōvinciā, *in the province*

Prōvinciā is in the ABLATIVE because the preposition **in,** meaning *in* or *on,* takes the ablative case.

VOCABULARY

oppidum, ī	*town*
Gallia, ae	*Gaul*
Gallus, ī	*a Gaul*
Rōmānus, ī	*a Roman*
Rōma, ae	*Rome*
propter, *prep. w. acc.*	*on account of*
cum, *prep. w. abl.*	*with*
post, *prep. w. acc.*	$\begin{cases} after \\ behind \end{cases}$
in, *prep. w. abl.*	$\begin{cases} in \\ on \end{cases}$

NOTE

The abbreviations used are: *prep.*, preposition, *w.*, with. In vocabulary study always learn WHAT CASE A PREPOSITION GOVERNS.

RELATED ENGLISH WORDS

The French are famous for their *Gallic* wit. In the *post-bellum* years.

EXERCISE 22
[Essential]

1. *Translate;*
2. *Explain the cases of the nouns:*

1. in oppidō
2. in silvā
3. cum Gallō
4. cum Marīā
5. propter glōriam Rōmae
6. post victōriam
7. in silvīs Galliae
8. cum nautā
9. propter perīcula oppidī
10. in terrā
11. propter victōriam
12. in portīs Rōmae
13. cum Deō
14. propter praemia Gallōrum
15. in caelō
16. post victōriam Rōmānōrum
17. cum amīcīs
18. in silvīs
19. in portīs oppidī
20. cum Rōmānīs

21. in Galliā
22. propter glōriam bellī
23. in prōvinciīs
24. in prōvinciā
25. cum servō
26. post bellum
27. cum Rōmānō
28. in rēgnō
29. in oppidīs
30. cum fīliīs

31. propter perīculum
32. in silvīs et oppidīs
33. post perīculum
34. cum Chrīstō
35. in bellō
36. cum Chrīstiānīs
37. cum Gallīs
38. propter bellum
39. post oppidum
40. in portā

EXERCISE 23
[Essential]
Translate:

1. with Mary
2. after the war
3. with God

4. on account of the war
5. in the town
6. after the danger

ROMA

7. on account of the reward	16. in the forests
8. with the Son of God	17. on land
9. on account of the Christians	18. in the provinces
10. in heaven	19. with the slave
11. on account of the kingdom	20. in danger
12. with friends	21. on account of power
13. in Gaul	22. with a Gaul
14. with the Romans	23. behind the town
15. with the sailors	24. on earth

25. on account of the fame of Rome

5. THE PREDICATE NOUN

Chrīstus est Fīlius Deī.
Christ is the Son of God.

We have seen that transitive verbs take an object in the AC-CUSATIVE CASE. In this sentence, however, we have a different kind of verb: **est,** *is.* The verb *to be* (of which *is* is a form) is called a LINKING verb because it *LINKS* two words together. IT DOES NOT TAKE AN ACCUSATIVE OBJECT. A noun linked to the subject is in the NOMINATIVE case. Such a noun is called the PREDICATE NOUN. **Fīlius** is a predicate noun in this sentence and is therefore in the NOMINATIVE case.

> RULE: AFTER A LINKING VERB THE PREDICATE
> NOUN IS PUT IN THE SAME CASE
> AS THE SUBJECT.

HOW TO DIAGRAM A SENTENCE CONTAINING A PREDICATE NOUN

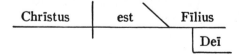

ASSIGNMENT: Learn the following forms of the verb *I AM* and their meanings:

sum	*I am*	sumus	*we are*
es	*you* (singular) *are*	estis	*you* (plural) *are*
est	*he, she, it is*	sunt	*they are*

FORMS OF THE VERB *SUM* MAY STAND ANY-WHERE IN THE SENTENCE.

EXERCISE 24
[Essential]

1. Translate;
2. Diagram Sentences 2, 4, and 7:

Warning. Some of the sentences in this exercise have no predicate noun.

1. "Estis fīliī Deī" (Words of Christ to His disciples).
2. Chrīstus est Fīlius Marīae. 3. Chrīstiānī sunt servī Deī.
4. Caelum est praemium Chrīstiānōrum. 5. Marīa est in Caelō cum Deō. 6. Bellum in prōvinciā est. 7. Sumus fīliī Deī.
8. Amīcus Deī es. 9. Gallī sunt in Galliā, sed Rōmānī nōn sunt in Galliā. 10. Gallī sunt in oppidīs et in silvīs. 11. Rōmānī gladiōs Gallīs nōn dedērunt. 12. Silvae in Galliā sunt. 13. Rōma nōn est in Galliā. 14. Propter bellum Gallī nōn sunt amīcī Rōmānōrum. 15. Gladiī sunt in oppidō. 16. Nautae estis.
17. Nautae in silvīs nōn sunt. 18. Cum amīcō in prōvinciā sum.
19. Silvae sunt post oppidum. 20. Nautae sunt Chrīstiānī. 21. In oppidō sumus. 22. Rōmānus servō praemium dedit. 23. Sunt Deī amīcī. 24. Chrīstiānus es sed servus Rōmānī es. 25. In Caelō nōn estis.

EXERCISE 25
[Essential]
Translate:

1. Christ is the Son of God.   2. Sailors see the sky but not the land.   3. Christians are servants of Christ.   4. We are friends of God.   5. Mary is with Christ in heaven.   6. The slaves are in the towns and in the forest.   7. Christians praise God on account of the glory of Christ.   8. The Gauls are in Gaul.   9. You are the sons of God.   10. You are a servant of Christ.   11. I am on the earth.   12. Heaven is the reward of the servants of Christ. 13. After the war—the rewards of victory!   14. Romans are in the provinces.   15. Mary is the "Gate of Heaven."   16. The servants are in the towns.   17. You are not in Gaul.

TALKING LATIN NO. 2

When a Roman thought something was pretty good (excellent, 'swell') he said, "Optimē!" or "Optimum est." But when something was pretty bad, he remarked in disgust, "Pessimē" or "Pessimum est." So when your teacher groans "Pessimē!" after your recitation DON'T SMILE HAPPILY.

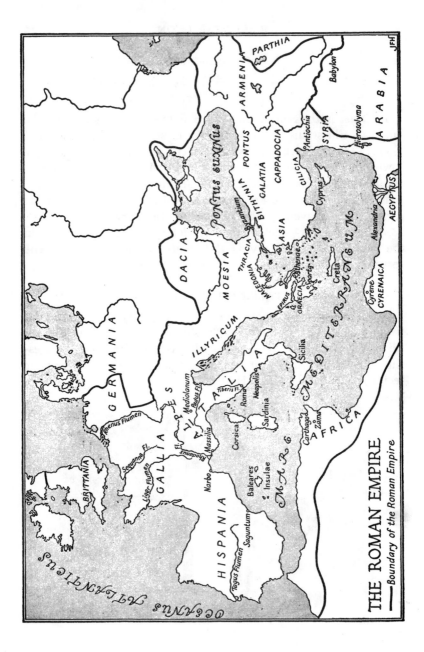

THE ROMAN EMPIRE
——— Boundary of the Roman Empire

6. USE OF *QUOD*, 'BECAUSE'

I am a servant of Christ because Christ is God.

Servus Chrīstī sum quod Chrīstus Deus est.

Quod, *because,* is a conjunction which joins a subordinate clause to a main clause. In this sentence *I am a servant of Christ* is the main clause; *because Christ is God* is a subordinate clause.

VOCABULARY

quod, *conj.*	*because*
itaque, *conj.*	{ *therefore* { *and so*
incolunt	*they inhabit*
vidētis	*you* (plural) *see*
vīcērunt	*they conquered*

NOTE

Quod and **itaque** NEVER change their spelling. **Itaque** is used at the beginning of a sentence as an introductory adverb.

EXERCISE 26
[Essential]

WHAT YOU SEE ON THE MAP

In tabulā[1] vidētis Rōmam et imperium Rōmānōrum. Rōmānī Rōmam incolunt. Prōvinciās imperiī Rōmānōrum vidētis. Galliam vidētis. Rōmānī Gallōs in bellīs vīcērunt. Gladiī nōn sunt in oppidīs Gallōrum quod Gallī post bellum gladiōs Rōmānīs dedērunt. Itaque post victōriās Rōmānōrum prōvincia in Galliā est. Prōvinciam Gallī et Rōmānī incolunt. Perīcula sunt in silvīs Galliae, quod Gallī nōn sunt amīcī Rōmānōrum. Gallī sunt servī Rōmānōrum, quod Rōmānī Gallōs vīcērunt. Itaque Gallī imperium Rōmānōrum nōn laudant, sed Rōmānī propter glōriam bellī imperium laudant.

---

[1] **tabula, ae:** *map.*

EXERCISE 27
[Essential]

Vidētis Chrīstiānōs. Vidētis Marīam et Chrīstum et Deum. Chrīstiānī in terrā sunt, sed Chrīstus et Marīa in Caelō cum Deō sunt. Perīcula Chrīstiānōrum in terrā sunt, sed praemia sunt in Caelō. Itaque Chrīstiāni in terrā ōrant. Marīa cum Chrīstiānīs ōrat quod Chrīstiānī fīliī Marīae sunt. Chrīstiānī Marīam laudant quod Chrīstus est fīlius Marīae. Chrīstum laudant quod fīlius Deī est.

READING NO. 2

LATIN, THE LANGUAGE OF ROME AND OF THE WORLD

We have seen that Latin is still widely in use in the Catholic Church. But who first spoke Latin and how did it become so important? Latin was the language of the people living in the region called Latium in ancient Italy. (See map, page 166.) Here was the city of Rome. There were dozens of other dialects spoken in Italy, but the language of Rome alone was destined to reach out into the world. For the Romans gradually conquered their neighbors; the soldiers from Rome marched to the southern shores as conquerors; their tread was heard in the Alps and in the African deserts. Gaul (the ancient name of France), Spain, northern Africa, the Mediterranean world—all were bound into one great empire under Rome.

So, just as Spanish and Portuguese have become the languages of South America because Spain and Portugal conquered and colonized there, Latin became the tongue of Gaul, Spain, northern Africa, and of Roman cities throughout the Empire. Even after the fall of the Roman Empire, Latin continued to be spoken in Europe. Throughout the Middle Ages it was the universal language of learning and science. Spanish, French, and Italian are all just modern editions of Latin and still show a close similarity to the ancient mother tongue. This is why one who knows Latin finds it easy to learn these modern languages.

For example, from the word **VICTŌRIA**, which you have had, the modern languages (even ones not derived from Latin) have the following derivatives or cognates:[1]

ENGLISH	Victory	United States, Canada, Great Britain. Ireland, South Africa, New Zealand, Australia
SPANISH	Victoria	Spain, Mexico, Central America, South America
PORTUGUESE	Vitória	Portugal, Brazil
FRENCH	Victoire	France, Belgium, Switzerland, French Canada
ITALIAN	Vittoria	Italy
RUMANIAN	Victorie	Rumania
DUTCH	Victorie	Holland
POLISH	Wiktorya	Poland

Read through the places listed here. Roman words—words that were heard thousands of years ago only in that small region called Latium—are now heard in all these places. Latin, the language of the Romans, has conquered far wider reaches of the world than Rome's generals ever dreamed of.

---

[1] Reprinted with permission from a chart prepared by B. L. Ullman for the American Classical League.

LESSON 3: THE THIRD DECLENSION

Here are some words which belong to the third declension:

NOMINATIVE	GENITIVE	MEANING
lēx	lēgis	*law*
homō	hominis	*man*
vēritās	vēritātis	*truth*
imperātor	imperātōris	*commander*

What do you notice about the endings of the nominative? Unlike the first and second declensions, the third declension has NO REGULAR ENDING in the nominative singular. How then will you be able to tell when a word belongs to this declension? (Give the general rule!)

> ALL NOUNS WHOSE GENITIVE SINGULAR ENDS IN *-IS* BELONG TO THE THIRD DECLENSION.

The STEM is found by dropping the **-is** of the genitive singular. Thus, genitive: lēgis, stem: lēg-.

1. GENDER IN THE THIRD DECLENSION

Nouns in the third declension may be masculine, feminine, or neuter. We shall study the masculine and feminine nouns first. You can tell whether a noun is masculine or feminine from the rules given in the GRAMMAR, Nos. 46-52.[1] Read these rules carefully and see whether you can determine the gender of the nouns in the vocabularies on pages 39 and 42. Now memorize the rules.

EXERCISE 28

Without looking in the GRAMMAR determine the gender for the nouns listed on pages 36, 44, and 51. Give the proper rules.

---

[1] There are many exceptions, to be marked *m.*, *f.*, or *n.* in the vocabularies.

2. RULES FOR NOUNS LIKE *LĒX* AND *PARS*

Look at Nos. 57 and 58 in the GRAMMAR. You will notice that two models are given for the masculine and feminine nouns of the third declension. They have exactly the same endings except in the nominative singular and in the GENITIVE PLURAL.

All masculine and feminine nouns of the third declension are declined like lēx EXCEPT THOSE in the GRAMMAR, Nos. 59-63. All masculine and feminine nouns covered by these rules are declined like **pars.**

ASSIGNMENT: Learn the rules for nouns declined like **pars,** GRAMMAR, Nos. 59-63.

EXERCISE 29

Which words on pages 44 and 47 are like lēx? Like **pars?**

3. THE DECLENSION OF *LĒX*

ASSIGNMENT: Memorize the declension of lēx, GRAMMAR, No. 57.

VOCABULARY

(All the words in this vocabuary are like lēx)

lēx, lēgis	*law*
rēx, rēgis	*king*
dux, ducis	*leader*
lūx, lūcis	*light*
homō, hominis	*man*
imperātor, imperātōris	*commander in chief* / *general*
vēritās, vēritātis	*truth*

RELATED ENGLISH WORDS

The *Duke* of York; a *regal* manner; the eternal *verities; Lucifer;* a *legal* dispute.

EXERCISE 30

1. Give the gender and the proper gender rules for each word in the vocabulary.
2. Decline each word in the vocabulary (but decline **vēritās** and **lūx** only in the singular). Follow these rules: (a) Find the declension from the genitive. (b) Find the stem by dropping the genitive ending. (c) Find the proper model (**lēx** or **pars**). (d) Add the endings as in the model.
3. Give the genitive plural of: (a) **lēx**, (b) **dux**, (c) **rēx**, (d) **homō**, (e) **imperātor**. Why are all these nouns like **lēx?**

EXERCISE 31

1. Tell what forms these are;
2. Translate:

1. lēgibus
2. rēgum
3. imperātōrī
4. ducum
5. lūce
6. ducēs
7. vēritātī
8. homō
9. imperātōrum
10. ducibus
11. hominum
12. vēritātem
13. rēgem
14. imperātōrem
15. lūcem
16. hominibus
17. duce
18. vēritāte
19. homine
20. rēgibus
21. lēgī

EXERCISE 32
Translate:

1. lūx vēritātis
2. rēx rēgum
3. rēx hominum
4. lēx Deī
5. rēx Chrīstiānōrum
6. propter lēgem Deī
7. cum rēge
8. propter vēritātem

EXERCISE 33
Translate:

1. behind the king
2. for men
3. the light of truth
4. for the commander in chief
5. on account of the law of Christ
6. with the leader of the Gauls

EXERCISE 34
[Essential]
1. Translate;
2. Underline the direct objects:

1. Chrīstus est Rēx Rēgum. 2. Hominēs lūcem vident.
3. Nautae sunt hominēs. (Why is **hominēs** nominative?)
4. Chrīstiānī vēritātem Chrīstī laudant. 5. Lūx in silvīs nōn
est. 6. Rōmānī lēgem et vēritātem Chrīstī nōn laudant. 7. Imperātōrēs Rōmānōrum Gallōs vīcērunt. 8. Gallōrum ducēs lēgem
et imperium Rōmānōrum nōn laudant. 9. Chrīstus est Rēx hominum quod Deus est. 10. Dux Rōmānōrum in Galliā est quod
bellum est in Galliā. (Explain the use of **quod.**) 11. Rōmānī
imperātōrī et ducibus praemia dedērunt quod Gallōs vīcērunt.
(Explain the case of **ducibus.**) 12. Rōmānī ducēs et rēgēs Gallōrum vīcērunt.

EXERCISE 35
Translate:

1. The commander in chief does not praise the leaders of the
Gauls. 2. Christ is the Light of Men because He gave men truth.
3. The Gauls do not praise the laws of the Romans. 4. Christ is
the King of Kings. 5. The leaders of the Romans are in Gaul.
And so the kings of the Gauls are servants of the Romans. 6. The
general sees the dangers of the war.

4. APPOSITIVES

Christ, the Son of God, is the King of Kings.
Chrīstus, Fīlius Deī, est Rēx Rēgum.

Christians praise Christ, the Son of God.
Chrīstiānī Chrīstum, Fīlium Deī, laudant.

In these sentences the word *Son* is a noun which is used to
explain the word *Christ.* Such a noun is said to be in APPOSI-
TION to the noun it explains and is called an APPOSITIVE.

Son is in apposition to *Christ* and is an appositive. Fīlius is in apposition to Chrīstus and is an appositive. An appositive is frequently set off by commas. Note that Chrīstus is in the nominative case because it is the subject of the sentence and that FĪLIUS IS IN THE SAME CASE; that Chrīstus is singular and FĪLIUS IS IN THE SAME NUMBER. In the same manner, explain the case and number of Fīlium in the second sentence above. How do you explain the case of imperator? (See illustration.)

CAESAR, IMPERATOR ROMANORUM

RULE: AN APPOSITIVE AGREES WITH ITS NOUN IN NUMBER AND CASE.

VOCABULARY

Caesar, Caesaris	*Caesar*
salūs, salūtis	*safety* / *welfare* / *salvation*
vōx, vōcis	*voice* / *cry*
audīvit	*he, she, it heard*

NOTE

What is the gender of Caesar, vōx, and salūs? Why? Why is vōx like lēx?

RELATED ENGLISH WORDS

Salutary advice; *vocal* lessons; the *Kaiser*.

HOW TO DIAGRAM A SENTENCE CONTAINING AN APPOSITIVE

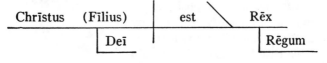

EXERCISE 36
[Essential]

1. Translate;
2. Diagram Sentences 2, 3, and 7:

1. Gallī Caesarī, imperātōrī Rōmānōrum, praemia nōn dedērunt. 2. Servus vōcem Caesaris imperātōris audīvit. 3. Deus, Rēx Caelī et terrae, salūtem hominibus dedit. 4. Caesar, dux Rōmānōrum, vōcēs Gallōrum in silvīs audīvit. 5. Propter salūtem hominum Chrīstus est homō. 6. Chrīstus, Fīlius Deī, est Fīlius Marīae. 7. Gallī, servī Rōmānōrum, Rōmānōs nōn laudant. 8. Chrīstiānī Chrīstum, Fīlium Marīae, laudant.

> Sānctus Jōannēs,[1] Chrīstī servus,
> vōcem Chrīstī audīvit:
> "Ego[2] sum Via[3] et Vēritās et Vīta."[4]

EXERCISE 37
Complete and translate:

1. Chrīstus, Rē............ hominum, in Caelō est. 2. Salūs hominum in Chrīstō, Fīli............ Deī, est. 3. Caesar, imperāt............ Rōmānōrum, in Galliā est. 4. Vōx Chrīstī, Fīli............ Deī, est vōx Deī. 5. Rōmānī Caesarem imperāt............ laudant.

---

[1] **Sānctus Jōannēs:** *Saint John; i.e.,* St. John the Evangelist, one of the twelve Apostles, the author of the Fourth Gospel. The sentence quoted was spoken by Christ at the Last Supper the night before He died.
[2] **Ego:** *I.*
[3] **Via, ae:** *the Way.*
[4] **Vīta, ae:** *the Life.*

EXERCISE 38

[Essential]

Translate:

1. Christ, the Son of God, is man on account of the salvation of men. 2. He heard the voice of Christ, the son of Mary. 3. Christ, the Son of God, is the King of Kings. 4. God gave a kingdom to Christ, the friend of men. 5. Christians praise Christ, the King and friend of men. 6. Caesar, the general of the Romans, heard the cries of the Gauls. 7. On account of the safety of the province Caesar, the commander in chief, is in Gaul.

EXERCISE 39

Name in Latin the objects pictured here:

EXERCISE 40

1. Tell what forms these are;
2. Translate:

1. imperātōrum	5. rēgum	9. hominum	13. fīliīs
2. Rōmānōrum	6. rēgnum	10. ducī	14. bellīs
3. amīcum	7. vēritātem	11. amīcī	15. lūcis
4. perīculum	8. Chrīstum	12. hominī	16. lēgis

5. THE EXPLETIVE *THERE*

There are dangers in Gaul.

There is a king in Gaul.

In these sentences *there* is an expletive. It merely introduces the sentence. The real subjects are *dangers* and *king*.

Do not confuse the EXPLETIVE *there* with the ADVERB *there,* as in the sentence, "Were you *there?*" In this sentence *there* is an adverb meaning *in that place.*

The expletive *there* is NOT TRANSLATED in Latin. *There is* and *there are* are expressed in Latin by EST or SUNT. *There* is not translated. Thus:

<u>Sunt</u> perīcula in Galliā.

<u>Est</u> rēx in Galliā.

VOCABULARY

virtūs, virtūtis	{ *courage* *virtue*
mīles, mīlitis	*soldier*
pāx, pācis	*peace*
via, ae	{ *road* *way*
populus, ī	{ *people* *nation*
mūnīvērunt	{ *they fortified* *they constructed* (*w.* viam *or* viās)

NOTE

1. To what declensions do the nouns in the vocabulary belong?
What gender are they? Why?

2. **Mūnīvērunt** means *they constructed* ONLY when it has
viam or **viās** for its object. Otherwise it means *they fortified*.

RELATED ENGLISH WORDS

Military measures. *Pacific* intentions. *Popular* government. He
came *via* the Panama Canal.

PROVERB

VŌX POPULĪ, VŌX DEĪ [1]

EXERCISE 41
[Essential]

Translate:

1. Sunt perīcula in silvīs Galliae. 2. Nōn est pāx in Galliā
quod Caesar cum mīlitibus in Galliā est. 3. Sunt viae in prōvinciā. 4. Populus ducem mīlitum propter virtūtem laudat.
5. Rōmānī viās in prōvinciā mūnīvērunt. 6. Est pāx in Caelō.
7. Sunt Chrīstiānī in Caelō. 8. In pāce et in bellō Chrīstiānī
ōrant. 9. Sunt mīlitēs in viā. 10. Caesar mīlitibus praemia virtūtis dedit quod Gallōs vīcērunt. 11. Ducēs Gallōrum oppida
mūnīvērunt.

EXERCISE 42
[Essential]

Translate:

1. There are roads in Gaul. 2. There is a war in the province.
3. There are soldiers in the forest. 4. The Romans constructed
roads. 5. There is not peace in Gaul because Caesar and the
soldiers are in Gaul. 6. On account of the courage of the soldiers

---

[1] In proverbs forms of the verb *to be* (**est, sunt,** *etc.*) are frequently omitted.
They should be supplied in the translation.

there is peace in the province.　7. They fortified the towns on account of the people's danger.　8. Christ is the Way and the Truth.　9. They praise the virtue of the nation.

TALKING LATIN NO. 3

When the Romans answered a question, they either repeated the sentence (with or without **nōn**) or used single words like our *yes* and *no*: **ita**, *thus, so,* **certē**, *certainly,* **minimē**, *least of all, by no means.* Your classroom conversation can be made very interesting by the use of these words. For example:

TIME: TODAY

TEACHER. "Did you do your homework?"
YOU *(brightly).* "Ita!"
TEACHER. "Is it all correct?"
YOU *(still brightly).* "Certē!"

TIME: TOMORROW

YOU. "Did you correct our homework?"
TEACHER *(not too brightly).* "Ita."
YOU. "Was mine correct?"
TEACHER *(grimly).* "MINIMĒ!"

6. THE DECLENSION OF *PARS*

ASSIGNMENT: Review the rules in GRAMMAR, Nos. 59-63. Learn the declension of **pars**, No. 58. Note that it is like **lēx** except in the nominative singular and the GENITIVE PLURAL.

VOCABULARY

pars, partis	*part*
collis, collis, *m.*	*hill*
hostis, hostis	*enemy* (in war)
gēns, gentis	*tribe*
caedēs, caedis	*slaughter*

NOTE

The plural of **hostis** is often used to translate the English singular *enemy*. **Collis** is an exception to the rules for gender; notice that it is masculine.

RELATED ENGLISH WORDS

The *gentiles; hostile* actions.

EXERCISE 43

1. Give the gender and the gender rule for each word in the vocabulary.
2. Give the genitive plural of each word in the vocabulary.
3. Decline (a) pars, (b) hostis, (c) gēns.

PĀX CHRĪSTĪ IN RĒGNŌ CHRĪSTĪ

(Motto of Pope Pius XI)

EXERCISE 44

1. Tell what forms the nouns are;
2. Translate:

1. pars hostium
2. propter caedem gentium
3. cum hostibus
4. in colle
5. post caedem Gallōrum
6. in oppidīs hostium
7. in collibus
8. rēx gentium
9. post collem
10. gentibus
11. post caedem hostium

HOSTES ROMANORUM

EXERCISE 45
Translate:

1. on account of the welfare of the tribes
2. part of the leaders and soldiers
3. with the general of the enemy
4. on account of the slaughter of the men
5. on the hill
6. with the enemy
7. in the way
8. the leaders of the tribes

EXERCISE 46
[Essential]

1. Translate;
2. Diagram Sentences 1, 2, 7, and 9:

1. Ducēs Rōmānōrum hostēs in colle vīcērunt. 2. Propter caedem mīlitum bellum in Galliā est. 3. Sunt perīcula in Galliā quod Gallī hostēs Rōmānōrum sunt. 4. Chrīstus est rēx populōrum et salūs hominum quod Deus est. 5. Pars hostium in silvīs est, sed pars est in colle. 6. In Galliā sunt collēs et silvae et oppida et viae. 7. Rōmānī rēgēs et gentēs Galliae vīcērunt. 8. Propter salūtem populī et pācem prōvinciārum Rōmānī viās mūnīvērunt. 9. Hominēs virtūtem et vēritātem laudant. 10. Post caedem hostium Caesar mīlitēs propter virtūtem laudat.

EXERCISE 47
[Essential]
Translate:

1. Part of the enemy is in the towns, but part is on the hill. 2. On account of the slaughter of the leaders of the tribe, the Gauls do not praise Caesar. 3. Christ is the King of tribes and nations. 4. There are hills behind the town. 5. After a victory there is a slaughter of part of the leaders of the tribe. 6. Part of the enemy is in the hills and forests.

EXERCISE 48
REVIEW

1. How can you tell the difference between the nominative singular and the ablative singular of the first declension?

2. Give the gender and the proper gender rule for:

nauta	lēx	Chrīstus
praemium	homō	vēritās

3. Translate, and give the rule for the case of the italicized words:

Chrīstus, *Fīlius* Deī, glōriam et *praemium amīcīs* Deī dedit.

7. REVIEW OF NOUNS LIKE *LĒX* AND *PARS*

Review GRAMMAR, Nos. 45-63. Review vocabulary, page 36.

VOCABULARY

frāter, frātris (frātrum)	*brother*
pater, patris (patrum)	*father*
māter, mātris (mātrum)	*mother*
mōns, montis, *m.*	*mountain*
clāmor, clāmōris	$\begin{cases} shouting \\ shout \end{cases}$
prīnceps, prīncipis	$\begin{cases} chief \\ leading\ man \end{cases}$
occīdērunt	*they killed*

NOTE

1. The genitive plural of **pater, māter, frāter** is put in parentheses to remind you that these words are exceptions to the rule for **-ium** words.

2. Notice that **mōns** is an exception to the gender rules.

RELATED ENGLISH WORDS

Paternal care; the crown *prince;* *maternal* affection; *clamorous* demands; *fraternal* love.

EXERCISE 49

1. Give the rules for gender for masculine and feminine nouns of the third declension. Give the gender of the third declension nouns in the vocabulary.

2. When are masculine and feminine nouns of the third declension declined like lēx? Like pars?

EXERCISE 50
Identify these forms:

1. oppidum
2. montium
3. nautārum
4. amīcōrum
5. mīlitum
6. mātrum
7. prīncipum
8. gentium
9. clāmōrum

EXERCISE 51
[Essential]

1. *Tell what case these nouns are;*
2. *Translate;*
3. *Give their nominative and genitive singular and their gender;*
4. *Give the genitive plural of all italicized words:*

1. propter virtūtem mīlitum
2. pāx populōrum et gentium
3. propter clāmōrem hostium
4. post caedem patrum et mātrum
5. propter lūcem et vēritātem Chrīstī
6. cum *imperātōre* Rōmānōrum
7. propter salūtem frātrum
8. in *colle*
9. in *montibus*
10. post *ducem*
11. cum *rēge*
12. *vōcēs* hominum
13. cum *parte* mīlitum
14. cum Caesare

NOTE ON READING LATIN

When you read a Latin sentence you have to puzzle out the meaning. Perhaps you look for the subject and the verb and translate them into English and so gradually find out what the Latin means. But a Roman boy or girl did not have to do this; they could UNDERSTAND the Latin words at once and IN

THE ORDER in which they were spoken or written. They read Latin just as you read English.

Now you can learn to read Latin that way too. It may take you a long time, but if you start now in the right way you will eventually be able to read Latin WITHOUT EVER THINK-ING OF ENGLISH WORDS. But it takes a lot of the right kind of practice. A football coach makes a boy hold a ball in a certain way, throw it in a certain way—over and over again—until the boy learns how to do it naturally, quickly, and correctly. So you too must practice the right way of reading Latin.

Now here is the way to practice reading Latin.

1. First read each Latin sentence slowly and thoughtfully, trying to understand it. At first you won't understand a thing. But do this each time anyway.

2. Then work out in translation all the words and phrases you didn't understand. At first you will have to work out the whole sentence.

3. Then REREAD the sentence several times, trying to put the MEANING into the Latin and to understand the Latin without thinking of English words. Do this over and over again until you UNDERSTAND the Latin in the Latin order. It will help to read the sentence aloud and to put as much meaning into your voice as possible. (Be sure to pronounce the words correctly!)

If you do this regularly NOW, Latin later on will be much easier and you will have the satisfaction of reading it quickly and easily. Try out this method on Exercise 52.

EXERCISE 52

1. Frātrēs Estis

Chrīstus est rēx hominum sed est frāter hominum, et Deus est rēx hominum sed est pater hominum. Itaque hominēs sunt frā-trēs. Itaque bellum est caedēs frātrum. Itaque Deus et Chrīstus bellum nōn laudant.

2. Caedēs Gallōrum

Rōmānī partem prīncipum Gallōrum occīdērunt. Itaque Deus clāmōrem mātrum et patrum et frātrum in silvīs et montibus Galliae audīvit.

3. In Galliā

In Galliā sunt silvae et montēs et collēs. Sunt oppida in collibus, sed pars gentium Gallōrum montēs et silvās incolunt.

4. Chrīstus, Dux Hominum

Chrīstus est dux hominum quod vēritātem et lēgem et lūcem hominibus dedit. Chrīstus est "Via" et "Vēritās."

5. "Our Tainted Nature's Solitary Boast"—Wordsworth

Marīa est Māter Chrīstī. Sed Chrīstus est Deus quod Fīlius Deī Patris est. Itaque Marīa est Māter Deī. Marīam, Mātrem Deī, Chrīstiānī laudant. Marīa est māter hominum quod Chrīstus in cruce[1] Marīam hominibus dedit. Itaque Chrīstiānī sunt fīliī et servī Marīae. Marīa est Porta Caelī.

MĪLES CHRĪSTĪ SUM

(Motto of the Archbishop of Indianapolis)

EXERCISE 53
[Essential]

1. He heard the shouting of the leading men. 2. They killed the chiefs of the tribe. 3. There are dangers in the mountains. 4. The general praises the mothers and fathers of the soldiers. 5. The brothers are with Caesar in Gaul. 6. They fortified the hills on account of the war. 7. The Romans constructed roads in the mountains.

---

[1] in cruce: *on the cross.*

8. THE DECLENSION OF *FLŪMEN*

VOCABULARY

flūmen, flūminis	*river*
iter, itineris, *n.*	$\begin{cases} journey \\ march \\ route \end{cases}$
corpus, corporis, *n.*	*body*
vulnus, vulneris, *n.*	*wound*
agmen, agminis	$\begin{cases} column \text{ (of soldiers)} \\ army \text{ (on the march)} \end{cases}$
nōmen, nōminis	*name*

RELATED ENGLISH WORDS

Corporal needs. An *itinerant* salesman. We *nominated* him for president.

To what declension do all the words in the vocabulary belong? To determine their genders study the rules, GRAMMAR, Nos. 51-52.

Without looking in the GRAMMAR see whether you can work out the declension of **flūmen** from the following hints:

1. **Flūmen** is declined exactly like **lēx** except in the nominative and accusative, singular and plural.

2. In all neuter nouns the accusative is always like the nominative.

3. The nominative singular of **flūmen** you know from the vocabulary. The nominative plural is **flūmin-a.**

ASSIGNMENT: Now compare your declension with the one in GRAMMAR, No. 64. Learn the declension of **flūmen** and decline the words in the vocabulary.

EXERCISE 54

1. Tell what forms these are;
2. Translate:

1. flūmina
2. in itinere
3. propter nōmen
4. in nōmine Patris

5. propter nōmen Chrīstī
6. nōminum
7. nōmen patris
8. nōmine
9. flūminibus
10. in flūmine
11. in agmine

12. agmina
13. in nōmine Deī
14. vulnera mīlitis
15. vulneribus
16. iter hostium
17. vulnerum
18. corporibus

EXERCISE 55
Translate:

1. in the river
2. on account of the wounds
3. on the journey
4. in the column
5. in the name of Mary
6. in the body
7. with the army

8. on the march
9. after the journey
10. the name of the river
11. on account of the law
12. with the generals
13. the safety of the tribes
14. on the mountain

EXERCISE 56
[Essential]
Translate:

1. Propter vulnera mīles in agmine nōn est. 2. Imperātor vulnera mīlitum videt. 3. Sunt corpora in flūmine. 4. In Galliā sunt flūmina et silvae. 5. Rōmānī in itinere sunt. 6. Sunt hostēs in silvīs et in montibus. Itaque in perīculō sumus. 7. Caesar agmen hostium videt. 8. Chrīstiānī nōmen Marīae laudant. 9. Agmen hostium in flūmine est. 10. Rōmānī Chrīstiānōs occīdērunt quod Chrīstiānī nōmen Chrīstī laudant.

EXERCISE 57
[Essential]
Translate:

1. There are bodies and swords in the river. 2. The column is in the mountains. 3. Christians pray in the name of Christ, the Son

of God.   4. There are brothers and fathers in the army.   5. There are dangers on the journey because the enemy is in the hills.   6. After the march they fortified the hill.   7. The route is in the mountains.   8. The sailors see the land and the sky.   9. The king prays on account of the welfare of the kingdom.

9. REVIEW OF THE THIRD DECLENSION

ASSIGNMENT: Review GRAMMAR, Nos. 45-64. Review vocabularies on pages 36, 39, 42, 44, 47, and 51.

VOCABULARY

mundus, ī	*world*
erat	*he, she, it was*
erant	*they were*

NOTE

Erat and **erant** (like **est** and **sunt**) sometimes mean *there was* and *there were.*

RELATED ENGLISH WORD

Mundane affairs.

EXERCISE 58

1. Give the genitive and gender and the gender rule;
2. Give the accusative singular;
3. Give the nominative plural;
4. Give the genitive plural:

nōmen	mīles	virtūs	vōx
rēx	caedēs	iter	frāter
vēritās	pater	prīnceps	corpus
māter	flūmen	pars	imperātor
mōns	clāmor	hostis	pāx
agmen	lūx	salūs	vulnus
dux	homō	collis	gēns

EXERCISE 59
[Essential]
Translate:

1. "Estis lūx mundī" (Words of Christ to His disciples). 2. Propter salūtem hominum Chrīstus erat in mundō. 3. Chrīstus lūcem et lēgem et salūtem et vēritātem hominibus dedit. 4. Caesar, imperātor Rōmānōrum, cum mīlitibus in Galliā erat. 5. Chrīstus est salūs mundī. 6. Servī nōmen rēgis laudant. 7. Agmen hostium in montibus erat. 8. Propter caedem prīncipum nōn erat pāx. 9. Propter vulnera mīlitēs in itinere nōn erant. 10. Deus, pater hominum, virtūtem laudat sed bella et caedem nōn laudat. 11. Dux vōcēs servōrum et clāmōrem mīlitum audīvit. 12. Post bellum corpora erant in collibus et in flūminibus, et imperātor clāmōrem mātrum audīvit. 13. Chrīstiānī frātrēs Chrīstī et mīlitēs Chrīstī sunt. 14. Rōmānī partem prīncipum Gallōrum occīdērunt. 15. Gentēs et populī Galliae imperium Rōmānōrum nōn laudant.

EXERCISE 60
[Essential]
Translate:

1. In the name of the king. 2. On account of the salvation of men. 3. On the journey. 4. In the mountains and the hills. 5. With the leading men of the tribes. 6. They see the light of the world. 7. After the slaughter of the leaders. 8. There were bodies in the road. 9. On account of the courage of the soldier. 10. He praises the virtues of Christians. 11. In peace and in war. 12. He heard the voice of the general. 13. They killed part of the enemy. 14. They praise the laws of the tribe. 15. Caesar gave rewards to the soldiers. 16. On account of the wounds of the chiefs. 17. The commander in chief heard the shouts of the fathers. 18. The column was in the river. 19. The mothers see the army. 20. On account of the welfare of the nation. 21. He heard the cries of the brothers. 22. God gave

truth to men. 23. On account of the safety of the column. 24. On the march. 25. There was a route in the mountains. 26. Caesar did not give swords to the chief. 27. The Gauls gave the commander in chief a reward.

EXERCISE 61

Write a Latin sentence for each of these pictures:

(Compare the Latin sentence beneath the picture on page 10.)

LESSON 4: THE FOURTH DECLENSION

1. THE DECLENSION OF *PORTUS*

Learn the declension of **portus, ūs,** GRAMMAR, No. 65, and the rule for gender, GRAMMAR, No. 66. Note that the **-us** is short in the nominative singular but long in other cases.

VOCABULARY

adventus, ūs	*arrival* / *coming*
equitātus, ūs	*cavalry*
exercitus, ūs	*army*
impetus, ūs	*attack*
metus, ūs	*fear*
spīritus, ūs	*breath* / *spirit*
portus, ūs	*harbor*
senātus, ūs	*senate*

NOTE

1. The **ūs** in the vocabulary stands of course for the full genitive form, *e. g.,* **adventus, ūs = adventus, adventūs.**

2. Be sure to note the difference between **portus, ūs** and **porta, ae.**

3. The Roman Senate was an aristocratic governing body somewhat like a combination of the United States Senate and the British House of Lords. In the time of the Republic the Senate was very powerful and really directed Roman policies. Under the emperors it had very little real power.

RELATED ENGLISH WORDS

The *port* of New York. The season of *Advent*. He gave the movement a strong *impetus*.

EXERCISE 62

1. Give the full genitive of the nouns in the vocabulary.
2. Decline the words in the vocabulary (but **adventus, equitātus,** and **metus** only in the singular).
3. Give the ablative singular of the words in the vocabulary.

EXERCISE 63

1. Tell what forms these are;
2. Translate:

1. post adventum Chrīstī
2. adventus Caesaris
3. in portū
4. portus prōvinciae
5. cum equitātū
6. in exercitū
7. post equitātum
8. exercitūs
9. in senātū

10. in prōvinciā
11. senātus
12. lēx senātūs
13. propter metum
14. amīcī senātūs
15. metus Caesaris
16. impetum
17. dux equitātūs
18. cum exercitū

EXERCISE 64

Translate:

1. on account of fear of danger
2. in the senate
3. with Caesar's army
4. after the coming of Christ

5. with the cavalry of the Gauls
6. the attack of the enemy
7. with the spirit of God
8. in the harbor

2. *IN* WITH THE ACCUSATIVE

The preposition **in** may take either the accusative or the ablative case. (You have already been using it with the ablative.)

1. Whenever there is MOVEMENT or MOTION expressed by the **in**, the ACCUSATIVE is used.

In silvam vēnit.
He came INTO the forest.

In hostēs impetum fēcērunt.
They made an attack AGAINST (UPON, ON) the enemy.

2. When there is no idea of movement or motion, the ABLA-TIVE is used.

In colle est.   **In silvā est.**
He is on the hill.   *He is in the forest.*

VOCABULARY

in, *prep. w. abl.*	$\begin{cases} in \\ on \end{cases}$
in, *prep. w. acc.*	$\begin{cases} in \\ into \\ against \\ upon \\ on \end{cases}$
nunc, *adverb*	*now*
autem, *conj., postpositive*	*however*
fēcērunt	*they made*
vēnit	*he, she, it came*
vēnērunt	*they came*

IN SILVAM VENIT.   IN HOSTES IMPETUM FECERUNT.

NOTE

Autem is postpositive. This means that it cannot stand first in a clause but must ALWAYS FOLLOW THE FIRST WORD OR PHRASE OF ITS CLAUSE. (See Sentence 4, Exercise 65.)

EXERCISE 65
[Essential]
Translate:

1. Nunc sunt portūs in Galliā. (Why is **Galliā** in the ablative?)
2. Post adventum Rōmānōrum bellum erat in Galliā.
3. Caesar cum equitātū in prōvinciam vēnit. (Why is **prōvinciam** in the accusative?)
4. Caesar autem cum exercitū nōn erat.
5. Propter metum Rōmānōrum Gallī in silvās vēnērunt.
6. Nautae portum vident.
7. Senātus Caesarem laudat quod Rōmānī hostēs vīcērunt.
8. Impetum in hostēs fēcērunt.

IN COLLE EST.   IN SILVA SUNT.

9. Post adventum equitātūs mīlitēs impetum in Gallōs fēcērunt.
10. Gallī in colle erant. In Gallōs autem Caesaris mīlitēs impetum fēcērunt. Ducēs et prīncipēs Gallōrum occīdērunt et Gallōs vīcērunt. Post bellum, propter metum Caesaris, hostēs impetum in Rōmānōs nōn fēcērunt.
11. Gallī senātum occīdērunt.

EXERCISE 66

1. *Tell what forms these are;*
2. *Translate:*

1. portibus	5. spīritū	9. portārum
2. portūs	6. portum	10. impetum
3. corpus	7. portam	11. rēgum
4. equitātū	8. portuum	12. metum

EXERCISE 67

CAEDĒS CHRĪSTIĀNŌRUM

Post Chrīstī adventum lūx vēritātis in mundō erat, sed Rōmānī amīcī Chrīstī et vēritātis nōn erant. Chrīstiānī autem amīcī Chrīstī erant. Erant multī[1] Chrīstiānī in imperiō Rōmānōrum. Erant in portibus et in oppidīs prōvinciārum et in silvīs et in montibus. Erant in exercitū et in equitātū et in senātū. Erant servī et mīlitēs; erant mātrēs et patrēs, Gallī et Rōmānī. Propter metum autem Chrīstī Rēgis et propter nōmen Deī Chrīstiānōrum Rōmānī Chrīstiānōs occīdērunt. Post caedem Chrīstiānōrum, Rōmānī nōn erant amīcī et servī Deī. Chrīstiānī autem, quod Rōmānī Chrīstiānōs propter lēgem Chrīstī occīdērunt, nunc in Caelō sunt cum Marīā et Chrīstō et glōriam Deī Patris vident.

Answer these questions:

1. What did Christ give men?
2. Did the Romans receive Christ's truth at once?

---

[1] multī: *many.*

3. Were there many Christians in the Roman Empire?
4. Where were they to be found?
5. What sort of persons were they?
6. What did the Romans do to the Christians?

EXERCISE 68
[Essential]
THE CONQUEST OF GAUL

The Gauls were not friends of Caesar and of the Senate. There-fore Caesar came into Gaul with the cavalry and the soldiers. The Gauls, however, on account of fear of Caesar, came into the forests and mountains. Caesar's army was in the forests of the enemy, and there were dangers. The Romans, however, made an attack upon the enemy. They killed the leaders and the leading men of the Gauls. They conquered the cavalry and the army of the Gauls, and fortified the harbors and the towns and the hills of Gaul. And so the Senate now praises Caesar on account of the fame of the war and the courage of the soldiers. On account of fear of the soldiers the Gauls are now friends and servants of the Senate.

EXERCISE 69
GOD IS EVERYWHERE

"Deus spīritus est." In Caelō et in terrā est. Mundum videt. Hominēs videt. Mīlitēs et nautās et servōs videt. Mātrēs et patrēs et frātrēs et fīliōs videt. Hominēs propter virtūtem laudat sed propter caedem nōn laudat.

LESSON 5: THE FIFTH DECLENSION

ASSIGNMENT: Learn the declension of **rēs**, GRAMMAR, No.
69 and the rule for gender, GRAMMAR, No. 70.

VOCABULARY

rēs, reī	*thing* *affair*
fidēs, fideī	*faith* *reliability* *faithfulness*
aciēs, aciēī	*battle line*
spēs, speī	*hope*
posuērunt	*they put* *they placed*

NOTE

When **posuērunt** is modified by an **in**-phrase, the **in** ALWAYS
takes the ablative.

RELATED ENGLISH WORDS

This is the *real* state of affairs. *Fidelity* to duty.

EXERCISE 70

1. Decline **aciēs** throughout.
2. Decline **spēs** and **fidēs** in the singular only.

EXERCISE 71

1. Tell what forms these are;
2. Translate:

1. in aciē
2. propter fidem
3. rēbus
4. propter spem
5. propter rem
6. rē
7. rērum
8. post aciem
9. aciēbus

EXERCISE 72
[Essential]
Translate:

1. Mīlitēs in aciē erant. 2. Rōmānī Chrīstiānōs propter fidem occīdērunt. 3. Mīlitēs spem victōriae in virtūte posuērunt. 4. Rōmānī in aciem hostium impetum fēcērunt. 5. Gallī aciem Rōmānōrum in colle vident. 6. In Chrīstō est spēs mundī. 7. Deus Chrīstiānōs propter fidem et virtūtem laudat. 8. Mīlitēs rem vident.

EXERCISE 73
[Essential]
Translate:

1. Caesar was in the battle line. 2. They praise the reliability of the soldier. 3. The Senate does not praise the affair. 4. The Gauls made an attack on the battle line of the Romans. 5. They placed hope in God.

EXERCISE 74
REVIEW

1. Give the genitive plural and the rule for:

   hostis   virtūs   homō   gēns

2. Give the gender and rule for:

   homō   nauta   pāx   equitātus
   rēs   māter   gēns   praemium
   fīlius   vēritās   servus   Rōmānus

LESSON 6: NOUNS WITH SPECIAL MEANINGS IN THE PLURAL

SOME LATIN nouns are used mainly in the plural but with a SINGULAR meaning:

castra, castrōrum   *camp*

impedīmenta, impedīmentōrum $\begin{cases} baggage \\ baggage\ train \end{cases}$

Some Latin nouns have different meanings in the singular and plural:

grātia, ae $\begin{cases} favor \\ influence \\ grace \text{ (in Christian Latin)} \end{cases}$

grātiae, grātiārum   *thanks*

cōpia, ae $\begin{cases} supply \\ abundance \end{cases}$

cōpiae, cōpiārum, f. $\begin{cases} troops \\ forces \text{ (a military term)} \end{cases}$

Learn also:

posuērunt $\begin{cases} they\ put \\ they\ placed \\ they\ pitched\ (w.\ \textbf{castra}) \end{cases}$

agunt   *they give* (*w.* **grātiās**)

NOTE

1. **Posuērunt** means *they pitched* ONLY when it has **castra** for its object. Remember that when an **in**-phrase modifies **posuērunt**, the **in** always governs the ablative.

2. **Agunt** means *give* ONLY when it has **grātiās** for its object.

3. **Grātia** is used in Christian Latin to mean *grace*, as in **grātia Deī,** *the grace of God.*

4. **Silva, ae,** as you know, means a *forest;* but it is generally used in the PLURAL and with the SAME MEANING as in the singular, like the English word *woods.*

5. Recall that the English singular *enemy* is often translated by the plural **hostēs.**

RELATED ENGLISH WORDS

A *copious* flow of water; *gratitude;* a *gracious* manner; a comfortable *position.*

EXERCISE 75
[Essential]
Translate:

1. Christians give thanks to God on account of the abundance of the grace of Christ.

2. On account of fear of Caesar the tribes did not make an attack on the camp.

3. There was a supply of swords in the camp.

4. The commander in chief was in favor with the king on account of the victory.

5. They made an attack on the camp.

6. The forces of the enemy were not in the province.

7. They put hope in the grace of Christ.

8. There was war in Gaul on account of the slaughter of the leading men. Caesar came into Gaul with troops and cavalry and a baggage train. The forces of the enemy were on a hill. The Romans, however, pitched camp behind the hill. The Gauls on account of fear of Caesar did not make an attack upon the camp. The Romans, however, made an attack on the Gauls. The Gauls placed hope in the cavalry, but the Romans killed the cavalry of the Gauls and captured[1] the hill. They captured[1] the leaders and the camp and the baggage of the Gauls. After the war there was peace in Gaul and the Romans came into the province.

---

[1] *captured:* **cēpērunt.**

EXERCISE 76

CASTRA RŌMĀNŌRUM

A Roman army never spent a single night outside a fortified camp. Towards the end of the day's march a detachment was sent ahead to mark out the site for the night's encampment. The plots assigned to the various divisions of the forces were indicated by colored flags. A rampart was always erected and a ditch dug. The camp was generally square and had four gates. The Roman legionnaire was as much a builder and a laborer as a fighting man. It was no doubt partly to this continuous training that he owed his remarkable steadiness and endurance in the field. The camp depicted on page 67 is rather more elaborate and permanent, yet the nightly encampments were constructed in the same general way.

Vidētis exercitum Rōmānōrum in castrīs. Vidētis mīlitēs et ducēs et imperātōrem. Vidētis gladiōs mīlitum. Impedīmenta nōn vidētis, sed impedīmenta sunt in castrīs. In castrīs est cōpia omnium[1] rērum. Mīlitēs castra in colle posuērunt sed nōn in silvīs. In castra agmen cum impedīmentīs vēnit. Hostēs autem impetum in castra fēcērunt, sed cōpiae Rōmānōrum hostēs vīcērunt. Nunc imperātor mīlitēs et ducēs propter virtūtem laudat, et ducēs propter victōriam grātiās mīlitibus agunt. Propter victōriam imperātor in grātiam cum senātū vēnit.

EXERCISE 77

"VAE VICTĪS!" ("WOE TO THE CONQUERED!")

Gallī erant hostēs Rōmānōrum. Itaque Rōmānī cum cōpiīs in Galliam vēnērunt et castra posuērunt. In castrīs erant mīlitēs et equitātus et servī et mīlitum impedīmenta. Cōpia gladiōrum in castrīs erat. Erant aciēs in collibus et montibus et silvīs. Gallī in Rōmānōs impetum fēcērunt; Rōmānī autem in Gallōs impetum fēcērunt. Rōmānī spem victōriae in virtūte posuērunt; Gallī spem salūtis in virtūte posuērunt. Rōmānī autem Gallōs vīcērunt:

---

[1] omnium: *of all.*

CASTRA ROMANORUM

partem prīncipum et ducum Gallōrum occīdērunt; portūs et
oppida Gallōrum cēpērunt.[1] Itaque Gallī cōpiam gladiōrum et
servōrum Rōmānīs dedērunt. Post bellum erat pāx in Galliā, sed
erant castra Rōmānōrum in Galliā et Gallī servī Rōmānōrum
erant. Imperātor Rōmānōrum erat Caesar. Senātus propter victōriam et mīlitum virtūtem Caesarem et exercitum laudat, et
Rōmānī Caesarī grātiās agunt.

EXERCISE 78

BROTHERS IN CHRIST

Propter Deī grātiam Chrīstiānī sumus. Itaque frātrēs sumus
propter lēgem Chrīstī: "Estis frātrēs."

---

[1] cēpērunt: *they captured.*

EXERCISE 79

WORD REVIEW

Name in Latin the objects pictured here:

EXERCISE 80

WHO IS CHRIST?

Chrīstus, Fīlius Deī, est fīlius Marīae. Itaque homō et Deus est. Chrīstus Rēx hominum est quod Deus est. In Chrīstō est salūs hominum, quod, propter salūtem hominum, in mundum vēnit. Est "Lūx Mundī" quod hominibus vēritātem dedit. Itaque Chrīstiānī grātiās Deō et Chrīstō agunt, et Chrīstum, Rēgem et Imperātōrem, laudant.

REVIEW OF UNIT ONE

EXERCISE 81

Give the

1. *genitive singular;*
2. *meaning;*
3. *gender and gender rule;*
4. *accusative singular;*
5. *genitive plural and its meaning:*

1. vulnus	12. bellum	23. terra	34. mīles
2. Chrīstiānus	13. hostis	24. gēns	35. populus
3. rēs	14. agmen	25. rēx	36. praemium
4. pars	15. Gallus	26. fīlius	37. virtūs
5. prōvincia	16. māter	27. silva	38. vōx
6. nōmen	17. flūmen	28. collis	39. nauta
7. frāter	18. rēgnum	29. amīcus	40. via
8. cōpia	19. Rōmānus	30. mōns	41. imperātor
9. perīculum	20. pater	31. victōria	42. gladius
10. porta	21. iter	32. homō	43. lēx
11. corpus	22. dux	33. servus	44. portus

EXERCISE 82

Give the

1. *genitive singular;*
2. *meaning;*
3. *gender and gender rule;*
4. *accusative singular;*
5. *ablative singular:*

1. lūx	5. Deus	9. exercitus	13. vēritās
2. Caesar	6. adventus	10. caedēs	14. gēns
3. fidēs	7. impetus	11. spēs	15. aciēs
4. mundus	8. glōria	12. metus	16. clāmor

EXERCISE 83
[Essential Drill]

1. Translate;
2. Explain the use of the italicized words:

1. Deus, pater hominum, in Caelō est. 2. Deus lēgem *hominibus* dedit. 3. Propter salūtem hominum Chrīstus homō in terrā erat. 4. Chrīstus est *lūx* mundī. 5. Chrīstus, *Fīlius* Deī, est rēx gentium et populōrum. 6. Post *adventum* Chrīstī vēritās erat in mundō. 7. Spīritus Deī in Chrīstō erat. 8. Rēgnum Chrīstī est rēgnum Caelī. 9. Chrīstiānī in nōmine Chrīstī ōrant. 10. Marīa in *rēgnō* Caelōrum cum Chrīstō glōriam Deī nunc videt. 11. Marīa, Māter Deī, est Porta Caelī. 12. Caelum est praemium virtūtis. 13. Deus *fidem* Chrīstiānōrum laudat. 14. Frātrēs estis. 15. Amīcus est amīcī servus. 16. Mīlitēs pācem laudant. 17. Rōma nōn est in Galliā, sed prōvincia Rōmānōrum est in Galliā. 18. Gallī Galliam incolunt. 19. Nautae portūs vident. 20. Rōmānī viās in prōvinciīs mūnīvērunt. 21. Chrīstiānī caedem prīncipum hostium nōn laudant. 22. Caesar imperium Galliae Gallīs nōn dedit. 23. Imperātor clāmōrem et vōcēs hostium audīvit. 24. Propter vulnera mīlitēs iter nōn fēcērunt. 25. Propter metum dux rēgem laudat. 26. Propter bellum *erant* mīlitēs et cōpia gladiōrum in oppidō. 27. Hostēs in montibus et collibus erant. 28. Corpora mīlitum in silvīs erant. 29. Partem equitātūs in flūmine occīdērunt. 30. Senātus et prīncipēs *exercituī* propter victōriam grātiās agunt. 31. Rōmānī spem in virtūte posuērunt. 32. Caesar cum cōpiīs et impedīmentīs in castra vēnit. 33. Propter grātiam Caesaris prīncipēs Gallōrum servōs Rōmānīs dedērunt. 34. Hostēs erant post aciem Rōmānōrum. Equitātus autem in *aciem* vēnit. Itaque Rōmānī hostēs vīcērunt et occīdērunt. 35. In silvās Galliae Caesar vēnit. Prīncipēs autem Gallōrum rem vīdērunt.[1] Itaque impetum in agmen Caesaris fēcērunt. 36. Mīlitēs in aciē ōrant quod in perīculō sunt.

---

[1] vīdērunt: *they saw.*

UNIT TWO

LESSON 7: ADJECTIVES OF THE FIRST AND SECOND DECLENSIONS

1. THE DECLENSION OF *MAGNUS, A, UM*

Adjectives, like nouns, are declined in Latin. But they have THREE GENDERS and therefore are declined IN EACH GENDER.

The adjectives are grouped into two main classes:

1. Those which use the endings of the FIRST and SECOND declensions.

2. Those which use the endings of the THIRD declension.

The adjective **magnus, magna, magnum** belongs to the first and second declensions. You already know all its endings. See whether you can write out its declension without looking in the GRAMMAR. First study these hints:

1. The stem is **magn-** (**magn-us**).

2. The masculine is exactly like **servus.**

3. The feminine is exactly like **terra.**

4. The neuter is exactly like **bellum.**

5. Put the genders in three columns like this:

MASCULINE	FEMININE	NEUTER
magn-us	magn-a	magn-um
etc.	*etc.*	*etc.*

After you have written out both the singular and plural, compare with GRAMMAR, No. 72. You now know the declension of all adjectives in **-us, -a, -um.**

ASSIGNMENT: Memorize the declension of **magnus, a, um,** GRAMMAR, No. 72.

VOCABULARY

magnus, a, um	{ *great* / *large*
altus, a, um	{ *high* / *deep*
bonus, a, um	*good*
longus, a, um	*long*
malus, a, um	*bad*
multus, a, um	*much* (pl., *many*)
sānctus, a, um	{ *holy* / *saint*
prīmus, a, um	*first*

RELATED ENGLISH WORDS

The welfare of the people should be the *primary* concern of statesmen. The *magnitude* of the task. *Altitude.*

2. AGREEMENT OF ADJECTIVES

EXAMPLES

magnam gentem, *a large tribe* (as object)
nautae bonī, *good sailors*
servōs malōs, *the bad slaves* (as object)
in flūminibus altīs, *in the deep rivers*

In the first example:

1. **Gēns** is FEMININE (sox); therefore **magn-** has a feminine ending.

2. **Gentem** is ACCUSATIVE SINGULAR feminine; therefore **magnam** is in the ACCUSATIVE SINGULAR feminine.

Explain the other examples in the same way.

RULE: ADJECTIVES AGREE WITH THEIR NOUNS
IN <u>GENDER</u>, <u>NUMBER</u>, AND <u>CASE</u>.

EXERCISE 84
Translate:

1. in altō flūmine
2. cum magnō exercitū
3. post magnum bellum
4. cum sānctā Marīā
5. in longā viā
6. cum hominibus bonīs
7. cum magnīs cōpiīs

8. cum multīs mīlitibus
9. in magnō perīculō
10. in altīs montibus
11. cum homine bonō
12. post longum iter
13. propter multa vulnera
14. cum servō malō

THE POSITION OF ADJECTIVES

Examine the position of the adjectives in the exercise above. Some follow the noun, some precede. Those that precede are generally adjectives answering the questions How large? How long? How high? How many? How small? These are adjectives of QUANTITY like **multus** and **magnus.**

> **RULE: ADJECTIVES OF QUANTITY <u>GENERALLY</u> PRECEDE THEIR NOUNS.**

Those that follow answer the question What kind?, like **malus, bonus,** *etc.* These are adjectives of QUALITY.

> **RULE: ADJECTIVES OF QUALITY <u>GENERALLY</u> FOLLOW THEIR NOUNS.**

Note. In Christian Latin **sānctus** generally precedes its noun:

Sāncta Marīa, *Holy Mary*

EXERCISE 85
Translate:

1. with many soldiers
2. in the high mountains

3. on account of the holy law of God

4. with a good man
5. large bodies
6. with the first Christians
7. bad laws
8. the deep rivers *(as object)*

9. the long way
10. on account of a great fear
    of the Romans
11. great shouting
12. Saint Mary

EXERCISE 86
[Essential]
Translate:

1. Multī Chrīstiānī in prīmā aciē erant. (Why is **aciē** ablative?) 2. Sāncta Marīa ōrat. 3. Longum agmen in altōs montēs vēnit. (Why is **montēs** accusative?) 4. Nauta malus nōn ōrat. 5. Dux bonus magnam virtūtem mīlitum laudat. (Explain the position of **bonus** and **magnam**.) 6. In longō agmine multī mīlitēs et impedīmenta sunt.

EXERCISE 87
Translate:

1. Good leaders praise peace. 2. The bad kings killed many Christians. 3. The long column was in the forests, but the first battle line was on the high mountains. 4. On account of the great fame of Rome, many men praise the laws of the Romans. 5. There are large mountains and deep rivers in America.[1] 6. We Christians are servants of Holy Mary.

3. PREDICATE ADJECTIVES

Adjectives may modify a noun directly, as we have seen in such expressions as:

in altō flūmine, *in the deep river*
homō bonus, *a good man*

These are called attributive adjectives.

---

[1] *America:* America, ae

But adjectives may also be linked to their noun by means of a linking verb like **sum**, *I am*, as:

Deus est <u>bonus</u>. *God is <u>good</u>.*

Lēgēs sunt <u>malae</u>. *The laws are <u>bad</u>.*

Estis <u>sānctī</u>. *You are <u>holy</u>.*

Such adjectives are called PREDICATE ADJECTIVES.

The rule of agreement is the SAME for attributive and predicate adjectives.

Predicate adjectives are put in diagrams in the same way as predicate nouns.

VOCABULARY

angustus, a, um	*narrow*
reliquus, a, um	$\begin{cases} remaining \\ the\ rest\ of \end{cases}$
tūtus, a, um	*safe*
Rōmānus, a, um	*Roman*
Chrīstiānus, a, um	*Christian*

RELATED ENGLISH WORDS

Relics of the Saints; a good *tutor*.

EXERCISE 88
[Essential]
Complete these sentences:

1. The way is narrow. Via est ....
2. God is good. Deus est ....
3. The soldiers are safe. Mīlitēs sunt ....
4. The camp was Roman. Castra erant ....
5. The soldiers were Christian. Mīlitēs erant ....
6. The laws were bad. Lēgēs erant ....
7. A part of the enemy was remaining. Pars hostium erat ....
8. You are holy. Estis ....
9. The river was deep. Flūmen erat ....

10. The Gauls were first. Gallī erant ....
11. He was holy. Erat ....
12. The victories of the enemy were not many. Victōriae hostium nōn erant ....
13. We are safe. Sumus ....
14. The Gauls' swords were large. Gladiī Gallōrum erant ....
15. The leader was bad. Dux erat ....
16. The road was long. Via erat ....
17. God is holy. Deus est ....
18. The sailors were safe. Nautae erant ....

"SALŪS POPULĪ SUPRĒMA[1] EST LĒX."—Cicero[2]

From this is derived the motto of the State of Missouri:

SALŪS POPULĪ SUPRĒMA[1] LĒX ESTŌ[3]

---

4. USE OF *PRŌ*

The preposition **prō** ALWAYS takes the ABLATIVE. In expressions of PLACE, **prō** means *in front of*.

Prō exercitū, *in front of the army*

Prō, especially with nouns naming persons, frequently means *on behalf of, for*.

Marīa prō hominibus ōrat.
Mary prays for (on behalf of) men.

Prō rēge impetum fēcērunt.
They made the attack for (on behalf of) the king.

---

[1] **suprēmus, a, um:** *highest.*
[2] Marcus Tullius Cicero (106-43 B.C.) was Rome's greatest orator. He was a lawyer of exceptional ability and a prominent politician. His orations have been models of style for two thousand years and strongly influenced the great French and English orators of modern times. He is also well known for his letters and essays.
[3] **estō:** *let . . . be.*

VOCABULARY

prō, *prep. w. abl.*	*in front of (before)* / *on behalf of (for)*
inopia, ae	*scarcity* / *want*
dominus, ī	*master* / *Lord*[1]
mūrus, ī	*wall*
frūmentum, ī	*grain* (pl., *crops*)
legiō, legiōnis, *f.*	*legion*

RELATED ENGLISH WORDS

Arguments *pro* and con; a *dominating* personality; *mural* decorations.

Glōria Patrī et Fīliō et Spīrituī Sānctō.[2]

EXERCISE 89
[Essential]

Translate:

1. Legiōnēs Rōmānae prō castrīs erant. 2. Sāncta Marīa prō hominibus malīs et bonīs ōrat. 3. Multī Gallī prō portīs castrōrum erant. 4. Prīncipēs prō mūrō altō erant. 5. Mīlitēs Rōmānī prō mūrō oppidī magnī castra posuērunt. 6. Chrīstiānī prō amīcīs ōrant. 7. Prō rēge bonō mīlitēs impetum in hostēs fēcērunt. 8. Erat magna inopia frūmentī in Galliā. 9. Reliquī mīlitēs Chrīstiānī in prīmā aciē prō silvīs erant. 10. Servī dominum bonum laudant.

---

[1] In Christian Latin Dominus, *Lord,* is used when referring to God or Christ.
[2] Sit, *be,* is understood in the Latin. Supply it in the English translation.

EXERCISE 90

[Essential]

Translate:

Erat magna inopia frūmentī in castrīs Rōmānīs quod Gallī Rōmānīs cōpiam frūmentī nōn dedērunt et frūmenta in Galliā nōn erant. Gallī nōn erant amīcī Rōmānōrum. Itaque Caesar cum cōpiīs et impedīmentīs in Galliam vēnit. Agmen Caesaris longum erat. Via in angustīs et altīs montibus erat. Itaque Gallī impetum in longum agmen fēcērunt, sed Gallōs legiōnēs Rōmānae vīcērunt. Itaque in oppidum tūtum vēnērunt reliquī Gallī. Rōmānī autem castra prō mūrō altō posuērunt. Prīma aciēs Caesaris prō castrīs erat. Gallī autem propter magnum metum Caesaris impetum in castra Rōmāna nōn fēcērunt. Itaque Rōmānī impetum in Gallōs fēcērunt et Gallōs vīcērunt. Multōs Gallōs et magnam partem prīncipum Galliae occīdērunt. Post victōriam Caesaris erat pāx in Galliā. Itaque Gallī magnam frūmentī cōpiam Rōmānīs dedērunt, et nōn erat inopia frūmentī in castrīs Rōmānīs.

SĀNCTUS, SĀNCTUS, SĀNCTUS, DOMINUS DEUS EXERCITUUM!

(A Title of God in the Old Testament)

EXERCISE 91

[Essential]

Translate:

1. In front of the large camp is a deep river. 2. The walls of the town are high. 3. Caesar was a great general. 4. There was a great scarcity of grain. 5. There were many legions with Caesar in Gaul. 6. Holy Mary prays for men. 7. Christ the Lord prays on behalf of the world. 8. Roman slaves do not praise the masters. 9. There are great crops in Gaul.

EXERCISE 92
[Essential Review]

1. Translate;
2. Explain position and agreement
of the italicized words:

1. Agmen *longum* erat. 2. *Reliquī* Gallī tūtī nōn erant.
3. Mīlitēs *Chrīstiānī* prō imperātōre *bonō* impetum in hostēs fēcērunt. 4. Via angusta *erat*. 5. *Longum* agmen in montēs altōs vēnit. 6. *Prīma* legiō in aciē erat. 7. *Magna* frūmentī inopia in *reliquīs* gentibus erat. 8. Hominēs *malī* prō reliquīs hominibus nōn ōrant. 9. Sunt *multa* flūmina in Galliā. 10. Dominus, homō *bonus* et sānctus, servīs frūmentum dedit. 11. Legiōnēs Rōmānae in aciē prō mūrō *altō* erant.

IN NŌMINE DOMINĪ
(Motto of the Bishop of Boise)

EXERCISE 93

Add the correct endings to the adjectives in the following phrases and translate:

1. propter lēgēs mal............
2. cum ducibus bon............
3. propter magn............ metum
4. in magn............ lūce
5. prō rēge Rōmān............
6. prō hominibus bon............
7. cum mult............ nautīs
8. propter vēritātem Chrīstiān............
9. propter magn............ virtūtem
10. in castra Rōmān............
11. in long............ viā
12. propter magn............ corpus

Dominī est terra!
Magna est glōria Dominī!
—Adapted from the *Roman Breviary*[1]

EXERCISE 94
Translate:

1. cum Caesare, imperātōre Rōmānō
2. propter salūtem populī Rōmānī
3. in altīs montibus
4. post magnam caedem
5. propter multa vulnera
6. propter salūtem reliquārum gentium
7. pro Sānctō Nōmine
8. in altō flūmine

---

[1] The *Roman Breviary* is a Latin work usually published in four volumes. It contains the Psalms, lives of the Saints, and various other selections and prayers. Every Roman Catholic priest is required to read certain sections each day.

LESSON 8: ADJECTIVES OF THE THIRD DECLENSION

1. THE DECLENSION OF *GRAVIS, E*

The second group of adjectives contains all those that use endings of the THIRD declension. Most of these adjectives are like **gravis, e.**

ASSIGNMENT: Learn the declension of **gravis** in GRAMMAR, No. 78. Notice that:

1. The ablative singular ends in **-ī.**
2. The neuter plural nominative and accusative end in **-ia.**
3. The genitive plural ends in **-ium.**

RULE: ALL ADJECTIVES WITH *-IS, -E* IN THE NOMINATIVE SINGULAR ARE DECLINED LIKE *GRAVIS, E.*

VOCABULARY

gravis, e	*heavy* / *severe* / *serious*
brevis, e	*short*
commūnis, e	*common*
difficilis, e	*difficult*
facilis, e	*easy*
fortis, e	*brave* / *strong*
nōbilis, e	*noble* / *renowned*
omnis, e	*all* / *every*

RELATED ENGLISH WORDS

Life is *brief.* The good of the *community. Fortified* positions.
God is *omnipresent.* A *grave* matter.

NOTE

Remember that ALL adjectives follow the rule for agreement
given on page 73.

EXERCISE 95

1. Decline in all genders: (a) facilis, (b) nōbilis, (c) omnis,
(d) brevis.

2. Decline in the neuter: (a) commūnis, (b) fortis, (c) gravis,
(d) difficilis.

3. Put the following in
      a. the ablative singular,
      b. the nominative plural,
      c. the genitive plural:

1. homō fortis	3. dux nōbilis	5. via difficilis
2. omnis Chrīstiānus	4. breve iter	6. bellum grave

4. Put the following groups in
      a. the accusative singular,
      b. the ablative singular:

1. salūs commūnis	4. metus gravis	7. vulnus grave
2. omnis Gallia	5. oppidum nōbile	8. via facilis
3. rēs gravis	6. omnis spēs	9. nōmen nōbile

5. Complete and translate:

a. in viā difficil............	g. propter metum grav............
b. cum omn............ cōpiīs	h. cum omn............ equitātū
c. prō rēge nōbil............	i. cum mīlitibus fort............
d. prō amīcō fort............	j. propter vulnera grav............
e. prō duce nōbil............	k. propter salūtem commūn............
f. post bellum grav............	l. post oppidum nōbil............

EXERCISE 96
[Essential]
Complete and translate:

1. Dominus Chrīstus, Rēx hominum, erat fort............ et nōbil.............
2. Spēs Gallōrum erat brev.............
3. Dux nōbil............ in prīmā aciē erat.
4. Prō castrīs mīlitēs fort............ erant.
5. Omn............ spem salūtis in virtūte posuērunt.
6. Chrīstiānī in nōmine Chrīstī omn............ spem salūtis posuērunt.
7. Propter rem grav............ Caesar in Galliam vēnit.
8. Propter salūtem commūn............ omnēs Gallī in prōvinciam impetum fēcērunt.
9. Propter montēs et silvās via erat difficil.............
10. Propter virtūtem Gallōrum rēs nōn erat facil.............

EXERCISE 97
[Essential]
Translate:

1. The danger was serious. 2. You are brave. 3. On account of the common salvation of men, Christ came into the world. 4. The way was difficult. 5. All men praise great courage. 6. There were strong soldiers and renowned leaders in the Roman army. 7. The journey was not easy. 8. The mountains are large and high. 9. Every general praises courage and faithfulness. 10. Caesar was a great and renowned general. 11. The victory was not easy. 12. The route was short. 13. Roman swords were heavy. 14. The affair was serious. 15. Christ is a noble lord and a brave leader; therefore all good and holy men praise Christ the Lord. 16. The Roman laws were severe. 17. The long and deep rivers of America[1] are renowned.

---

[1] *America:* America, ae.

2. ADJECTIVES GOVERNING CASES

He is eager for power.

Mary is full of grace.

The province is next to the Gauls.

In these sentences the prepositional phrases *for power, of grace, to the Gauls,* modify the adjectives *eager, full, next.* These prepositional phrases which modify adjectives are often translated into Latin by the genitive or dative or ablative WITHOUT A PREPOSITION. THE PROPER CASE TO BE USED IS DETERMINED BY THE ADJECTIVE. Thus **cupidus** always takes the genitive case. It makes no difference whether the English is *eager FOR power* or *desirous OF power*—cupidus ALWAYS has the GENITIVE case. Likewise, **finitimus,** *next (to),* always has the DATIVE. **Plēnus,** however, takes either the genitive or the ablative.

The sentences written above must be translated:

> **Imperiī cupidus est.**
>
> **Marīa est grātiā (grātiae) plēna.**
>
> **Prōvincia Gallīs fīnitima est.**

When an adjective of this kind is given in the vocabularies, it will always be followed by an abbreviation to indicate the case to be used. Be sure to learn this when you learn the adjective.

VOCABULARY

cupidus, a, um ; *w. gen.*	*eager* *desirous*
plēnus, a, um ; *w. gen. or abl.*	*full*
fīnitimus, a, um ; *w. dat.*	*neighboring* *next*
similis, e ; *w. gen. or dat.*	*like* *similar*

NOTE

These adjectives are sometimes used WITHOUT a modifying phrase as: **gentēs fīnitimae,** *neighboring tribes.*

RELATED ENGLISH WORDS

The *cupidity* of the miser; a *plenary* indulgence.

EXERCISE 98
[Essential]

Translate:

1. Gallī glōriae cupidī erant. 2. Fīlius similis patris est. 3. Gallī fīnitimī erant prōvinciae. 4. Marīa est grātiā plēna. 5. Gallia plēna Rōmānōrum erat. 6. Oppidum plēnum erat mīlitum et gladiōrum. 7. Prōvincia plēna est omnium rērum bonārum. 8. Caelum est plēnum glōriae Deī. 9. Cupidī sumus omnium rērum bonārum. 10. Fīnitimī Galliae erant. 11. Sānctī hominēs Chrīstō similēs sunt.

PONS ROMANUS

EXERCISE 99

Complete these sentences:

1. The camp is full of swords. Castra plēna sunt ....
2. The enemy were eager for victory. Hostēs cupidī erant ....
3. The tribes were next to Gaul. Gentēs erant fīnitimae ....
4. The Gauls were not like the Romans. Gallī nōn erant similēs ....
5. They killed the leaders of the neighboring tribes. Ducēs gentium .... occīdērunt.
6. A sailor is not like a soldier. Nauta nōn est similis ....
7. The Gauls are desirous of war. Gallī cupidī sunt ....

3. THE DECLENSION OF *JĒSŪS*

VOCABULARY

Jēsūs, ū	*Jesus*
et . . . et	*both . . . and*
quid	*what?*
prīmā lūce	*at dawn*
urbs, urbis	*city*
pōns, pontis, *m.*	*bridge*
signum, ī	{ *standard* *signal* *sign*
eques, equitis	*horseman* (pl., *cavalry*)

NOTE

1. **Quid** is used in asking questions:

   Quid est in urbe? *What is in the city?*
   Quid vidētis? *What do you see?*

2. **Lūce** is the ablative of **lūx; prīmā** (from **prīmus, a, um**) agrees with it. **Prīmā lūce** literally means *with* or *at the first light;* hence, *at dawn.*

3. The plural of *horseman* is *horsemen,* which is the same as *cavalry;* hence the meaning for **equitēs** given in the vocabulary.

4. **Jēsūs** is declined:

Nom.	Jēsūs
Gen.	Jēsū
Dat.	Jēsū
Acc.	Jēsūm
Abl.	Jēsū

RELATED ENGLISH WORDS

The *urban* population; an *equestrian* statue.

OMNIA PRŌ JĒSŪ

(Motto of the Bishop of Tucson)

EXERCISE 100

[Essential]

Translate:

Nōmen Jēsū est Sānctum Nōmen. Est nōmen nōbile et speī plēnum. In nōmine Jēsū omnēs Chrīstiānī ōrant; Jēsūm omnēs laudant; Jēsū omnēs grātiās agunt; Jēsūm omnēs in Caelō cum Marīā vident. In nōmine Jēsū prīmī Chrīstiānī Rōmānōs vīcērunt. Propter Jēsūm Deus Pater prīmīs Chrīstiānīs praemium victōriae dedit. Itaque Jēsūs Chrīstus est et Dominus et Rēx omnium hominum.

EXERCISE 101

[Essential]

Translate:

1. Chrīstiānī et Jēsūm Chrīstum et Marīam laudant. 2. Rōma est urbs et magna et nōbilis. 3. Caesar et glōriae et imperiī cupidus erat. 4. Prīmā lūce equitēs fortēs impetum in reliquōs hostēs fēcērunt. 5. Propter perīcula gravia et multa mīlitum vulnera Rōmānī iter breve in prōvinciam fēcērunt.

AGMEN ROMANUM

The soldier in the left foreground is 'modeling' the standard Roman outfit. The long *pīlum* which he holds is much like the modern javelin used in track competition; his *gladius*—the two-edged sword for hand-to-hand fighting—hangs from his shoulder. He is protected by helmet, breastplate, and shield. He would thus be prepared for actual service in the field; on the march the helmet was carried in the pack and the shield was generally inclosed in a bag to protect it.

EXERCISE 102

Translate:

Quid vidētis in pictūrā?[1] In pictūrā vidētis agmen Rōmānum. Agmen longum est, sed vidētis partem agminis. Vidētis signa legiōnum et gladiōs mīlitum. Pars agminis est in ponte. Equitēs autem nōn sunt in ponte. Vidētis imperātōrem. Prīmus vēnit. In agmine sunt impedīmenta. In impedīmentis est cōpia frūmentī et omnium rērum. Vidētis urbem et mūrum altum.

---

[1] pictūra, ae: *picture.*

EXERCISE 103
[Essential]
Translate:

1. There are many bridges on the long and deep rivers of America.[1] 2. The Roman soldiers killed many Christians on account of the name of Jesus. 3. There are great and renowned cities in America.[1] 4. Christians put all hope and faith in the Lord Jesus Christ. 5. Both sailors and soldiers praise God. 6. The city of Rome is large and renowned. (Do not use the genitive for *of Rome;* names of cities are put in apposition to **urbs.**) 7. The general gave the signal at dawn, and so the cavalry made an attack on the enemy and killed a large part of the leading men of the tribe. 8. You see the standards of the legions. 9. The wounds of the brave soldiers are many and serious. 10. The enemy killed the Roman horseman. 11. They fortified the bridges. 12. What do the Christians praise?

SIGNUM CRUCIS[2]
In nōmine Patris et Fīliī et Spīritūs Sānctī.
Āmēn.[3]

READING NO. 3

A LATIN QUIZ PROGRAM

Quid est victōria?
>—Est praemium virtūtis.

Quid est bellum?
>—Est caedēs frātrum.

Quid est mīles?
>—Est mūrus[4] imperiī.

---

[1] *America:* America, ae.

[2] **crux, crucis:** *cross.*

[3] Āmēn is a Hebrew word meaning "So be it!" The congregation, or the server in the name of the congregation, answers Āmēn to show that the people are united with the prayer of the priest.

[4] In this sentence **mūrus** may be translated *bulwark.*

MASTERY REVIEW VOCABULARY NO. 1

[Units One and Two

FIRST DECLENSION

NOUNS LIKE *TERRA, AE*

cōpia, ae	*supply* *abundance*
cōpiae, cōpiārum, *f.*	*troops* *forces* (a military term)
Gallia, ae	*Gaul*
glōria, ae	*fame* *glory*
grātia, ae	*favor* *influence* *grace* (in Christian Latin)
grātiae, grātiārum	*thanks*
inopia, ae	*scarcity* *want*
Marīa, ae	*Mary*
nauta, ae	*sailor*
porta, ae	*gate*
prōvincia, ae	*province*
Rōma, ae	*Rome*
silva, ae[1]	*forest*
terra, ae	*earth* *land*
via, ae	*road* *way*
victōria, ae	*victory*

---

[1] Generally used in the plural in Latin with same meaning as in the singular.

SECOND DECLENSION

NOUNS LIKE *SERVUS, i*

amīcus, ī	*friend*
Chrīstiānus, ī	*Christian*
Chrīstus, ī	*Christ*
Deus, Deī	*God*
dominus, ī	$\begin{cases} \textit{master} \\ \textit{Lord}^1 \end{cases}$
fīlius, ī	*son*
Gallus, ī	*a Gaul*
gladius, ī	*sword*
mundus, ī	*world*
mūrus, ī	*wall*
populus, ī	$\begin{cases} \textit{people} \\ \textit{nation} \end{cases}$
Rōmānus, ī	*a Roman*
servus, ī	$\begin{cases} \textit{slave} \\ \textit{servant} \end{cases}$

NOUNS LIKE *BELLUM, Ī*

bellum, ī	*war*
caelum, ī	$\begin{cases} \textit{sky} \\ \textit{heaven}^2 \end{cases}$
frūmentum, ī	*grain* (pl., *crops*)
imperium, ī	$\begin{cases} \textit{command} \\ \textit{power} \\ \textit{empire} \end{cases}$
oppidum, ī	*town*
perīculum, ī	*danger*
praemium, ī	*reward*

---

[1] In Christian Latin Dominus, *Lord,* is used when referring to God or Christ.
[2] When **Caelum** is used to mean the Christian heaven the *c* will be capitalized.

rēgnum, ī	{ *kingdom* / *royal power*
signum, ī	{ *standard* / *signal* / *sign*

NOUNS LIKE THE PLURAL OF *BELLUM*

castra, castrōrum	*camp*
impedīmenta, impedīmentōrum	{ *baggage* / *baggage train*

THIRD DECLENSION

MASCULINE AND FEMININE NOUNS LIKE *LĒX, LĒGIS*

Caesar, Caesaris	*Caesar*
clāmor, clāmōris	{ *shouting* / *shout*
dux, ducis	*leader*
eques, equitis	*horseman* (pl., *cavalry*)[1]
frāter, frātris (frātrum)[2]	*brother*
homō, hominis	*man*
imperātor, imperātōris	{ *commander in chief* / *general*
legiō, legiōnis, *f.*	*legion*
lēx, lēgis	*law*
lūx, lūcis	*light*
māter, mātris (mātrum)[2]	*mother*
mīles, mīlitis	*soldier*
pater, patris (patrum)[2]	*father*
pāx, pācis	*peace*

---

[1] The plural of *horseman* is *horsemen*, which is the same as *cavalry;* hence the meaning for **equitēs** given in the vocabulary.

[2] The genitive plural of **frāter, māter,** and **pater** is put in parentheses to remind you that these words are exceptions to the rule for -ium words.

prīnceps, prīncipis	*chief* *leading man*
rēx, rēgis	*king*
salūs, salūtis	*safety* *welfare* *salvation*
vēritās, vēritātis	*truth*
virtūs, virtūtis	*courage* *virtue*
vōx, vōcis	*voice* *cry*

MASCULINE AND FEMININE NOUNS LIKE *PARS, PARTIS*

caedēs, caedis	*slaughter*
collis, collis, *m.*	*hill*
gēns, gentis	*tribe*
hostis, hostis[1]	*enemy* (in war)
mōns, montis, *m.*	*mountain*
pars, partis	*part*
pōns, pontis, *m.*	*bridge*
urbs, urbis	*city*

NEUTER NOUNS LIKE *FLŪMEN, FLŪMINIS*

agmen, agminis	*column* (of soldiers) *army* (on the march)
corpus, corporis, *n.*	*body*
flūmen, flūminis	*river*
iter, itineris, *n.*	*journey* *march* *route*
nōmen, nōminis	*name*
vulnus, vulneris, *n.*	*wound*

---

[1] The plural of hostis is used to translate the English *enemy* unless ONE soldier of the enemy is meant.

FOURTH DECLENSION
NOUNS LIKE *PORTUS, ŪS*

adventus, ūs	*arrival* / *coming*
equitātus, ūs	*cavalry*
exercitus, ūs	*army*
impetus, ūs	*attack*
metus, ūs	*fear*
portus, ūs	*harbor*
senātus, ūs[1]	*senate*
spīritus, ūs	*breath* / *spirit*

FIFTH DECLENSION
NOUNS LIKE *RĒS, REĪ*

aciēs, aciēī	*battle line*
fidēs, fideī	*faith* / *reliability* / *faithfulness*
rēs, reī	*thing* / *affair*
spēs, speī	*hope*

---

[1] The Roman Senate was an aristocratic governing body somewhat like a combination of the United States Senate and the British House of Lords. In the time of the Republic the Senate was very powerful and really directed Roman policies. Under the emperors it had very little real power.

ADJECTIVES OF THE FIRST AND SECOND DECLENSIONS

LIKE *MAGNUS, A, UM*

altus, a, um	*high* *deep*
angustus, a, um	*narrow*
bonus, a, um	*good*
Chrīstiānus, a, um	*Christian*
cupidus, a, um; *w. gen.*	*eager* *desirous*
fīnitimus, a, um; *w. dat.*	*neighboring* *next*
longus, a, um	*long*
magnus, a, um	*great* *large*
malus, a, um	*bad*
multus, a, um	*much* (pl., *many*)
plēnus, a, um; *w. gen. or abl.*	*full*
prīmus, a, um	*first*
reliquus, a, um	*remaining* *the rest of*
Rōmānus, a, um	*Roman*
sānctus, a, um	*holy* *saint*
tūtus, a, um	*safe*

ADJECTIVES OF THE THIRD DECLENSION

LIKE *GRAVIS, E*

brevis, e	*short*
commūnis, e	*common*
difficilis, e	*difficult*
facilis, e	*easy*

fortis, e	$\begin{cases} brave \\ strong \end{cases}$
gravis, e	$\begin{cases} heavy \\ severe \\ serious \end{cases}$
nōbilis, e	$\begin{cases} noble \\ renowned \end{cases}$
omnis, e	$\begin{cases} all \\ every \end{cases}$
similis, e; *w. gen. or dat.*	$\begin{cases} like \\ similar \end{cases}$

PREPOSITIONS WITH THE ACCUSATIVE

in, *prep. w. acc.*	$\begin{cases} in \\ into \\ against \\ upon \\ on \end{cases}$
post, *prep. w. acc.*	$\begin{cases} after \\ behind \end{cases}$
propter, *prep. w. acc.*	*on account of*

PREPOSITIONS WITH THE ABLATIVE

cum, *prep. w. abl.*	*with*
in, *prep. w. abl.*	$\begin{cases} in \\ on \end{cases}$
prō, *prep. w. abl.*	$\begin{cases} in \ front \ of \ (before) \\ on \ behalf \ of \ (for) \end{cases}$

CONJUNCTIONS

autem, *conj., postpositive*[1]	*however*
et, *conjunction*	*and*
et . . . et	*both . . . and*
itaque, *conjunction*[2]	{ *therefore* *and so*
quod, *conjunction*	*because*
sed, *conjunction*	*but*

ADVERBS

nōn, *adv.*	*not*
nunc, *adv.*	*now*

OTHER WORDS

Jēsūs, ū[3]	*Jesus*
prīmā lūce[4]	*at dawn*
quid[5]	*what?*

---

[1] **Autem** is postpositive. This means that it cannot stand first in a clause but must *always follow the first word or phrase of a clause.*

[2] **Itaque** is used at the beginning of a sentence as an introductory adverb.

[3] **Jēsūs** is declined: Jēsūs, Jēsū, Jēsū, Jēsūm, Jēsū.

[4] **Lūce** is the ablative of **lūx**; **prīmā** (from **prīmus, a, um**) agrees with it. **Prīmā lūce** literally means *at the first light;* hence, *at dawn.*

[5] **Quid** is used in asking questions: **Quid est in urbe?** *What is in the city?* **Quid vidētis?** *What do you see?*

UNIT THREE

LESSON 9: THE FIRST CONJUGATION

INTRODUCTION

If you closed your eyes and "tuned in" on all the conversation going on in a room between classes you might hear something like this:

"He *was running* down the side line . . . *dove* for him but . . . *saw* a swell show last night at . . . we*'re going* over to Charlie's house tonight . . . *did* it in ten minutes . . . she *said* . . . *don't care* what . . ."

All are saying something, and all, without realizing it, are using VERBS. We could not say anything at all unless we had verbs.

They are the strong words of language because they express ACTION. And if you stop to think about it, they are amazing words, grammar's quick-change artists, because in sentence after sentence they appear and re-appear with different spellings and in different combinations. Let us study their changes.

1. VERBS CHANGE THEIR FORM TO EXPRESS DIFFER-ENT *TIME*.

    I *played* ball yesterday.

    I *am playing* ball.

    I *shall play* ball tomorrow.

In each of these sentences the verb expresses the same action *(playing)*, but there is a difference in each sen-

FILIUS DUCIS

99

tence. What is it? The action is shown as happening at different TIMES. *Played* expresses PAST time; *am playing* expresses PRESENT time; *shall play* expresses FUTURE time. THE KIND OF TIME EXPRESSED BY A VERB IS CALLED ITS *TENSE*.

IN BOTH ENGLISH AND LATIN, VERBS CHANGE THEIR FORM TO EXPRESS TENSE.

---

2. VERBS CHANGE THEIR FORM TO EXPRESS DIF-FERENT *PERSONS*.

> I *play* ball.
>
> He *plays* ball.

Again there is a difference between *play* and *plays,* but not in the time expressed. They are both PRESENT tense. The change here shows PERSON. *Play* is used with the first person, *I ;* *plays* with the third person, *he.* (You cannot say "He play ball" unless you are a native of Borneo and speak pidgin English.)

IN BOTH ENGLISH AND LATIN, VERBS CHANGE THEIR FORM TO SHOW PERSON.

---

3. VERBS CHANGE THEIR FORM TO EXPRESS DIF-FERENT *NUMBERS*.

> He *plays* ball.
>
> They *play* ball.

Here the tense (present) and the person (third) are the same in both sentences. This change is to show NUMBER. *Plays* is the third person SINGULAR (one) ; *play* is third person PLURAL (more than one).

IN BOTH ENGLISH AND LATIN, VERBS CHANGE THEIR FORM TO SHOW NUMBER.

Verbs also have MOOD and VOICE, but these will be explained later. For the present we shall study the indicative mood, active voice. You need only remember that the indicative mood is used in ordinary statements and questions.

1. PRINCIPAL PARTS: THE FIRST CONJUGATION

When we studied the nouns we saw that it was very important to know the GENITIVE because this case gives us the STEM.

Now, the Latin verb uses SEVERAL stems, and to know these we must learn the PRINCIPAL PARTS OF A VERB. THE PRINCIPAL PARTS are the four main forms on whose STEMS all the other forms of the verb are built up. The principal parts of a regular verb are:

1. The first person singular
   present indicative active: **laudō,** *I praise*
2. The present infinitive active: **laudāre,** *to praise*
3. The first person singular
   perfect indicative active: **laudāvī,** *I praised*
4. The perfect participle passive: **laudātus,** *having been praised*

We saw that nouns were divided into groups called declensions. Now, regular verbs are divided into FOUR main groups and these are called CONJUGATIONS. There is a MODEL verb for each group. The conjugation to which a verb belongs is shown by the ending of the SECOND principal part, the PRESENT INFINITIVE ACTIVE: **laudāre.**

**ALL VERBS WHOSE PRESENT INFINITIVE ACTIVE
ENDS IN -ĀRE BELONG TO THE FIRST
CONJUGATION.**

EXERCISE 104

From this group of present infinitives, pick out the verbs which belong to the first conjugation:

1. laudāre	4. audīre	7. occupāre
2. monēre	5. oppugnāre	8. mūnīre
3. pācāre	6. dīcere	9. parāre

NOTE

Most verbs of the first conjugation form their principal parts by changing the -ō of the first principal part to -āre, -āvī, -ātus, thus:

laud-ō, laud-āre, laud-āvī, laud-ātus

par-ō, par-āre, par-āvī, par-ātus

EXERCISE 105

Give the principal parts of these first-conjugation verbs:

occupō   oppugnō   ōrō

2. PRESENT INDICATIVE ACTIVE OF *LAUDŌ*

The PRESENT TENSE expresses action in PRESENT TIME. Study the meanings in GRAMMAR, No. 162.

The PRESENT TENSE is always formed on the PRESENT *STEM*. The present stem is found by dropping the ending -āre of the infinitive, thus:

Infinitive: **LAUD-ĀRE**   Present STEM: **LAUD-**

ASSIGNMENT: Study the present tense of **laudō** with its meanings in GRAMMAR, No. 162. Notice the following:

1. Except in the first person singular the ENDINGS BEGIN with a. (The first conjugation is the *A*-CONJUGATION.)

2. You know already that the Latin verb expresses persons *(I, you, he-she-it, we, they)* in its ENDING. If you drop the **a**

from the endings you have the following table of FINAL PER-
SONAL SIGNS:

	SINGULAR			PLURAL	
1.	*(I)*	....		*(we)*	-mus
2.	*(you)*	-s		*(you)*	-tis
3.	*(he, she, it)*	-t		*(they)*	-nt

(Generally ō or m is a sign of the first person singular, *I.*)

3. The present tense has three forms in English.
   1. You praise
   2. You are praising
      (showing that the action is GOING ON)
   3. You do praise (used (1) in questions;
                   e. g., Do you praise?
               (2) for emphasis;
                   e. g., You *do* praise.
               (3) in negative sentences.
                   e. g., You *do not* praise.)

ALL THESE are expressed in Latin by the SAME form:
laudās.

> **Laudās.** *You praise.*
> **Laudās.** *You are praising.*
> **Quid laudās?** *What do you praise?*
> **Laudās!** *You do praise!*
> **Nōn laudās.** *You do not praise, are not praising.*

VOCABULARY

laudō, *1, tr.*	*praise*
occupō, *1, tr.*	*seize*
oppugnō, *1, tr.*	*attack* *assault*
ōrō, *1, tr.*	*beg* *pray*
parō, *1, tr.*	*prepare* *get ready*

NOTE

1. Whenever the principal parts are not printed in full in the vocabulary, the verb forms its parts regularly like the model for its conjugation. Thus **occupō** is like **laudō: occupō, OCCU-PĀRE, OCCUPĀVĪ, OCCUPĀTUS,** *1, tr.* IN ALL TESTS AND RECITATIONS GIVE THE FULL PRINCIPAL PARTS.

2. The abbreviation *tr.* stands for TRANSITIVE and shows that the verb takes a direct OBJECT in the ACCUSATIVE case. Always learn from the vocabulary whether a verb is TRANSITIVE or INTRANSITIVE.

RELATED ENGLISH WORDS

He *lauded* the President's program. American soldiers *occupied* many islands in the Pacific.

EXERCISE 106

1. Give the principal parts of the verbs in the vocabulary.
2. Tell why they are like **laudō.**
3. Conjugate them in the present indicative active. To do this:
   a. Find PRESENT STEM (drop -**āre** of infinitive).
   b. Add the endings of **laudō,** *i. e.,* -**ō**, -**ās**, -**at,** *etc.*

EXERCISE 107

1. Tell what forms these are;
2. Give three English translations for each form:

1. ōrant	3. occupās	6. parāmus	9. ōrās
2. oppugnant	4. ōrātis	7. occupat	10. parō
	5. ōrat	8. occupāmus	

EXERCISE 108

Add the required personal signs:

1. *They* are preparing war.   Bellum para............
2. *He* is attacking the camp.   Castra oppugna......... ..
3. *You* do praise God.   Deum laudā......... ...

4. *They* pray for (their) friends.   Prō amīcīs ōra..............
5. *We* prepare swords.   Gladiōs parā..............
6. *I* praise Christ.   Chrīstum laud..............

EXERCISE 109
Translate:

1. He is praying. 2. You are preparing. 3. What does he praise? 4. We are praying. 5. They seize towns. 6. They are attacking the town. 7. They praise virtue. 8. He prepares swords. 9. She prays. 10. What do they praise?

3. AGREEMENT OF VERBS

Marīa ōrat. *Mary prays.*

Rōmānī Caesarem laudant. *The Romans praise Caesar.*

The subject of the first sentence is Marīa. Marīa is third person and singular. THEREFORE the verb is third person and singular. (Note the final personal sign -t.)

The subject of the second sentence is Rōmānī. Rōmānī is third person and plural. THEREFORE the verb is third person and plural. (Note the final personal sign -nt.)

RULE: A FINITE VERB AGREES WITH ITS SUBJECT IN PERSON AND NUMBER.

EXERCISE 110
1. Add the required personal signs;
2. Translate:

1. Rōmānī Caesarem lauda..............
2. Caesar legiōnem prīmam nōn lauda..............
3. Hostēs bellum para..............
4. Dux nōbilis urbem et portum occupa..............
5. Mīlitēs castra oppugna..............

Romani amici Christianorum non erant.

EXERCISE 111
[Essential]
PRAY ALWAYS!

Translate:

Omnēs hominēs bonī ōrant sed hominēs malī nōn ōrant. Chrīstiānī in nōmine Chrīstī ōrant. Rēx bonus prō rēgnō et mīlitibus ōrat. Dux bonus prō mīlitibus ōrat. Et mīlitēs et nautae propter bellī perīcula ōrant. Et patrēs et mātrēs prō fīliīs ōrant. Fīliī prō patribus et mātribus ōrant. Amīcī prō amīcīs ōrant. Chrīstus prō omnibus hominibus ōrat.

Cum[1] ōrāmus, Deum laudāmus. Omnēs Chrīstiānī Deum, pa-

---

[1] **Cum** is here a conjunction. Translate *when.*

trem omnium hominum, laudant, quod multās rēs bonās hominibus[1] parat. Mīlitēs post victōriam et salūtem Deum laudant; patrēs et mātrēs Deum propter pācem et fīliōrum salūtem laudant.

EXERCISE 112
[Essential]
Translate:

Rēgēs et ducēs malī bellum parant. Rēx malus, glōriae et rēgnī cupidus, gladiōs et legiōnēs parat. Castra gladiōrum et frūmentī plēna parat. Urbēs et oppida fīnitima oppugnat et occupat. Mīlitēs rēgis malī et silvās et collēs occupant. Cupidī sunt victōriae sed nōn pācis. Deus autem mīlitibus et rēgibus malīs praemia nōn parat!

EXERCISE 113
[Essential]
Translate:

Estis hominēs bonī. Itaque pācem et virtūtem laudātis et prō omnibus hominibus ōrātis. Bellum nōn parātis quod nōn estis glōriae et victōriae cupidī. Urbēs fīnitimās nōn oppugnātis; oppida gentium fīnitimārum nōn occupātis; gladiōs et legiōnēs nōn propter bellum sed propter pācem parātis.

EXERCISE 114
Translate:

1. Chrīstiānī prō omnibus hominibus ōrāmus. (With what does **Chrīstiānī** agree?) 2. Mīlitēs fortēs laudās. 3. Urbem nōn oppugnās. 4. Cōpiam gladiōrum parās. 5. Chrīstiānī Spīritum Sānctum laudāmus. (With what does **Chrīstiānī** agree?) 6. Hominem fortem et sānctum omnēs laudātis. (With what does **omnēs** agree?)

---

[1] When *to* will not translate the dative into good English use *for*.

EXERCISE 115
[Essential]
Translate:

1. Roman generals praise the courage and reliability of brave soldiers. Brave Roman soldiers prepare a supply of swords. They storm cities and towns. They seize hills and mountains and bridges. They are the "bulwark *(mūrus, ī)* of empire." In the courage of the brave legions is all hope of victory and safety.

2. You are all Christians. Therefore do you all praise Jesus Christ, the Son of God, and Mary, the Mother of Christ. You pray for all men, for soldiers and sailors, for leading men and slaves. You pray in the name of Jesus Christ, and you praise the Father and the Son and the Holy Spirit.

3. We are praising Caesar because he is a great and brave general. (*Great* in this sentence does not mean *large* but *famous* or *outstanding.* Therefore it is not an adjective of quantity here.)

4. The leader is attacking the camp.

5. They are preparing war.

6. We praise peace, but we do not praise war.

7. The leaders are getting grain and swords ready. (*Are getting . . . ready* = one Latin word!)

EXERCISE 116
[Essential Review]

1. Give the genitive plural of: (a) collis, (b) frāter, (c) prīnceps, (d) gravis.

2. Give the reasons for the endings you used in Question 1.

3. Translate; parse **portīs**: Mīlitēs prō portīs sunt.

4. IMPERFECT INDICATIVE ACTIVE OF *LAUDŌ*

The imperfect tense in Latin expresses action as GOING ON in PAST time. For example: "I *was eating* dinner between six and seven yesterday evening." I could say, "I *ate* dinner between six and seven yesterday," but the verb *ate* would not express the CONTINUANCE of the action. *Was eating* is translated into Latin by the IMPERFECT tense.

ASSIGNMENT: Study the meanings given in GRAMMAR, No. 163 and learn **laudābam,** *etc.* Note that:

1. The imperfect of a verb is formed on the PRESENT STEM.

2. The ending has the a of the first conjugation.

3. The FINAL PERSONAL SIGNS are the same as for the present tense.

4. The ending contains a *TENSE SIGN:* **ba** (*e. g.,* **laud-ā-BA-t**), which is ALWAYS THE SIGN OF THE IMPERFECT TENSE. (The Latin verb is thus a sort of CODE which you can learn to decipher.)

VOCABULARY

pugnō, *1, intr.*	*fight*
superō, *1, tr.*	$\begin{cases} overcome \\ conquer \\ surpass \end{cases}$
portō, *1, tr.*	*carry*
centuriō, centuriōnis	*a centurion*[1]
numerus, ī	*number*

RELATED ENGLISH WORDS

He gave a large tip to the *porter.* Some boys are *pugnacious* by nature. Every *century* has its saints. Roman *numerals. Import* and *export* taxes.

RELATED LATIN WORD

Oppugnō

---

[1] A centurion was a Roman army officer in charge of 100 men. The rank was similar to that of our captain.

CENTURIO

EXERCISE 117

1. Give the principal parts of the verbs in the vocabulary.
2. Give their present stems.
3. Conjugate them in the present indicative.
4. Conjugate them in the imperfect indicative.

EXERCISE 118

1. Tell what forms these are;
2. Translate:

1.	portābat	8.	superābat
2.	ōrābant	9.	laudābam
3.	occupābant	10.	laudābāmus
4.	pugnābant	11.	pugnābat
5.	laudābās	12.	laudābant
6.	laudābat	13.	portābant
7.	superābant	14.	parābant

EXERCISE 119

1. Point out the imperfects by identifying the tense sign;
2. Point out the third-person plural verbs by identifying the final personal sign;
3. Translate:

Note. All Latin words which end in -nt are VERBS in the THIRD PERSON PLURAL.

1. oppugnābant	7. superant	13. parāmus
2. portat	8. superat	14. occupant
3. pugnant	9. occupābat	15. ōrābat
4. parābat	10. portant	16. laudābātis
5. pugnat	11. portābant	17. oppugnābat
6. laudābant	12. laudās	18. parābās

EXERCISE 120
[Essential]

1. Add the correct final personal signs;
2. Translate:

1. Equitēs fortēs cum magnō hostium numerō pugnāba.............
2. Chrīstiānī Chrīstum, rēgem omnium gentium, laudāba...........
3. Centuriōnēs frūmentum nōn portāba............
4. Altus mōns collēs superāba............
5. Populus Rōmānus victōriās legiōnum reliquārum laudāba............
6. Chrīstiānī bonī prō frātribus ōrāba............
7. Equitātus Rōmānus Gallōs virtūte[1] superāba............
8. Magnus centuriōnum numerus in prīmā aciē pugnāba...........

EXERCISE 121
[Essential]

Translate:

1. The slaves were carrying the grain into the towns. 2. The Roman legions were fighting with the tribes of Gaul. 3. The cavalry were conquering a large number of Gauls. 4. The centurion was fighting in the first battle line. 5. Caesar was overcoming the enemy.

EXERCISE 122

1. Identify the final personal signs;
2. Translate:

1. laudābam	6. parābat	11. laudābās
2. portābat	7. portat	12. pugnābant
3. laudābātis	8. superant	13. portant
4. ōrābat	9. oppugnābat	14. occupābat
5. superat	10. pugnābat	15. parābant

---

[1] Translate: *in courage.*

EXERCISE 123
[Essential Review]

1. What is the gender of: (a) centuriō, (b) legiō, (c) mōns? Give the rule.
2. Give the nominative plural of: (a) legiō, (b) virtūs, (c) corpus, (d) gravis.
3. Translate; parse **servīs**:
    Centuriōnēs servīs gladiōs nōn dedērunt.

5. FUTURE INDICATIVE ACTIVE OF *LAUDŌ*

The future tense expresses action that WILL take place. Study the meanings in GRAMMAR, No. 164. Learn the model verb. You need not learn the meanings given in the parentheses. Note that:

1. The future tense is formed on the PRESENT STEM.
2. The ending has the **a** of the first conjugation.
3. The final personal signs are the same as for the present and the imperfect tenses.
4. The ending contains a tense sign, **bi** (*e. g.*, **laud-ā-BI-t**), which is the sign of the future in the FIRST and SECOND conjugations.

VOCABULARY

dō, dare, dedī, datus, *1, tr.*	*give*
vocō, *1, tr.*	*call*
interim, *adverb*	*meanwhile*
mors, mortis	*death*
hīberna, hībernōrum	*winter quarters*

NOTE

1. **Dō** forms its perfect stem differently from **laudō**. Therefore you must memorize the principal parts. It is also peculiar in this, that the **a** which begins the endings is short throughout the indicative except in the second person singular present indicative active (**dās**).
2. **Hīberna**, like **castra**, is declined only in the plural.

RELATED ENGLISH WORDS

A *mortal* wound. Some animals *hibernate* during the winter. A *vocation* to the priesthood.

RELATED LATIN WORD

Marīa vōcem Chrīstī audīvit.

EXERCISE 124

1. Conjugate the verbs of the vocabulary in the present, imperfect, and future tenses of the indicative active. 2. Conjugate in the future indicative active: (a) parō, (b) occupō, (c) superō, (d) portō, (e) pugnō, (f) ōrō.

EXERCISE 125

1. Tell what forms these are;
2. Translate:

1. superābit	7. dabis	13. laudābimus
2. laudābō	8. laudābis	14. vocābunt
3. dabō	9. pugnābimus	15. superābit
4. parābunt	10. laudābit	16. pugnābunt
5. laudābunt	11. laudābitis	17. dabitis
6. occupābitis	12. vocābis	18. vocābit

EXERCISE 126

[Essential]

Translate:

1. Omnibus gentibus Deus vēritātem dabit. 2. Interim imperātor centuriōnēs in hīberna vocābit. 3. Deus hominēs sānctōs post mortem in Caelum vocābit. 4. Prīncipēs reliquārum gentium propter mortis metum frūmentum Rōmānīs dabunt. 5. Servī frūmentum in hīberna portābunt. 6. Centuriō prīncipēs in hīberna vocābit.

EXERCISE 127
[Essential]
Translate:

1. We shall praise God in heaven. 2. Bad kings will prepare for war. (Omit *for* in Latin.) 3. You will praise Rome. 4. I shall praise the Lord God of Hosts. (Hosts = armies.) 5. God will give great rewards to all good men. 6. Caesar will call the soldiers into the winter quarters. 7. After the death of Caesar, the Gauls were servants of the Romans. 8. Meanwhile the centurion will call the legions into the battle line.

EXERCISE 128
[Essential Review]

1. Translate, and explain the case of **imperātor:**
   Caesar erat imperātor Rōmānōrum.

2. What is the gender of: (a) mors, (b) rēx, (c) vēritās? Give the rule.

3. Give the ablative singular of: (a) mors, (b) **centuriō,** (c) gravis, (d) senātus, (e) rēgnum, (f) vōx, (g) fidēs.

6. QUESTIONS

VOCABULARY

ubi, *adv.*	*where?*
quis, *pronoun*	*who?*
quid, *pronoun*	*what?*
cūr, *adv.*	*why?*
locus, ī (*pl.,* loca, locōrum)	*place*
aliēnus, a, um	$\begin{cases} \textit{unfavorable} \\ \textit{another's} \\ \textit{foreign} \end{cases}$

NOTE
1. The abbreviation *adv.* stands for *adverb.*

2. **Locus** becomes a neuter noun in the plural: **loca.** When **locus** is modified by an adjective the preposition **in** may be omitted with the ablative case.

In an unfavorable place, **locō aliēnō**

RELATED ENGLISH WORDS

The politician has *alienated* many of his friends. A *local* election. Some *aliens* are deported by the government.

INTERROGATIVE ADVERBS AND PRONOUNS IN QUESTIONS

Questions may be asked in Latin by using interrogative adverbs or pronouns just as in English.

Ubi es? *Where are you?*

Quis pugnābat? *Who was fighting?*

Quid parās? *What are you preparing?*

Cūr Caesarem laudās? *Why do you praise Caesar?*

EXERCISE 129
[Essential]
Translate:

1. Quis Caesarem post caedem prīncipum Galliae laudābit?
2. Cūr senātum vocās? 3. Ubi sunt hīberna hostium? 4. Quis Deum nōn laudat? 5. Ubi sunt cōpiae Rōmānae? 6. Cūr locō aliēnō castra posuērunt? 7. Cūr urbēs aliēnās occupat? 8. Cūr gentēs aliēnae bellum parābant? 9. Cūr omnia loca occupābat?

EXERCISE 130
Translate:

1. Why were the soldiers fighting in an unfavorable place?
2. Who will surpass the great general Caesar? 3. What were they preparing? 4. Who is seizing foreign harbors and cities?
5. Where will they fight at dawn? 6. A man eager for fame does not praise another's courage.

EXERCISE 131
[Essential]

1. Translate;
2. Write Latin answers for all the questions to which no answers are given:

1. Cūr Deum laudāmus?
   Ans. Deum laudāmus quod Deus bonus est et Dominus Caelī et terrae.

2. Cūr Rōmānī cum Gallīs pugnābant?
   Ans. Rōmānī cum Gallīs propter caedem centuriōnum pugnābant.

3. Cūr Caesarem Rōmānī laudābant?

4. Cūr Chrīstiānī Spīritum Sānctum laudant?

5. Cūr Chrīstiānī Marīam laudant?

6. Cūr ōrāmus in nōmine Jēsū Chrīstī?

7. Quis magnam frūmentī cōpiam portābat?
   Ans. Servus magnam frūmentī cōpiam portābat.

8. Quid parat dux bonus?
   Ans. Dux bonus parat gladiōs et frūmentī cōpiam.

9. Quis prō duce bonō pugnābit?

10. Quis servum vocābat?
    Ans. Dominus servum vocābat.

11. Quis erat imperātor Rōmānōrum in Galliā?

12. Quis magna praemia hominibus bonīs dabit?

13. Quid in bellō occupant ducēs bonī?

14. Quis est Chrīstus?

15. Quis ōrat prō omnibus hominibus?

16. Ubi nunc ōrat Marīa?
    Ans. Marīa nunc ōrat in Caelō.

17. Ubi est Deus?
    Ans. Deus est in Caelō et terrā et omnī locō.

18. Ubi Caesar pugnābat?

19. Ubi sunt impedīmenta Rōmānōrum?

20. Ubi Deus praemium hominibus sānctīs post mortem dabit?

7. THE INTERROGATIVE PARTICLE -*NE*

When no interrogative adverb or pronoun is used, questions may be asked by putting the most emphatic word (generally the VERB) first and adding -*NE*.

Was he praising Caesar? <u>Laudābatne</u> Caesarem?
Do you fight for the king? <u>Pugnāsne</u> prō rēge?
Were they friends of the Romans? <u>Erantne</u> amīcī Rōmānōrum?

VOCABULARY

ōrātiō, ōrātiōnis	{ *speech* / *prayer*
semper, *adv.*	*always*
sīcut, *conj.*	*as*
in prīncipiō	*in the beginning*
in saecula saeculōrum	{ *world without end* / *forever*
-ne	particle used in questions

NOTE
Ōrātiō means *prayer* only in Christian Latin.

RELATED ENGLISH WORDS
The priest reads the *orations* after the Kyrie Eleison.

RELATED LATIN WORD
Marīa prō omnibus hominibus ōrat.

ASSIGNMENT: Review neuter nouns of the third declension in the Mastery Review Vocabulary (pages 91-98).

EXERCISE 132
[Essential Drill]
Translate:

1. Pugnābantne semper Rōmānī? 2. Parābantne frūmentum post longum iter? 3. Montēs et silvās et flūmina Galliae laudā-

bitis. 4. Pugnābantne in itinere Rōmānī cum Gallīs? 5. Erantne post bellum multa corpora in flūminibus et silvīs? 6. Suntne impedīmenta et legiōnēs in agmine? 7. Laudābāsne nōmen Marīae? 8. Propter vulnera longum iter nōn fēcērunt. 9. Superatne exercitus Rōmānus Gallōs? 10. Ōrābantne semper hominēs sānctī? 11. Lēgem et vēritātem Chrīstī semper laudābō. 12. Datne imperātor signum? 13. Dantne Rōmānī cōpiam frūmentī Gallīs post ōrātiōnem prīncipis? 14. Vocābitne prīmā lūce centuriō equitēs? 15. Ōrantne Chrīstiānī in nōmine Chrīstī? 16. Fēcēruntne semper Gallī impetum in agmina Rōmānōrum? 17. Eratne magnus pōns in altō flūmine? 18. Oppugnābantne Gallī hīberna? 19. Victōriam et glōriam Chrīstī laudābāmus. 20. Laudābatne imperātor centuriōnem propter magnam virtūtem et multa vulnera? 21. Dantne rēgēs magna praemia amīcīs? 22. Occupābitne collēs? 23. Interim, propter grātiam Caesaris, Gallī frūmentum in hīberna portant. 24. Ōrābatne nauta propter vulnerum metum? 25. Parābatne dux frūmentum et gladiōs? 26. Chrīstum, Rēgem glōriae, laudābimus. 27. Quis loca occupābat? 28. Pugnābatne equitātus in silvīs? 29. Portābantne servī magnum gladiōrum numerum? 30. Propter metum vulnerum et mortis, nautae et mīlitēs in bellō semper ōrant. 31. Deus ōrātiōnēs multōrum Chrīstiānōrum audīvit. 32. Pugnābantne equitēs locō aliēnō et angustō?

ŌRĀTIŌ CHRĪSTIĀNA "DOXOLOGIA"

A doxology is a prayer in which "glory" is offered to the Blessed Trinity. Of the many doxologies which date from very early Christian times the following is most familiar:

Glōria Patrī et Fīliō et Spīrituī Sānctō,[1]
Sīcut erat in prīncipiō et nunc et semper et in saecula saeculōrum. Āmēn.

---

[1] Sit, *be*, or *may . . . be*, is understood in the first line. Supply *be* in translation.

EXERCISE 133

Translate:

1. Do you always praise the names of Jesus and Mary? 2. Shall we praise God in heaven? 3. Christians pray always, as Christ advised[1] His[2] friends. 4. On account of the prayers of Christians, God will give grace to many men. 5. On account of the general's speech, the chiefs of the tribes will prepare (for) war. 6. In the beginning of the war the Romans were conquering the enemy. 7. Are there many long and renowned rivers in America?[3] 8. Was the journey long and difficult? 9. On account of the many serious wounds of the soldiers, the army made[4] a short march into winter quarters. 10. Was the route full of dangers? 11. Were the columns of Caesar safe in Gaul? 12. Will God call all good men into heaven after death? 13. Was the place unfavorable? 14. What were the Roman slaves begging (for)?[5] 15. Was there a large number of slaves in the Roman Empire? 16. Were the Romans conquering all the tribes of Gaul? 17. The slaves were carrying the body of the chief. 18. Will American[6] sailors and soldiers seize foreign harbors and cities? 19. A Roman column was assaulting the camp. 20. Meanwhile, where were the remaining Gauls fighting?

---

[1] *advised:* monuit.
[2] *his:* suus, a, um.
[3] *America:* America, ae.
[4] *made:* fēcit.
[5] Omit *for* in Latin.
[6] *American:* Americānus, a, um.

LESSON 10: THE PRESENT, IMPERFECT, AND FUTURE INDICATIVE ACTIVE OF *MONEŌ*

The principal parts of regular verbs of the second conjugation are formed by dropping the -eō of the first person present indicative and adding -ēre, -uī, -itus.[1]

mon-eō, mon-ēre, mon-uī, mon-itus
hab-eō, hab-ēre, hab-uī, hab-itus

Many second-conjugation verbs, however, are irregular in their principal parts. These will be written out in full in the vocabularies and must be memorized. But the present infinitive active ALWAYS ends in -ĒRE (with the first ē long!).

ALL VERBS WHOSE PRESENT INFINITIVE ACTIVE ENDS IN *-ĒRE* BELONG TO THE SECOND CONJUGATION.

VOCABULARY

moneō, 2, *tr.*	{ *warn* / *advise*
timeō, timēre, timuī, 2, *tr.*	*fear*
terreō, 2, *tr.*	*terrify*
habeō, 2, *tr.*	*have*
arma, armōrum	*arms*

NOTE
1. **Timeō** has no fourth principal part.
2. **Arma** is a neuter plural of the second declension.

RELATED ENGLISH WORDS
A *timorous* soul; a *timid* person; *rearmament*.

---

[1] When the verb is intransitive, the fourth principal part ends in -itum.

120

Now that you know the model **laudō, moneō** is quite easy:

1. Find the stem by dropping the ending of the present infinitive active, thus: **monēre, STEM: mon-.**

2. Add **-eō** for the first person present indicative active.

3. For the other endings use the endings of the first conjugation but change the first **a** of the endings to **e.**

ASSIGNMENT: Write out the present, imperfect, and future of **moneō** without looking in the book. Then compare with the model, GRAMMAR, Nos. 165, 168, and 171. Learn the model.

EXERCISE 134

1. Why do the verbs in the vocabulary belong to the *second* conjugation?

2. Give the full principal parts of these verbs.

3. Write the third person singular and third person plural of the present, imperfect, and future of these verbs.

EXERCISE 135
[Drill on Present Tense]

1. Tell what forms these are;

2. Give three English meanings for each form:

1. timet	5. monētis	9. monēmus
2. moneō	6. monet	10. monent
3. monēs	7. habet	11. terret
4. terrent	8. timent	12. habent

EXERCISE 136
[Drill on Imperfect Tense]

1. Tell what forms these are;

2. Translate:

1. monēbant	5. timēbant	9. monēbās
2. terrēbat	6. monēbātis	10. monēbat
3. monēbam	7. monēbāmus	11. terrēbant
4. habēbant	8. timēbat	12. habēbat

EXERCISE 137
[Drill on Future Tense]
1. Tell what forms these are;
2. Translate:

1. monēbunt	4. monēbitis	7. habēbit
2. timēbō	5. monēbit	8. terrēbunt
3. monēbis	6. monēbō	9. timēbimus

EXERCISE 138
Translate:

1. Timēs. 2. Ducem monēbit. 3. Hostēs terrēbat. 4. Frātrem monēbant. 5. Imperium habent. 6. Populum terrent. 7. Partem habēbat. 8. Equitātum timēbitis.

EXERCISE 139
1. Fill in the required personal signs;
2. Translate:

1. Clāmor hostium mīlitēs Rōmānōs nōn terre............, quod Rōmānī fortēs sunt.
2. Multī hominēs in pāce fortēs sunt; in bellō autem hostēs timēbu.............
3. Servī propter metum dominum monēbu.............
4. Metus Deī hominēs malōs terre.............
5. Propter grātiam Caesaris Gallī Rōmānōs monēba.............
6. Omnēs hominēs vulnera et mortem time.............
7. Legiōnēs magnam armōrum cōpiam habēba.............

EXERCISE 140
[Essential]
Translate:

1. Omnēs hominēs rēs difficilēs timent. 2. Propter rem gravem centuriōnēs imperātōrem monēbunt. 3. Clāmor hostium locīs difficilibus et angustīs legiōnēs terret. 4. Rēx malus rēs aliēnās habet. 5. Populus Rōmānus perīcula gravia et rēs difficilēs nōn timēbat. 6. Multae gentēs arma nōn habent.

EXERCISE 141
[Essential Review]

1. Give the nominative plural of: (a) legiō, (b) **flūmen,**
(c) corpus, (d) centuriō, (e) facilis.
2. Translate: They are eager for victory and renown.
3. Translate; explain the case of **castra:**
    Frūmentum in castra portābat.

EXERCISE 142
[Honor Work]

PEARL HARBOR

The enemy were always preparing (for) war because they
were eager for empire and fame and victory. However, they were
fearing the American[1] forces; they were fearing the American[1]
sailors and soldiers. The leading men of the enemy were warning
and terrifying the nation: "The Americans[2] are eager for empire.
They have a large supply of arms and a large number of sailors
and soldiers. They will attack the harbors and the towns. And
so we shall prepare a supply of arms and of all things. We shall
fight with the legions of the enemy and we shall conquer." And so
they were preparing (for) war.

In America,[3] however, there was peace. The American[1] people
were not eager for war; the generals were not desirous of the glory
of war. Not many leading men were warning the Senate and the
people.

On December 7, 1941,[4] the enemy made an attack on Pearl[5]
Harbor. They killed many sailors and soldiers. There was war!

Now, however, we are conquering the enemy; we are terrifying
the tribes of Japan.[6] Brave sailors and soldiers are fighting for

---

[1] *American:* **Americānus, a, um.**
[2] *Americans:* **Americānī, Americānōrum.**
[3] *America:* **America, ae.**
[4] *December 7, 1941:* **ante diem septimum Īdūs Decembrēs, 1941.**
[5] *Pearl:* **Margarītārius, a, um.**
[6] *Japan:* **Japōnia, ae.**

America. They are fighting in places unfavorable and full of great dangers; but they are eager now for victory, the reward of courage. They will conquer the enemy!

EXERCISE 143

*Complete these sentences with a Latin verb
describing the action in the pictures:*

1. Rōmānī urbem ....
2. Servī gladiōs ....
3. Caesar servum ....
4. Equitēs hostēs ....
5. Servus prīncipem ....
6. Rōmānī cum Gallīs ....

1

2

3

4

5

6

LESSON 11: PERSONAL PRONOUNS

1. Pronouns of the FIRST person are those which refer to the SPEAKER OR WRITER. In English they are: I (ME), WE (US).

2. Pronouns of the SECOND person are those which refer to the person spoken TO. In English they are: YOU (THOU, THEE, YE).

3. Pronouns of the THIRD person are those which refer to the person or thing spoken or written ABOUT. In English they are: HE (HIM), SHE (HER), IT, THEY (THEM).

1. PRONOUNS OF THE FIRST PERSON

ASSIGNMENT: Learn the declension of **ego,** *I,* and **nōs,** *we,* GRAMMAR, No. 123. Study the English meanings carefully.

VOCABULARY

ego, meī	*I*
nōs, nostrī	*we*
video, vidēre, vīdī, vīsus, 2, *tr.*	*see*
saepe, *adv.*	*often*

NOTE

Video forms its principal parts differently from the model **moneō.** Memorize all the parts given here.

RELATED ENGLISH WORDS

An inflated *ego.* Napoleon was *egotistical. Visual* aids. The shepherds saw a *vision* of angels.

ASSIGNMENT: Review the forms of **sum,** present tense, GRAMMAR, No. 346.

EXERCISE 144

1. Tell what forms these are;
2. Translate:

1. videt	5. mihi	9. nōs
2. meī	6. vidēbat	10. vident
3. vidēbimus	7. nōbīs	11. vidēbit
4. ego	8. vidēbant	12. mē

EXERCISE 145
[Essential]

AN IMAGINARY LETTER FROM A CENTURION NAMED MARCUS,
SERVING WITH CAESAR IN GAUL, TO HIS MOTHER

Translate:

Mārcus Centuriō Rōmānus Mātrī
Salūtem Dat.[1]

Ego nunc cum exercitū in Galliā sum. Magnus exercitus in Galliā est quod Gallī cum Rōmānīs pugnant. Caesar, homō fortis, est imperātor omnium legiōnum. Caesarem ego laudō quod dux bonus est—omnia[2] videt; omnia[2] parat.

Ego in periculō nunc nōn sum. Nōs in castrīs sumus. Hostēs castra Rōmāna nōn oppugnant quod fortēs nōn sunt. Galba[3] mēcum in castrīs est. Homō bonus est et mihi amīcus.

Nōs saepe pugnābāmus cum Gallīs et superābāmus. Itaque nunc multī Gallī servī sunt et nōbīscum in castrīs sunt. Nōbīs frūmentum dant. Impedīmenta in castra portant et multās rēs nōbīs parant.

Post prīmam victōriam mē Caesar in castrīs propter virtūtem

---

[1] Roman letters frequently opened with the greeting **salūtem dat,** *gives greeting,* and closed with **valē,** *farewell (good-by).*

[2] Adjectives are sometimes used as nouns. **Omnia** is so used here and means *all things* or *everything.*

[3] **Galba, ae:** *Galba* (a Roman proper name).

MARCUS

et fidem laudābat.[1] Prīmā lūce hostēs in nōs impetum fēcērunt. Et ego et Galba in prīmā aciē pugnābāmus, et multī Gallī nōbīscum pugnābant, sed nōs nōn terrēbant, nōn superābant. Caesar nōs vidēbat. Itaque Caesar nōs propter virtūtem laudābat. Magnam glōriam ego nunc habeō, et post bellum Caesar mihi magnum praemium dabit. Laudāsne fīlium? Valē![2]

EXERCISE 146

1. Express all the italicized pronouns;
2. Translate:

1. He is warning *me*. 2. *We* shall warn the Senate and the leading men. 3. *I* am seizing the hill, but Caesar is seizing the bridge. 4. He sees *us*. 5. *I* praise the Holy Spirit. 6. They are fighting on *my* behalf.[3] 7. He is fighting with *me*. 8. The Gauls were giving *us* rewards. 9. Will he give *me* a reward? 10. They were fighting with *us*. 11. The Christians are praying for *me*. 12. Holy Mary prays for *us*. 13. *We* shall see the Father and the Son and the Holy Spirit in heaven. 14. Many brave soldiers are fighting with *me*. 15. Does God give *us* grace?

---

[1] Polybius, a Greek historian writing in the second century B. C., speaks thus of the encouragement given young soldiers in the Roman army: "After a battle in which some of them have distinguished themselves, the general calls an assembly of the troops, and bringing forward those whom he considers to have displayed conspicuous valor, first of all speaks in laudatory terms of the courageous deeds of each and of anything else in their previous conduct which deserves commendation, and afterwards distributes . . . rewards."—From Grant Showerman: *Rome and the Romans*. By permission of The Macmillan Company, Publishers.

[2] See Note 1 on page 126.

[3] Translate: *on behalf of me*.

2. PRONOUNS OF THE SECOND PERSON

ASSIGNMENT: Learn the declension of tū, *you*, and vōs, *you*, GRAMMAR, No. 124. Study the English meanings carefully. Notice that the English uses the SAME forms for the singular and plural while the Latin has different forms.

VOCABULARY

tū, tuī	*you* (sing.)
vōs, vestrī	*you* (pl.)
teneō, tenēre, tenuī, tentus, 2, *tr.*	*hold*
moveō, movēre, mōvī, mōtus, 2, *tr.*	*move*
tamen, *adv.*	*nevertheless*
neque, *conj.*	{ *nor* *and . . . not*

RELATED ENGLISH WORDS

Napoleon possessed a *tenacious* and indomitable will. *Motion* pictures.

REVIEW VOCABULARY

imperātor, imperātōris { *commander in chief* *general* *emperor*[1]

EXERCISE 147

1. Translate;
2. Express the italicized pronouns:

1. *I* shall give *you* (sing.) a reward. 2. The Lord fights for *you* (pl.). 3. God will give *you* (pl.) a reward, heaven. 4. *I* was warning *you* (sing.). 5. The master is calling *you* (sing.). 6. The Lord is with *you* (sing.). 7. *You* (pl.) will praise the victory of Christ. 8. *You* (sing.) will warn the leader. 9. Does the fear of death move *you* (sing.)? 10. *We* shall pray for *you* (pl.).

---

[1] Imperator in nonmilitary language is to be translated as *emperor*.

EXERCISE 148

AN EXAMINATION OF PROFESSED CHRISTIANS
BY A ROMAN JUDGE[1]

The proconsul, the judge, is seated. A group of Christians is brought in.

PROCONSUL *(addressing the first of the group)*. Esne tū Chrīstiānus?

CHRISTIAN. Ego Chrīstiānus sum.

PROCONSUL *(addressing a second Christian)*. Et tū—esne tū Chrīstiāna?

SECOND CHRISTIAN. Chrīstiāna et[2] ego sum. Omnēs nōs Chrīstiānī sumus.

PROCONSUL. Quid? Vōs omnēs Chrīstiānī estis?

FIRST CHRISTIAN. Sumus.

PROCONSUL. Cūr vōs deōs Rōmānōrum nōn laudātis?

FIRST CHRISTIAN. Nōs deōs Rōmānōrum nōn laudāmus quod vērī[3] nōn sunt.

PROCONSUL. Vōs moneō! Sī[4] deōs Rōmānōrum laudābitis, praemia vōbīs dabō—*(threateningly)* sed . . .

SECOND CHRISTIAN. Metus mortis et vulnerum nōs nōn movet. Nōs laudāmus Dominum Caelī et terrae, "Rēgem Rēgum et Imperātōrem Omnium Gentium."[5] Chrīstus prō nōbīs ōrābat.[6] Grātia Chrīstī in nōbīs est. Itaque quid nōs terrēbit? Tē nōn timēmus.

PROCONSUL *(scornfully)*. Chrīstus! Quis est Chrīstus? Rōmānī Chrīstum occīdērunt quod malus homō erat.

---

[1] This is an imaginary account, but much of it has been suggested by actual trials as recorded in the authentic *Acts* of the early martyrs.

[2] Et here means *also*.

[3] vērus, a, um: *true*.

[4] sī: *if*.

[5] These words were actually said at Carthage by a Christian martyr named Speratus. Saturninus was the examining official.

[6] At the Last Supper Christ expressly prayed for all believers: "Yet not for these [the Apostles] only do I pray, but for those also who through their word are to believe in Me" (John 17:20-21).

"CHRISTUS NOS IN CAELUM VOCAT."

FIRST CHRISTIAN. Chrīstus est Fīlius Deī et tamen frāter omnium hominum.

PROCONSUL *(impatiently)*. Cūr vōs imperātōrem Rōmānum nōn laudātis?

FIRST CHRISTIAN. Nōs semper imperātōrem Rōmānum laudāmus sed caedem hominum sānctōrum nōn laudāmus neque laudābimus. Tamen prō imperātōre semper ōrāmus et ōrābimus. Nōs Chrīstiānī—sīcut Chrīstus nōs monēbat—prō omnibus hominibus, prō rēgibus, prīncipibus, mīlitibus, servīs ōrāmus.

PROCONSUL. Vōs tamen moneō! Post mortem *(sarcastically)* quid vōs habēbitis?

FIRST CHRISTIAN. Tū nōs nōn movēbis. Fidem et vēritātem Chrīstī nōs tenēmus et semper tenēbimus. Chrīstus est salūs hominum. In Chrīstō est spēs omnium gentium. Post mortem magnum praemium nōbīs dabit; nōs cum Chrīstō in Caelō Patrem et Fīlium et Spīritum Sānctum vidēbimus in saecula saeculōrum. THE OTHER CHRISTIANS. Āmēn!

PROCONSUL. Ubi est Deus Chrīstiānōrum? Ego Deum Chrīstiānōrum nōn vidēbam neque videō.

SECOND CHRISTIAN. In omnī locō est sed nunc nōs Deum nōn vidēmus. Deus corpus nōn est. Tamen post mortem tū vidēbis, neque tibi praemium dabit.

PROCONSUL (angrily). Mehercule![1] Monētisne vōs mē? Metus Deī Chrīstiānōrum mē nōn terret neque terrēbit. (Solemnly.) Ego autem imperium habeō! Vōs terrēbunt mīlitum Rōmānōrum gladiī!

CHRISTIANS. Gladius nōs nōn terret neque imperium mundī. Imperium autem Deī nōs terret et movet. In Deō est salūs.

PROCONSUL (firmly). Estisne omnēs Chrīstiānī?

CHRISTIANS (loudly). Nōs sumus Chrīstiānī omnēs.

PROCONSUL. Itaque omnēs hōs[2] Chrīstiānōs "gladiō animadvertī placet."[3]

CHRISTIANS. Deō grātiās! Prō tē ōrābimus. (The Christians are taken away.) Chrīstus nōs in Caelum vocat!

EXERCISE 149
[Essential Review]

1. What is the rule for accent in Latin?
2. Indicate the accent in these words and explain: (a) laudābat, (b) impedīmenta.
3. Translate: There are dangers in the forest.

---

[1] Mehercule!: By Hercules! (a common Roman exclamation).
[2] hōs: these.
[3] This is a technical legal phrase. "It is decreed that all these Christians be punished by the sword."

DOMINUS MEUS,[1] ET DEUS MEUS[1]

3. PRONOUNS OF THE THIRD PERSON

When used as the personal pronoun of the third person, **is, ea, id** has the meaning *he, she,* or *it*. Since Latin pronouns must agree in GENDER and NUMBER with the Latin words to which they refer, a masculine or feminine Latin form is often translated by the English *it*.

He saw the army and feared it. **Vīdit exercitum et timuit eum.**

ASSIGNMENT. Learn the declension of **is, ea, id,** *he, she, it* and **eī, eae, ea,** *they, those,* GRAMMAR, Nos. 128-129. Study the English meanings carefully. Note that the plural can be formed by adding the endings of **magnī, ae, a** to the stem **e-**. Study the rule for agreement of pronouns in GRAMMAR, No. 479.

---

[1] **meus, a, um:** *my.* (These were the words uttered by St. Thomas when he saw the risen Savior.)

VOCABULARY

is, ea, id	he, she, it
sustineō, sustinēre, sustinuī, sustentus, 2, tr.	{ sustain withstand
fīnēs, fīnium, m.	territory

NOTE

Fīnēs is a *plural* noun of the third declension.

RELATED LATIN WORDS

Teneō; fīnitimus.

EXERCISE 150

1. *Tell what forms these are;*
2. *Translate:*

1. sustinēbat   3. vidēbat   5. sustinēbant   7. sustinent
2. sustinet   4. habēbant   6. sustinēbit   8. habēmus

EXERCISE 151
[Essential]

1. *Translate;*
2. *Point out the words to which the italicized pronouns refer and explain the agreement:*

1. Caesarem laudābās. Itaque *is* tibi praemium dabit. 2. Caesar agmen hostium nōn videt. Monēbisne *eum*? 3. Marīa sāncta erat. Itaque Deus *eī* praemium dedit. 4. Hostēs in hīberna impetum fēcērunt. Mīlitēs autem fortēs impetum *eōrum* sustinēbant. 5. Marīa est Māter Deī. Itaque *eam* Chrīstiānī laudāmus. 6. Amīcus est in perīculō. Itaque prō *eō* ōrābimus. 7. Hostēs oppidum occupant. Tenēbuntne *id*? 8. Hostēs bellum parant, sed impetum *eōrum* sustinēbimus. 9. Caesar ducēs Gallōrum in hīberna vocat; sed *eī* nōn sunt amīcī senātūs et populī Rōmānī. 10. Mātrēs bonae sunt. Virtūs *eārum* magna est. Nōs *eās* semper laudāmus, et Deus *eīs* magna praemia dabit. 11. Caesar est imperātor Rōmānus, sed senātus virtūtem *ējus* nōn laudat.

12. Caesar oppidum Gallōrum occupābit, sed tū *eōs* nōn monē-bis. 13. Multī hominēs sānctī sunt. *Eīs* Deus praemia dabit. 14. Chrīstus est fīlius Marīae et nunc in Caelō cum *eā* est. 15. Mī-litēs semper in perīculō sunt. Itaque prō *eīs* ōrāmus. 16. Caesar in castrīs est. *Eī* servus gladium dat. 17. Omnēs Gallī in armīs sunt. Spem victōriae in virtūte posuērunt. Equitēs *eōrum* fortēs sunt. Cōpia frūmentī in oppidīs *eōrum* est. Et pontēs et collēs tenent. *Ea* Caesar audīvit; eōs tamen nōn timet.

EXERCISE 152

1. Translate;
2. Express all the italicized pronouns:

Warning. Remember that the pronoun must agree in *gender* and *number* with the *Latin* word to which it refers.

1. The Senate praises Caesar because *he* fights for the Roman people in the territory of the Gauls. 2. The roads are good. The Romans constructed *them*. 3. Caesar was fighting with the Gauls in *their* territory. He was seizing *their* towns and cities. The Gauls were not withstanding *his* attacks. 4. *We* praise Christ and Mary, *His* mother. *She* was holy. God gave *her* a great reward. All holy men will see *her* and *her* Son in heaven. *They* will all pray with *her* for *us*. 5. The Gauls were not friends of the Romans. The Gauls were not giving *them* grain, and they were not praising *them*. The Gauls were fighting with *them*. 6. Christ is the light of the world and the salvation of all men. We praise *Him* now on earth, and with *Him* we shall praise God in heaven forever. 7. We praise the Roman legions on account of *their* victories. *They* were fighting for the Senate and the Roman people. The Gauls were fighting with *them* but *they* conquered the Gauls. Caesar was *their* commander in chief and was praising *them* on account of *their* courage and reliability. Therefore the Senate gave *them* great rewards. 8. The enemy are carrying grain and arms into the town. Will *they* hold *it?* 9. The Gauls are preparing a camp. In *it* they will fight for the common welfare of Gaul. Never-theless they will not hold *it*. Caesar will overcome *them* and seize

it. 10. The winter quarters of the Romans were in the territory of the enemy. The enemy were attacking and were seizing *them.* 11. The Gauls often made an attack on the Roman columns, but the Romans were withstanding *their* attacks.

SUSTINEŌ ĀLĀS[1]

(Motto of the Technical Ground Command of the U. S. Army Air Corps)

---

4. DIRECT REFLEXIVE PRONOUNS

We pray for OURSELVES.

A good man does not praise HIMSELF.

In these sentences the pronouns *himself* and *ourselves* REFER BACK to the subject; that is, they stand for the SAME person (or persons) as the SUBJECT.

A PRONOUN THAT REFERS BACK TO THE SUBJECT OF ITS OWN CLAUSE IS CALLED A DIRECT REFLEXIVE.

The oblique cases (the genitive, dative, accusative, and ablative) of the regular pronouns which you have learned, **ego, nōs, tū, vōs,** are used as the DIRECT REFLEXIVES of the FIRST and SECOND persons.

We pray for <u>ourselves</u>. **Prō <u>nōbīs</u> ōrāmus.**

But when a pronoun of the THIRD PERSON refers back to the subject of its own clause, the proper form of **suī** must be used instead of **is, ea, id.**

A good man does not praise <u>himself</u>. **Homō bonus <u>sē</u> nōn laudat.**

ASSIGNMENT: Learn the declension of **suī,** GRAMMAR, No. 127. Notice that each form can mean *himself, herself, itself,* or *themselves* according to the MEANING of the word to which it refers.

---

[1] **āla, ae:** *wing.*

JESUS CHRISTUS, DEUS ET HOMO

Christ is the model of all Christian virtues. "Come," He said, "follow Me."
We follow Him by imitating His virtues and thus becoming, as the Saints did,
"other Christs."

Eī sē laudābant. *They were praising themselves.*

Marīa sē nōn laudat. *Mary does not praise herself.*

Caesar sē laudābat. *Caesar was praising himself.*

Legiō sē laudābat. *The legion was praising itself.*

VOCABULARY

suī
$\left\{\begin{array}{l} himself \\ herself \\ itself \\ themselves \end{array}\right.$

etiam, *adv.*   *also*

enim, *conj., postp.*   *for*

EXERCISE 153
Translate:

1. We often pray for ourselves. 2. He prays for himself.
3. You pray for yourself. 4. They pray for themselves. 5. They praise him. 6. The legion prays for itself. 7. I pray for myself.
8. He sees them. 9. You pray for yourselves. 10. She does not praise him. 11. She prays for herself. 12. We have the grace of God in us.

EXERCISE 154
[Essential]
Translate:

1. Holy men do not praise themselves. 2. Mothers praise not themselves but their sons. (Omit *their* in translating.) 3. Men often do not see themselves as we see them. 4. Christians often pray for themselves and for all men. For God gives them and all men grace on account of their prayers. 5. Caesar was not praising himself. 6. The legion also was praising itself. 7. Now Mary does not pray for herself but for us, for she is in heaven and is also the mother of all men. 8. The Gauls often killed themselves after the victories of the Romans.

EXERCISE 155

[Essential]

VIRTŪS RŌMĀNA ET VIRTŪS CHRĪSTIĀNA

The Romans had many virtues and the best of the Romans were upright and idealistic men. Among these was the famous Roman orator and politician, Marcus Tullius Cicero. But they were not Christians and therefore the great Christian virtue of humility was unknown to them. They did not, of course, have our personal devotion to Christ nor our loving submission to God. Their ideal was a natural one, good in many ways, but far inferior to the supernatural ideal which shines forth in our Master and our Model, Jesus Christ.

1. Translate;
2. Point out the words to which the italicized pronouns refer and explain your translation of these pronouns:

Mārcus Tullius Cicerō, ōrātor[1] magnus et bonus, vēritātem et virtūtem saepe laudābat. Dē[2] virtūte "Virtūs propter *sē*," inquit,[3] "laudātur."[4] In ōrātiōnibus hominēs bonōs saepe laudābat, malōs autem nōn laudābat. Multa perīcula sustinēbat; mortem et gladiōs nōn timēbat; nōmen populī Rōmānī semper laudābat.

Cicerō tamen Chrīstiānus nōn erat. (Post *ejus* mortem[5] Chrīstus in terram vēnit.) Itaque Cicerō, glōriae cupidus, *sē* saepe laudābat. Omnēs Rōmānī saepe *sē* laudābant. Senātus *sē* laudābat. Etiam imperātōrēs et ducēs Rōmānī *sē* laudābant. Hominēs sānctī autem nōn *sē* sed Deum laudant, sīcut Marīa, Māter omnium Chrīstiānōrum, *sē* nōn laudābat. *Ea* post Annuntiātiōnem[6] ōrābat:

---

[1] ōrātor, ōrātōris: *an orator* (Cf. ōrātiō).
[2] dē, *prep. w. abl.: concerning.*
[3] inquit: *he said.*
[4] laudātur: *is praised.*
[5] Cicero lived 106-43 B.C.
[6] Annuntiātiō, Annuntiātiōnis: *the Annunciation by the Angel Gabriel.*

Magnificat[1] anima[2] mea Dominum

. . . . quia[3] fēcit[4] mihi magna . . . .

et sānctum nōmen ējus (est).

Cicerō et omnēs Rōmānī spem in *sē* posuērunt. Chrīstiānī autem spem nōn in *sē* sed in grātiā Chrīstī pōnunt.[5] Cicerō multa et gravia perīcula sustinēbat quod et bonus erat et glōriae cupidus. Chrīstiānī autem perīcula sustinent quod Chrīstum *sē*cum habent. Chrīstiānī enim Jēsūm Chrīstum in *sē* "portant." Itaque nōmen Chrīstiānōrum erat etiam "Chrīstophorī."[6]

---

[1] magnificat: *doth magnify.*

[2] anima mea: *my soul.*

[3] quia = quod.

[4] fēcit: *he has done.*

[5] pōnunt: *place.*

[6] Chrīstophorus is from a Greek word meaning "Christ-bearer." Our name Christopher is derived from this.

LESSON 12: PRESENT SYSTEM ACTIVE OF THE THIRD CONJUGATION

1. PRINCIPAL PARTS OF THE THIRD CONJUGATION

The principal parts of verbs of the third conjugation must be memorized from the vocabularies. There is no general rule for their formation.

The present infinitive active, however, always ends in -ere (with the first e *short*!). This is the sign of the third conjugation.

How then can you tell the difference between the second and the third conjugation?

EXERCISE 156

Tell what conjugation each of these infinitives belongs to:

1. dēfendere
2. parāre
3. monēre
4. dūcere

5. gerere
6. pugnāre
7. sustinēre
8. īnstruere

9. dare
10. movēre
11. mittere
12. terrēre

2. PRESENT INDICATIVE ACTIVE OF *MITTŌ*

ASSIGNMENT: Study the model for the present indicative active in GRAMMAR, No. 166. Note that:

1. The final personal signs are the same as for the other conjugations.

2. The third person plural has U in the ending.

VOCABULARY

dūcō, dūcere, dūxī, ductus, 3, tr.
$\left\{\begin{array}{l}lead \\ guide\end{array}\right.$

gerō, gerere, gessī, gestus, 3, tr.
$\left\{\begin{array}{l}carry \\ carry on \\ wage \text{ (w. bellum)}\end{array}\right.$

140

dēfendō, dēfendere, dēfendī, dēfēnsus, *3, tr.*   *defend*

īnstruō, īnstruere, īnstrūxī, īnstrūctus, *3, tr.*   { *draw up*
                                                       { *equip*

mittō, mittere, mīsī, missus, *3, tr.*   *send*

fortiter, *adv.*   { *bravely*
                     { *strongly*

RELATED ENGLISH WORDS

What is the difference between a *missive* and a *missile?* It is safer to builo *viaducts* over railroad tracks. St. Francis Xavier was a great Catholic *missionary.* St. Francis Borgia was the *Duke* of Gandía before he became a Jesuit.

RELATED LATIN WORDS

Chrīstus est **dux** omnium hominum. Caesar erat **fortis.**

EXERCISE 157

1. Why do all the verbs in the vocabulary belong to the third conjugation?

2. Conjugate **mittō** and **dūcō** throughout the present; give three meanings for each form.

3. Give the third person, singular and plural, present of: (a) gerō, (b) dēfendō, (c) īnstruō.

EXERCISE 158

1. Pick out the third persons plural by the final personal signs;

2. Translate, giving three meanings for each form:

1. dēfendunt	7. gerunt	13. mittimus
2. mittis	8. dūcit	14. īnstruunt
3. dēfendit	9. īnstruit	15. mittitis
4. mittunt	10. dēfendimus	16. dēfendis
5. dūcunt	11. mittō	17. dūcimus
6. mittit	12. gerit	18. geris

EXERCISE 159
[Essential]

A SHORT SHORT-STORY—A ROMAN "SPOTTER"

1. Mīles Rōmānus hostēs videt. Hostēs autem eum nōn vident.
2. Mīles servum in castra mittit.
3. Servus Caesarem in castrīs monet. "Hostēs in flūmine sunt; perīculum nōbīs est!"
4. Caesar ducēs et centuriōnēs vocat.
5. Centuriōnēs mīlitēs vocant. Eōs prō castrīs īnstruunt.
6. Caesar mīlitēs dūcit. "Hostēs nōs terrēbimus! Fortiter pugnābimus!
7. Interim hostēs mīlitem Rōmānum vident. Is autem sē fortiter dēfendit.
8. Vident hostēs legiōnem et Caesarem. Metus Caesaris eōs terret. "Caesar est! Superābit nōs! Perīculum est!" Prīncipēs hostium cōpiās īnstruunt. Sē dēfendunt.
9. Rōmānī rem fortiter gerunt et hostēs superant. Hostēs sē Caesarī dant.
10. Caesar mīlitēs et hostēs in castra dūcit; omnēs mīlitēs īnstruit et laudat.

EXERCISE 160
[Essential]

Translate:

1. The Roman legions defend themselves bravely because they are eager for the glory of war. 2. Caesar is leading the army into the territory of the enemy; the enemy sees and fears him. 3. The Romans always wage war bravely with the enemy. 4. The centurion is drawing up the legion in front of the wall. 5. Does he send centurions to the neighboring tribes? 6. Caesar carries a sword. 7. The Romans often carry on war with the neighboring peoples and tribes. 8. Is the slave guiding the column into a narrow and difficult place? 9. The general is strongly warning the Senate. 10. The king is equipping an army; we, however, shall conquer him and his army.

3. IMPERFECT INDICATIVE ACTIVE OF *MITTŌ*

The endings of the imperfect in the third conjugation are EXACTLY like those of the SECOND conjugation.

ASSIGNMENT: Learn the model, GRAMMAR, No. 169.

VOCABULARY

vincō, vincere, vīcī, victus, *3, tr.*	*conquer*
petō, petere, petīvī, petītus, *3, tr.*	$\begin{cases} seek \\ beg \\ request \end{cases}$
pellō, pellere, pepulī, pulsus, *3, tr.*	$\begin{cases} drive \\ repulse \\ rout \end{cases}$
litterae, litterārum	$\begin{cases} letter \text{ } (i.\,e.,\text{ an epistle}) \\ dispatch \end{cases}$

NOTE

Litterae is a plural noun of the first declension (like **cōpiae**).

RELATED ENGLISH WORDS

A *petition* presented to Congress; a *victorious* general.

RELATED LATIN WORD

Imperātōrēs propter **victōriās** laudāmus.

EXERCISE 161

Conjugate in the imperfect indicative active: (a) vincō, (b) mittō, (c) petō, (d) dēfendō.

EXERCISE 162

1. Pick out the third person singular forms by the final personal signs;
2. Translate:

1. pellit	3. īnstruēbat	5. petēbant
2. gerēbant	4. vincēbant	6. pellunt

7. petunt	13. mittēbat	19. vincit
8. pellēbam	14. mittēbam	20. dūcēbant
9. mittēbās	15. petēbat	21. gerēbat
10. mittēbāmus	16. mittēbant	22. vincēbat
11. pellēbant	17. vincunt	23. īnstruēbant
12. dūcēbat	18. mittēbātis	24. pellitis

EXERCISE 163

1. Add the correct final personal signs to the verbs;
2. Translate:

1. Gallī bellum cum Rōmānīs gerēba............ sed eōs nōn vincēba.............
2. Gallī post victōriam Caesaris pācem petēba.............
3. Chrīstus mundum vinci.............
4. Ego hostēs in pontem pellēba.............
5. Hostēs mīlitēs prō castrīs īnstruēba.............
6. Mittēba............ne Caesar litterās?
7. Rēx pācem petēba.............
8. Mīlitēs fortēs hostēs pellu.............

EXERCISE 164
Translate:

1. Propter metum Rōmānōrum Gallī bellum cum eīs gerēbant. Rōmānī autem semper vincēbant. 2. Nōs frūmentum petēbāmus. Vōs frūmentum nōn mittēbātis. 3. Legiōnēs Rōmānae hostēs semper vincunt. 4. Caesar ˙Gallōs pellit.

EXERCISE 165
Translate:

1. The general was sending a dispatch and was begging (for) a supply of rations[1] and swords. 2. We were often routing the enemy. We were often conquering them. Nevertheless they were carrying on the war and defending themselves bravely. 3. They

---

[1] *rations:* **frūmentum, ī.** Grain was the main provision of a Roman army.

were driving the first battle line into a deep river. 4. The general is sending a letter. A slave will carry[1] it into the province.

4. FUTURE INDICATIVE ACTIVE OF *MITTŌ*

The future indicative active of the third conjugation is quite different from that of the first and second. The personal signs are the SAME, but there is NO TENSE SIGN and the VOWEL of the ending changes.

ASSIGNMENT: Study the model, GRAMMAR, No. 172, carefully.

VOCABULARY

pōnō, pōnere, posuī, positus, *3, tr.*	$\begin{cases} put \\ place \\ set \\ pitch \ (\textbf{w. castra}) \end{cases}$
contendō, contendere, contendī, *3, intr.*	$\begin{cases} strive \\ contend \\ hasten \end{cases}$
agō, agere, ēgī, āctus, *3, tr.*	$\begin{cases} drive \\ do \\ act \\ treat \end{cases}$
ibi, *adv.*	*there*
dē, *prep. w. abl.*	$\begin{cases} concerning \\ about \end{cases}$

NOTE

1. **Pōnō** means *pitch* only when it is used of a camp. When an in-phrase is used to modify **pōnō,** in always takes the *ABLATIVE.*

2. **Contendō** has no fourth principal part.

3. **Agō** is not the helping verb *do,* as in "I *did love*" or "I *do fight*"; it is an independent verb, as in "I *did* it."

---

[1] Use **portō.**

EXERCISE 166
Translate:

1. mittent	7. mittet	13. aget
2. mittētis	8. contendēbat	14. pōnit
3. contendit	9. mittēs	15. pōnēbat
4. mittēmus	10. agēbat	16. agam
5. pōnēbant	11. pōnunt	17. contendēbant
6. agit	12. mittam	18. contendunt

EXERCISE 167
[Essential]
Translate:

1. Vōs legiōnēs in castra mittētis. 2. Litterās dē multīs rēbus mittēmus. 3. Rōmānī cum Gallīs semper contendunt. 4. Ubi Rōmānī castra pōnent? 5. Ego frūmentum nōn mittam. 6. Mittēsne servōs? 7. Ibi castra pōnent. 8. Reliquī Gallī prīmā lūce in montēs contendent. 9. Spem salūtis in virtūte pōnet. 10. Eōs in flūmen agam. 11. Senātus dē rē gravī aget.

EXERCISE 168
Translate:

1. We shall pitch the camp there. 2. They will treat with the tribe about peace. 3. He will hasten with all the troops into the town. 4. They will contend with the Gauls. 5. They will put faith in the courage of the remaining legions.

LESSON 13: PRESENT SYSTEM ACTIVE OF THE FOURTH CONJUGATION

To form the principal parts of regular verbs of the fourth conjugation, drop the -iō of the first person singular present indicative and add -īre, -īvī, -ītus (notice the long ī). Thus:

aud-iō, aud-īre, aud-īvī, aud-ītus

ASSIGNMENT: Study the present tense of audiō, GRAMMAR, No. 167.

To find the endings of the imperfect and future indicative of the FOURTH conjugation put an i before the endings of the THIRD. Instead of the endings -ēbam, -ēbās, *etc.*, the fourth has -iēbam, -iēbās, *etc.*; instead of -am, -ēs, *etc.*, it has -iam, -iēs, *etc.* See if you can write out the imperfect and future of audiō without looking in the GRAMMAR.

ASSIGNMENT: Learn the models, GRAMMAR, Nos. 170 and 173.

VOCABULARY

audiō, *4, tr.*	hear
mūniō, *4, tr.*	fortify / construct (*w.* viam *or* viās)
veniō, venīre, vēnī, ventum, *4, intr.*	come
conveniō, convenīre, convēnī, conventum, *4, intr.*	come together / assemble
per, *prep. w. acc.*	through

NOTE

Veniō (as is clear from its meaning) is intransitive; *i. e.*, it cannot take an object in the accusative case. The fourth principal part of INTRANSITIVE verbs is written -um, not -us (**ventum**). This will be explained later.

RELATED ENGLISH WORDS

Munitions of war. The Senate *convened* to discuss the treaty. The 1944 Democratic *convention* nominated Roosevelt and Truman. The *auditorium* was packed.

RELATED LATIN WORD

Adventus

EXERCISE 169
[Present Tense]
Translate:

1. audiunt	5. audiō	9. audit
2. mūnit	6. mūniunt	10. veniunt
3. audīs	7. audītis	11. audīmus
4. venit	8. conveniunt	12. convenītis

EXERCISE 170
[Imperfect and Future Tenses]
Translate:

1. audiam	8. veniētis	15. audiet
2. audiēbātis	9. audiam	16. audiēbam
3. veniēs	10. convenient	17. venient
4. audiēbāmus	11. audient	18. veniēbās
5. audiēs	12. veniam	19. conveniēbant
6. veniet	13. audiētis	20. veniēbat
7. audiēbās	14. veniēbant	

EXERCISE 171
[Drill]
Translate:

1. Metus vōs terret. 2. Senātus conveniet. 3. Impetum sustinēbant. 4. Portum vident. 5. Equitātum timēbunt. 6. Castra pōnunt. 7. Dē victōriā contendent. 8. Oppidum mūniunt. 9. Centuriōnem vocābit. 10. Sē dēfendit. 11. Exercitum in

Galliam mittet. 12. Per silvās veniēbant. 13. Dē rē agēbant. 14. Vōcem audit. 15. Spīritus Deī eum dūcit. 16. Bellum gerēbat. 17. Adventus Caesaris vōs terrēbit. 18. Deum laudat. 19. Collem occupābit. 20. Cōpiās īnstruit. 21. Vōs eōs superābitis. 22. Urbem oppugnābat. 23. Ōrātis. 24. Arma parābant. 25. Ego servōs nōn habēbam. 26. Vōs monēbō. 27. Pontem tenēbunt. 28. Signum portābunt. 29. Fortiter pugnant. 30. Gladiōs dabit. 31. Ego hostēs vincam. 32. Castra movētis. 33. Pācem petam. 34. Equitēs pellitis. 35. Ōrātiōnem audiēbant.

EXERCISE 172
Translate:

1. Ducēs oppida et pontēs saepe mūniunt. 2. Pars hostium per silvās venit; pars autem eōrum per prōvinciam venit. 3. Audīsne vōcēs servōrum? 4. Rōmānī propter commūnem salūtem longās viās per prōvinciās mūniēbant. 5. Clāmōrem equitum audiēbāmus. 6. Imperātor in senātum veniet. Ōrātiōnem ējus senātus audiet. 7. Ducēs et prīncipēs Gallōrum in oppidum convenient. 8. Prīmā lūce senātus in locum tūtum conveniet. Dē rē gravī aget. 9. Interim Caesar cum omnibus cōpiīs per prōvinciam veniēbat. 10. Equitēs Caesarem dē ējus perīculō monēbant. Itaque castra mūnit.

EXERCISE 173
Translate:

1. They are assembling in the camp. 2. The Romans were constructing long roads. 3. They were fortifying the bridges. 4. They will come together at dawn. 5. Are the Romans coming into the territory of the enemy? 6. Do they hear the cries and shouting of the cavalry? 7. Will the column come through the province? 8. The leaders of the tribe were assembling in the mountains. 9. Will they defend the Roman law? 10. The light and truth of Christ guide me. 11. They were hearing the speech of the chief. 12. After the arrival of Caesar the Gauls were fortifying the towns. 13. The general was praising the centurions

on account of their courage and faithfulness. 14. The enemy were bravely defending themselves. 15. There were slaves in the hills. 16. Part of the leading men are now assembling. 17. The Gauls will fear the cavalry after the slaughter of the chiefs. 18. They came into favor with the king on account of the victory. 19. They were treating with the commander in chief about peace. 20. The army was coming through the forest. 21. They will pitch the camp there. But Caesar will attack it. 22. We shall pray in the name of Jesus Christ. Therefore God will give us grace. 23. We praise the holy wounds of Christ. 24. We shall seek peace and salvation through Christ. 25. You will come into Gaul and you will see deep rivers and great mountains, towns and large cities. You will see brave and renowned chiefs. There is an abundance of grain in the cities. You will praise Gaul and the Gauls.

EXERCISE 174

DĒ SENĀTŪ

Translate:

In senātū Rōmānō sunt multī hominēs nōbilēs et fortēs. Senātus Populusque[1] Rōmānus imperium multārum gentium et prōvinciārum habet. Senātus saepe convenit. In senātum rēgēs gentium aliēnārum saepe veniunt. Pācem saepe petunt; saepe cōpiam armōrum et frūmentī petunt. Prīncipēs Rōmānī saepe in senātum veniunt. Dē rēbus gravibus et dē salūte populī Rōmānī saepe agunt. Dē lēgibus, dē bellīs, dē prōvinciīs agunt. Omnēs gentēs aliēnae senātum timent.

---

[1] Populusque = et Populus. Senātus Populusque Rōmānus (usually abbreviated: SPQR) was the official title of the Roman government. It regularly takes a *singular* verb.

LESSON 14: PRESENT SYSTEM INDICATIVE
OF *SUM*

1. PRESENT, IMPERFECT, AND FUTURE INDICATIVE
OF *SUM*

ASSIGNMENT: Review the present indicative of **sum,** GRAMMAR, No. 346. Learn the imperfect and future indicative, GRAMMAR, Nos. 347 and 348. Note that:

1. The final personal signs are the same as in the four conjugations.

2. The third person plural of the future is **erunt.**

VOCABULARY

sum, esse, fuī, futūrus, *intr.*	*am*
undique, *adv.*	$\begin{cases} \textit{from all sides} \\ \textit{on all sides} \end{cases}$
tēlum, ī	*dart*

NOTE

Sum has no PASSIVE; therefore it has no perfect participle *passive.* The future active participle is given as the fourth principal part. We shall study these participles later.

ASSIGNMENT: Review the list of adjectives on pages 96 and 97, and the rules of agreement, GRAMMAR, Nos. 474 and 477.

EXERCISE 175
[Essential]
Translate:

1. Rome was a large and renowned city. 2. The enemy were on all sides. 3. Many rivers of Gaul were deep and long. 4. Will you be brave? 5. There are mountains on all sides. 6. The Roman camp was full of swords and darts. 7. We shall be with God in heaven. 8. We were eager for the grace of God. 9. You

are Christians and sons of God. 10. I am a soldier of Christ. 11. The way is narrow and difficult. 12. The mountains of Gaul are high. 13. Caesar's journeys were often long and difficult. 14. You will be safe on account of the grace of God. 15. Christ is a good and noble leader. 16. The Romans were eager for fame. 17. Are you like Christ? 18. There will be many holy men in heaven. 19. The Gauls are next to the province. 20. The glory of Rome will always be great. 21. We are Christians and God's servants. 22. Many kings were bad. 23. The remaining soldiers were safe. 24. Were you in the first battle line? 25. I was not with Caesar. 26. Not all Christians are like Christ. 27. There are many and large cities in the province.

EXERCISE 176

Translate:

1. Propter metum hostium in castrīs Caesaris sumus. 2. Undique erat clāmor hostium. 3. Erat perīculum grave in prōvinciā. 4. Gallī semper sunt cupidī imperiī. 5. Omnēs hominēs cupidī sunt glōriae. 6. Erantne tēla in castrīs? 7. Undique erant montēs

ROMAN SHIPS

et silvae. 8. In Caelō cum Christō erimus. 9. Erantne montēs altī et difficilēs? 10. Caesar erat imperiī cupidus. 11. Estne Christus fīlius et Marīae et Deī? 12. Estne Marīa grātiā plēna? 13. "Vōs autem omnēs frātrēs estis." (Words of Christ to His disciples.) 14. Eratne Christus in mundō propter nōs? 15. In silvīs nōn erāmus. 16. Caesar in prīmā aciē erat. 17. Erō fortis. 18. Eram in Galliā cum exercitū. 19. Esne eques? Esne mīles? 20. Omnēs hominēs sānctī Christō similēs sunt.

2. COMPOUNDS OF *SUM*

VOCABULARY

absum, abesse, āfuī, āfutūrus, *intr.;* ab (ā) *w. abl.*	am away am distant
longē, *adv.*	far by far

NOTE

Absum is a compound of the preposition **ab** and the verb **sum.** Therefore it is conjugated like SUM. The place away from which something is, is expressed by the preposition **ab** (**ā** before consonants), *from,* and the ablative. Thus:

Caesar was away from the camp. **Caesar ā castrīs aberat.**

RELATED ENGLISH WORD

Many members of Congress were *absent.*

RELATED LATIN WORD

Via **longa** erat.

EXERCISE 177

Translate:

1. Hīberna ab oppidō Gallōrum nōn longē aberant. 2. Caesar longē aberat ā castrīs. 3. Hīberna nōn longē absunt ā Caesare.

4. Legiōnēs aberunt.   5. Caesar aberat.   6. Rōma longē abest ā nōbīs.   7. Deus ā nōbīs nōn longē abest.   8. Bellum et mortis perīculum longē ā Caelō absunt.

EXERCISE 178
Translate:

1. I am away from the camp.   2. He was not far away from the town.   3. They were far away from the river.   4. The river is not far distant from the forest.   5. Gaul is far away from you.

LESSON 15: THE PERFECT SYSTEM ACTIVE

1. THE PERFECT ACTIVE STEM

The perfect system of the indicative active includes the perfect, pluperfect, and future perfect tenses.

These are all formed on the PERFECT ACTIVE STEM.

The perfect active stem is found by dropping the ending -ī of the third principal part:

laudāv-ī	*stem:* laudāv-
monu-ī	*stem:* monu-
mīs-ī	*stem:* mīs-
audīv-ī	*stem:* audīv-
fu-ī	*stem:* fu-

2. THE PERFECT INDICATIVE ACTIVE

The PERFECT tense expresses a past act. There are three forms in English:

1. I *praised*.

2. I *did praise* (used in questions, in negative statements, and for emphasis).

3. I *have praised* (action completed in present time; called the PRESENT PERFECT).

For all these, Latin has one form: the PERFECT INDICATIVE ACTIVE.

The perfect indicative active of ALL LATIN VERBS, REGULAR AND IRREGULAR, is formed by:

1. Finding the perfect stem from the third principal part;

2. Adding the endings shown in the model, GRAMMAR, No. 174.

Note that the final personal signs are the same as in the present system except in the first person and second person singular, laudāv-ī and laudāv-istī.

ASSIGNMENT: Learn the conjugation of laudāvī, monuī, mīsī, audīvī, and fuī, GRAMMAR, Nos. 174, 177-179, and 349.

VOCABULARY

collocō, *1, tr.*	{ place station
maneō, manēre, mānsī, mānsūrus, *2, intr.*	remain
compleō, complēre, complēvī, complētus, *2, tr.; w. abl.*	fill (with)
cēdō, cēdere, cessī, cessūrus, *3, intr.*	{ give way yield
atque (ac), *conj.*	and

NOTE

When compleō is modified by a *with*-phrase, this *with*-phrase is translated by the ablative *without* a preposition. Hence the notation *w. abl.*

He filled the camp <u>*with grain*</u>. Castra frūmentō complēvit.

RELATED ENGLISH WORDS

Mexico *ceded* California to the United States. The destroyer has its full *complement* of men.

RELATED LATIN WORDS

Marīa est grātiā plēna. In locum tūtum vēnit.

EXERCISE 179

1. *Give the perfect stem;*
2. *Give the third person singular and plural of the perfect indicative active, and translate each three ways:*

1.	laudō	7.	portō	13.	habeō	19.	dūcō
2.	occupō	8.	dō	14.	videō	20.	gerō
3.	oppugnō	9.	vocō	15.	teneō	21.	vincō
4.	parō	10.	moneō	16.	moveō	22.	petō
5.	pugnō	11.	timeō	17.	sustineō	23.	pellō
6.	superō	12.	terreō	18.	dēfendō	24.	pōnō

25. contendō	28. veniō	31. sum	34. maneō
26. audiō	29. conveniō	32. absum	35. compleō
27. mūniō	30. agō	33. collocō	36. cēdō

EXERCISE 180

1. *Tell what forms these are;*
2. *Translate:*

1. vīdērunt	13. complēvērunt	25. mittimus
2. cessērunt	14. audīvimus	26. collocat
3. audīvistis	15. oppugnāvērunt	27. fuī
4. mānsit	16. fuistī	28. portāvērunt
5. terruērunt	17. laudāvī	29. collocāvērunt
6. cessit	18. vīcit	30. superāvērunt
7. fuit	19. petīvērunt	31. mīsī
8. monuimus	20. parāvērunt	32. vocāvērunt
9. complēvit	21. fuimus	33. fuērunt
10. mūnīvērunt	22. laudāvistī	34. collocābat
11. mānsērunt	23. collocāvit	35. sustinuērunt
12. mīsērunt	24. monuērunt	36. dēfendērunt

EXERCISE 181
[Essential]

A DREAM OF JUDGMENT

This was my dream. I was in the midst of light, a light brilliant and intense, so intense that it seemed to penetrate and reveal the depths of the soul. And I was aware of a Presence at the very center of the light and I knew with a strange inner conviction that there stood the Angel of Judgment. After a breathless moment, I became aware of other presences, felt rather than saw them. Were they angels? Were they souls? Then the Angel spoke in a voice like the sound of many waters, like no voice ever heard upon earth.

THE VOICE OF THE ANGEL. Quis es?

SECOND VOICE *(harsh and unpleasant).* Ego rēx sum. Rēgnum et imperium Rōmānōrum in terrā tenuī.

Voice of the Angel. Petisne nunc praemium et glōriam?

Second Voice. Ego petō. Ego magnam glōriam in terrā habuī et semper habēbō. Mē omnēs hominēs laudāvērunt. Imperātor magnus fuī. Multa bella fortiter gessī. Dux bonus, omnēs rēs parāvī; frūmentum et arma parāvī; castra et oppida mūnīvī; mīlitēs īnstrūxī et collocāvī. In mē mīlitēs spem semper posuērunt. Ego saepe in prīmā aciē cum mīlitibus pugnāvī. Ego eōs per montēs et silvās dūxī. In Galliā et in omnibus prōvinciīs cum hostibus contendī. Mē metus hostium nōn mōvit neque terruit. Fīnēs multārum gentium occupāvī. Ego et multa oppida et magnās urbēs oppugnāvī. Prōvinciās Rōmānās et eārum urbēs fortiter dēfendī. Hostēs nōminis Rōmānī terruī atque impetūs eōrum fortiter sustinuī. Equitēs et mīlitēs in eōs mīsī—hostēs semper cessērunt. Hostēs pepulī et in bellīs eōs superāvī et vīcī.

The Voice of the Angel. Homō sē fortiter laudat!

Second Voice. Propter mē gentēs prōvinciīs fīnitimae legiōnēs Rōmānās timuērunt; eae saepe prīncipēs in castra Rōmānōrum dē pāce mīsērunt. Mēcum prīncipēs et rēgēs dē pāce ēgērunt. Mihi sē dedērunt. Prīncipēs Gallōrum in castra vocāvī. In castra convēnērunt! Frūmentum petīvī. Magnam cōpiam in castra portāvērunt. Omnēs hominēs mē timuērunt. Omnēs gentēs nōmen rēgis Rōmānī audīvērunt.

Voice of the Angel. *(There was a deeper earnestness in the voice.)* Cūr cum multīs gentibus bellum gessistī? Cūr eās pepulistī, terruistī, vīcistī?

Vox Regis. *(And his voice seemed to swell as though he were speaking in the Roman Senate.)* Propter glōriam et salūtem Senātūs Populīque[1] Rōmānī!

(Suddenly another voice broke in, harsh with malicious hatred.)

Third Voice. Nōn! Nōn propter ea! sed quod cupidus fuit glōriae et imperiī! Pācem nōn petīvit, sed gladiōs et bella et caedem petīvit. Flūmina et silvās et oppida corporibus complēvit; mīlitēs et nautās caedī dedit quod SIBI glōriam petīvit. Praemium eī dabō EGO.

---

[1] Populīque = et Populī.

SANCTUS MICHAEL[1]

Vox Regis *(shaken and fearful).* Quis es tū?

THIRD VOICE. Aaah! Mē nōn vīdistī, sed nōn longē ā tē āfuī. Omnia vīdī. Tē autem nōn monuī. *(A shrill, diabolical laugh.)* Tēcum semper in terrā fuī—nunc mēcum manēbis in saecula saeculōrum!

(A black shadow passed swiftly across the light . . . a shriek, and then again the peace and the brilliance. Then I knew that another had entered.)

VOICE OF THE ANGEL. Quis es? THE NEW VOICE. Chrīstiānus sum. VOICE OF THE ANGEL. Quid petis? Petisne glōriam cum Chrīstō? CHRISTIANUS. Deum et Chrīstum petō. *(Then silence.)*

THE GUARDIAN ANGEL. Is sē nōn dēfendet neque laudābit. Ego autem semper cum eō fuī. Servus imperātōris Rōmānī fuit. Lēgem autem Chrīstī fortiter tenuit; in nōmine Chrīstī ōrāvit. Imperātor autem eum, quod Chrīstiānus fuit, in vinculīs[2] tenuit. Metus autem mortis et vulnerum eum nōn mōvit neque terruit. Spem in grātiā Chrīstī posuit et fidem semper tenuit. Itaque Rōmānī ?um occīdērunt.

(The light grew slowly more intense and a new voice, stronger and more tender, spoke:)

Intrā[3] in gaudium[4] Dominī tuī.[5]

(Vōcēs undique audīvī:)

Glōria Patrī et Fīliō et Spīrituī Sānctō sīcut erat in prīncipiō et nunc et semper et in saecula saeculōrum. Āmēn.

The vision faded.

---

[1] Sānctus Michael: *St. Michael the Archangel.*
[2] vinculum, ī: *chain.*
[3] intrā: *enter!*
[4] gaudium, ī: *joy.*
[5] tuus, a, um: *your.*

EXERCISE 182
[Essential]
Translate:

1. Caesar stationed soldiers on the bridge and in front of the camp. 2. Christ did not remain on earth. 3. They filled the walls with men. 4. Caesar prepared a supply of grain. 5. The Romans did not often yield to the enemy. 6. Where have you been? 7. The Senate often praised Caesar on account of his victories. 8. Caesar did not fear danger and death. 9. There were many Romans in Gaul. 10. Did the Romans overcome the Gauls? 11. Did they treat with the chief about peace? 12. The leading men of the Gauls assembled at dawn. 13. The cavalry did not yield, but withstood the attack bravely. 14. Who conquered the Gauls and seized their cities and towns? 15. The Gauls did not praise Caesar, but they feared him. 16. Have you seen Rome?

3. PLUPERFECT AND FUTURE PERFECT INDICATIVE ACTIVE

VOCABULARY

incitō, *1, tr.*	*incite* / *arouse*
adjuvō, adjuvāre, adjūvī, adjūtus, *1, tr.*	*help* / *aid*
servō, *1, tr.*	*guard* / *keep*
perturbō, *1, tr.*	*confuse* / *disturb*
incendō, incendere, incendī, incēnsus, *3, tr.*	*set fire to* / *burn*
tum, *adv.*	*then* / *at that time*

RELATED ENGLISH WORDS
Incendiary bombs. The general's *adjutant*. He was very *perturbed*.

ASSIGNMENT: Learn the models in GRAMMAR, Nos. 175-176 and 180-185, for the pluperfect indicative active and the future perfect indicative active. Notice that the PERFECT stem is used and that the endings are the SAME in all conjugations.

EXERCISE 183
[Essential]

1. Translate;
2. Explain the case of the italicized nouns:

1. Prīncipēs gentēs *prōvinciae* fīnitimās incitāverant quod *victōriae* cupidī erant. 2. Interim equitēs *reliquōs* Gallōs perturbāverant. 3. Chrīstiānī bonī fidem et vēritātem Chrīstī servāverant. 4. Imperātor urbēs et oppida incenderat. 5. Multī Gallī legiōnēs Rōmānās adjūverant. 6. Dux hostium collēs *hominibus* complēverat. 7. Equitēs agmen hostium perturbāverant. 8. Virtūs Rōmam servāverat. 9. Caesar et collēs et pontēs prīmā lūce occupāverat. 10. Senātus prōvinciam *Caesarī* dederat.

EXERCISE 184
[Essential]
Translate:

1. The king had aroused the slaves. 2. God had helped them. 3. They had kept the faith. 4. The cavalry had confused the enemy. 5. The slaves had burned the town. 6. They had called the leading men of Gaul into the Senate. 7. He had stationed the cavalry in the forest. The enemy made an attack on them.

EXERCISE 185
Translate:

1. The Senate praised Caesar. 2. The Gauls had always feared Caesar. 3. The cavalry terrified the enemy. 4. The soldiers had burned the crops. 5. The slaves had helped the enemy. 6. They kept the faith. 7. They did not yield. 8. They have held the city. 9. They moved camp. 10. He seized the bridge. 11. They

had prepared many darts. 12. The slaves had had arms.
13. They saw the Roman column. 14. They did not withstand
the attack. 15. He defended himself. 16. They sent arms into
Gaul. 17. The slaves had carried grain into the camp. 18. The
Romans overcame the Gauls. 19. They had prayed for the
king. 20. He has called the chiefs.

UNIT FOUR

LESSON 16: ADDITIONAL NOUNS AND ADJECTIVES OF THE FIRST AND SECOND DECLENSIONS

1. DECLENSION OF *PUER, AGER,* AND *VIR*

There are, in the second declension, a few MASCULINE nouns that do not end in **-us.** These are:

> PUER, PUERĪ, *boy,* and similar words;
> AGER, AGRĪ, *field,* and similar words;
> VIR, VIRĪ, *man.*

How can you tell that these words belong to the second declension? Find the stems of **puer, ager,** and **vir.** NOTICE THE DIFFERENCE IN THEIR STEMS! Except in the nominative singular, all these words have the SAME ENDINGS AS SERVUS, Ī. Now complete these declensions without looking in the GRAMMAR:

puer	ager	vir
puer-ī	agr-ī	vir-ī
etc.	*etc.*	*etc.*

ASSIGNMENT: Study GRAMMAR, Nos. 41-43.

VOCABULARY

puer, puerī	*boy*
ager, agrī	*field*
vir, virī	*man*
Italia, ae	*Italy*
fortūna, ae	*fortune*
ita, *adv.*	{ *so* *thus*
trāns, *prep. w. acc.*	*across*

163

NOTE

Homō means a human being, a man as opposed to an animal; **vir** means a man as opposed to a woman or a child.

Chrīstus propter nōs homines in mundum vēnit.
Christ came into the world on account of us men.

Men here means the human race; Christ came for both men and women, hence **homines.**

Caesar erat vir fortis.
Caesar was a brave man.

Vir is used because Caesar is not a woman and has manly, virile qualities.

Hereafter use **homō** only when *a human being* or *man* in general is meant.

RELATED ENGLISH WORDS

A *puerile* remark. A *virile* character. The *agrarian* party. Lindbergh made the first solo *trans*atlantic flight.

EXERCISE 186

Translate:

1. With good boys. 2. On behalf of noble men. 3. Into good fields. 4. A field full of boys. 5. In the fields. 6. With a brave man. 7. In a large field. 8. A boy similar to a brave man. 9. On account of the glory of brave men. 10. Through the fields of the Gauls. 11. The death of a brave man. 12. On account of the slaughter of mothers and boys. 13. The good fortune of a brave and noble man.

EXERCISE 187

[Essential]

Translate:

1. Virī Rōmānī fortēs erant et fortiter cum hostibus pugnā vērunt. Ita Rōmam servāvērunt. Fortūna enim virōs fortēs ad-juvat. 2. Multī hostēs trāns montēs in Italiam vēnērunt. *Eōs*

tamen Rōmānī vīcērunt. 3. Puer bonus est glōria mātris. Omnēs enim patrēs et mātrēs puerōs bonōs semper laudant sed puerōs malōs nōn laudant. 4. Tum, post adventum exercitūs Rōmānī, erat magna frūmentī inopia in Galliā. Rōmānī enim frūmenta in agrīs incenderant. 5. In Italiā *erant* agrī bonī, virī nōbilēs, puerī bonī. 6. Imperātor Rōmānus cum omnibus cōpiīs in agrōs hostium vēnit. Frūmenta incendit; oppida et urbēs oppugnāvit; virōs et puerōs in castra dūxit.

REVIEW QUESTIONS ON EXERCISE 187

The words to which these questions refer are italicized in Exercise 187.

Sentence 2 : Give the rule for the agreement of **eōs.**
Sentence 5 : Explain the translation of **erant.**

EXERCISE 188

This exercise reviews all the verbs of the first conjugation and drills on the present indicative.

Translate:

1. All men praise good fortune. 2. Hannibal,[1] a brave and renowned man, has come across the mountains and is seizing a large part of Italy. 3. Good boys often pray. 4. The boys are preparing arms. 5. They have come across the river into the fields and are burning the crops. 6. He is placing troops in the fields of the enemy. 7. Brave men are fighting for us. 8. He is stationing men in the fields of Italy. 9. Thus do we brave soldiers keep the glory of the Roman name. 10. The boys are helping the men in the fields. 11. Who is calling the boy? 12. Is the boy carrying a dispatch into Italy? 13. What are you giving the boy? 14. Did they overcome the Gauls? 15. What does the boy carry? 16. Who is inciting the tribes of Gaul? 17. We do not help bad men. 18. He is stationing the soldiers before the gate of the camp. 19. They are storming the cities of Italy.

---

[1] *Hannibal:* **Hannibal, Hannibalis.**

Rhenus Fl.
GALLIA
ALPES
Rhodanus Fl.
Flumen
Padus
Genua
Aquileia
ILLYRICUM
ITALIA
Florentia
Arnus Fl.
ETRURIA
UMBRIA
Tiberis Fl.
CORSICA
Roma
Ostia
LATIUM
APULIA
Cannae
Neapolis
Tarentum
SARDINIA
Messana
Rhegium
SICILIA
Syracusae
MARE MEDITERRANEUM
Carthago
Zama
ROMA
JFH

READING NO. 4

DĒ ITALIĀ ET DĒ GALLIĀ

Italia est terra et magna et bona. Vidēsne Italiam in tabulā?[1]
Estne Italia magna? Estne longa? In Italiā erat Rōma, urbs et
magna et nōbilis. Vidēsne Rōmam in tabulā?[1] Rōma in flūmine
Tiberī est. Vidēsne flūmen in tabulā?[1] In Italiā erant multae et
magnae urbēs, flūmina longa, montēs altī. Erant etiam agrī frūmentōrum plēnī. In agrīs Italiae Rōmānī multa bella cum fīnitimīs gentibus gesserant et tandem[2] omnem Italiam vīcerant. Ita
imperium Italiae Rōmānī tenuērunt. In omnibus Italiae partibus
omnēs virī et puerī nōmen Rōmānum et laudābant et dēfendēbant.
Alpēs[3] sunt montēs magnī et altī. Vidēsne montēs in tabulā?[1]
Trāns Alpēs tum erant et Prōvincia Rōmāna et Gallia. Multī
imperātōrēs trāns montēs in Italiam vēnērunt. Hannibal,[4] vir
fortis et nōbilis, per montēs difficilēs cum omnibus cōpiīs in
Italiam vēnit et ita in Italiae agrīs cum Rōmānīs bellum gessit.
Tum Caesar legiōnēs Rōmānās trāns montēs in agrōs Gallōrum
dūxit. Napoleon etiam, imperātor fortis, cum magnīs cōpiīs trāns
montēs in Italiam contendit et omnem Italiam occupāvit.

Rōma, sīcut in tabulā[1] vidēs, longē abest ā Galliā. In Galliā
erant etiam urbēs et oppida et agrī bonī. Erant flūmina et montēs.
Eōs in tabulā[1] vidēs. Vidēs etiam fīnēs Prōvinciae Rōmānae.
Ējus imperium Caesar tenuit et cum Gallīs bella gessit. Post victōriās Caesaris Rōmānī imperium omnis Galliae tenuērunt.

MĀTER ITALIAE—RŌMA

—Florus[5]

---

[1] tabula, ae: *map.*
[2] tandem, *adv.: finally.*
[3] Alpēs, Alpium: *the Alps.*
[4] Hannibal, Hannibalis: *Hannibal* (a great Carthaginian general).
[5] L. Annaeus Florus, a Roman historian.

2. DECLENSION OF *MISER* AND *INTEGER*

There are, in the first and second declensions, a few adjectives whose masculine is like **puer** or **ager.**

LIKE PUER: miser, miser-a, miser-um, *wretched*
    STEM: miser-

LIKE AGER: integer, integr-a, integr-um, *fresh, uninjured*
    STEM: integr-

ENDINGS: The endings for **miser** and **integer** are exactly like those of **magnus** except in the nominative masculine singular, **miser, integer.**

ASSIGNMENT: Decline **miser** and **integer** without looking in the GRAMMAR. Then study GRAMMAR, Nos. 74-76.

VOCABULARY

miser, misera, miserum	*wretched*
līber, lībera, līberum	*free*
integer, integra, integrum	{*fresh* *uninjured* *whole*
proelium, ī	*battle*
cīvitās, cīvitātis	*state*

NOTE

The ablative of **proelium** is generally used *without* in in such expressions as: *in many battles,* **multīs proeliīs.**

RELATED ENGLISH WORDS

Lincoln *liberated* the slaves. A *miserable* fellow. The number one is an *integer.*

EXERCISE 189

Decline:

1. servus miser
2. legiō integra
3. rēs misera
4. oppidum līberum

EXERCISE 190
Translate:

1. With fresh forces. 2. For free men. 3. Against the wretched Gauls. 4. With fresh legions. 5. In a free state. 6. With the wretched slaves. 7. After the victory of free men. 8. On account of a wretched fortune. 9. On account of the glory of a free state.

DOMINUS ERIT TĒCUM IN OMNĪ TEMPORE[1]
ET LOCŌ.
—From the *Following of Christ*[2]

EXERCISE 191
[Essential]
Translate:

1. Virī nōbilēs et līberī cīvitātem Americānam[3] servāvērunt. 2. Rōmānī, *virī* fortēs et līberī, Gallōs miserōs multīs proeliīs vīcērunt. Rōmānōs enim etiam fortūna adjūvit. 3. Ducēs legiōnēs integrās in prīmā aciē collocant. 4. Rōmānī oppida Gallōrum oppugnāvērunt; agrōs *eōrum* occupāvērunt; frūmenta incendērunt; prīncipēs, ducēs, mātrēs, patrēs, virōs, puerōs, occīdērunt. Ita *eōs* vīcērunt. 5. Hannibal,[4] vir fortis et nōbilis, cum omnibus cōpiīs trāns montēs in agrōs Italiae contendit. Cum eō Rōmānī fortiter contendērunt. Urbēs et oppida Italiae dēfendērunt. Post multa proelia et magnam caedem Rōmānī eum superāvērunt. Ita glōriam nōminis Rōmānī servāvērunt.

---

[1] tempus, temporis, *n.: time.*

[2] *The Following of Christ* is a book of religious meditations and instructions composed by the educator Gerard Groote after his conversion and entry into religious life (about A. D. 1386), and either written down or at least edited by his disciple Thomas à Kempis (1379-1471). Next to the New Testament, the volume is the most famous and influential Christian religious work ever written.

[3] Americānus, a, um: *American.*

[4] Hannibal, Hannibalis: *Hannibal.*

REVIEW QUESTIONS ON EXERCISE 191
*The words to which these questions
refer are italicized in Exercise 191*

Sentence 2: Explain the use of **virī**.
Sentence 4: Give the rule for the agreement of **eōrum** and **eōs**. Explain.

MONTĀNĪ[1] SEMPER LĪBERĪ

(Motto of West Virginia)

EXERCISE 192
*This exercise reviews all third-conjugation
verbs and drills on the imperfect.*

Translate:

1. He was leading fresh troops into the battle. 2. The chief was defending the wretched Gauls. 3. The Romans were conquering free states. 4. The Romans conquered the Gauls in many battles. 5. After the battle they were burning the crops and the towns. 6. The soldiers, brave and free men, were repulsing the enemy. 7. He was treating with the master concerning his wretched slave. 8. They were pitching camp after the battle. 9. The fresh legions were not yielding. 10. He was hastening into Gaul with fresh forces. 11. The slaves were not carrying arms. 12. The wretched Gauls were seeking peace. 13. Was he sending a dispatch into Italy? 14. After the battle he was drawing up the uninjured troops. 15. We Americans[2] were defending a free state. 16. They were sending boys and men into the fields. 17. We Americans shall always be free.

---

[1] **montānī, montānōrum:** *mountaineer:.*

[2] From now on proper nouns and adjectives will ordinarily not be given in footnotes. If necessary, they may be found in the vocabularies in the back of the book.

EXERCISE 193

Answer in complete Latin sentences:

1. Suntne servī līberī?
2. Estne cīvitās Americāna lībera?
3. Erantne servī Rōmānī miserī?
4. Esne vir līber?
5. Esne puer miser?
6. Eratne Washingtonius vir fortis et nōbilis?

READING NO. 5

RŌMA AETERNA

Rome first appeared in our history as a small country village on the Tiber. In the course of centuries of expansion, however, she built up a vast and well-organized empire. The city on the seven hills grew into a city of splendor and became the capital of the western world. What was the secret of Rome's success? The Romans certainly were practical men, gifted in organization. They were builders whose roads survived for centuries, whose monuments of masonry still stand today. All of these things and many others contributed to their success. But behind all there was the driving power of the Roman spirit. Throughout their history the Romans displayed a tenacity of purpose, a stubborn determination, that no odds and no disasters could overcome. There were many dark days in the history of Rome, but the Roman people never despaired. The great achievements of Rome's heroes became part of the Roman tradition and the Roman spirit. No wonder then that the Romans became convinced that fortune had chosen Rome for an eternal destiny of power. This conviction they crystallized in the phrase **Rōma aeterna,** *eternal Rome.*

Translate:

Rōmānī spem salūtis et victōriae semper in virtūte pōnēbant. In bellīs omnia parābant; oppida et castra mūniēbant; mīlitēs et equitēs habēbant; frūmentī cōpiam parābant. Saepe ducēs et imperātōrēs magnī et nōbilēs erant. Sed nōn propter ea omnia

ROMA AETERNA

Rōmānī vīcērunt. Multae enim gentēs ea omnia habēbant sed hostēs nōn vīcērunt. Rōmānī tamen hostēs multōs et magnōs vīcērunt. Hostēs saepe castra oppugnāverant, legiōnēs vīcerant, agrōs et urbēs occupāverant. Senātus Populusque[1] Rōmānus tamen pācem nōn petīvit. Prīncipēs in senātū dē pāce nōn ēgērunt. Victōriae et imperiī et glōriae cupidī erant. Itaque Rōmānī hostēs semper vīcērunt. Victōria erat Rōmānōrum propter virtūtem Rōmānam. Itaque glōria nōminis Rōmānī magna fuit et Rōmam aeternam[2] et Rōmānī et gentēs aliēnae laudāvērunt.

> ## RŌMA
> Māter rēgumque[3] ducumque

---

[1] Populusque = et Populus.
[2] aeternus, a, um: *eternal.*
[3] rēgumque ducumque = et rēgum et ducum.

3. POSSESSIVE ADJECTIVES OF THE FIRST AND SECOND PERSONS

The possessive adjectives of the FIRST PERSON are:

meus, a, um $\quad\begin{cases} my \\ mine \end{cases}$

noster, nostra, nostrum $\quad\begin{cases} our \\ ours \end{cases}$

The possessive adjectives of the SECOND PERSON are:

tuus, a, um $\quad\begin{cases} your \text{ (when referring to} \\ yours \qquad \text{ONE person)} \end{cases}$

vester, vestra, vestrum $\quad\begin{cases} your \text{ (when referring to MORE} \\ yours \qquad \text{THAN ONE person)} \end{cases}$

1. DECLENSION:

Meus, a, um and **tuus, a, um** are declined like **magnus, a, um.**
Noster, nostra, nostrum and **vester, vestra, vestrum** are declined like **integer, integra, integrum.**

EXERCISE 194

Decline: (a) tuus, (b) meus, (c) vester, (d) noster.

2. AGREEMENT:

As adjectives the possessive adjectives AGREE WITH THE NOUN THEY MODIFY.

       mīlitēs meī, *my soldiers*
       propter virtūtēs tuās, *on account of your virtues*
       rēx noster, *our king*
       in oppidō vestrō, *in your town*

EXERCISE 195

Decline in singular and plural:

1. amīcus meus   3. virtūs tua
2. rēx noster   4. oppidum vestrum

MOMENTS AT MASS NO. 1

Frequently during Mass the priest turns to the people and says:

DOMINUS VŌBĪSCUM!

and the server, in the name of the people, answers:

ET CUM SPĪRITŪ TUŌ!

3. EXAMPLES OF USAGE:

Vōs propter virtūtēs vestrās laudō. *I praise you for your virtues.*
(I am speaking to MORE THAN ONE person; hence vōs is used
and so vestr- must also be used. Vestrās is feminine accusative
plural because it AGREES with virtūtēs.)

Mātrem tuam laudō. *I praise your mother.*
(I am speaking to ONE person; hence tu- must be used. Tuam
is feminine accusative singular because it AGREES WITH mātrem.)

Mīlitēs meōs laudant. *They praise my soldiers.*
(ONE person is speaking; hence me- must be used. Meōs is
masculine accusative plural because it AGREES WITH mīlitēs.)

EXERCISE 196
Translate:

1. On account of your fortune. 2. In our fields. 3. With our
brave men. 4. After my death. 5. In your state. 6. On account
of the glory of our fathers.

EXERCISE 197
[Essential]
Translate:

1. Patrēs nostrī, virī et līberī et fortēs, multīs proeliīs cum
hostibus contendērunt. Ita cīvitātem nostram et dēfendērunt et
servāvērunt. Itaque nunc cīvitātem et nōbilem et līberam habēmus. 2. Vōbīscum dē salūte mīlitum vestrōrum agēmus. 3. Tē
propter caedem servōrum miserōrum nōn laudō neque virtūtem
tuam laudō. 4. In prīmam aciem legiōnēs meās integrās mittam.
5. Oppida vestra et urbēs vestrās oppugnābimus. Frūmenta incendēmus. Puerōs vestrōs et mātrēs vestrās terrēbimus. Ita mīlitēs
vestrōs vincēmus. 6. Bellum difficile et perīculōrum plēnum est.
Hostēs trāns montēs veniunt. In agrōs vestrōs veniunt. Cum eīs
fortiter pugnābitis neque dē pāce cum eīs agētis. Fortūna etiam
vōs adjuvābit.

"MĀTER DEĪ EST MĀTER MEA!"

—St. Stanislaus Kostka[1]

EXERCISE 198
[Essential]
This exercise reviews all second-conjugation verbs.
Translate:

1. Our brave soldiers do not fear your attacks. 2. I shall warn your commander in chief. 3. Our state shall always be free. 4. Our cavalry will terrify your soldiers. 5. We shall see your fields and your cities. 6. Our soldiers, brave and free men, were holding the hill. 7. We shall move our camp at dawn. 8. They will not withstand our cavalry. 9. I shall remain in my city. 10. You were filling the wall with your men. 11. Your slave is warning me. 12. Do you hear our cavalry? 13. Are you holding your camp? 14. Will our men withstand their attack? 15. I do not fear your soldiers, for our brave men will withstand them.

READING NO. 6

THE SECOND PUNIC WAR

In the third century before Christ, Carthage, a city on the northern coast of Africa, was the center of a powerful empire. It was the one rival of the growing power of Rome in the western Mediterranean, and it was therefore inevitable that these two nations should meet in a final struggle for power. This struggle came in the Second Punic War (218-202), a war in which Roman courage and Roman endurance were tested to the utmost. Later generations of Romans were to look back to the hard years of this war as Americans look back to Valley Forge or Englishmen to the German Blitz of World War II.

---

[1] Stanislaus Kostka was the son of a prominent Polish nobleman. Born in 1550, he entered the Society of Jesus after having a vision of the Blessed Virgin with her Infant Son. He died while yet a novice in 1568.

The war began when a Carthaginian army under Hannibal—one of the greatest generals of all history—attacked a Roman ally in Spain. At the very outset Hannibal conceived the daring and unexpected plan of crossing the Pyrenees and the Alps and invading Italy from the north.

Translate:

Hannibal, vir fortis et nōbilis, tum erat Carthāginiēnsium[1] imperātor. Hostis populī Rōmānī semper fuerat. Victōriae et imperiī cupidus fuit. Itaque cum Rōmānīs bellum fortiter gerēbat. Is cum magnō exercitū in Hispāniā erat. Magnum numerum mīlitum et equitum et elephantōrum[2] sēcum habēbat. Cum omnibus cōpiīs per Galliam contendit (nōndum enim erat prōvincia Rōmāna in Galliā). Per silvās magnās mīlitēs dūxit. Trāns flūmina alta exercitum dūxit. Alpēs altī et magnī montēs erant. Via per eōs difficilis et angusta fuit. Multae Gallōrum gentēs cum eō bellum gerēbant. Is tamen Gallōs multīs proeliīs pepulit et cum mīlitibus et impedīmentīs et elephantīs[2] per montēs in Italiam vēnit.

This was a terrible surprise to the Romans, who, meanwhile, had been planning an expedition to Africa. No one had expected Hannibal to transport such an army with its elephants and all its equipment across the mountain barrier that guarded the north.

As Hannibal stood on the southern slopes of the Alps and saw Italy before him at last, he spoke to his exhausted and discouraged men in some such fashion as this:

"Italia est! In Italiā sunt agrī bonī et cōpia omnium rērum. Sunt etiam oppida et multae et magnae urbēs. Eās Rōmānī nunc tenent, sed nōs Rōmānōs superābimus. Urbēs et agrōs tenēbimus, etiam Rōmam occupābimus. Rōmānī fortēs sunt, sed nōs etiam sumus fortēs. Nōs nōn superābunt. Itaque omnem victōriae spem in virtūte pōnēmus! Fortūna etiam nōs adjuvābit; fortūna enim fortēs semper adjuvat. Post victōriam magna vōbīs praemia dabō et magnam habēbimus bellī glōriam!"

---

[1] **Carthāginiēnsēs, Carthāginiēnsium:** *Carthaginians.*
[2] **elephantus, ī:** *elephant.*

QUESTIONS ON READING NO. 6

Answer in Latin:

1. Quis fuit Hannibal?
2. Eratne vir fortis?
3. Ubi fuit?
4. Quid sēcum habuit?
5. Vēnitne in Italiam?

UNIT FIVE

LESSON 17: PRESENT SYSTEM PASSIVE OF THE FIRST CONJUGATION; AGENCY

1. ACTIVE AND PASSIVE VOICE

The boy throws the ball.

The boy is throwing the ball.

The boy does throw the ball.

Is the boy throwing the ball?

Does the boy throw the ball?

All these sentences say or ask WHO IS DOING THE ACTION, *i. e.,* who is throwing. Hence, the verbs in all these sentences are in the ACTIVE VOICE because the SUBJECT—the boy—ACTS.

WHEN IS A VERB IN THE ACTIVE VOICE?

WHEN THE SUBJECT IS THE PERSON OR THING THAT <u>DOES</u> THE ACTION.

All the verbs you have studied so far have been in the ACTIVE VOICE.

Is the ball being thrown?

The ball is being thrown.

These sentences say or ask to what the action is being done. The verbs in these sentences are in the PASSIVE VOICE because the SUBJECT—the ball—RECEIVES THE ACTION.

WHEN IS A VERB IN THE PASSIVE VOICE?
WHEN THE SUBJECT IS THE PERSON OR THING TO WHICH THE ACTION IS DONE.

EXERCISE 199

Point out the voice of the verbs in these sentences:

1. America *is being praised* by many nations. 2. Christ *was crucified* by Roman soldiers. 3. The martyrs *kept* the faith. 4. The faith *was kept* by the martyrs. 5. I *am praying.* 6. When St. Augustine *was dying,* his own city *was being attacked* by the Vandals. 7. *Will* America *be kept* free? 8. Rome *had been captured* by the Gauls early in its history. 9. *Is* God *being served* by all men? 10. We *have* often *been told* of the exploits of our heroic pilots. 11. We *have* often *heard* of the heroism of our soldiers.

2. FINAL PERSONAL SIGNS IN THE PASSIVE

When we studied the present system ACTIVE we found the following final personal signs:

1. *I*	$\begin{cases}\text{-ō} \\ \text{-m}\end{cases}$		*we*	**-mus**
2. *you*	**-s**		*you*	**-tis**
3. *he, she, it*	**-t**		*they*	**-nt**

Now, the present, imperfect, and future indicative active (of all conjugations) become PASSIVE by changing these final personal signs as follows:

1.	**-ō**	to **-or**		**-mus**	to **-mur**
	-m	to **-r**			
2.	**-s**	to **-ris**		**-tis**	to **-minī**
3.	**-t**	to **-tur**		**-nt**	to **-ntur**

EXAMPLES:

laudō, *I am praising*	becomes laudor, *I am being praised*
laudābam, *I was praising*	becomes laudābar, *I was being praised*
laudās, *you are praising*	becomes laudāris, *you are being praised*
laudat, *he is praising*	becomes laudātur, *he is being praised*
laudāmus, *we are praising*	becomes laudāmur, *we are being praised*
laudātis, *you are praising*	becomes laudāminī, *you are being praised*
laudant, *they are praising*	becomes laudantur, *they are being praised*

EXERCISE 200

1. Translate the active form here given;
2. Change the active form to the corresponding passive form:

EXAMPLE:	Active Form	Meaning	Passive Form
	laudō	*I am praising*	laudor

1. vocō	13. laudābit	25. collocābunt
2. terreō	14. laudāmus	26. mūniunt
3. audiēbam	15. vincēmus	27. laudātis
4. terrēbam	16. audiēbāmus	28. audiunt
5. laudābō	17. monēmus	29. mittimus
6. monēbō	18. laudābimus	30. laudāmus
7. dās	19. laudātis	31. audītis
8. monēs	20. pōnitis	32. laudant
9. agit	21. perturbātis	33. laudās
10. sustinet	22. adjuvābātis	34. moneō
11. mittit	23. monēbunt	35. mittō
12. vincit	24. dūcēbant	

3. PRESENT SYSTEM PASSIVE OF THE FIRST CONJUGATION

ASSIGNMENT: Study the present, imperfect, and future indicative passive of the first conjugation, GRAMMAR, Nos. 243-245. Notice that one form does not follow the rules given for final personal signs in Section 2. The exception is future tense, second person singular: **laudābis** becomes **laudāberis**.

VOCABULARY

administrō, *1, tr.*	*manage* / *attend to*
appellō, *1, tr.*	*address* / *call (upon)*
cōnfirmō, *1, tr.*	*encourage* / *strengthen*

RELATED ENGLISH WORDS

The sacrament of *confirmation*. The president of the United States should be a good *administrator*.

REVIEW VOCABULARY

dō, dare, dedī, datus, *1, tr.*	*give*
adjuvō, adjuvāre, adjūvī, adjūtus, *1, tr.*	*help* / *aid*
collocō, *1, tr.*	*place* / *station*
oppugnō, *1, tr.*	*attack* / *assault* / *storm*

EXERCISE 201

Give the third person, singular and plural, of the present, imperfect, and future indicative passive of the words in the vocabulary. Translate each form given.

EXERCISE 202
Translate:

1. administrātur	5. collocātur	9. adjuvantur
2. appellātur	6. laudāberis	10. appellābāmur
3. oppugnantur	7. cōnfirmābantur	11. laudāmur
4. cōnfirmātur	8. administrābantur	12. datur

EXERCISE 203

1. Change to the passive;
2. Translate both passive and active forms:

1. cōnfirmō	6. cōnfirmat	11. cōnfirmābunt
2. appellābam	7. administrābat	12. collocant
3. cōnfirmābant	8. adjuvābit	13. cōnfirmant
4. dabat	9. appellāmus	14. dat
5. administrās	10. adjuvātis	15. collocābās

EXERCISE 204

Translate:

1. Marīa appellābātur. 2. Prōvincia administrābitur. 3. Amīcī cōnfirmantur. 4. Gallia administrātur. 5. Rōmānī cōnfirmābantur. 6. Mundus administrātur. 7. Bella administrantur. 8. Deus Rēx hominum appellātur. 9. Imperātor appellābitur. 10. Pāx cōnfirmābitur. 11. Prīncipēs appellantur. 12. Virtūs legiōnum cōnfirmābātur. 13. Spīritus Sānctus appellātur. 14. Rēs administrābātur. 15. Spēs victōriae cōnfirmātur. 16. Centuriōnēs appellābuntur. 17. Virī fortēs cōnfirmābuntur. 18. Rōma nōn oppugnābitur. 19. Terra et caelum laudantur. 20. Litterae ducis hostī dantur. 21. Nautae nōn adjuvābantur. 22. Hīberna oppugnābantur. 23. Signum legiōnibus datur. 24. Glōria Deō dabitur. 25. Magnus servōrum numerus eī dabātur. 26. Salūs et vēritās nōbīs per Chrīstum dantur. 27. Praemia mīlitibus dabuntur. 28. Victōria nautārum laudābitur. 29. Multī hominēs in colle collocābuntur. 30. Gentēs fīnitimae adjuvantur. 31. Pars mīlitum in fīnibus hostium collocātur. 32. Puerī malī nōn laudantur. 33. Arma Caesarī dabantur. 34. Oppidum oppugnābitur. 35. Populus Rōmānus adjuvābātur. 36. Mīlitēs in mūrō collocantur. 37. Fortūna bona laudābātur. 38. Propter grātiam Caesaris frūmentum Rōmānīs datur. 39. Nōmen Deī semper laudābitur. 40. Propter metum vulnerum et mortis, mīlitēs Deum appellant. 41. Mīlitēs in ponte collocantur. 42. Jēsūs Chrīstus, Dominus noster, laudābitur.

EXERCISE 205
[Essential]
Translate:

1. Pāx saepe propter metum vulnerum et mortis laudātur. 2. Erant virī fortēs et līberī in exercitū Caesaris. Eī laudābantur; fortiter enim urbēs et oppida oppugnāvērunt. 3. Cōnfirmābiturne pāx post proelia et bella et caedēs? 4. In perīculō Deus semper appellātur. 5. Omnēs rēs fortiter administrābantur quod Caesar, vir fortis et nōbilis, imperātor erat Rōmānōrum. 6. Aut[1] Lincoln aut[1] Washingtonius prīnceps fuit omnium ducum Americānōrum. Itaque eī laudantur et semper laudābuntur. 7. Cūr puerī malī nōn laudantur? 8. Glōria Deō per Jēsūm Chrīstum datur. 9. Mīlitēs et in silvīs et in agrīs collocābantur; in eōs hostēs impetum fēcērunt. 10. Rēx malus nōn adjuvābitur. 11. Mīlitēs propter virtūtem laudantur. Centuriōnēs etiam propter virtūtem et fidem laudantur. Ducēs et imperātōrēs rēs fortiter administrant. Itaque eī etiam laudantur. 12. Chrīstiānī bonī et in pāce et in bellō lēgem Chrīstī servant. Itaque eīs magnum praemium in Caelō dabitur. 13. Vōs estis Americānī. Et līberī et fortēs estis. Itaque semper laudāminī. 14. Ducēs nōn laudābantur. Longē enim aberant ā proeliīs et castrīs.

EXERCISE 206
Translate:

1. The centurions are being addressed. 2. God will be called upon. 3. The affair is being managed. 4. Peace was being strengthened. 5. Soldiers are being stationed in the fields. 6. The cities are being stormed. 7. The soldier is being helped. 8. Grain will be given the soldiers. 9. Our friends will be encouraged. 10. Our soldiers were being helped. 11. The army is being strengthened. 12. Our faith will be strengthened. 13. The war is being managed. 14. You will be praised. 15. We are being encouraged. 16. They were being helped.

---

[1] aut . . . aut: *either . . . or.*

4. THE ABLATIVE OF AGENT

When the verb is PASSIVE, the SUBJECT is the person or thing TO WHICH THE ACTION IS DONE. The PERSON WHO DOES THE ACTION—the LIVING AGENT—is expressed in Latin as in English by a PREPOSITIONAL PHRASE:

Deus ab hominibus laudātur.
God is being praised by men.

Bellum ā duce administrātur.
The war is being managed by the leader.

The preposition used is **ab,** *by,* which is generally written **ā** before a word beginning with any consonant except *h.*
Ab (ā) ALWAYS takes the ABLATIVE case.

ab omnibus hominibus, *by all men*
ā duce, *by the leader*
ab hominibus, *by men*

ASSIGNMENT: Learn the rule, GRAMMAR, No. 764.

NOTE

Remember that you have already learned a different meaning and use for **ab (ā).** When **ab (ā)** is used in a prepositional phrase modifying **ABSUM,** it must be translated *FROM.* Thus:

Mōns ā flūmine longē abest.
The mountain is far away from the river.

VOCABULARY

cōnservō, *1, tr.*	{ *preserve* { *spare*
nam, *conj.*	*for* (when *for* means *because* and introduces a REASON)
ab (ā), *prep. w. abl.*	{ *by* (expressing agency) { *from* (*w.* absum)

REVIEW VOCABULARY

voco, *1, tr.*   *call*
occupo, *1, tr.*   *seize*

EXERCISE 207

Complete these phrases with ā *whenever possible; otherwise use* ab:

1. By the king.   .... rēge.
2. By the enemy.   .... hostibus.
3. By the cavalry.   .... equitibus.
4. By Mary.   .... Marīā.
5. By all slaves.   .... omnibus servīs.
6. By the leader of the enemy.   .... hostium duce.

OPPIDUM A MILITIBUS OPPUGNATUM EST.

EXERCISE 208
[Essential]

1. Translate;
2. Underline the ablatives of the agent:

Warning. One sentence contains a "booby-trap."

1. Pāx ā mīlitibus saepe nōn cōnservātur, nam glōriae bellī cupidī sunt. 2. Imperium ā Caesare, virō fortī et bonō, administrābitur. 3. Cōpia frūmentī ā servīs nōn cōnservābātur. 4. Post proelium nōs ab imperātōre cōnfirmābāmur. 5. Laudanturne sānctī hominēs ā virīs bonīs? 6. Rōma ab Americā longē abest. 7. Silvae ab equitibus occupābuntur. 8. Laudāturne Senātus Rōmānus ā multīs virīs? 9. Omnēs rēs ā duce bonō administrābantur. 10. Centuriōnēs ab imperātōre appellābantur. 11. Imperātor ā senātū vocābitur.

EXERCISE 209
Translate:

1. Our free state will be preserved by free and brave men. 2. All the soldiers will be called into the battle by the commander in chief; for the number of the enemy is large, and they are eager for victory. 3. The faith was being kept by many renowned Christians. 4. Many foreign fields were being seized by the Roman soldiers. 5. The leaders of the Gauls were often called by Caesar. 6. The slaves were being called by the master. 7. The American state is being praised by all free men.

EXERCISE 210
Translate:

QUESTION. Administrāturne mundus ā Deō?

ANSWER. Mundus ā Deō et cōnservātur et administrātur. Nam Deus in prīncipiō caelum et terram et omnēs rēs propter nōs hominēs fēcit[1] et est hominum Pater. Nōs hominēs ā Deō cōn-

---

[1] **fēcit**: *he made.*

servāmur, et nōbīs omnēs rēs ā Deō dantur. Vēritās et salūs nōbīs ā Deō dantur; frūmentum et omnium rērum cōpia nōbīs[1] ā Deō et parantur et cōnservantur. Itaque in mortis perīculō ā nautīs Deus appellātur; in bellī perīculīs ā mīlitibus appellātur; ā mātribus et patribus, ā virīs et puerīs, ā Chrīstiānīs et ab omnibus hominibus semper et in omnibus locīs appellātur. Nam Deus bonus est, et hominēs ab Eō semper adjuvantur et cōnfirmantur. Itaque Deus semper ab hominibus bonīs et sānctīs laudātur, nam Pater omnium hominum est.

EXERCISE 211
Translate:

Tum imperium populī Rōmānī ā Caesare occupābātur. Vir fortis erat, nam ab eō et hostēs superābantur et amīcī cōnfirmābantur. Post ējus mortem pāx ab imperātōribus Rōmānīs per arma et legiōnēs cōnfirmābātur. Nōn omnēs autem hominēs līberī erant, nam multī hominēs erant servī miserī. Pāx Rōmāna ab imperātōribus cōnfirmābātur, sed lībertās[2] omnium hominum ā Rōmānīs nōn cōnservābātur.

EXERCISE 212
Translate:

Cīvitās Americāna ā mīlitibus fortibus cōnservātur et semper cōnservābitur. Mīlitēs Americānī ab hostibus etiam fortibus nōn superābuntur. Virī Americānī propter virtūtem et fidem ā nōbīs et ab omnibus hominibus semper laudābuntur.

READING NO. 7

HANNIBAL IN ITALY!

Hannibal trāns magnōs et altōs montēs exercitum dūxerat. Hostis populī Rōmānī in Italiā erat. Itaque Rōmānī in magnō

---

[1] Translate *for us*.
[2] lībertās, lībertātis: *liberty* (cf. līber).

perīculō erant. Exercitus Rōmānus in Hispāniā[1] erat. Scīpiō[2] cum legiōnibus Rōmānīs
in Galliā fuerat. Is autem exercitum in Hispāniam[1] mīsit
et in Italiam contendit.
Gallī partēs Italiae Alpibus
fīnitimās tenēbant. Eī hostēs
erant populī Rōmānī et saepe
cum Rōmānīs bellum gesse-
rant. Itaque in eōrum fīnēs
Hannibal exercitum dūxit et
ab eīs adjuvābātur. Ibi Scīpiō,[2] dux Rōmānōrum, cum
Hannibale pugnāvit sed Hannibal eum vīcit. Rōmānī tamen pācem nōn petīvērunt.

HANNIBAL IN ITALIA EST!

Many of the Gauls who dwelt in northern Italy were now in
insurrection around the Roman army. A second army sent out
from Rome effected a juncture with Scipio, but the position of
the legions remained critical. Scipio had been wounded in the
first battle with Hannibal, and a lesser man, Tiberius Sempronius,
was now in command. For political reasons Sempronius was eager
to fight a pitched battle with the Carthaginian army. Hannibal
understood the character of this man. On a cold and bleak December day a screen of Carthaginian horse, retreating by order,
drew the Roman cavalry across the swollen river Trebia. Sempronius thought his chance had come. He hurriedly sent his army
through the icy waters of the Trebia.

Suddenly in the mist the Romans found themselves confronted
by the main force of the enemy.

Itaque equitēs et Rōmānōrum et hostium fortiter pugnābant.

---

[1] Hispānia, ae: *Spain.*
[2] Scīpiō, Scīpiōnis: *Scipio* (a Roman family name).

Interim imperātor Rōmānus cōpiās in proelium mīsit. Elephantī[1] et equitēs hostium equitēs Rōmānōs terruērunt et superāvērunt. Tum in mīlitēs hostium legiōnēs Rōmānae impetum fēcērunt. Mīlitēs Rōmānī fortēs erant et fortiter pugnābant. Tamen ab hoste superābantur. Tum pars mīlitum hostium ā tergō[2] impetum in Rōmānōs fēcit.[3] *(These had been placed in ambush by Hannibal with orders to attack the Roman rear.)* Itaque hostēs undique impetum in Rōmānōs fēcērunt. Tamen pars Rōmānōrum per hostēs vēnit *(this group was 10,000 in number)* et tūta in oppidum Rōmānum vēnit. Gallī et Carthāginiēnsēs[4] reliquōs Rōmānōs omnēs occīdērunt. Nōn multī Rōmānī tūtī in castra vēnērunt. Victōria Hannibalis fuit. Fortūna hostēs, nōn Rōmānōs, adjūverat.

Answer in complete Latin sentences of at least three words:

1. Vēneratne Hannibal trāns Alpēs?
2. Ubi erant exercitūs Rōmānī?
3. Quis erat imperātor Rōmānōrum?
4. Superāvēruntne equitēs Rōmānī hostēs?
5. Vīcēruntne Rōmānī?

EXERCISE 213

[Honor Work]

AN IMAGINARY SPEECH

Imagine that Rome is at war (and it generally was!). The political opponents of the government are criticizing the war policy of the administration and its generals. A spokesman for the government rises in the Roman senate and speaks:

Translate into Latin:

"The war is being managed by a brave leader. Before[5] the war all things were being prepared by him; grain and arms were being

---

[1] elephantus, ī: *elephant.*
[2] ā tergō: *from the rear.*
[3] fēcit: *made.*
[4] Carthāginiēnsēs, Carthāginiēnsium: *the Carthaginians.*
[5] *before:* ante, *prep. w. acc.*

carried into the towns of the province by the slaves; hills and bridges were being seized by the legions; the courage of the soldiers was being strengthened by the centurions. Now, in the dangers of war, the general of the Roman legions is praised by both Roman soldiers and the enemy. For he has frightened the enemy, and their fear is the glory of a Roman general. Why is he not praised by the Roman Senate? Why is he not helped by you all? GOOD men are now praising him and good men will always praise him."

Reply to this speech:

Imagine that you are a leader of one of the parties opposed to the government. Write a short speech in Latin answering the arguments given above. USE WORDS AND CONSTRUCTIONS YOU KNOW. DON'T USE ANY CONSTRUCTION ABOUT WHICH YOU ARE DOUBTFUL.

LESSON 18: PRESENT SYSTEM PASSIVE OF THE SECOND CONJUGATION; ABLATIVE OF MEANS

1. PRESENT SYSTEM PASSIVE OF THE SECOND CONJUGATION

ASSIGNMENT: Study the present, imperfect, and future indicative passive of the second conjugation, GRAMMAR, Nos. 246, 249, and 252. Notice that there is ONE change which does not follow the rules for final personal signs given in Section 2 of Lesson 17. **Monēbis** becomes **monēberis**.

VOCABULARY

contineō, continēre, continuī, contentus, 2, *tr.*	*restrain* *hold in*
obtineō, obtinēre, obtinuī, obtentus, 2, *tr.*	*hold* *occupy*
aut, *conj.*	*or*
aut . . . aut, *conjs.*	*either . . . or*
neque . . . neque, *conjs.*	*neither . . . nor*
posteā, *adv.*	*afterwards*

RELATED ENGLISH WORD

A *container*.

RELATED LATIN WORDS

Post; ea.

REVIEW VOCABULARY

terreō, 2, *tr.*	*terrify*
teneō, tenēre, tenuī, tentus, 2, *tr.*	*hold*
videō, vidēre, vīdī, vīsus, 2, *tr.*	*see*

EXERCISE 214

1. Write out the full principal parts of **terreō**.

2. Give the third person, singular and plural, of the present, imperfect, and future indicative passive of all the words in the vocabulary. Translate each form given.

EXERCISE 215
Translate:

1. continentur
2. obtinēbātur
3. terrēberis
4. tenētur
5. terrentur

6. vidētur
7. obtinēbitur
8. terrēbantur
9. continēbāminī
10. tenēbuntur

EXERCISE 216
Translate:

1. Hostēs ab equitibus Rōmānīs saepe terrentur. 2. Impetus hostium ā mīlitibus fortibus sustinēbitur. 3. Multī puerī in agrīs vidēbantur. 4. Virī nōbilēs et magnī neque terrēbuntur neque superābuntur. 5. Collis mīlitibus integrīs complētur. 6. Reliquī hostēs ā Rōmānīs undique tenēbantur. 7. Posteā signum ā centuriōne movēbitur. 8. Hostēs propter metum gravem terrēbantur. 9. Virī sānctī mortis metū nōn terrēbuntur. 10. Montēs altī undique ab Helvētiīs¹ videntur. 11. Hostēs undique continentur. 12. Locus clāmōre miserōrum mīlitum complēbātur. 13. Posteā imperium ā Caesare obtinēbātur. 14. Rēgnum ā rēge glōriae cupidō saepe obtinētur. 15. Pōns ā mīlitibus fortibus tenētur. 16. Gallī prōvinciae fīnitimī terrentur. 17. Propter metum mortis neque movēbantur neque terrēbantur. 18. Impetus sustinētur. 19. Legiōnēs Rōmānae nōn terrentur. 20. Rōmānī ā Gallīs, virīs fortibus, nōn terrentur. 21. Omnēs mīlitēs in castrīs continēbuntur. 22. Posteā castra trāns flūmen movēbuntur. 23. Puer terrēbātur

---

¹ **Helvētiī, Helvētiōrum**: *the Helvetians* (the inhabitants of ancient Switzerland).

quod ā patre et mātre longē āfuit. 24. Virī līberī nōn continēbantur. 25. Oppidum frūmentī plēnum obtinēbitur.

EXERCISE 217
[Essential]
Translate:

1. The soldiers were being restrained by the commander in chief.
2. The power is being held by Caesar. 3. The enemy are being
terrified by the cavalry. 4. The Roman column will be seen by
the Gauls. 5. The town will be either held by us or seized by
the enemy. 6. The bridge is being held by the cavalry. 7. Afterwards the royal power will be held by him. 8. We shall be terrified neither by the soldiers nor by the cavalry. 9. They were
being held in by the cavalry.

2. THE ABLATIVE OF MEANS

We have seen that the living agent is expressed by **ab (ā) with**
the ablative.

The ablative WITHOUT A PREPOSITION is used to express:

1. The NON-LIVING AGENT.

> **Montibus continēbantur.**
> *They were held in by mountains.*
> (BUT: **Ab hoste continēbantur.**
> *They were being held in by the enemy.*)

> **Hostēs vōcibus mīlitum terrēbantur.**
> *The enemy were being terrified by the cries of the soldiers.*

2. The MEANS or INSTRUMENT with which something is
done.

> **Rōmānī tēlīs hīberna dēfendērunt.**
> *The Romans defended the winter quarter* $\left\{ \begin{array}{l} \textit{with} \\ \textit{by means of} \end{array} \right\}$ *darts.*

ASSIGNMENT: Learn the rule, GRAMMAR, No. 765.

EXERCISE 218
[Essential]
1. Translate;
2. Explain the italicized cases:

1. Chrīstiānī Deum et *vōce* et *virtūte* laudant. 2. Rōmānī Chrīstiānōs *gladiīs* nōn vīcērunt. 3. Rēs Rōmāna *armīs* et *virtūte* cōnservābātur. 4. Rōmānī hīberna *tēlīs* et *gladiīs* semper dēfendērunt. 5. Virtūs equitum fortium *praemiīs* cōnfirmābātur. 6. Interim centuriōnēs *litterīs* Caesaris monēbuntur. 7. Helvētiī[1] *montibus* altīs et magnō *flūmine* undique continentur.

EXERCISE 219

*All the prepositional phrases in these sentences
are to be translated by the ablative of means.*

Translate:

1. They defended the camp *with darts*. 2. The soldiers' courage will be strengthened *by* the centurion's *speech*. 3. They fought *with swords*. 4. The Roman state was being preserved *by the courage* of the Roman Senate and people. 5. The Romans fortified cities *by means of walls*.

READING NO. 8

HANNIBAL ANNIHILATES A ROMAN ARMY!

Victōria Hannibalis magna fuit. Senātus Populusque Rōmānus tamen pācem nōn petēbat. Integrās cōpiās parāvērunt. Arma et tēla parābantur.

A new general, Gaius Flaminius, was now in command of the Roman forces. Hannibal crossed the Apennines into Etruria, marched through terrain made almost impassable by the spring rains, and took up a strong position before Flaminius, who had planned to block the mountain passes, knew he had managed the crossing. Hannibal, to incite the Romans to fight on his own

---

[1] Helvētiī, Helvētiōrum: *Helvetians.*

terms, marched past the Roman camp, pillaging and wasting the land all around. This was too much for the headstrong Flaminius. Though his army was inferior, he pursued the Carthaginians. The road along which the Carthaginians were marching enters, as it skirts Lake Trasimene, a narrow strip of plain enclosed by surrounding hills which come close down to the shore of the lake. Here Hannibal took up a strong position to await the pursuing Romans.

In colle Hannibal magnum numerum mīlitum collocāvit; equitēs autem in dextrā[1] et sinistrā[2] parte collocāvit. *(Besides, a mist concealed his positions.)* Itaque imperātor Rōmānus, proeliī et victōriae cupidus, exercitum Rōmānum in loca angusta dūxit. Subitō[3] Rōmānī hostēs vīdērunt. Undique ab hostibus continēbantur. Nōn erat spēs salūtis. Rōmānī et tēlīs terrēbantur et ab equitibus perturbābantur. Tum hostēs undique in Rōmānōs impetum fēcērunt. Caedēs Rōmānōrum magna fuit. Locus clāmōre Rōmānōrum miserōrum complēbātur. Pars tamen Rōmānōrum per hostēs vēnit. Eōs autem equitēs hostium posteā occīdērunt.

In this battle—a slaughter rather than a battle—the Romans lost an entire army, 15,000 killed and 15,000 captured. The Carthaginians lost only 1,500 men, and these mainly from their Gallic auxiliaries.

Victōria hostium magna fuit. Perīculum Rōmānōrum grave erat. Tamen etiam tum Rōmānī dē pāce cum hostibus nōn ēgērunt. Spem salūtis in virtūte pōnēbant.

As an officer in Caesar's army was to say later, "Romans never ask terms of peace from an armed foe." Such was the invincible spirit of Rome.

---

[1] **dexter, dextra, dextrum:** *right.*
[2] **sinister, sinistra, sinistrum:** *left.*
[3] **subitō,** *adv.: suddenly.*

LESSON 19: PRESENT SYSTEM PASSIVE
OF THE THIRD CONJUGATION

1. PRESENT SYSTEM PASSIVE OF THE THIRD CONJUGATION

The rules for changes in the final personal signs apply also to the present system indicative PASSIVE of the THIRD conjugation.

ASSIGNMENT: Learn the model verbs, GRAMMAR, Nos. 247, 250, and 253.

VOCABULARY

trādō, trādere, trādidī, trāditus, *3, tr.*	*hand over*
dīmittō, dīmittere, dīmīsī, dīmissus, *3, tr.*	*send away* / *dismiss*
occīdō, occīdere, occīdī, occīsus, *3, tr.*	*kill*
sine, *prep. w. abl.*	*without*
ferē, *adv.*	*almost*

REVIEW VOCABULARY

dēfendō, dēfendere, dēfendī, dēfēnsus, *3, tr.*	*defend*
dūcō, dūcere, dūxī, ductus, *3, tr.*	*lead* / *guide*
pellō, pellere, pepulī, pulsus, *3, tr.*	*drive* / *repulse* / *rout*
vincō, vincere, vīcī, victus, *3, tr.*	*conquer*
agō, agere, ēgī, āctus, *3, tr.*	*drive* / *do* / *act* / *treat* / *give* (*w.* **grātiās**)

NOTE

The phrase **grātiās agō** means *I give thanks* or *I thank* and takes an indirect object.

Tibi grātiās agimus. *We thank you (We give thanks to you).*

EXERCISE 220

Give the third persons, singular and plural, present, imperfect and future indicative passive of all the verbs in the vocabulary.

EXERCISE 221
Translate:

1. trādēbātur	5. pōnuntur	9. pelluntur
2. dīmittēbātur	6. dīmitteris	10. dūcitur
3. occīduntur	7. occīdēbantur	11. vincēbātur
4. dūcentur	8. incenditur	12. trādēbantur

EXERCISE 222
1. Change to the passive;
2. Translate both active and passive forms:

1. trādam	6. trādet	11. occīdēs
2. dīmittēbat	7. occīdēmus	12. dūcent
3. occīdunt	8. pōnēbās	13. incendit
4. dēfenditis	9. trādit	14. pellēbant
5. dīmittit	10. dīmittō	15. sustinētis

EXERCISE 223
Translate:

1. Prīncipēs hostium senātuī trāduntur. 2. Gallus occīditur. 3. Homō malus ā senātū occīdētur. 4. Italia ā Rōmānīs dēfenditur. 5. Gallī et pelluntur et occīdentur. 6. Agmen in fīnēs hostium dūcitur. 7. Grātiae Deō aguntur. 8. Equitēs in gentēs fīnitimās dīmittēbantur. 9. Vōs in Galliam mittiminī. 10. Rōma dēfendētur. 11. Servī saepe occīduntur. 12. Omnēs ferē gentēs fīnitimae vincuntur. 13. Agmen ā Caesare dūcitur. 14. Hostēs tamen vincentur. 15. Urbs hostibus nōn trādētur. 16. Equitēs in

gentēs reliquās dīmittuntur. 17. Castra tēlīs dēfendēbantur.
18. Rōmānī neque pellentur neque occīdentur. 19. Rēgēs glōriae
cupidī cum gentibus fīnitimīs bellum saepe gerunt. 20. Frūmenta
in agrīs saepe incenduntur.

EXERCISE 224
Translate:

1. The enemy's cavalry was being killed by darts. 2. The
Senate is being dismissed. 3. Almost all the swords and darts will
be handed over by the leaders of the Gauls. 4. Almost all the
tribes of Gaul were being conquered by the Romans. 5. Our
cities and towns are being defended by brave soldiers. 6. The
army will be led into Gaul by the general. 7. The enemy's cavalry
will be repulsed by our cavalry. 8. The Gauls were fighting
without hope. 9. Thanks are being given to the Senate.

2. ABLATIVES OF AGENCY AND MEANS COMPARED

Study these differences between the ablative of agency and the
ablative of means:

THE ABLATIVE OF THE AGENT:

1. ALWAYS has the preposition **ab** (ā) in Latin.

2. ALWAYS expresses a LIVING AGENT (a person, soldiers,
Caesar, lions, an army, *etc.*).

3. ALWAYS has the preposition *by* in English.

Deus ā Chrīstiānīs laudātur. *God is (being) praised by Christians.*

THE ABLATIVE OF MEANS:

1. NEVER has a preposition in Latin.

2. Generally expresses a THING (a sword, courage, shouting,
etc.).

3. Generally has *by* or *with* in English.

Servī tēlīs (gladiō) occīdēbantur.
The slaves were being killed by darts (with a sword).

EXERCISE 225
[Essential]

1. Translate;
2. Explain the italicized forms:

Warning. One sentence conceals several "booby-traps."

1. Silvae saepe in bellō ab *hostibus* incenduntur. 2. Rōma *virtūte* legiōnum cōnservābātur. 3. Centuriōnēs in omnēs ferē gentēs fīnitimās ā *Caesare* dīmittuntur. 4. Cōpiae Rōmānae ā *Gallīs* nōn pelluntur. 5. Virtūs mīlitum *spē* victōriae semper cōnfirmātur. 6. Post proelium prīncipēs hostium ā *Rōmānīs* saepe occīdēbantur. 7. Prīncipēs ā *Caesare* nōn dīmittentur. 8. *Tēlīs* occīditur. 9. Mīles Rōmānus hostem videt. Eum *tēlīs* occīdit. 10. Mīlitēs undique dūcentur; castra in *colle* pōnentur; arma et frūmentum in *castra* portābuntur.

EXERCISE 226
[Essential]

1. Translate;
2. Explain the italicized forms:

Warning. Some of these sentences have the ablative of means; some have the ablative of agency.

1. All things were being attended to *by the general.* 2. They fortified the camp *with a wall.* 3. He killed the leading men *with a sword.* 4. Peace was being strengthened *by the courage* of the legions. 5. They were being defended *by Roman cavalry.* 6. The city was being handed over *by the Gauls.* 7. He conquered the enemy *by the courage* of the Roman soldiers. 8. The leading men are being sent away *by the Roman general.*

READING NO. 9

SCIPIO INVADES AFRICA!

Hannibal continued to win victories in the open field, but he could not break the spirit of Rome. Gradually the superior resources of the Romans and their dogged determination began to tell. The Carthaginians withdrew their forces from Italy and

HANNIBAL ELEPHANTOS HABEBAT.

Sicily, and at last Publius Cornelius Scipio, son of the Scipio who had first faced Hannibal in northern Italy, led an invasion of Africa itself. (This was in 204 B. C.; the war had opened in 218 B. C.) The final battle of the war was fought at Zama in northern Africa, probably in the spring of 202 B. C.

Hannibal magnum mīlitum numerum habuit sed nōn ita multōs equitēs. Scīpiō nōn ita multōs mīlitēs habēbat, multōs autem equitēs. Hannibal etiam elephantōs[1] habēbat. *(There were said to be about eighty.)* Rōmānī elephantōs nōn habēbant.

Hannibal planned to drive his elephants in an opening charge against the Roman foot soldiers to throw them into disorder. The Carthaginian cavalry, stationed on the flanks, was meanwhile to retreat and draw the superior cavalry of the Romans off the field, thus leaving Hannibal free to attack the disordered legions with numerically superior infantry.

How did Scipio meet this attack?

(Continued on page 204)

---

[1] **elephantus, ī:** *elephant.*

LESSON 20: PRESENT SYSTEM PASSIVE OF THE FOURTH CONJUGATION; ACCOMPANIMENT

1. PRESENT SYSTEM PASSIVE OF THE FOURTH CONJUGATION

The rules for final personal signs in the passive apply also to the fourth conjugation.

ASSIGNMENT: Study GRAMMAR, Nos. 248, 251, and 254.

REVIEW VOCABULARY

audiō, *4, tr.*	*hear*
mūniō, *4, tr.*	{ *fortify* / *construct (w.* / *viam or* viās)
veniō, venīre, vēnī, ventum, *4, intr.*	*come*
conveniō, convenīre, convēnī, conventum, *4, intr.*	{ *come together* / *assemble*

EXERCISE 227
Translate:

1. audītur	4. mūnientur	7. audiētur
2. mūniuntur	5. audior	8. mūniēbātur
3. audiēbātur	6. mūniēbantur	9. audiuntur

EXERCISE 228
[Essential]

1. Translate;
2. Explain the construction of the italicized words:

1. Castra ā *Rōmānīs* semper *mūniēbantur.* 2. Quid ā vōbīs audītur? 3. Cum *Caesare* per *montēs* in *Galliam* vēnī. 4. Urbs ā rēge *victōriae* cupidō mūnītur. 5. Chrīstō, *Fīliō Deī,* grātiās agimus. 6. Interim et collēs et pontēs ā legiōnibus mūniēbantur. 7. *Fuit* metus in *castrīs quod* clāmor hostium audiēbātur.

8. *Puerīs* malīs praemia nōn dabuntur. 9. *Ubi* est Rōma? 10. Fīlius saepe est *patris* similis. 11. Gentēs *finibus hostium* fīnitimae saepe cōpiam armōrum petunt. 12. Fuitne Lincoln *Washingtoniō* similis? 13. Legiōnēs integrae in *hostēs* mittuntur. 14. Clāmor nautārum *reliquōrum* audiēbātur. 15. Marīa est *grātiā* plēna. 16. Silvae *perīculōrum* plēnae sunt. 17. Propter hostium *metum* legiōnēs prō *portīs* īnstruēbantur. 18. Urbs *mūrō* mūnītur. 19. Quis prō *rēge* pugnābit? 20. Impedīmenta magna erant. 21. Post *bellum* fuit pāx. 22. Caesar fuit Rōmānōrum *imperātor*. 23. *Loca* angusta et difficilia fuērunt. 24. Rōma ā *Galliā longē* abest. 25. Oppidum mīlitibus complēbātur. 26. Mīles similis *ducī* nōn erat. 27. Rōmānī Rōmam *virtūte* et armīs semper dēfendērunt. 28. *Cūr* iter per montēs nōn fēcērunt? 29. Mīlitēs undique tēla in hostēs mīsērunt. 30. Dux rēgnum occupāvit.

2. ABLATIVE OF ACCOMPANIMENT

Do not confuse the ABLATIVE OF MEANS with the ABLATIVE OF ACCOMPANIMENT:

When *with* expresses association, pointing out the person or thing ín company with which something is or is done, the ABLATIVE WITH CUM MUST BE USED. This is called the ABLATIVE OF ACCOMPANIMENT.

> *He came with the Roman.*
> **Cum Rōmānō vēnit.**
> (*i. e.*, He came IN COMPANY WITH the Roman.)
>
> *The swords are in the camp with the darts.*
> **Gladiī in castrīs CUM TĒLĪS sunt.**
> (*i. e.*, They are TOGETHER WITH the darts.)
>
> (BUT: *He is being killed with a sword.*
> **Gladiō occīditur.**)
> (*i. e.*, He is being killed BY MEANS OF A SWORD.
> The sword is the instrument or *means*.)

ASSIGNMENT: Learn the rule for accompaniment in GRAMMAR, No. 772.

CUM ROMANIS VENIT.

GLADIO OCCIDITUR.

EXERCISE 229

Some of the with-*phrases in these sentences are to be translated by the ablative of MEANS, some by the ablative of ACCOMPANIMENT.*

Translate:

1. They fought *with* swords. 2. Caesar was fighting *with* the Gauls. 3. The cavalry was in the camp *with* the soldiers. 4. The camp was being fortified *with* a wall. 5. Mary is in heaven *with* God. 6. They terrified the cavalry *with* (their) shouting.

READING NO. 10

THE BATTLE OF ZAMA—HANNIBAL'S LAST STAND

Et Hannibal et Scīpiō mīlitēs īnstrūxērunt. Virtūs et spēs mīlitum ōrātiōnibus imperātōrum cōnfirmābantur. "Spem in virtūte pōnēmus! Fortiter pugnābimus! Aut vincēmus aut vincēmur!"

Hannibal lined up his eighty elephants in front of his main army. In the first line behind them he placed his 12,000 mercenary troops, men drawn from many lands and held together by devotion to their great leader. In the second line he stationed 15,000 new Carthaginian levies. Behind these he held in re-

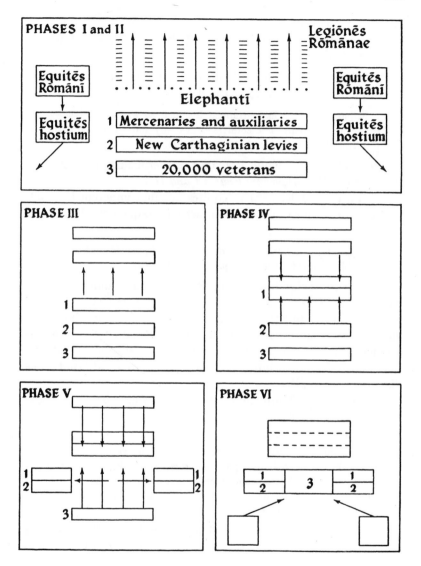

serve 20,000 veteran troops to strike the final blow for victory.
The cavalry were massed on either flank. *(See diagram: Phases
I and II.)*

Hannibal signum dedit. Elephantī[1] in aciem Rōmānam mittē-
bantur. *(See diagram: Phases I and II.)*

Scipio, however, had arranged his men so as to leave lanes
between his troops. The soldiers thus easily shifted to allow the
elephants to run harmlessly between them.

Itaque elephantī[1] neque Rōmānōs terruērunt neque aciem per-
turbāvērunt. *(See diagram: Phases I and II.)*
Interim equitēs Rōmānī in equitēs hostium impetum fēcērunt.
Hostēs autem impetum nōn sustinuērunt. Itaque equitēs hostium
cessērunt.

Thus both cavalries rushed off the field as Hannibal had
probably planned. *(See diagram: Phases I and II.)*

Tum prīma aciēs hostium in Rōmānōs ab Hannibale mittēbātur. *(See diagram: Phase III.)* Rēs gladiō gerēbātur. Et Rōmānī et hostēs fortiter pugnābant. Vōcēs et clāmor hominum
undique audiēbantur. Multī et hostēs et Rōmānī tēlīs et gladiīs
occīdēbantur. Mīlitēs tamen Rōmānī impetum sustinēbant. Itaque
et Scīpiō et Hannibal integrōs mīlitēs in proelium mīsērunt. *(See
diagram: Phase IV.)*
Rōmānī autem ā mīlitibus integrīs nōn superābantur. Itaque
hostēs in magnō perīculō erant.

Both armies were now in great confusion and both attempted
to re-form. Hannibal pushed his third line of veterans to the
front and rejoined battle. *(See diagram: Phase V.)* The battle
raged on through long and bloody hours. Finally the Roman
cavalry, having left off pursuit, probably according to instructions, returned to the field.

Tum equitēs Rōmānī ā tergō[2] impetum in hostēs fēcērunt. *(See
diagram: Phase VI.)* Itaque hostēs ā Rōmānīs undique continē-

---

[1] elephantus, ī: *elephant.*
[2] ā tergō: *from the rear.*

bantur. Magna erat caedēs hostium miserōrum. Rōmānī enim omnēs ferē hostēs aut occīdērunt aut cēpērunt.[1] *(Hannibal, however, escaped capture and fled from the field.)* Post proelium hostēs pācem petīvērunt. Ita, post multās hostium victōriās et magnam Rōmānōrum caedem, Rōmānī hostēs virtūte et armīs vīcērunt.

---

[1] cēpērunt: *(they) captured.*

LESSON 21: THE PERFECT SYSTEM OF THE INDICATIVE PASSIVE

The perfect, pluperfect, and future perfect tenses passive are COMPOUND tenses in Latin. They are formed by using the PERFECT PARTICIPLE PASSIVE as a predicate adjective with the verb **sum,** *am.*

The PERFECT indicative passive is compounded of the perfect participle passive (the fourth principal part in -us) and the present indicative of the verb *to be.*

The perfect participle passive is declined like **magnus, a, um** and agrees with the subject of the sentence, just like a predicate adjective. Explain all the underlined endings in these examples:

Ego laudātus sum. *I was praised.*

Tū laudātus es. *You were praised.*

Marīa ā Chrīstiānīs laudāta est. *Mary was praised by the Christians.*

Nōs laudātī sumus. *We were praised.*

Vōs laudātī estis. *You were praised.*

Mīlitēs laudātī sunt. *The soldiers were praised.*

Mātrēs laudātae sunt. *The mothers were praised.*

Flūmina laudāta sunt. *The rivers were praised.*

In forming the PERFECT SYSTEM OF THE PASSIVE in all conjugations follow this rule:

1. Take the PERFECT PARTICIPLE PASSIVE of the verb (the fourth principal part of transitive verbs).

2. Add, as a separate word, the required form of the verb **sum.**

ASSIGNMENT: Study the model verbs, GRAMMAR, Nos. 255-266.

VOCABULARY

vehementer, *adv.*	{ greatly { violently
explōrō, *1, tr.*	{ reconnoiter { find out
premō, premere, pressī, pressus, *3, tr.*	{ press { press hard
retineō, retinēre, retinuī, retentus, *2, tr.*	{ hold back { keep
comparō, *1, tr.*	{ get { prepare

EXERCISE 230

Conjugate in the perfect system indicative active: (a) cōnservō, (b) retineō, (c) premō, (d) mūniō.

EXERCISE 231

Give the perfect participles passive
(the fourth principal part) of:

1. laudō	17. parō	32. pōnō
2. moneō	18. vincō	33. mūniō
3. superō	19. appellō	34. collocō
4. habeō	20. petō	35. cōnfirmō
5. portō	21. dō	36. incendō
6. dēfendō	22. agō	37. adjuvō
7. occupō	23. administrō	38. videō
8. dūcō	24. moveō	39. pellō
9. gerō	25. vocō	40. perturbō
10. oppugnō	26. comparō	41. obtineō
11. trādō	27. retineō	42. cōnservō
12. audiō	28. occīdō	43. incitō
13. terreō	29. explōrō	44. servō
14. īnstruō	30. dīmittō	45. contineō
15. mittō	31. sustineō	46. premō
16. compleō		

EXERCISE 232

Conjugate **sum** in the (1) present indicative, (2) imperfect indicative, (3) future indicative.

EXERCISE 233

Add the proper endings to the participles and translate:

Note. Remember that in a compound tense the perfect participle passive agrees in number and gender with the subject of the sentence.

1. Vōs laudāt............ estis.
2. Oppidum trādit............ est.
3. Prīncipēs retent............ sunt.
4. Cōpia frūmentī comparāt............ est.
5. Omnia loca explōrāt............ sunt.
6. Hostēs press............ sunt.
7. Tū laudāt............ es.
8. Nōs laudāt............ sumus.
9. Vōcēs audīt............ sunt.
10. Nautae retent............ sunt.
11. Exercitus superāt............ est.
12. Castra mōt............ sunt.

EXERCISE 234

Add the proper form of the verb **sum:**

1. You have been praised. Vōs laudātī ....
2. They have been conquered. Victī ....
3. You have been warned. Tū monitus ....
4. The courage of the soldiers has been strengthened. Virtūs mīlitum cōnfirmāta ....
5. All the places had been reconnoitered. Omnia loca explōrāta ....
6. We had been held back. Nōs retentī ....
7. It has been prepared. Comparātum ....
8. The camp has been fortified. Castra mūnīta ....

EXERCISE 235
[Essential]
Translate:

1. Vōs laudātī erātis. 2. Tū monitus es. 3. Equitēs superātī sunt. 4. Pōns incēnsus est. 5. Frūmentum portātum est. 6. Castra dēfēnsa sunt. 7. Omnia ferē loca occupāta erant. 8. Eī pulsī sunt. 9. Ductī sumus. 10. Ea gesta sunt. 11. Oppidum oppugnātum erat. 12. Arma eīs trādita sunt. 13. Audītī estis. 14. Vehementer territī erāmus. 15. Mīlitēs īnstructī sunt. 16. Litterae missae sunt. 17. Mōns hominibus complētus erat. 18. Tēla parāta sunt. 19. Victī sumus. 20. Appellātī erātis. 21. Pāx petīta est. 22. Frūmentum eīs datum est. 23. Actum est. 24. Rēs administrāta est. 25. Castra mōta erant. 26. Centuriōnēs vocātī erant. 27. Gallī pressī sunt. 28. Cōpia tēlōrum comparāta erat. 29. Ducēs retentī sunt. 30. Occīsī sunt. 31. Montēs explōrātī erant. 32. Prīncipēs dīmissī erant. 33. Impetus sustentus erat. 34. Spēs in virtūte posita est. 35. Oppidum mūnītum est. 36. Legiōnēs ibi collocātae sunt. 37. Omnēs rēs comparātae erant. 38. Pāx cōnfirmāta est. 39. Territī sumus. 40. Frūmenta in agrīs incēnsa sunt. 41. Adjūtus sum. 42. Pulsī estis. 43. Vīsus es. 44. Pulsus est. 45. Vehementer perturbātus eram. 46. Obtentum est imperium. 47. Lēx cōnservāta nōn est. 48. Gentēs fīnitimae incitātae erant. 49. Legiō prīma pressa est. 50. Signum servātum erat. 51. Undique contentī sumus. 52. Pressī sunt.

EXERCISE 236
[Drill]
Translate:

1. I was praised by Caesar. 2. You were warned by the slave. 3. We were conquered by the enemy. 4. A large number of slaves was had by the Romans. 5. Grain had been carried into the winter quarters. 6. The town had been bravely defended. 7. The hills were seized by the cavalry. 8. The Romans were led by a brave general. 9. War had been waged with the Gauls.

10. The city had been attacked. 11. We were handed over to the enemy by the leader. 12. The speech was heard by the chiefs. 13. You had been terrified by the darts. 14. The legions were drawn up by Caesar. 15. The letter was sent by the chief. 16. The wall was filled with men. 17. Arms had been gotten. 18. We were not conquered. 19. God had been called upon. 20. Peace was sought. 21. The swords were given to the soldiers. 22. The enemy was driven into the forest. 23. The war was managed by a brave general. 24. The camp had been moved into a safe place. 25. The centurions had been called by the general. 26. The enemy was routed by darts. 27. All things had been got ready. 28. The king had been held back. 29. The leaders had been killed by swords. 30. All the places had been reconnoitered. 31. The slaves were dismissed. 32. The attack was withstood by the battle line. 33. The camp had been pitched there. 34. The camp was fortified with a wall. 35. A horseman had been stationed on the bridge. 36. Peace had been strengthened. 37. The grain had been burned by the Romans. 38. They were helped by both slaves and free men. 39. Soldiers had assembled. 40. He had been seen by the horseman. 41. The cavalry were repulsed. 42. The first battle line was disturbed. 43. The royal power was held by a good man. 44. The state had been preserved by brave men. 45. The legion was sent into the camp. 46. The faith has been kept by many Christians. 47. The soldiers were restrained by the leaders.

EXERCISE 237

OMNIA BELLA SIMILIA SUNT

Translate:

1. Propter bellum gladiī et tēla ā Rōmānīs comparāta erant; hodiē[1] etiam multa et magna arma ab Americānīs comparantur.

2. In castrīs Rōmānōrum saepe fuit magna omnium rērum inopia; in castrīs Americānīs etiam saepe est rērum inopia.

---

[1] hodiē, *adv.: today.*

3. In bellīs Rōmānōrum omnia loca ab equitibus saepe explōrāta sunt; in bellīs autem hodiernīs[1] omnia loca ab aviātōribus[2] explōrantur.

4. Tum hostēs ab equitātū saepe pressī sunt; hodiē[3] hostēs ab armigerīs[4] premuntur.

5. Bellum Gallicum[5] ā Caesare administrātum est. Quis bellum commūne hodiē[3] administrat?

6. Caesar, imperātor Rōmānōrum, propter victōriam laudātus est. Laudābunturne ducēs Americānī propter victōriam?

READING NO. 11

PICTURES FROM THE PAST

An Imaginary Interview with a Centurion

The professor cleared his throat. We waited expectantly. "Gentlemen," he said, "I have invited you here tonight to see the first demonstration of my electrical wave detector. This machine cannot only gather and combine into a picture the waves being sent off from any part of the earth at the present time, but it can detect even the smallest remnants of waves which, sent off at some past time, are yet vibrating in the universal medium of all electrical waves. However, this is not an explanation of a theory but a demonstration of success. Watch carefully. I set this control for time *(with growing excitement we watched him turning the dial)*, and this *(he began moving a larger dial on the huge machine)* for space. Now, I throw the power switch. *(A large screen or mirror became suddenly illumined with splotches of changing colors.)* This should put our picture at approximately 58 B. C. somewhere in southern Gaul."

"I have not yet," he added apologetically, "succeeded in exactly correlating my controls with the longitudes and latitudes of the earth's surface." As he was speaking, the screen had

---

[1] hodiernus, a, um: *modern.*
[2] aviātor, aviātōris: *airman.*
[3] hodiē, *adv.: today.*
[4] armigerum, ī: *tank.*
[5] Gallicus, a, um: *Gallic.*

focused into a very realistic picture of a wild forest. The movement of a breeze through the trees was quite discernible. There
was a gasp of astonishment, but the professor held up his hand.
"Now," he said, "I set the sound control." A roar of static rose
from a speaker to the left of the screen, then settled down to the
quiet sounds of a forest—no, there was something else—growing
louder—the sound of horses and the clang of metal. Then, before
our amazed eyes, a troop of cavalry rode onto the scene. The
leader, a bronzed, sturdy man who rode his horse with the assur-
ance of long custom, halted, and gazed off to the left. In the
silence that followed we heard something else—distant cries, a
shouting as if a whole army were in an uproar—then, yes, the
centurion (he looked just like a picture of a centurion I had seen
in a high-school Latin book) turned his head in our direction.
He became paralyzed with amazement. But the professor was
almost leaping with excitement. "He sees us! It works! It works!"
He rushed to the machine and began pulling several levers.
"Perhaps," he muttered, "perhaps the sound can be reversed
too, but then, . . . " He stepped back and cleared his throat.

"Estisne vōs" *(yes, the professor had been a good Latin student in high school),* "estisne vōs mīlitēs Rōmānī?" *(We held our breath. Slowly the paralysis of surprise passed, and we saw the centurion open his mouth. . . . yes, then we heard):*

CENTURIO. Nōs equitēs Rōmānī sumus. Vōs autem . . .

PROFESSOR *(excitedly interruping him).* Ubi estis?

C. In Galliā sumus. In agrīs hostium sumus. Nunc, sīcut vidē-tis, in magnīs silvīs sumus.

P. Quis imperātor vester est?

C. Caesar, vir et nōbilis et fortis, imperātor noster est. Bellum ab eō fortiter administrātur.

P. Bellum? Geriturne bellum?

C. Ita. Cum Gallīs legiōnēs Rōmānae nunc pugnant. *(He pointed off to the left.)* Audīturne ā vōbīs clāmor et hostium et Rōmānōrum?

P. Parāvēruntne Gallī bellum? Erantne cupidī bellī?

C. Ita. Victōriae et bellī glōriae cupidī erant. Itaque ante[1] bellum arma et tēla ā Gallīs parāta sunt. Virtūs eōrum ā ducibus et prīncipibus cōnfirmāta est. Oppida et urbēs ab eīs mūnītae sunt. Frūmentum in oppida et ā Gallīs et ab eōrum servīs por-tātum est. Ita omnēs rēs parātae erant.

P. Quid autem nunc agunt Gallī?

C. Tēlīs et armīs oppida et agrōs dēfendunt. Collēs et pontēs ab eīs occupantur, nam bellum nōbīscum gerunt.

P. Et Caesar? Quid is ante[1] bellum ēgit?

C. Castra in colle ab eō posita sunt. Frūmentum in castra ā servīs portātum est. Arma et tēla etiam ab eō parāta sunt. Equi-tēs ā Caesare in fīnēs hostium dīmittēbantur. Omnia loca ab eīs explōrāta sunt. Castra nostra mūrō mūnīvimus. Caesar virtūtem et spem mīlitum ōrātiōne et praemiīs cōnfirmāvit.

P. Vincenturne Gallī ā vōbīs?

C. Ita. *(He roared with laughter.)* Gallī fortiter pugnant, sed nōs nōn vincent. Nōs armīs et virtūte eōs vincēmus. Rōmānī

---

[1] ante, *prep. w. acc.: before.*

enim neque vincuntur neque dē pāce cum hostibus agunt. En![1]
(He pointed towards the shouting.) Jam[2] nunc ā mīlitibus Rōmānīs Gallī et terrentur et occīduntur. Caedēs! Urbēs *(with a
sweeping gesture)*, oppida, collēs, silvae, portūs, agrī ab exercitū
Rōmānō occupābuntur. Imperium omnis Galliae ā Caesare obtinēbitur! Gladiīs *(his voice became harsh)* rem gerēmus! Multī
Gallī ā nōbīs occīdentur. Frūmenta ab equitibus Rōmānīs incendentur; pontēs et oppida ā legiōnibus incendentur. Post bellum frūmentum et servī et arma ā Gallīs nōbīs trādentur. Ita pāx
in Galliā cōnfirmābitur. Victōria nostra erit! *(He tossed up his
head proudly.)* Victōria! Ah!

P.   Quid autem vōs nunc agitis?

C.   In proelium ā Caesare mittimur. Ecce nōs post aciem hostium sumus. Per silvās longā viā vēnimus et . . . *(Suddenly there
was the high piercing note of a trumpet, once—and again.)*
Signum est! Signum ā Caesare datur! *(He threw up his arm.)*
In hostēs!

The whole troop rushed madly off the scene towards the left.
I shivered for the Gauls. The cry of panic rose and mounted,
shrill, of men in ultimate pain. Then the professor switched off
the power. We sat there long in silence.

---

[1] **en:** *behold.*
[2] **jam,** *adv.: already.*

MASTERY REVIEW VOCABULARY NO. 2

[Units Three, Four, and Five]

FIRST CONJUGATION

VERBS LIKE *LAUDŌ*

adjuvō, adjuvāre, adjūvī, adjūtus, *1, tr.*[1]	{ *help* / *aid* }
administrō, *1, tr.*	{ *manage* / *attend to* }
appellō, *1, tr.*	{ *address* / *call (upon)* }
collocō, *1, tr.*	{ *place* / *station* }
comparō, *1, tr.*	{ *get* / *prepare* }
cōnfirmō, *1, tr.*	{ *encourage* / *strengthen* }
cōnservō, *1, tr.*	{ *preserve* / *spare* }
dō, dare, dedī, datus, *1, tr.*[1]	*give*
explōrō, *1, tr.*	{ *reconnoiter* / *find out* }
incitō, *1, tr.*	{ *incite* / *arouse* }
laudō, *1, tr.*	*praise*
occupō, *1, tr.*	*seize*
oppugnō, *1, tr.*	{ *attack* / *assault* / *storm* }

---

[1] Adjuvō and dō form their perfect stems differently from laudō. Therefore you must memorize the principal parts. Dō is also peculiar in that the a which begins the endings is short throughout the indicative except in the second person singular present indicative active, dās.

ōrō, *1, tr.*	{ *beg* { *pray*
parō, *1, tr.*	{ *prepare* { *get ready*
perturbō, *1, tr.*	{ *confuse* { *disturb*
portō, *1, tr.*	*carry*
pugnō, *1, intr.*	*fight*
servō, *1, tr.*	{ *guard* { *keep*
superō, *1, tr.*	{ *overcome* { *conquer* { *surpass*
vocō, *1, tr.*	*call*

SECOND CONJUGATION

VERBS LIKE *MONEŌ*

compleō, complēre, complēvī, complētus, 2, *tr.; w. abl.*[1]	*fill (with)*
contineō, continēre, continuī, contentus, *2, tr.*	{ *restrain* { *hold in*
habeō, *2, tr.*	*have*
maneō, manēre, mānsī, mānsūrus, *2, intr.*	*remain*
moneō, *2, tr.*	{ *warn* { *advise*
moveō, movēre, mōvī, mōtus, *2, tr.*	*move*
obtineō, obtinēre, obtinuī, obtentus, *2, tr.*	{ *hold* { *occupy*
retineō, retinēre, retinuī, retentus, *2, tr.*	{ *hold back* { *keep*
sustineō, sustinēre, sustinuī, sustentus, *2, tr.*	{ *sustain* { *withstand*

[1] When compleō is modified by a *with*-phrase, this *with*-phrase is translated
by the ablative *without* a preposition. Hence the notation *"w. abl."*

teneō, tenēre, tenuī, tentus, *2, tr.*   *hold*
terreō, *2, tr.*   *terrify*
timeō, timēre, timuī, *2, tr.*[1]   *fear*
videō, vidēre, vīdī, vīsus, *2, tr.*   *see*

THIRD CONJUGATION
VERBS LIKE *MITTŌ*

agō, agere, ēgī, āctus, *3, tr.*
$\left\{\begin{array}{l} drive \\ do \\ act \\ treat \\ give\ (w.\ \text{grātiās}) \end{array}\right.$

cēdō, cēdere, cessī, cessūrus, *3, intr.*
$\left\{\begin{array}{l} give\ way \\ yield \end{array}\right.$

contendō, contendere, contendī, *3, intr.*
$\left\{\begin{array}{l} strive \\ contend \\ hasten \end{array}\right.$

dēfendō, dēfendere, dēfendī, dēfēnsus, *3, tr.*   *defend*

dīmittō, dīmittere, dīmīsī, dīmissus, *3, tr.*
$\left\{\begin{array}{l} send\ away \\ dismiss \end{array}\right.$

dūcō, dūcere, dūxī, ductus, *3, tr.*
$\left\{\begin{array}{l} lead \\ guide \end{array}\right.$

gerō, gerere, gessī, gestus, *3, tr.*
$\left\{\begin{array}{l} carry \\ carry\ on \\ wage\ (w.\ \text{bellum}) \end{array}\right.$

incendō, incendere, incendī, incēnsus, *3, tr.*
$\left\{\begin{array}{l} set\ fire\ to \\ burn \end{array}\right.$

īnstruō, īnstruere, īnstrūxī, īnstrūctus, *3, tr.*
$\left\{\begin{array}{l} draw\ up \\ equip \end{array}\right.$

mittō, mittere, mīsī, missus, *3, tr.*   *send*
occīdō, occīdere, occīdī, occīsus, *3, tr.*   *kill*

pellō, pellere, pepulī, pulsus, *3, tr.*
$\left\{\begin{array}{l} drive \\ repulse \\ rout \end{array}\right.$

---

[1] Timeō has no fourth principal part.

petō, petere, petīvī, petītus, *3, tr.* { *seek* / *beg* / *request* }

pōnō, pōnere, posuī, positus, *3, tr.*[1] { *put* / *place* / *set* / *pitch (w. castra)* }

premō, premere, pressī, pressus, *3, tr.* { *press* / *press hard* }

trādō, trādere, trādidī, trāditus, *3, tr.*　　*hand over*

vincō, vincere, vīcī, victus, *3, tr.*　　*conquer*

FOURTH CONJUGATION
VERBS LIKE *AUDIŌ*

audiō, *4, tr.*　　*hear*

conveniō, convenīre, convēnī, conventum, *4, intr.*　　{ *come together* / *assemble* }

mūniō, *4, tr.*　　{ *fortify* / *construct (w. viam or viās)* }

veniō, venīre, vēnī, ventum, *4, intr.*　　*come*

IRREGULAR VERBS

absum, abesse, āfuī, āfutūrus, *intr.;* ab (ā) *w. abl.*[2]　　{ *am away* / *am distant* }

sum, esse, fuī, futūrus, *intr.*[3]　　*am*

---

[1] Pōnō means *pitch* only when it is used of a camp. When an *in*-phrase is used to modify pōnō, the in always takes the ABLATIVE.

[2] Absum is a compound of the preposition ab and the verb sum. Therefore it is conjugated LIKE SUM. The place away from which something is, is expressed by the preposition ab (ā before consonants), *from*, and the ablative.

[3] Sum has no PASSIVE; therefore it has no perfect participle *passive;* the future participle active is given as the fourth principal part. We shall study these participles later.

NOUNS OF THE FIRST DECLENSION

fortūna, ae	*fortune*
Italia, ae	*Italy*
litterae, litterārum[1]	$\begin{cases} letter\ (i.\ e.,\ an \\ \quad epistle) \\ dispatch \end{cases}$

NOUNS OF THE SECOND DECLENSION (MASCULINE)

ager, agrī	*field*
locus, ī (*pl.*, loca, locōrum)[2]	*place*
numerus, ī	*number*
puer, puerī	*boy*
vir, virī[3]	*man*

NOUNS OF THE SECOND DECLENSION (NEUTER)

arma, armōrum[4]	*arms*
hīberna, hībernōrum[5]	*winter quarters*
proelium, ī[6]	*battle*
tēlum, ī	*dart*

---

[1] Litterae is a plural noun of the first declension (like cōpiae).

[2] Locus becomes a neuter noun in the plural: loca. When locus is modified by an adjective, the preposition in is frequently omitted with the ablative. *In an unfavorable place,* locō aliēnō.

[3] Vir means a man as opposed to a woman or a child. Homō means a human being, a man as opposed to an animal.

[4] Arma is a neuter plural of the second declension (like castra).

[5] Hīberna, like castra, is declined only in the plural.

[6] The ablative of proelium is generally used *without* in in such expressions as: *in many battles,* multīs proeliīs.

NOUNS OF THE THIRD DECLENSION

centuriō, centuriōnis	*a centurion*[1]
cīvitās, cīvitātis	*state*
fīnēs, fīnium, *m.*[2]	*territory*
mors, mortis	*death*
ōrātiō, ōrātiōnis	{ *speech* / *prayer*[3] }

ADJECTIVES OF THE FIRST AND SECOND DECLENSIONS

aliēnus, a, um	{ *unfavorable* / *another's* / *foreign* }
integer, integra, integrum	{ *fresh* / *uninjured* / *whole* }
līber, lībera, līberum	*free*
miser, misera, miserum	*wretched*

PRONOUNS

ego, meī	*I*
is, ea, id	*he, she, it*
meus, a, um	{ *my* / *mine* }
nōs, nostrī	*we*
noster, nostra, nostrum	{ *our* / *ours* }
quid	*what?*
quis	*who?*

---

[1] A Roman army officer in charge of one hundred men. The rank was similar to that of our captain.

[2] Fīnēs is a plural noun like partēs.

[3] Ōrātiō means *prayer* only in Christian Latin.

suī	$\begin{cases} himself \\ herself \\ itself \\ themselves \end{cases}$
tū, tuī	you (sing.)
tuus, a, um	$\begin{cases} your \text{ (when referring to} \\ yours \qquad \text{ONE person)} \end{cases}$
vester, vestra, vestrum	$\begin{cases} your \text{ (when referring to MORE} \\ yours \qquad \text{THAN ONE person)} \end{cases}$
vōs, vestrī	you (pl.)

ADVERBS

cūr, adv.	why?
etiam, adv.	also
ferē, adv.	almost
fortiter, adv.	$\begin{cases} bravely \\ strongly \end{cases}$
ibi, adv.	there
interim, adv.	meanwhile
ita, adv.	$\begin{cases} so \\ thus \end{cases}$
longē, adv.	$\begin{cases} far \\ by\ far \end{cases}$
posteā, adv.	afterwards
saepe, adv.	often
semper, adv.	always
tamen, adv.	nevertheless
tum, adv.	$\begin{cases} then \\ at\ that\ time \end{cases}$
ubi, adv.	where?
undique, adv.	$\begin{cases} from\ all\ sides \\ on\ all\ sides \end{cases}$
vehementer, adv.	$\begin{cases} greatly \\ violently \end{cases}$

CONJUNCTIONS

atque (ac), *conj.*	*and*
aut, *conj.*	*or*
aut . . . aut, *conjs.*	*either . . . or*
enim, *conj., postp.*	*for*
nam, *conj.*	*for*[1]
neque, *conj.*	$\begin{cases} nor \\ and \ldots not \end{cases}$
neque . . . neque, *conjs.*	*neither . . . nor*
sīcut, *conj.*	*as*

PREPOSITIONS

ab (ā), *prep. w. abl.*	$\begin{cases} by \text{ (expressing agency)} \\ from \text{ (w. absum)} \end{cases}$
dē, *prep. w. abl.*	$\begin{cases} concerning \\ about \end{cases}$
per, *prep. w. acc.*	*through*
sine, *prep. w. abl.*	*without*
trāns, *prep. w. acc.*	*across*

OTHER WORDS

in prīncipiō	*in the beginning*
in saecula saeculōrum	$\begin{cases} world \ without \ end \\ forever \end{cases}$
-ne	particle used in questions

---

[1] When *for* means *because* and introduces a REASON.

UNIT SIX

LESSON 22: THE PRESENT SUBJUNCTIVE; PURPOSE CLAUSES

INTRODUCTION

We have studied the INDICATIVE MOOD. We saw that it was used in ordinary STATEMENTS OF FACT and in DIRECT QUESTIONS.

We shall now study the SUBJUNCTIVE MOOD. This mood is used in many special constructions, both in main clauses and in subordinate clauses. Latin uses the subjunctive in sentences where the English uses auxiliary (or helping) verbs, such as *may*, *might*, *should*, and the like. But Latin also uses the subjunctive where English uses the indicative. The MEANING of the subjunctive, therefore, will have to be learned as we study the DIFFERENT LATIN CONSTRUCTIONS REQUIRING THE SUBJUNCTIVE.

1. THE PRESENT SUBJUNCTIVE ACTIVE

ASSIGNMENT: Study the present tense of the subjunctive in the four conjugations, GRAMMAR, Nos. 186, 194-196. Learn the meaning in purpose clauses. Note that (1) the *vowels* which begin the endings are not the usual ones in each conjugation, (2) the final personal signs are regular.

EXERCISE 238
[First Conjugation]
What forms are these?

1. collocet	5. pugnent	9. laudet
2. det	6. perturbēmus	10. appellet
3. perturbet	7. occupent	11. cōnfirmet
4. laudēs	8. perturbent	12. laudētis

EXERCISE 239
[Second Conjugation]
What forms are these?

1. moneās	4. habeat	7. teneat
2. terreant	5. moneāmus	8. moneātis
3. sustineat	6. terreātis	9. obtineant

EXERCISE 240
[Third Conjugation]
What forms are these?

1. mittāmus	5. dēfendat	9. īnstruant
2. dūcant	6. cēdant	10. incendat
3. pellat	7. pōnātis	11. vincant
4. petant	8. pellant	12. mittās

EXERCISE 241
[Fourth Conjugation]
What forms are these?

1. audiāmus	4. audiās	7. veniant
2. veniat	5. conveniant	8. mūniat
3. mūniant	6. audiātis	9. audiam

2. MOOD IN PURPOSE CLAUSES

He is fighting in order that he may defend the city.

Pugnat ut urbem dēfendat.

"He is fighting" is a MAIN clause.

"In order that" introduces a SUBORDINATE clause.

"In order that he may defend the city" is a SUBORDINATE clause. This subordinate clause expresses the PURPOSE of his fighting. It answers the QUESTION: "For what purpose is he fighting?" ANSWER: "In order that he may defend the city."

A subordinate clause expressing PURPOSE is called a PURPOSE CLAUSE.

> RULE: A PURPOSE CLAUSE IS INTRODUCED BY
> *UT* ('IN ORDER THAT'). THE VERB IN THE PUR-
> POSE CLAUSE IS PUT IN THE SUBJUNCTIVE.

A purpose clause is an ADVERBIAL clause. It expresses the
PURPOSE of the action in the main clause, and so, like an adverb, modifies the main verb.

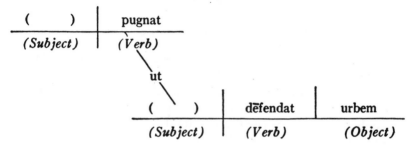

VOCABULARY

vīta, ae	*life*
vallum, ī	{ *wall* { *rampart*
amīcitia, ae	*friendship*
fossa, ae	*ditch*
celeriter, *adv.*	*swiftly*

RELATED ENGLISH WORDS
Vital; amicable; vitamin; celerity.

RELATED LATIN WORD
Amīcus

> LAUDĀBŌ DEUM MEUM IN VĪTĀ MEĀ.
> —From the *Roman Breviary*

EXERCISE 242

1. *Translate;*
2. *Point out the MAIN clauses;*
3. *Point out the SUBORDINATE PURPOSE clauses;*
4. *Diagram Sentences 1 and 2:*

1. Castra vallō mūnit ut ea dēfendat. 2. Damusne praemia amīcīs ut amīcitiam cōnfirmēmus? 3. Fortiter pugnō ut vītam meam cōnservem. 4. Hīberna fossā mūniunt ut impetum hostium sustineant. 5. Equitēs celeriter veniunt ut frūmenta incendant.

3. PRIMARY TENSES

The present, future, and future perfect in the INDICATIVE are called PRIMARY TENSES. When the verb of the main clause is in a PRIMARY tense, the PRESENT subjunctive must be used in a PURPOSE clause. In these sentences **pugnat, pugnābit,** and **pugnāverit** are PRIMARY tenses. Therefore **dēfendat** is in the PRESENT subjunctive.

Pugnat ut urbem dēfendat.
He is fighting in order that he may defend the city.

Pugnābit ut urbem dēfendat.
He will fight in order that he may defend the city.

Pugnāverit ut urbem dēfendat.
He will have fought in order that he may defend the city.

RULE: WHEN THE MAIN VERB IS IN A PRIMARY TENSE, USE THE PRESENT SUBJUNCTIVE IN THE PURPOSE CLAUSE.

EXERCISE 243

In which sentences should the present subjunctive be used?

1. Pugnāvit ut .... 2. Pugnāverās ut .... 3. Veniet ut .... 4. Hostēs terret ut .... 5. Praemium eīs dedit

ut .... 6. Pugnat ut .... 7. Veniō ut .... 8. Pugnāverit ut ....

We can express purpose in English in DIFFERENT ways:

>He fights *in order that* he *may* defend the city.
>He fights *that* he *may* defend the city.
>He fights *in order to* defend the city.
>He fights *to* defend the city.

All these MEAN the same thing and MAY be translated into
Latin in the same way:

Pugnat ut urbem dēfendat.

EXERCISE 244
[Essential]
Translate each sentence in four different ways:

1. Mīlitēs glōriae cupidī pugnant ut hostēs vincant. 2. Pugnā-
buntne virī līberī semper ut cīvitātem nostram servent? 3. Arma
ā nōbīs parantur ut vītās nostrās cōnservēmus. 4. Castra vallō
et fossā mūniunt ut impetum hostium sustineant. 5. Amīcitiam
cum omnibus gentibus cōnfirmābimus ut pācem cum eīs servēmus.

EXERCISE 245
Translate:

1. They fight to defend the lives of good men. 2. He fortifies
the hill with a rampart to hold it. 3. They are sending grain in
order to strengthen peace. 4. They help the Romans in order to
strengthen friendship with them.

In virtūte posita est vēra[1] fēlīcitās.[2]
—Seneca[3]

---

[1] **vērus, a, um:** *true.*
[2] **fēlīcitās, fēlīcitātis:** *happiness.*
[3] Lucius Annaeus Seneca, a Roman philosopher, essayist, and dramatist (died
A. D. 65).

4. NEGATIVE PURPOSE CLAUSES

He fights in order that the enemy may not burn the city.
He fights lest the enemy burn the city.

Pugnat nē hostēs urbem incendant.

A purpose is expressed in the subordinate clause of these sentences, but the purpose is NEGATIVE *(NOT, LEST)*.

> **RULE: WHEN THE PURPOSE CLAUSE IS NEGATIVE, *NĒ* ('IN ORDER THAT . . . NOT,' 'LEST') IS USED INSTEAD OF *UT NŌN*.**

Notice that the meaning of **nē** is *in order that . . . NOT*. Therefore in the example the English *not* is translated in the word **nē**.

ASSIGNMENT: Learn the present subjunctive of **sum**, GRAMMAR, No. 352.

VOCABULARY

exspectō, *1, tr.*	wait for wait
novus, a, um	new
diū, *adv.*	a long time long
ācriter, *adv.*	bitterly eagerly
expugnō, *1, tr.*	storm take by storm

RELATED ENGLISH WORDS

Great *expectations* The *acrid* smell of burning sulphur. I am *expecting* a friend. Not so many years ago the radio was a *novelty*.

RELATED LATIN WORDS

Diū pugnāvimus. Oppidum oppugnāvit.

EXERCISE 246

1. Translate;
2. Point out the main clause;
3. Point out the subordinate clause;
4. Explain the tense in the subordinate clause;
5. Diagram Sentences 1 and 2:

1. Frūmentum in castra ā servīs portātur nē inopia frūmentī sit. 2. Continetne mīlitēs in castrīs ut cōpiās novās exspectet? 3. In agrōs hostium venit ut eōs terreat. 4. Gallī diū et ācriter pugnant nē Rōmānī frūmenta incendant. 5. Virtūtem mīlitum ōrātiōne cōnfirmat ut victōriae cupidī sint. 6. Praemia prīncipibus dat ut amīcitiam cum eōrum gentibus cōnfirmet. 7. Gallī pugnant nē servī sint. 8. Centuriō frātrem adjuvat nē hostēs eum occīdant. 9. Castra vallō et fossā mūnit nē hostēs ea expugnent.

EXERCISE 247

Translate:

1. They fight in order to conquer. 2. They assault the town in order to take it by storm. 3. They are coming to hear the speech. 4. They are seizing the bridge to burn it. 5. They will come to see Rome. 6. They pray in order to be good. 7. They will fortify the town lest the enemy take it by storm. 8. They warn the chief in order to preserve his life. 9. He fights in order to be king. 10. They are yielding lest there be a slaughter. 11. They station soldiers to defend the bridge. 12. They are handing over arms to strengthen peace. 13. They prepare arms to wage war. 14. He will come to kill the commander in chief. 15. He is coming to seek peace. 16. He will remain to wait for new legions.

EXERCISE 248
[Essential]
Translate:

1. God helps us in order that the enemy may not overcome us. 2. Mary prays for us that we may have the grace of God.

3. I shall fight bravely and long to preserve your life. 4. He is fortifying the camp with a ditch to defend it. 5. We are waiting for Caesar lest the enemy conquer us. 6. Is he leading new legions into Gaul to take the cities (by storm)? 7. He is burning the crops in order that there may be a scarcity of grain in Gaul. 8. He is strengthening friendship with all tribes lest there be war. 9. They are coming to storm the town. 10. The enemy is pressing them hard. Therefore they will give way lest the enemy kill them.[1] 11. They are assembling to hear the king.

EXERCISE 249

1. Identify and translate these forms;
2. Use each in a Latin sentence:

1. contendat	8. pellat	15. dūcat
2. vincam	9. exspectābit	16. cōnfirmat
3. timeant	10. veniat	17. appellēs
4. expugnant	11. veniet	18. geris
5. laudet	12. vincit	19. occupent
6. vincet	13. adjuvet	20. occīdant
7. pugnat	14. dēfendant	21. adjuvant

VĪTA SINE LITTERĪS[2] MORS EST.

NOTE ON TRANSLATION

Very often several meanings are given for a Latin word in the vocabularies. In translating you should choose the meaning that makes GOOD SENSE. For example, in the following sentences **altus** must be translated in different ways. Explain how you know which meaning to use.

1. Hannibal cōpiās trāns montēs *altōs* dūxit.
2. Hannibal cōpiās trāns flūmina *alta* dūxit.

---

[1] *Them:* translate here by **sē.**
[2] **Litterīs** here does not mean *letters, i. e.,* an epistle, but *literature* or *writing.*

EXERCISE 250

[Essential Review]

Translate and explain the case of the italicized words:

1. *Multī* hominēs in *Italiam* veniunt ut Rōmam videant. 2. Hominēs celeriter conveniunt ut rēs *novās* et audiant et videant. 3. Mīlitēs diū et fortiter pugnant ut victōriae glōriam comparent. 4. Mīlitēs cum *hostibus* ācriter contendunt ut *eōs* pellant atque occīdant. 5. Dominus malus ā servīs *miserīs* laudātur ut vītam *eōrum* servet. 6. Caesar, *vir* bonus et fortis, cum mīlitibus in *aciē* saepe pugnat ut eōrum *virtūtem* cōnfirmet. 7. Castra vallō et fossā ā Rōmānīs mūniuntur nē hostēs *ea* expugnent. 8. Ducēs *mīlitibus* saepe et grātiās agunt et praemia dant ut fortiter pugnent. 9. Suntne imperātōrēs saepe *glōriae* atque victōriae cupidī?

READING NO. 12

WOE TO THE WEAK!

TIME. About 55 B. C.

PLACE. A town somewhere in Gaul. The gates are shut; a few Gauls are seen standing about. Suddenly horses are heard approaching. The guards at the gate are on the alert.

GUARD. Quis es?

VOICE OUTSIDE THE GATE. Centuriō Rōmānus sum. Veniō ut cum prīncipibus dē rē gravī agam.

GUARD. Eōs vocābimus. *(A slave is sent off. Several elderly and distinguished Gauls return. The gates are opened. A Roman centurion and several horsemen ride in.)*

PRINCIPES. Cūr venītis? Quid petitis?

CENTURIO. Venīmus ut cōpiam frūmentī petāmus. Est frūmentī inopia in castrīs nostrīs. Itaque Caesar nōs mittit ut frūmentum comparēmus.

PRINCIPES. Nōs autem nōn magnam frūmentī cōpiam habēmus neque sunt frūmenta in agrīs.

CENTURIO *(firmly)*. Dabitis tamen nōbīs. Estisne amīcī populī

"Frumentum Petimus."

Rōmānī? Nōbīs frūmentum dabitis . . . ut amīcī semper sītis populī Rōmānī.

Principes. Nōs etiam homines sumus. Puerī et mātrēs et . . .

Centurio (*interrupting and speaking slowly and threateningly*). Gēns vōbīs fīnitima frūmentum nōbīs nōn dedit. Jam oppida et urbēs eōrum expugnantur et incenduntur; puerī et virī occīduntur; mātrēs in castra dūcuntur ut servae[1] sint. Vōs tamen amīcī (*ironically*) estis populī Rōmānī! (*Interim multī Gallī convēnērunt. A murmur of resentment runs through the crowd. The chiefs look about uncertainly.*)

Principes. Nōs amīcī Caesaris et populī Rōmānī semper fuimus. Etiam equitēs mīsimus. Cum eō bellum nōn gessimus. Pācem cum Caesare et populō Rōmānō semper servāvimus.

Centurio (*insolently*). Itaque cūr exspectātis? Frūmentum nunc petimus!

Principes (*in despair*). Cōpiam autem nōn habēmus!

Voices from the Crowd. Nōn dabimus! Pugnābimus! (*The crowd moves menacingly towards the centurion. He whirls his horse about and charges through the opening. The gates slam shut behind him. There is a long silence.*)

Princeps (*fearfully*). Veniet Caesar!

(*Such scenes were common not only in Caesar's wars with the Gauls but in all wars when the might of arms crushed the rights of the innocent and the weak.*)

---

[1] serva, ae: *a female slave.*

LESSON 23: THE IMPERFECT SUBJUNCTIVE ACTIVE

1. IMPERFECT SUBJUNCTIVE ACTIVE OF THE FOUR CONJUGATIONS

ASSIGNMENT: Learn the imperfect subjunctive, GRAMMAR, Nos. 187, 197-199.

Note. Here is an easy way to remember the imperfect subjunctive: ADD THE REGULAR FINAL PERSONAL SIGNS (-m, etc.) TO THE PRESENT INFINITIVE. For example:

1. laudāre + -m = laudārem
2. laudāre + -s = laudārēs, *etc.*

VOCABULARY

tribūnus, ī	*tribune*
cōnsilium, ī	$\begin{cases} plan \\ counsel \end{cases}$
concilium, ī	*council*
lēgātus, ī	$\begin{cases} envoy \\ lieutenant \end{cases}$
lātus, a, um	*wide*
facile, *adv.*	*easily*

NOTE

Tribūnus is often used with the genitive mīlitum. Tribūnus mīlitum (literally, *a tribune of soldiers*) is to be translated *a military tribune*. The military tribune was an officer a rank above the centurion.

RELATED ENGLISH WORDS

The American *Legation*. The *latitude* and the longitude of the earth. The papal *legate*. His manner was *facile*. Control of the air *facilitates* military victories. Practice can produce remarkable *facility*.

RELATED LATIN WORD

Iter per prōvinciam **facile** erat.

EXERCISE 251
[First Conjugation]
What forms are these?

1. exspectāret	5. ōrāret	9. portāret
2. parāret	6. laudārem	10. superārent
3. appellārent	7. pugnārent	11. exspectārent
4. oppugnārent	8. laudārēmus	12. laudārētis

EXERCISE 252
[Second Conjugation]
What forms are these?

1. habēret	5. monērēmus	9. monērem
2. obtinērent	6. movēret	10. vidērem
3. monērētis	7. sustinērent	11. terrēret
4. terrērent	8. tenēret	12. complērent

EXERCISE 253
[Third Conjugation]
What forms are these?

1. peterent	5. mitterēmus	9. gererent
2. gereret	6. mitterēs	10. incenderet
3. mitterem	7. trāderent	11. īnstruerent
4. premeret	8. cēderent	12. contenderet

EXERCISE 254
[Fourth Conjugation]
What forms are these?

1. audīrēmus	3. mūnīret	5. mūnīrent
2. venīret	4. audīrētis	6. convenīrent

| 7. audīrem | 9. convenīrētis | 11. audīrent |
| 8. audīrēs | 10. venīrent | 12. convenīret |

EXERCISE 255
[General]
What forms are these?

1. vincit	6. sint	11. vidēret
2. expugnet	7. audīret	12. portārent
3. pelleret	8. contenderent	13. sītis
4. veniet	9. veniam	14. audiat
5. exspectēmus	10. oppugnat	15. portet

2. SECONDARY TENSES

The imperfect, perfect, and pluperfect indicative are SEC-ONDARY TENSES.

When the main verb is in a SECONDARY tense, use the IMPERFECT subjunctive in the purpose clause.

Pugnāvit ut castra occupāret.

He fought in order that he might seize the camp.

He fought that he might seize the camp.

He fought in order to seize the camp.

He fought to seize the camp.

RULE

PURPOSE CLAUSES ARE INTRODUCED BY *UT* (NEGATIVE: *NĒ*);
USE THE SUBJUNCTIVE;
USE THE PRESENT SUBJUNCTIVE WHEN THE MAIN VERB IS PRIMARY;
USE THE IMPERFECT SUBJUNCTIVE WHEN THE MAIN VERB IS SECONDARY.

Pugnābat ut castra <u>occupāret</u>.

He was fighting <u>in order that</u> he <u>might</u> seize the camp.

Pugnāverat ut castra <u>occupāret</u>.

He had fought <u>in order that</u> he <u>might</u> seize the camp.

EXERCISE 256
[Essential]

1. Translate;
2. Parse the italicized words;
3. Diagram Sentence 1:

1. Caesar legiōnēs novās et integrās saepe exspectāvit ut hostēs facile *vinceret*. 2. Gallī oppidum vallō altō et *fossā* lātā mūnīvērunt nē Rōmānī *id expugnārent*. 3. Lēgātus centuriōnēs et tribūnōs mīlitum appellāvit ut fortiter et diū *pugnārent*. 4. Dūxitne Hannibal omnēs cōpiās trāns lāta flūmina et per montēs altōs ut cum Rōmānīs in Italiā bellum *gereret?* 5. Jēsūs Chrīstus, Deī Fīlius, in mundum vēnit ut vītam et salūtem nōbīs *daret*. 6. Gallī saepe lēgātōs in castra Caesaris mīsērunt ut pācem et amīcitiam *peterent*. 7. Concilium saepe ab imperātōribus vocātur ut dē rē gravī in conciliō *agant*. 8. Dux lēgātīs praemia dedit ut cōnsilium laudārent.

EXERCISE 257
[Drill]
Translate:

1. They fought in order to conquer. 2. They assaulted the town in order to take it (by storm). 3. They seized the bridge to burn it. 4. They came to hear the plan. 5. They came to see Rome. 6. They prayed in order to be good. 7. They fortify the town lest the enemy storm it. 8. They warned the chief in order to spare his life. 9. He waged war in order to seize the royal power. 10. They are yielding lest there be a slaughter. 11. They stationed horsemen to defend the hill.

12. They handed over the arms in order to preserve peace.
13. They prepared arms in order to wage war. 14. The chiefs
were dismissed lest the tribes wage war. 15. He came to kill
the king. 16. The soldiers were drawn up to defend the city.
17. He waited for Caesar in order to conquer the enemy. 18. He
came to seek peace. 19. They assembled to hear the speech.
20. He remained to wait for the chief.

EXERCISE 258
[Essential]
Translate:

1. The Romans fortified the camp with a wide ditch lest the
enemy should easily take it (by storm). 2. Caesar, in the council,
often strengthened the courage of the lieutenants and military
tribunes in order that they might fight bravely. 3. They fought
bitterly lest the enemy storm the town. 4. After a war were the
chiefs and leaders of the enemy often killed by Caesar? 5. The
lieutenant held the soldiers in the camp lest the enemy should
see the plans. 6. Caesar stationed soldiers on the bridge lest the
enemy should come across the wide river.

READING NO. 13

DĒ FRĀTRUM FORTIUM MORTE

A STORY BASED ON THE REPORT OF THE AFFAIR MADE BY CAESAR.

In hōc[1] proeliō multī equitēs occīsī sunt; in[2] eīs vir fortis et
nōbilis, Pīsō Aquītānus. Is amīcus erat Populī Rōmānī. Ējus
frāter in proeliō vulnerātus[3] erat et ab hostibus premēbātur. Nōn
erat spēs salūtis. Pīsō id vīdit; vīdit frātrem; vīdit hostēs. Tamen
in hostēs contendit ut frātrem adjuvāret. Ab hostibus autem
circumventus[4] est atque occīsus est. Tum frāter Pīsōnis morte

---

[1] hōc: *this.*
[2] in here means *among.*
[3] vulnerō, *1, tr.: wound.*
[4] circumveniō: *surround.*

ACRITER PUGNAVERUNT

ējus vehementer mōtus est et in hostēs contendit. Ācriter pugnāvit; tamen is etiam ab hostibus occīsus est. Ita occīsī sunt frātrēs
fortēs et bonī. Laudāmusne eōs?

Answer in complete Latin sentences:

1. Quis fuit Pīsō Aquītānus?
2. Quis ab hostibus premēbātur?
3. Quis in hostēs contendit?
4. Cūr in hostēs sē mīsit?
5. Estne Pīsō Aquītānus occīsus?
6. Estne frāter ējus occīsus?

EXERCISE 259
[Review]

1. Name the primary and secondary tenses of the indicative.
2. Give the rule for the ablative of means.

3. ADJECTIVES USED AS NOUNS; IMPERFECT SUBJUNCTIVE OF *SUM*

ASSIGNMENT: Study the use of adjectives as nouns (GRAMMAR, Nos. 845-848) and the imperfect subjunctive of **sum,** (GRAMMAR, No. 353).

VOCABULARY

labor, labōris	{ *effort* / *toil*
ōrdō, ōrdinis, *m.*	*rank* (of soldiers)
obses, obsidis, *c.*	*hostage*
inter, *prep. w. acc.*	{ *between* / *among*
statim, *adv.*	{ *at once* / *immediately*

NOTE

Obses is marked *c* (= common gender); that is, it may be either masculine or feminine, as hostages were men and women. However, use it as masculine unless it clearly refers to women.

RELATED ENGLISH WORDS
Line the men up in *order*. Hard *labor*. *Interstate* commerce.

REVIEW VOCABULARY

sum, esse, fuī, futūrus, *intr.*	*am*
absum, abesse, āfuī, āfutūrus, *intr.;* ab (ā) *w. abl.*	{ *am away* / *am distant*
ab (ā), *prep. w. abl.*	{ *from* (*w.* **absum**) / *by* (agency)

IDIOM STUDY

Inter is a preposition which governs the accusative. It means *between* or *among*. Study its idiomatic use with REFLEXIVE PRONOUNS and DŌ.

Obsidēs inter nōs damus.

(Literally, *We are giving hostages among ourselves.*)
We are exchanging hostages.

Obsidēs inter vōs datis.

(Literally, *You are giving hostages among yourselves.*)
You are exchanging hostages.

Gentēs Galliae obsidēs inter sē dant.

(Literally, *The tribes of Gaul are giving hostages among themselves.*)
The tribes of Gaul are exchanging hostages.

Therefore **dō, dare, dedī, datus,** *1, tr.*, with **inter** and the proper REFLEXIVE pronoun means *exchange*.

PROPTER TĒ OMNIA AGŌ ET SUSTINEŌ.

—From the *Following of Christ*

EXERCISE 260
[Essential]

1. Translate;
2. Explain the use of the italicized words:

1. Laudāturne Deus *ab* omnibus *sānctīs?* 2. Gallī saepe obsidēs inter *sē* dedērunt ut pācem cōnfirmārent. 3. *Fortēs* propter metum nōn cēdunt. 4. Caesar, vir fortis, *omnia* fortiter ēgit. 5. Caesar multa bella gessit ut imperātor et prīnceps esset. 6. Adjuvatne Deus *fortēs?* 7. *Nostrī* fortiter et ācriter semper pugnant ut līberam cīvitātem nostram cōnservent. 8. Fortēs

fortūna adjuvat *(a Roman proverb).* 9. Nostrī cessērunt nē magna caedēs esset. 10. Omnia *virtūte* agō ut bonus servus Chrīstī sim. 11. Lēgātus in agrōs statim contendit *nē* longē ā proeliō abesset. 12. Sānctī labōrēs gravēs propter Chrīstum sustinent. 13. Hostēs equitēs in aciem statim mīsērunt ut ōrdinēs nostrōrum perturbārent. 14. Prīncipēs obsidēs inter sē dabant ut pāx in Galliā esset. 15. Prīncipēs Galliae semper inter sē dē imperiō omnis Galliae contendēbant. 16. Erat iter et difficile et angustum inter montēs et flūmen. 17. Ducēs inter sē in conciliō dē rē gravī agunt.

LABOR OMNIA VINCIT.

(Motto of the State of Oklahoma)

EXERCISE 261
[Essential]
Translate:

1. Meanwhile cavalry were sent by the general into the territory of the enemy to find out their plans. 2. The Romans often fortified the camp with a wall lest the Gauls take it (by storm.) 3. The Gauls strengthened peace by means of hostages. 4. Cavalry were immediately sent against the enemy in order to disturb their ranks. 5. They often exchanged hostages that they might preserve peace and friendship. 6. A council assembled in the town at once in order that the chiefs might treat among themselves about peace and war.

EXERCISE 262
[Review]

1. What is the rule for the ablative of means?
2. What is the rule for the ablative of the agent?
3. Name the primary tenses of the indicative.

OBSIDES

READING NO. 14

DĒ OBSIDIBUS

Gallī obsidēs inter sē saepe dedērunt ut amīcitiam et pācem cōnfirmārent. Itaque per obsidēs amīcitia cōnfirmāta est atque ita pāx in Galliā est cōnfirmāta. Gallī saepe obsidēs etiam Rōmānīs dedērunt ut fidem cōnfirmārent. Rōmānī autem obsidēs Gallīs nōn dedērunt, nam, omnis Galliae imperiī cupidī, gentēs Galliae armīs et virtūte vīcerant. Itaque Gallī Rōmānōs timēbant et cum eīs bella saepe gessērunt nē obsidēs eīs darent.

Obsidēs autem puerī et virī et mātrēs et patrēs erant. Saepe etiam erant fīliī prīncipum et rēgum Gallōrum. Līberī autem nōn erant obsidēs. Eōs enim Rōmānī in castrīs et hībernīs et oppidīs tenēbant ut propter eōrum salūtem Gallī pācem servārent. Itaque obsidēs saepe miserī erant. Nam, sī[1] post pācem Gallī

---

[1] sī: *if.*

bellum cum Rōmānīs gessērunt, Rōmānī omnēs eōrum obsidēs occīdēbant ut posteā[1] Gallī propter metum fidem servārent. Ita Gallī caede obsidum saepe territī sunt et bellum cum Rōmānīs saepe nōn gessērunt ut obsidum vītās cōnservārent.

Answer in complete Latin sentences:

1. Cūr Gallī inter sē obsidēs dedērunt?
2. Cūr Gallī Rōmānīs obsidēs dabant?
3. Erantne obsidēs līberī?
4. Ubi tenēbantur obsidēs ā Rōmānīs?
5. Erantne obsidēs saepe miserī? Cūr?

"DUCIS IN CŌNSILIŌ POSITA EST VIRTŪS MĪLITUM."

—Publilius Syrus

---

[1] **posteā,** *adv.: afterwards.*

LESSON 24: RELATIVE CLAUSES; THE USE OF *AD*

1. *QUĪ, QUAE, QUOD*

The RELATIVE PRONOUN in English is:

1. *WHO (whose, whom)* for PERSONS;
2. *WHICH* for THINGS;
3. *THAT* for PERSONS or THINGS.

The RELATIVE PRONOUN introduces a SUBORDINATE ADJECTIVE CLAUSE.

> The Gaul—who was in the camp—was a slave.
>
> Those—who fight bravely—do not always win.

The MAIN clauses are:

> The Gaul was a slave.
>
> Those do not always win.

The SUBORDINATE clauses are:

> who was in the camp
>
> who fight bravely

These subordinate clauses are ADJECTIVE clauses because, like an adjective, they modify (describe) a noun *(the Gaul)* or a pronoun *(those)*.

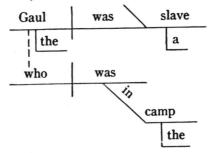

In English the relative pronoun:

1. May be EXPRESSED:

    1. *The Gaul—who was in the camp—was a slave.*

    2. *The column—which was in the forest—was long.*

    3. *The column—that was in the forest—was long.*

2. May be IMPLIED:

    4. *The Gaul—I saw—was a slave.*

Note. *Whom* is understood after Gaul. The full sentence would read:

    The Gaul—whom I saw—was a slave.

In Latin the relative pronoun—**quī, quae, quod**—is ALWAYS EXPRESSED.

    1. **Gallus—quī in castrīs erat—servus erat.**

    2. **Agmen—quod in silvīs erat—longum erat.**

    3. **Agmen—quod in silvīs erat—longum erat.**

    4. **Gallus—quem vīdī—servus erat.**

Note. Quem is masculine singular because it must AGREE with its antecedent, **Gallus**, in GENDER and NUMBER. But **quem** is in the ACCUSATIVE case because it is the object of **vīdī**, the verb in its own clause.

THE GENERAL RULE FOR THE AGREEMENT OF PRONOUNS (GRAMMAR, NO. 479) APPLIES TO RELATIVE PRONOUNS ALSO.

The ANTECEDENT of a relative pronoun (*i. e.,* the word to which the pronoun refers) is sometimes UNDERSTOOD in Latin when it would be in the nominative case. Express the antecedent when translating into English.

    Quī fortiter pugnant, bellī glōriam habent.

    THOSE who fight bravely have the glory of war.

ASSIGNMENT: Learn the declension of **quī, quae, quod** (GRAMMAR, No. 139) and the rule for the agreement of pronouns (GRAMMAR, No. 479).

VOCABULARY

quī, quae, quod	$\begin{cases} who \ (whose, \ whom) \\ which \\ that \end{cases}$
auxilium, ī	$\begin{cases} help \\ aid \end{cases}$
auxilia, auxiliōrum	*reinforcements*
memoria, ae	*memory*
memoriā teneō, tenēre, tenuī, tentus, 2, tr.	$\begin{cases} keep \ in \ memory \\ remember \end{cases}$

RELATED ENGLISH WORDS

The pilot turned on the *auxiliary* motor. They held a *memorial* service.

EXERCISE 263

Supply the correct form of the relative pronoun:

1. Caesar, who was a great general, conquered the Gauls.
   Caesar, ... imperātor magnus fuit, Gallōs vīcit.
2. The Gauls whose leaders Caesar killed were not friends of the Romans.
   Gallī .... ducēs Caesar occīdit amīcī Rōmānōrum nōn fuērunt.
3. Caesar, whose victories we all praise, was a great general.
   Caesar, ... victōriās omnēs laudāmus, imperātor magnus fuit.
4. God, to whom we give thanks, is our Father.
   Deus, ... grātiās agimus, Pater noster est.
5. The soldiers to whom Caesar gave rewards were brave.
   Mīlitēs .... Caesar praemia dedit fortēs erant.

6. Caesar, whom the Romans praised, was a great general.
   Caesar, ... Rōmānī laudāvērunt, imperātor magnus
   fuit.
7. The Gauls whom Caesar conquered fought bravely.
   Gallī .... Caesar vīcit fortiter pugnāvērunt.
8. The Gauls with whom Caesar fought were brave.
   Gallī ....-cum Caesar pugnāvit fortēs erant.
9. The war about which the Senate sent letters into Gaul was
   long and difficult.
   Bellum dē .... senātus litterās in Galliam mīsit longum
   et difficile fuit.
10. The town that Caesar stormed was large.
    Oppidum .... Caesar oppugnāvit magnum fuit.
11. The army with which Caesar came into Gaul was large.
    Exercitus ....-cum Caesar in Galliam vēnit magnus erat.
12. The victory for which Caesar was eager was not easy.
    Victōria .... Caesar cupidus erat facilis nōn erat.
13. The Gauls burned the baggage that was in the camp.
    Gallī impedīmenta .... in castrīs erant incendērunt.

EXERCISE 264
[Essential]

1. *Translate;*
2. *Explain the case and agreement of the italicized
   relative pronouns;* •
3. *Diagram Sentences 1 and 2:*

1. Rōmānī Chrīstum, *quī* erat Fīlius Deī, occīdērunt. 2. Marīa,
quam laudāmus, Māter Deī est. 3. Gentēs *quae* prōvinciae fīnitimae erant lēgātōs mīsērunt ut auxilium peterent. 4. Legiō
quae trāns flūmen fuerat in silvās statim missa est ut hostēs pel-
leret. 5. Bella *quae* patrēs nostrī gessērunt memoriā semper
tenēbimus. 6. Oppidum in *quō* frūmentum erat ā Rōmānīs op-
pugnābātur. 7. Imperātōrēs *quōrum* memoriam laudāmus fortēs
erant. 8. Lēgātus obsidēs *quōs* in castrīs tenēbat occīdit ut Gallōs
terrēret. 9. Ego, *quī* Rōmānus sum, tibi nōn cēdam. 10. Caesar

auxilia in silvās statim mīsit nē hostēs nostrōs vincerent.
11. Lēgātus servum *cui* hostēs gladium dederant occīdit.
12. Hīberna in *quibus* Rōmānī sunt angusta sunt. 13. Dabisne
nōbīs, *quī* Gallī sumus, frūmentum? 14. Rēgem prō *quō* pugnāvī
omnēs hominēs memoriā tenēbunt. 15. Rōmānī eōs *quibuscum*
pugnāverant saepe occīdēbant. 16. Caesar, *quōcum* eram, mihi
praemia dedit. 17. *Quī* lēgem Chrīstī servant, sānctī sunt.
18. Gentēs in *quārum* fīnēs Caesar vēnit fortiter cum eō pugnāvērunt. 19. Legiōnēs *quās* trāns flūmen lātum prīmā lūce vīderam
ā Caesare in castra ductae sunt. 20. Caesar imperium *cūjus*
cupidus erat obtinuit.

EXERCISE 265
[Essential]

1. Translate;
*2. Explain the agreement and the case of all relative
pronouns in the Latin translation:*

1. The Romans always killed slaves who had helped the enemy.
2. The mountains of Gaul, across which Caesar often led the
Roman forces, were high. 3. Caesar often killed the leaders of
the tribes with which he fought. 4. Caesar led the troops across
many rivers which were long and deep. 5. Christ, who is the
Son of God, was killed by the Romans. 6. The legion which was
in the forest was fighting bravely. 7. The legion to which the
Gauls gave grain was led into winter quarters. 8. The legion the
centurions of which were brave conquered the enemy. 9. The
legions which Caesar led into the province were brave. 10. The
legion with which the Gauls fought was brave. 11. The soldiers
whose courage Caesar praised are in winter quarters. 12. The
soldiers to whom the general gave thanks had withstood many
attacks of the enemy. 13. The Gauls often bravely defended the
towns which the Romans stormed. 14. The territory of the
enemy into which Caesar led all the Roman forces was full of
dangers. 15. The affair concerning which Caesar was treating
with the Gauls was serious. 16. The forest through which Caesar

often led the Roman legions was full of dangers. 17. The Roman people on whose behalf Caesar fought was great and renowned. 18. Caesar seized many cities from which Rome was far distant. 19. The roads which were constructed by the Romans were long and safe. 20. The things on account of which peoples and tribes wage war are serious. 21. Caesar immediately gave the soldiers the grain which the slaves had carried into the camp. 22. Caesar conquered the soldiers with whom the enemy had filled the bridge. 23. I, who am a Christian, will always praise Christ and Mary. 24. We all praise Caesar, whose victories were many and great. 25. The Gauls were storming the camp which had been pitched in their territory. 26. Caesar held the power for which he had been eager. 27. To you who are enemies of the Roman name I shall give neither grain nor arms. 28. We soldiers who fight for Rome are eager for victory and fame. 29. The hill on which the Romans pitched the camp is high.

EXERCISE 266

Translate:

1. "Bis[1] vincit quī sē vincit in victōriā."—*Publilius Syrus.*

   a. What is the antecedent of **quī**?

   b. Why is **sē** used instead of **eum**?

2. "Omnēs enim fīliī Deī estis per fidem quae est in Chrīstō Jēsū."—*St. Paul.*

   a. Explain the case of **fīliī.**

   b. With what does **omnēs** agree?

3. Jēsūs Chrīstus, quī prō nōbīs mortem semel[2] vīcit, semper mortem in nōbīs vincit.

   a. Give the rule for the case of **mortem.**

4. Templum[3] Deī sānctum est, quod estis vōs.—*Adapted from St. Paul.*

---

[1] **bis,** *adv.: twice.*

[2] **semel,** *adv.: once.*

[3] **templum, ī:** *temple.*

READING NO. 15

THE MOST IMPORTANT "PER" IN THE HISTORY OF THE LATIN LANGUAGE

Jesus Christ is our Savior. This means that all grace and salvation comes to us *through* Him. Without Him we can do nothing. He has brought us back to God through His death on the cross, and this is why today the cross surmounts our churches and the crucifix stands above all our altars.

Per Jēsūm Chrīstum grātiam Deī habēmus. Per Jēsūm Chrīstum et per ējus mortem salūtem et spem glōriae habēmus. Per eum in terrā tūtī sumus; per eum in Caelum post mortem veniēmus.

Therefore most of the public prayers of the Church today end with this or a similar formula:

. . . per Dominum nostrum Jēsūm Chrīstum Fīlium tuum, quī tēcum vīvit[1] et rēgnat[2] in ūnitāte[3] Spīritūs Sānctī Deus per omnia saecula[4] saeculōrum.[4]

The *per* which begins this formula is therefore the most important and significant *per* that has ever been written or spoken.

----

[1] vīvit: *lives*
[2] rēgnat: *reigns.*
[3] ūnitās, ūnitātis: *unity.*
[4] saeculum, ī: *age.*

2. THE USE OF *AD*

We have studied a number of prepositions, some governing the ablative case, others the accusative. The preposition *in*, for example, used with the accusative case after verbs of motion, means *into, in, onto, upon.*

In flūmen pulsī sunt. *They were driven into the river.*

In castra contendit. *He hastened into the camp.*

Another preposition which takes the ACCUSATIVE is **ad.** This word has several meanings and uses.

1. **Ad** is used with verbs of motion (and occasionally others like **pertineō**) to mean *to* or *up to.*

Ad flūmen pulsī sunt. *They were driven to the river.*

Ad castra contendit. *He hastened (up) to the camp.*

Ea omnia ad bellum pertinent.
All those things pertain to war.

2. **Ad** is used in expressions of time to mean *to, until.*

Ad noctem pugnāvērunt. *They fought until night.*

3. **Ad** sometimes also means *at*, both with verbs of motion and with other verbs.

Ad flūmen pervēnērunt. *They arrived at the river.*

Ad flūmen castra posuērunt. *They pitched camp at the river.*

4. **Ad** is used with certain adjectives to mean *for.*

Ad omnia parātus. *Prepared for all things.*

Ad bellum ūtilia. *Things useful for war.*

5. **Ad** is sometimes strengthened by the adverb **usque,** *all the way.* Usque can be frequently left untranslated.

Usque ad urbem contendērunt.
They hastened to (all the way to) the city.

VOCABULARY

ad, *prep. w. acc.*	*to* *until* *at* *for* (with adjectives)
usque, *adv.*	*all the way*
perveniō, pervenīre, pervēnī, perventum, *4, intr.;* in *or* ad *w. acc.*	*arrive*
pertineō, pertinēre, pertinuī, *2, intr.;* ad *w. acc.*	*pertain to* *stretch to*
parātus a, um; *w.* ad	*prepared (for)*
ūtilis, e; *w.* ad	*useful (for)*
nox, noctis	*night*

RELATED ENGLISH WORDS

A *pertinent* remark. No one doubts the *utility* of water power. China has never been able to *utilize* all its resources. The bat is a *nocturnal* animal. Usque is a Latin *adverb*.

RELATED LATIN WORDS

Veniō; teneō; parō.

REVIEW VOCABULARY

in, *prep. w. abl.*	*in* *on*
in, *prep. w. acc.*	*in* *into* *against* *upon* *onto* *on*
portō, *1, tr.*	*carry*
moveō, movēre, mōvī, mōtus, *2, tr.*	*move*
contendō, contendere, contendī, *3, intr.*	*strive* *contend* *hasten*

IDIOM STUDY

A verb is used impersonally when it has no DEFINITE SUB-JECT. In English we use the indefinite *IT* as a subject for impersonal verbs.

It rains.

In this sentence *it* does not refer to any definite thing.

In Latin many verbs are used impersonally in various constructions. When a verb is used impersonally it is always in the THIRD PERSON SINGULAR, and, in compound tenses, the participle is always NEUTER SINGULAR. For the present learn only these two common expressions:

Ācriter pugnātum est.
(Literally, *It was fought bitterly.*)
There was bitter fighting,
(or) *They fought bitterly.*

Ad flūmen perventum est.
(Literally, *It was arrived at the river.*)
They arrived at the river.

Always translate Latin impersonal verbs into GOOD ENGLISH. The Romans used many verbs impersonally which we cannot so use in English.

EXERCISE 267
[Drill on the use of **ad** and **in**]

1. Translate;
2. Explain the meaning of the prepositions:

1. *In* fīnēs hostium pervēnērunt. 2. *Ad* flūmen pervēnērunt. 3. *Ad* flūmen pugnāvērunt. 4. *Usque ad* noctem pugnāvērunt. 5. Arma *ad* bellum ūtilia sunt. 6. Prīmā lūce *ad* castra perventum est. 7. Prīmā lūce *in* castra pervēnit. 8. Erat inopia omnium rērum *in* hībernīs nostrīs. 9. *Ad* impedīmenta ācriter pugnātum est. 10. Mīlitēs *ad* omnia parātī erant. 11. *In* locum tūtum castra mōvit. 12. Frūmentum *in* castra portābātur. 13. Dūxitne mīlitēs *in* urbem? 14. Dūxitne mīlitēs *usque ad* urbem?

15. Mīlitēs Rōmānī, *ad* mortem parātī, prō portīs īnstrūctī sunt.
16. *In* silvās contendēbat. 17. *Ad* silvās contendēbat. 18. Eōs *in* prōvinciam mīsit. 19. Eōs *ad* prōvinciam mīsit. 20. *In* loca aliēna mīlitēs dūxit. 21. *In* hīberna lēgātum mīsit. *22. Ad* Caesarem lēgātōs mīsērunt. 23. Mīles *in* pontem missus est. 24. Mīles *ad* pontem missus est. 25. Caesar undique prīncipēs *ad* sē vocāvit. 26. *Ad* flūmen perventum est.

EXERCISE 268
[Essential]
Translate:

1. Ad impedīmenta ācriter usque ad noctem pugnātum est. 2. Lēgātī in castra celeriter pervēnērunt ut auxilium peterent. 3. Mittēsne litterās et lēgātōs ad mē? 4. Chrīstiānī propter Chrīstum ad labōrem et mortem parātī sunt. 5. Omnia quae ad bellum pertinent ab hostibus nostrīs comparantur; itaque nōs etiam ea quae ad bellum ūtilia sunt comparābimus. 6. Hostēs, glōriae cupidī, usque ad castra nostra vēnērunt. 7. Ducēs dē omnibus rēbus quae ad mīlitum salūtem pertinent in cōnsiliō inter sē agunt. 8. Mīlitēs ad labōrem praemiīs facile incitantur. 9. Prīmā lūce ad fīnēs hostium perventum est. 10. Ibi flūmen lātum erat, sed pōns pertinuit ad urbem quam lēgātus tenēbat. 11. Imperātor omnēs lēgātōs et mīlitēs ad sē statim vocāvit. 12. Tribūnōs mīlitum ad omnēs cīvitātēs fīnitimās dīmīsit ut praemiīs et ōrātiōnibus amīcitiam cum eīs cōnfirmārent.

EXERCISE 269
[Essential]
Translate:

1. They arrived at a river which was wide and deep. 2. There was bitter fighting[1] at the river. 3. They hastened to Caesar to help him. 4. Did the Romans fight until night? 5. Are the soldiers prepared for battle? 6. Swords and arms are useful for

---

[1] Use a Latin idiomatic expression.

war.   7. They prepared everything which pertained to the journey.   8. They stationed soldiers on the bridge which stretched to Rome.   9. They hastened to the river to defend the bridge. 10. The fresh legions were sent against the Gauls by the lieutenant.   11. They hastened to the hill and fortified it with a rampart and a ditch lest the enemy seize it.

WARNING!

Do not confuse **ad** and the dative of the indirect object. **Ad,** *to,* is used with VERBS OF MOTION. The indirect object is rarely used with verbs of motion.

He came to us. **Ad nōs vēnit.**

He gave rewards to us. **Nōbīs praemia dedit.**

SEMPER PARĀTUS
(Motto of the United States Coast Guard)

EXERCISE 270
[Drill]
Translate:

1. They handed over the arms *to* the Romans.   2. They hastened *to* the Romans.   3. They gave hostages *to* the Romans. 4. They carried grain *to* the army.   5. He called the lieutenants *to* him.   6. He sent envoys *to* all the neighboring tribes.

EXERCISE 271
[Review]

1. Give the rule for the ablative of accompaniment.
2. Give the rule for the ablative of agency.
3. Name the secondary tenses of the indicative.
4. Explain the use of **sānctī**:

Omnēs sānctī Deum laudant.

258 FIRST YEAR LATIN

3. RELATIVE CLAUSES OF PURPOSE

A RELATIVE CLAUSE is very frequently used in Latin instead of an ut-clause to EXPRESS PURPOSE.

The rules for MOOD and TENSE are the same in relative clauses of purpose as in ut-clauses of purpose.

Equitēs mīsit quī cōnsilia cognōscerent.

He sent cavalry
$\left\{\begin{array}{l} \textit{who should learn the plans.} \\ \textit{in order that they might learn the plans.} \\ \textit{in order to learn the plans.} \\ \textit{that they might learn the plans.} \\ \textit{to learn the plans.} \end{array}\right.$

A relative clause of purpose should be used instead of an ut-clause whenever possible. It may be used whenever the relative pronoun can, WITHOUT CHANGING THE MEANING, be made to agree with a noun or pronoun in the main clause, thus:

1. *He sent envoys to seek peace.*

Before translating into English, change to:

2. *He sent envoys WHO should seek peace.*

Lēgātōs mīsit QUĪ pācem PETERENT.

Sentences 1 and 2 MEAN THE SAME THING, but Sentence 2 shows how the sentence should be translated into Latin.

EXCEPTION. A relative clause of purpose cannot be used when the relative pronoun would have to agree with the SUBJECT of an ACTIVE MAIN VERB.

He came to see Rome. **Vēnit ut Rōmam vidēret.**

This cannot be changed to: *He came who should see Rome.*

A relative clause may be used to express purpose.
Mood: SUBJUNCTIVE.
Tense: Same as in *ut*-clauses of purpose.

VOCABULARY

dēdūcō, dēdūcere, dēdūxī, dēductus, 3, tr.	*lead* / *lead away*
cognōscō, cognōscere, cognōvī, cognitus, 3, tr.	*learn* / *find out*
nuntius, ī	*messenger* / *message*
nātūra, ae	*nature*
-que, *conj.*	*and*
injūria, ae	*injustice* / *wrong*

NOTE

The conjunction **-que** is always added to the first word tha follows the *and*.

Marīa sānctīque Deī. *Mary and the Saints of God.*

Senātus Populusque Rōmānus. *The Roman Senate and People.*

If **et** were used these would be:

Marīa et sānctī Deī; Senātus et Populus Rōmānus.

You have now learned three words for *and:*

1. **et,** which is the ordinary conjunction in Latin;

2. **atque,** which is more emphatic and emphasizes the second part of the combination;

3. **-que,** which joins things that are more closely associated.

RELATED ENGLISH WORDS

The *injured* party brought suit. Sherlock Holmes solved crimes by *deduction*. A papal *nuncio*.

RELATED LATIN WORD

Dūcō

Injūria nōn excūsat[1] injūriam.

[1] **excūsō,** *1, tr.: excuse.*

EXERCISE 272
[Essential]
1. Translate;
2. Diagram Sentences 1 and 2:

1. Hostēs servum in castra Caesaris mīsērunt quī cōnsilia ējus cognōsceret. 2. Dux mīlitēs ad omnia parātōs in aciem dēdūxit quī hostium cōpiās sustinērent. 3. Nuntium ad tē mittam quī dē injūriīs tēcum agat. 4. Dux mīlitēs ad collem statim mīsit quī eum vallō fossāque mūnīrent. 5. Mīsitne rēx ad Caesarem nuntium quī auxilium peteret? 6. Equitēs ad flūmen mīsit quī locī nātūram cognōscerent. 7. Propter injūriās lēgātum mīsit quī obsidēs occīderet.

"Deō autem grātiās,[1] quī dedit nōbīs victōriam per Dominum nostrum Jēsūm Chrīstum."

—Vōx Sānctī Paulī

EXERCISE 273
[Essential]
Translate:

(Use a relative clause of purpose *whenever possible*.)

1. They immediately sent envoys into the camp of Caesar to seek peace. 2. A messenger was sent to Caesar to beg help. 3. In front of the gate he stationed soldiers who were prepared for everything. 4. Soldiers were stationed on the bridge to defend it. 5. The chief came to seek grain. 6. He fortified the camp with a rampart lest the enemy storm it. 7. He sent a lieutenant into Italy to lead away the new legions into Gaul.

EXERCISE 274
[Review]

1. What is the rule for the ablative of agency?
2. What is the rule for the ablative of means?

---
[1] **Agō** or **agimus** is understood in this sentence.

3. Name the secondary tenses of the indicative.

4. How are verbs used impersonally in Latin? Give an example.

READING NO. 16

HOW A HOSTILE KING HONORED THE HEROIC PATRIOTISM OF MUCIUS SCAEVOLA

Porsenna[1] rēgnum Etruscōrum[2] obtinēbat. Is erat vir fortis et imperiī atque glōriae cupidus. Itaque cum Rōmānīs dē imperiō Italiae contendit et Rōmam magnīs cōpiīs oppugnābat. Rōmānī autem cōpiam frūmentī nōn habēbant et vehementer terrēbantur. Erat autem in numerō Rōmānōrum vir fortis, Mūcius Scaevola.[3] Ab eō virtūs Rōmānōrum cōnfirmābātur. Eīs enim, "In castra Etruscōrum,"[2] inquit,[4] "contendam et Porsennam[1] rēgem occīdam. Ita Rōmam servābō."

Itaque in eōrum castra tūtus pervēnit. *(However, he had never seen the King, and so by mistake he killed one of the court officials instead of Porsenna.)* Itaque Etruscī eum ad rēgem dūxērunt. Porsenna[1] autem perīculō vehementer mōtus est. Itaque Mūciō,[3] "Ad mē vēnistī," inquit,[4] "ut mē occīderēs. Vītam meam petīvistī. Id nōn sine auxiliō neque sine cōnsiliō ēgistī. Sī[5] dē cōnsiliīs vestrīs mē monueris, vītam tuam servābō et tē dīmittam."

Mūcius autem rēgī, "Omnēs Rōmānī," inquit,[4] "ad mortem parātī sunt. Perīculō mortis nōn movēbuntur. Multī mittentur in castra ad tē quī tē occīdant. Nōn vītam sed cīvitātem nostram servābimus. Ego enim neque ā tē terreor neque metū mortis terrēbor."

Erat autem ibi ante[6] rēgem ignis.[7] Tum Mūcius, ut rēx vir-

---

[1] Porsenna, ae: *Porsenna* (a proper name).

[2] Etruscī, Etruscōrum: *the Etruscans* (a people who dwelt north of Rome).

[3] Mūcius (ī) Scaevola (ae): *Mucius Scaevola.*

[4] inquit: *he said.* Inquit, as here, is always put after the first words of a direct quotation.

[5] sī: *if.*

[6] ante, *prep. w. acc.: before.*

[7] ignis, is, *m.: fire.*

MUCIUS MANUM IN IGNE POSUIT.

tūtem Rōmānam cognōsceret, manum dexteram[1] in igne[2] statim posuit neque dolōre[3] superātus est. Porsenna autem virtūte Mūciī vehementer mōtus est. Itaque ējus et vītam cōnservāvit et virtūtem laudāvit. Eum etiam in castra Rōmānōrum dīmīsit. Post id rēx lēgātōs ad imperātōrem Rōmānum mīsit quī pācem peterent. Ita cīvitās Rōmāna virtūte Mūciī servāta est.

---

[1] manum dexteram: *right hand.*
[2] ignis, is, *m.: fire.*
[3] dolor, dolōris: *pain.*

4. PURPOSE CLAUSES INTRODUCED BY *QUŌ*

When a purpose clause contains a COMPARATIVE, **quō** is used instead of **ut** but not instead of **nē**. Quō in these clauses never changes its spelling. We shall study comparatives later. For the present remember only that the sign of a comparative is the adverb *more* or the ending *-er*. These are comparative adverbs:

> **diūtius,** *longer*
> **facilius,** *more easily*

He sent reinforcements that the legion might more easily conquer the enemy.

Auxilia mīsit quō facilius legiō hostēs vinceret.

But:

He sent reinforcements lest the enemy fight longer.

Auxilia mīsit nē diūtius hostēs pugnārent.

Note. The comparative stands regularly IMMEDIATELY AFTER the **quō** or **nē**.

MEMORIZE THE COMPLETE RULE FOR PURPOSE
CLAUSES, GRAMMAR, NO. 546.

VOCABULARY

diūtius, *comparative adv.*	*longer*
facilius, *comparative adv.*	*more easily*
appropinquō, *1, intr.; w.* ad *or dat.*	draw near to / approach
vastō, *1, tr.*	lay waste / ravage
custōs, custōdis	*guard*

NOTE

1. Guards are usually soldiers. Therefore what gender is **custōs**?

2. **Appropinquō** is intransitive. The English object of *approach* or *draw near to* is expressed in Latin by **AD** with the accusative or by the DATIVE. This is the meaning of the notation: "*intr.; w.* **ad** *or* **dat.**" in the vocabulary.

Hostēs ad hīberna (hībernīs) appropinquant.
The enemy draws near to the winter quarters.
(or) *The enemy approaches the winter quarters.*

RELATED ENGLISH WORDS

Modern war brings terrible *devastation*. The police took the criminal into *custody*. I am the *custodian* of this property.

RELATED LATIN WORDS

Facilis; facile.

EXERCISE 275
[Essential]

1. Translate;
2. Diagram Sentence 1:

1. Lēgātus custōdēs ad flūmen statim collocāvit quō facilius pontem dēfenderent. 2. Ducēs Rōmānī agrōs Gallōrum vastābant nē diūtius bellum gererent. 3. Caesar centuriōnēs et tribūnōs mīlitum saepe appellābat quō diūtius pugnārent. 4. Imperātor auxilium in prīmam aciem mīsit quō diūtius et facilius mīlitēs hostēs pellerent. 5. Equitēs ad mūrum appropinquāvērunt; mīlitēs autem portae appropinquāvērunt.

EXERCISE 276
[Essential]
Translate:

1. They killed the guards that they might more easily approach the camp. 2. They killed the hostages that the enemy might not fight longer. 3. They drove the enemy into the town that they might more easily lay waste the fields. 4. The lieutenant gave rewards to the soldiers that they might fight longer. 5. They stationed guards on the bridge to defend it more easily. 6. They

fortified the winter quarters with a rampart and a ditch that they might repulse the enemy more easily.

EXERCISE 277
[Review]

1. Parse the italicized words:

Rēgēs saepe sunt *glōriae cupidī.*

2. Give the rule for the ablative of means.

ARMĪS VĪCIT; VITIĪS[1] VICTUS EST.

—Seneca writing of Alexander the Great

READING NO. 17

REPORT FROM THE FRONT

The radio has brought the great events of the world into our own parlors. Ringside and battlefront broadcasts keep us up with the news as it happens. Let us imagine that we are ancient Romans, seated in our home at Rome and listening to a broadcast direct from a winter quarters of Caesar's army in Gaul.

"Your announcer is Quintus Titurius Mucius, with the Second Legion in their Belgian winter quarters. Your friends here have been enjoying a very quiet winter. The Belgians *(clāmōrēs subitō[2] per radiophōniam[3] ā nōbīs audiuntur)* . . . *(Excitedly)* Friends, this is it . . . Hostēs appropinquant. Hībernīs nostrīs appropinquant! . . . Usque ad portās celeriter appropinquant! Audītis clāmōrem et hostium et nostrōrum. Prīncipēs et ducēs, virī fortēs, etiam cum eīs appropinquant. Etiam Rēgem eōrum videō! Custōdēs nostrōs statim gladiīs occīdunt et eōs quī in mūrō sunt tēlīs occīdunt quō facilius hīberna oppugnent. Nostrī omnēs statim ad arma vocantur. *(Vōcēs centuriōnum per radiophōniam[3]*

---

[1] vitium, ī: *vice.*
[2] subitō, *adv.: suddenly.*
[3] radiophōnia, ae: *radio.*

audiuntur.) Tribūnī mīlitum mūrōs hominibus complent! Equitēs
per portās celeriter mittuntur. Ācriter cum Gallīs pugnant! . . .
(Magnus clāmor subitō[1] *audītur.)* Rēx . . . Rēx hostium tēlīs
occīsus est! Nunc hostēs pelluntur! Cēdunt! Silvās petunt!
Sed lēgātus noster, vir bonus et fortis, equitēs nunc mittit quī
eōs omnēs occīdant. Friends, it's all over and may that be a
lesson to them. Fortūna legiōnēs Rōmānās semper adjuvat."

NOTE ON TRANSLATION

The English meanings given in the vocabularies for Latin
words give only the basic or general meaning of the Latin. Frequently in translating from Latin into English you should use
some other English word, generally a synonym, which expresses
the same MEANING as the Latin word but which sounds better
in English. Remember your translations should always MAKE
SENSE and be GOOD ENGLISH.

For example, you have learned that **magnus, a, um** means
large or *great*. The Romans used **magnus** much more frequently
than we do *large* or *great*. We would often use different adjectives
in English to modify different nouns. Thus **magna spēs** would
be better translated by *high hope* than by *large hope* or *great
hope*.

EXERCISE 278

*See whether you can pick the best English adjectives from
this list to translate* **magnus** *in the following phrases.*

ENGLISH ADJECTIVES: *hard, bright, large, loud* (to be used
twice), *extreme, extensive, bloody.*

Example: **magna spēs**
Translation: *high hope*

1. magnus clāmor
2. magnus labor
3. magna vōx
4. magna caedēs
5. magna inopia
6. magnae silvae
7. magnus numerus
8. magna lūx

---

[1] **subitō,** *adv.: suddenly.*

UNIT SEVEN

LESSON 25: DIRECT QUESTIONS

INTRODUCTION

Ordinary-questions which are addressed directly to a person are called DIRECT QUESTIONS and are generally in the indicative mood.

Direct questions, as we have seen, may be introduced by:

1. Interrogative adverbs: **Cūr vēnistī?** *Why have you come?*
2. Interrogative particles: **Vidēsne?** *Do you see?*
3. Interrogative adjectives and pronouns: **Quid vīdistī?** *What did you see?*

1. INTERROGATIVE ADVERBS

Questions may be introduced by INTERROGATIVE ADVERBS.

Ubi fuistī? *Where were you?*

Cūr vēnit? *Why did he come?*

Since these words are adverbs, they are not declined and never change their spelling.

VOCABULARY

ubi	*where?*
cūr	*why?*
unde	*whence?* / *from what place?* / *where . . . from?*
quō	*whither?* / *where . . . (to)?* / *to what place?*

267

NOTE

Ubi and quō can translate the English *where.* Ubi can be used only when the *where* refers to place IN WHICH and implies REST; quō can be used only when *where* refers to place TO WHICH and implies MOTION or direction. Unde can be used only of place FROM WHICH and implies MOTION or direction.

Ubi es? *Where are you?*

Quō contendis? *Where are you hastening?*

Unde venīs? *Where do you come from?*

EXERCISE 279

Translate:

1. Ubi erās? 2. Quō contendis? 3. Unde vēnistī? 4. Cūr Caesar bellum cum Gallīs gessit? 5. Quō lēgātus ā senātū missus est? 6. Cūr sunt Chrīstiānī et ad labōrēs et ad mortem parātī? 7. Cūr Gallī saepe obsidēs inter sē dedērunt? 8. Cūr victōriās patrum nostrōrum semper memoriā tenēbimus? 9. Cūr nōs Americānī amīcitiam cum omnibus gentibus cōnfirmāmus? 10. Cūr grātiās Deō agimus? 11. Cūr Rōmānī hīberna vallō fossāque mūnīvērunt?

EXERCISE 280

Answer in complete Latin sentences as shown in Sentence 1:

(Consult map on page 166)

1. Ubi est urbs Rōma? (ANSWER. Urbs Rōma est in Italiā.) 2. Ubi est flūmen Tiberis? 3. Ubi sunt Alpēs? 4. Ubi erat prōvincia cūjus imperium Caesar obtinēbat? 5. Ubi erant Gallī? 6. Ubi Caesar, imperātor Rōmānus, cum Gallīs bellum gessit? 7. Quō Caesar ā senātū missus est?

Per magnōs labōrēs ad magna praemia perveniēmus.

—Adapted from the *Roman Breviary*

EXERCISE 281
[Essential]
Translate:

1. Where were the guards? 2. Whence have you led the new forces? 3. Where have you hastened from? 4. Where will the lieutenant lead the legions? 5. Whither will you hasten? 6. To what place are you sending the envoys? 7. Why did you yield to the enemy? 8. Why did the Romans fortify the camp with a ditch and a rampart?

EXERCISE 282
[Review]

1. Give the complete rule for purpose clauses.

2. INTERROGATIVE PARTICLES

ASSIGNMENT: Study GRAMMAR, Nos. 502-503.

VOCABULARY

certus, a, um	certain sure
barbarus, a, um	barbarian
apud, *prep. w. acc.*	among in the presence of
plūrimum, *adv.*	very much very
valeō, valēre, valuī, valitūrus, 2, *intr.*	am strong am well am influential
cernō, cernere, 3, tr.	distinguish see

NOTE

Barbarus can, of course, be used as a noun to mean *barbarian:*

Barbarī pulsī sunt. *The barbarians were routed.*

RELATED ENGLISH WORDS

A *valid* argument; a *valiant* warrior.

EXERCISE 283

[Essential]

Translate, and give the "expected" answer in complete Latin sentences:

1. Valēsne? 2. Num mīlitēs sine certā spē fortiter pugnant? 3. Nōnne legiōnēs Rōmānae barbarōs facile superāvērunt? 4. Nōnne virī quī fortēs sunt apud barbarōs plūrimum valent? 5. Num amīcus certus et fortis facile cernitur? 6. Nōnne vir fortis in mortis perīculō facile cernitur? 7. Nōnne victōriās legiōnum Rōmānārum laudābis? 8. Num Columbus sine magnō labōre ad terrās novās pervēnit? 9. Vīdistīne Rōmam? Veniēsne in Italiam ut eam videās? 10. Nōnne ācriter pugnābimus ut cīvitātem nostram dēfendāmus? 11. Nōnne Caesar plūrimum apud Rōmānōs valēbit? 12. Num imperātōrēs apud Americānōs plūrimum valent? 13. Nōnne amīcī apud amīcōs plūrimum valent?

EXERCISE 284

Translate:

1. Was the chief influential among the Romans on account of his faithfulness?

2. You won't hand over the arms to the Romans, will you?

3. You will defend our free nation, won't you?

4. The lieutenant said:[1] "You see the battle line of the barbarians. They are prepared both for death and for victory. Surely you don't fear them, soldiers! You are brave, are you not? You are Romans, are you not? Will you fight bravely for the Roman name? Are you not fighting with a sure hope of victory? Is not the cavalry prepared for battle? Haven't we a large supply of arms and darts? What do you fear? Do you fear death? But men who are eager for glory are always prepared for either death

---

[1] *said:* inquit (after first words of quotation).

or victory. We are Romans; they are barbarians and Gauls. Barbarians will not conquer a Roman legion, will they? Is not Caesar our leader? Do not the barbarians also praise Caesar, do they not fear him? They will fight without a sure hope of victory. They will not withstand your attack. They will yield. They will be routed. Your victory will be the glory of the Roman Senate and People."

EXERCISE 285

[Review]

1. Give the complete rule for purpose clauses.
2. Give the rule of agreement for relative pronouns.

3. THE INTERROGATIVE PRONOUN

> *Who are you?*
>
> *To whom did you give the sword?*
>
> *What did you see?*
>
> *Whose towns did he burn?*

In these sentences *who, whom, what, whose* are INTERROGATIVES because they introduce a question. (**Interrogō** in Latin means *I ask, I question.*)

Who, whom, what, whose are PRONOUNS because they take the place of the person or thing to which they refer. They do not DIRECTLY modify a noun.

The Latin interrogative pronoun is **QUIS, QUID,** *who, what.*

ASSIGNMENT: Learn the declension of **quis, quid** in GRAMMAR, No. 140.

Study the translations of the examples given above:

Quis es?

Cui gladium dedistī?

Quid vīdistī?

Quōrum oppida incendit?

VOCABULARY

quis, quid	*who?* *what?*
ostendō, ostendere, ostendī, ostentus, *3, tr.*	*show*
trādūcō, trādūcere, trādūxī, trāductus, *3, tr.; two* accs. or acc. and trāns w. acc.	*lead across*
clam, *adv.*	*secretly*
socius, ī	*ally*

NOTE

With trādūcō the thing OVER WHICH the direct object is led, is put either (1) in the accusative, or (2) with trāns in the accusative.

> Exercitum flūmen trādūxit.
> Exercitum trāns flūmen trādūxit.
> *He led the army across the river.*

RELATED ENGLISH WORD

A *society* of nations.

AMĪCUS CERTUS IN RĒ INCERTĀ[1] CERNITUR.

—Ennius

EXERCISE 286
[Essential]
Translate:

1. Quibuscum pugnāvit Caesar? 2. Cui Gallī obsidēs dedērunt? 3. Quī erant Caesaris sociī? 4. Legiō sē barbarīs nōn ostendit ut clam in castra pervenīret. 5. Quis plūrimum apud Americānōs nunc valet? 6. Quis exercitum flūmen trādūxit? 7. Quis exercitum trāns montēs altōs et flūmina lāta trādūxit ut in Italiā cum Rōmānīs bellum gereret? 8. Quis lēgem sānctam et lūcem vēritātis nōbīs dedit? 9. Cui castra nostra ostendistī?

---

[1] incertus, a, um: *uncertain, dubious.*

WASHINGTONIUS EXERCITUM TRANS FLUMEN TRADUCIT.

EXERCISE 287
Translate:

(When the English may be either singular or plural
translate both ways in Latin.)

1. To whom did you give the reward?   2. With whom were
you?   3. Whom did you see?   4. Whose courage do you praise?
5. What do you seek?   6. What (things) did you hear?   7. What
did he show you?   8. Who came secretly into the camp?   9. Who
are your allies?   10. For what are you prepared?   11. To whom
did you send help?

EXERCISE 288
[Honor Work]
Translate:

Washington,[1] a brave and noble man whose courage **we all**
keep in memory, was the American general in our first war. He

---

[1] *Washington:* Washingtonius, ī.

led the troops across the river Delaware[1] to conquer the Germans[2] who were in the British[3] army. It was night. The soldiers were neither seen nor heard by the enemy. Thus he swiftly and easily conquered the enemy. We shall all praise Washington's[4] plan and courage, shall we not?

Answer in Latin:

1. Quis fuit Washingtonius?
2. Quī eum laudant?
3. Quibuscum bellum gessit?
4. Cernēbanturne ējus mīlitēs ab hostibus?
5. Quōs vīcit Washingtonius?

EXERCISE 289
[Review]

1. Give the rule for agreement of relative pronouns.
2. When is quō used to introduce a purpose clause?
3. Give the rule for the ablative of means.

4. THE INTERROGATIVE ADJECTIVE

Which men did you see?

Quōs virōs vīdistī?

Quōs here modifies and agrees with virōs. It is used, therefore, as an ADJECTIVE and not as a pronoun. It is an INTERROGATIVE because it introduces a question.

The INTERROGATIVE ADJECTIVE in Latin is declined exactly like the relative pronoun.

But in the NOMINATIVE MASCULINE SINGULAR quis is generally used as an adjective for *which* or *what,* quī for *what sort of, what kind of.*

---

[1] *Delaware:* Delawarēnse, Delawarēnsis.
[2] *Germans:* Germānī, Germānōrum.
[3] *British:* Britannicus, a, um.
[4] *Washington:* Washingtonius, ī.

VOCABULARY

quī, quae, quod {which? / what?}

REVIEW VOCABULARY

vocō, 1, tr.; two accs.   call

appellō, 1, tr.; two accs. {call / call upon / address}

ostendō, ostendere, ostendī, ostentus, 3, tr.   show

nōmen, nōminis   name

IDIOM STUDY

Verbs of calling, naming, making, showing, *etc.*, may take two accusatives, one of the direct object, the other a predicate accusative.

Tē amīcum vocō.
I call you friend.

(Ego)	vocō	tē / amīcum

Caesarem imperātōrem appellāvērunt.
They called Caesar general.

But when **nōmen** is used, **nōmen** is in the ablative.

Caesarem nōmine imperātōris appellāvērunt.
They called Caesar by the name of general.

Caesar centuriōnēs nōmine appellāvit.
Caesar called upon the centurions by name.

EXERCISE 290

Translate:

1. With which allies? 2. With the army of which king? 3. On account of what wrongs? 4. In which towns? 5. In what camp? 6. Among which tribes? 7. Up to what river? 8. By what name did they call you? 9. What guards did he station? 10. What

man called Caesar king? 11. In what place did he pitch camp?
12. To what messenger did he give the letters? 13. To which
envoys did he send the letters? 14. Christ called us brothers.
15. For what are arms useful? 16. Which town are we approaching? 17. What rivers are wide and deep? 18. What tribes are
exchanging hostages? 19. To what town does the bridge stretch?
20. To what guard did he show himself? 21. To what king do
they give thanks? 22. In what thing do they put hope?

EXERCISE 291
[Essential]
QUIZ ON AMERICAN HISTORY
Can you score 100%?

1. Propter quās injūriās nōs bellum cum Japōnibus gessimus?
2. Quis nuntius quem omnēs memoriā tenēmus per oppida contendit ut omnēs adventum Britannōrum exspectārent?
3. Quis imperātor Americānus trāns flūmen quod Delaware vocāmus exercitum trādūxit ut ad castra hostium clam pervenīret?
4. Cui gentī[1] grātiās Americānī ēgimus propter auxilium quod
in prīmō nostrō bellō ad nōs mīsit?
5. Quis dux cōpiās nostrās in Bataan dēdūxit quō diūtius cum
Japōnibus pugnāret?
6. In quō bellō hostēs urbem Washington incendērunt?
7. Quem ducem mīlitēs "Stonewall" appellāvērunt?
8. Quī Gallī prīmī vīdērunt flūmen quod Mississippi vocāmus?

EXERCISE 292
[Essential]
Translate:

1. Augustus prīmus imperātor[2] Rōmānus fuit. Augustus autem
nōn rēgem sed prīncipem sē vocāvit, nam Rōmānī nōmen rēgis
timuērunt.

---

[1] **gēns** here means *nation*.
[2] **imperātor** here means *emperor*.

2. Omnēs Americānī Washingtonium "Patrem Patriae"[1] appellāvērunt. Washingtonius enim cīvitātem nostram dēfendit atque cōnservāvit sīcut patrēs fīliōs dēfendunt atque cōnservant.

3. Rēx et imperātor Germānōrum sē "Caesarem"[2] appellāvit.

Answer in complete Latin sentences:

1. Quō nōmine Augustus sē vocāvit?
2. Quō nōmine Americānī Washingtonium appellāvērunt?
3. Quis rēx "Caesarem" sē appellāvit?

READING NO. 18

A GALLIC CAPTIVE

A Gallic captive is brought before the *lēgātus* for questioning. The Roman camp is in the wilds of Belgium, a land of thick forests and fierce tribes. There have been rumors of rebellion against the Roman army of occupation. The *lēgātus* is leading a relief expedition and it is important for him to get full information concerning the enemy.

LEGATUS. Quis es? Unde vēnistī?
GALLUS *(with grim laugh).* Nōn cognōvī.
LEGATUS. Ha! Nōn cognōvistī! Nōnne tū Gallus es?
GALLUS. Nōn cognōvī.
LEGATUS. Ubi sunt cōpiae vestrae? Quī sunt sociī vestrī?
GALLUS. Nōn cognōvī.
LEGATUS. Tū ad mortem dūcēris! Num ad mortem parātus es?
GALLUS. Ita. Ad mortem parātus sum. Ea quae petis nōn tibi ostendam. *(The legate summons the torturers. They torture the Gaul.)*
LEGATUS *(sarcastically).* Id diū sustinēbis, nam ad mortem parātus es.
GALLUS. Ēheu! Ēheu! Ēheu![3]
LEGATUS. Quid? Num timēs? Nōnne fortis es? Nōnne ad

---

[1] patria, ae: *country, fatherland.*
[2] The word *Kaiser* is a German form for Caesar.
[3] ēheu, ēheu: an interjection expressing grief or pain.

mortem parātus? *(The torturing stops; the Gaul lies exhausted on the ground.)*

LEGATUS. Itaque nunc ad mortem dūcēris.

GALLUS. Ēheu! Ēheu! Nōn! Nōn!

LEGATUS *(smiling).* Quid est? Num cognōvistī?

GALLUS. Cognōvī.

LEGATUS. Quis plūrimum apud gentēs vestrās valet? Quem prīncipem et ducem vocātis?

GALLUS. Ambiorīgem[1] et Catuvulcum.[2]

LEGATUS. Quī sunt sociī gentis tuae?

GALLUS. Omnēs Galliae gentēs atque Germānī.

LEGATUS. Germānī!

GALLUS. Ita est! Cōpiās trāns flūmen Rhēnum trādūcunt et celeriter in fīnēs nostrōs pervenient.

LEGATUS. Ubi nunc sunt cōpiae vestrae?

GALLUS. In silvīs ad flūmen castra posuērunt.

LEGATUS. Num cōpiam frūmentī habent? Omnia frūmenta quae in agrīs erant incendimus atque magna cōpia in hīberna portāta est.

GALLUS. Ita. Magnam cōpiam habent. Sociī inter sē obsidēs dedērunt et ad nōs frūmentum mīsērunt. Habent etiam cōpiam armōrum et tēlōrum. Nam expugnāvimus hīberna Rōmāna quae in fīnibus nostrīs posita erant.

LEGATUS. Quid? Num hīberna Rōmāna expugnāvistis? Quae castra? Num castra Rōmāna expugnāvistis?

GALLUS. Expugnāvimus. Magna fuit caedēs.

LEGATUS. Per deōs immortālēs![3] Propter injūriās agrōs vestrōs vastābimus; oppida incendēmus; mātrēs et patrēs et puerōs occīdēmus!

GALLUS. Mīlitēs nostrī etiam ad bellum parātī sunt. Eōs nōn vincētis.

---

[1] Ambiorīx, Ambiorīgis: *Ambiorix.*

[2] Catuvulcus, ī: *Catuvulcus.*

[3] **per deōs immortālēs:** *by the immortal gods.*

LEGATUS. Cūr hīberna expugnāvistis? Nōnne pāx et amīcitia fuit inter gentēs vestrās et Populum Rōmānum?

GALLUS. Ita, sed Rōmānōs timēmus. Semper frūmentum petunt; arma petunt; servōs petunt; obsidēs petunt. Imperiī et bellī semper sunt cupidī. Vītās nostrās et cīvitātēs nostrās līberās dēfendimus.

LEGATUS *(angrily)*. Quod in fidē cum Populō Rōmānō nōn mānsistis, vōs omnēs occīdēminī! Et tū *(he shakes his finger at the prostrate Gaul)* prīmus ad mortem dūcēris. *(He addresses the guards.)* Statim ad mortem!

EXERCISE 293
[Review]

1. Give the complete rule for purpose clauses.
2. Give the rule for the ablative of means.
3. Translate, and explain the translation of the italicized phrases:
   a. He sent help *to the first battle line*.
   b. They handed over their arms *to the enemy*.

LESSON 26: THE PERFECT SYSTEM ACTIVE OF THE SUBJUNCTIVE

1. PERFECT AND PLUPERFECT SUBJUNCTIVE ACTIVE

The perfect and pluperfect subjunctive of all LATIN VERBS. regular and irregular, are formed in the same way.

1. Find the perfect stem

$$\left\{\begin{array}{l}\text{laudāv-} \\ \text{monu-} \\ \text{mīs-} \\ \text{audīv-} \\ \text{fu-}\end{array}\right.$$

2. Add the endings shown in GRAMMAR, Nos. 200-207.

VOCABULARY

incolō, incolere, incoluī, *3, tr.*	$\left\{\begin{array}{l}\textit{inhabit} \\ \textit{dwell in}\end{array}\right.$
cōnsistō, cōnsistere, cōnstitī, *3, intr.*	$\left\{\begin{array}{l}\textit{halt} \\ \textit{take a position}\end{array}\right.$

EXERCISE 294

1. Give the perfect stem;
2. Give the third person, singular and plural, of the perfect and pluperfect subjunctive:

1. perveniō	7. pertineō	13. incolō
2. retineō	8. agō	14. compleō
3. administrō	9. cēdō	15. contineō
4. veniō	10. cōnfirmō	16. contendō
5. moneō	11. cōnsistō	17. īnstruō
6. pellō	12. appropinquō	18. comparō

EXERCISE 295

What forms are these?

1. fuisset	9. cognōvissent	17. constitissēs
2. cognōverit	10. exspectāverit	18. cesserīs
3. incoluisset	11. pervēnisset	19. audiverītis
4. mīserim	12. dēdūxisset	20. monuissent
5. expugnāvisset	13. cōnstitisset	21. pervēnerit
6. laudāverit	14. vastāvissent	22. ēgissent
7. cōnstiterint	15. appropinquāvisset	23. īnstrūxissem
8. vīcerint	16. incoluerint	24. mīsissēmus

2. INDIRECT QUESTIONS; PRIMARY SEQUENCE

As we have seen, a question asked directly is called a DIRECT QUESTION.

Estne Deus bonus? *Is God good?*

Valēsne? *Are you well?*

When a question, however, DEPENDS on a verb of ASKING, SAYING, THINKING, and the like, it is called an INDIRECT QUESTION.

Rogō sitne Deus bonus. *I ask whether God is good.*

Rogō valeāsne. *I ask whether you are well.*

Sitne Deus bonus and **valeāsne** are INDIRECT QUESTIONS because they depend on the verb **rogō**.

Indirect questions are NOUN CLAUSES because they are used as the OBJECT of a verb (**rogō**).

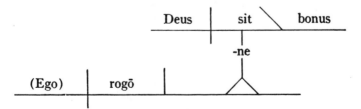

Indirect questions may be introduced by the same adverbs, adjectives, pronouns, and particles as direct questions, but:

-Ne and **num** in indirect questions mean *whether (if)*.

Nōnne is seldom used.

Quī is sometimes used for **quis**.

> *He asks whether Caesar conquered the Gauls.*
> **Rogat num Caesar Gallōs vīcerit.**
>
> *He asks who Caesar was.*
> **Rogat quis Caesar fuerit.**
>
> *He asks where we are.*
> **Rogat ubi sīmus.**

The TENSE in indirect questions is determined by the rule: TENSE BY SEQUENCE.

**THE MOOD IN INDIRECT QUESTIONS IS ALWAYS
SUBJUNCTIVE.**

ASSIGNMENT: Learn the general rule, GRAMMAR, Nos. 524-526.

IN PRIMARY SEQUENCE:

1. Use the PRESENT subjunctive when the action of the verb in the indirect question happens AT THE SAME TIME as the action of the main verb.

> *Caesar asks whether the soldiers are fighting.*
> **Caesar rogat num mīlitēs pugnent.**

2. Use the PERFECT subjunctive when the action of the verb in the indirect question happens BEFORE the action of the main verb.

> *Caesar asks whether the soldiers were fighting (fought).*
> **Caesar rogat num mīlitēs pugnāverint.**

VOCABULARY

rogō, 1, tr.	*ask*
quaerō, quaerere, quaesīvī, quaesītus, 3, tr.	$\begin{cases} seek \\ ask \end{cases}$
quantus, a, um, *interrogative adj.*	$\begin{cases} how\ large? \\ how\ great? \end{cases}$
mūnītiō, mūnītiōnis	*fortification*
genus, generis, n.	$\begin{cases} kind \\ race \end{cases}$
aqua, ae	*water*

RELATED ENGLISH WORDS

The prisoner of war was *interrogated*. He was asked many *questions*. Modern wars require a great *quantity* of *munitions*. What is the *genus* of this tree? The Romans built many long *aqueducts*. *Aquatic* sports are much in favor at the Florida beaches. *Rogation* days.

RELATED LATIN WORD

Mūniō

Alcohol is called

AQUA VĪTAE.

EXERCISE 296

1. Point out the indirect question;
2. Point out the introductory word;
3. Explain the mood and tense in the indirect question;
4. Diagram Sentences 1 and 5;
5. Translate:

1. Rogat num cōpiam aquae habeāmus. 2. Rogat num Caesar Gallōs vīcerit. 3. Quaeret ubi hostēs cōnstiterint. 4. Quaeret ubi cōpia aquae sit. 5. Rogat quis imperātor sit. 6. Quaerit quōs

Caesar vīcerit. 7. Rogābit valeantne mīlitēs. 8. Quaeret vīceritne Caesar barbarōs. 9. Rogat quae genera hominum Americam incolant. 10. Quaerit quae genera hominum Galliam tum incoluerint. 11. Quaeret quantās mūnītiōnēs hostēs parāverint. 12. Rogābit quae mūnītiōnum genera nōs parēmus. 13. Rogat quae gentēs Galliam incolant. 14. Quaerit quae gentēs prōvinciam incoluerint.

EXERCISE 297
[Imitation]

Imitate the word order and structure of the model in translating:

MODEL: **Rogō quōs mīlitēs vīderit.**
I ask what soldiers he saw.

1. I ask what hostages he killed. 2. I ask what general he praised. 3. I ask what plans he has learned. 4. I ask what hills he has occupied.

MODEL: **Rogat ubi mīlitēs sint.**
He asks where the soldiers are.

1. I ask where the general is. 2. I ask where the enemy is. 3. I ask where the fortifications are. 4. I ask where the winter quarters are.

EXERCISE 298
[Review]

1. Translate, and explain the translation of the italicized phrases:

    a. They sent letters *to the Senate.*

    b. They gave rewards *to the slave.*

2. Give the rule for the agreement of relative pronouns.

3. Translate; parse **ad** and **pugnātum est:** Ad flūmen diū pugnātum est.

4. Give the complete rule for purpose clauses.

READING NO. 19

[Essential]

WAR INFORMATION

It is of vital importance for a general to have the fullest possible information about the enemy before committing his troops to battle. Many military disasters have been due to ignorance either of the enemy's force and disposition or of the detail of the battleground. When the Battle of Gettysburg opened, Lee's scouts were away on a foraging expedition. The Union army was therefore able to reconnoiter and seize the most strategic points on the field and fight the action from chosen positions. Lee's army was terribly defeated.

Today every resource is used to discover vital war information. Hitler's invasion of Poland was backed by scientific study of every pertinent detail. Even the weather conditions had been calculated. During the years preceding the invasion of Europe in World War II, Allied experts studied the minutest detail of the invasion coast of Fortress Europe. Planes, spies, maps, scientists, travelers, refugees—all were used to place before the general staff the fullest possible information.

Military experts have always recognized the importance of such information. Caesar, too, though he lacked maps of modern technical excellence, as well as planes and swift-moving scouting cars, made extensive inquiries before launching a campaign. There were Roman spies, Gallic refugees, merchants—all of whom he consulted. The Roman army sent out cavalry and special scouts *(explōrātōrēs)* to study the terrain *(nātūra locī)* and the disposition of the opposing forces.

What then would a general wish to know?

Ante[1] proelium imperātor lēgātōs et tribūnōs mīlitum in concilium vocat. In conciliō quaerit quantum numerum et equitum et mīlitum hostēs habeant, ubi castra hostium sint, quantās parāverint mūnītiōnēs; num cōpiam aquae et frūmentī habeant; quantam armōrum cōpiam habeant. Quaerit etiam quae sint por-

---

[1] **ante,** *prep. w. acc.: before.*

CONCILIUM

tūs et flūmina et montēs in hostium fīnibus; quae genera hominum eās partēs incolant; num omnia quae ad bellum pertinent parāverint; num fortēs sint et cupidī bellī glōriae; num ācriter pugnent; quōs ducēs habeant, num bonī sint. Ante[1] proelia imperātor equitēs mittit quī nātūram locī explōrent et cognōscant ubi hostēs cōnstiterint. Cognōscit num aciem īnstrūxerint; num ad proelium sint parātī.

Ita Caesar et omnēs magnī ducēs saepe hostēs superāvērunt quod omnia quae ad proelium pertinent cognōverant.

3. SECONDARY SEQUENCE

We have seen that the MOOD in indirect questions is always subjunctive and that the TENSE is determined by the rule: TENSE BY SEQUENCE. Review the general rule, GRAMMAR, Nos. 524-526.

IN SECONDARY SEQUENCE:

1. Use the IMPERFECT subjunctive when the action of the verb in the indirect question happens AT THE SAME TIME as the action of the main verb.

Caesar rogāvit num mīlitēs pugnārent.

Caesar asked whether the soldiers were fighting.

2. Use the PLUPERFECT subjunctive when the action of

---

[1] ante, *prep. w. acc.: before.*

the verb in the indirect question happens BEFORE the action of the main verb.

Caesar rogāvit num mīlitēs pugnāvissent.
Caesar asked whether the soldiers had fought.

VOCABULARY

cōgō, cōgere, coēgī, coāctus, *3, tr.*	*collect* *force*
vērus, a, um	*true*
inquit	*he says* *he said*

NOTE

Inquit is always used with DIRECT quotations; that is, with quotations enclosed in QUOTATION MARKS:

Chrīstus, "Vōs," inquit, "frātrēs estis."
Christ said, "You are brothers."

This is a *direct* quotation because it contains the EXACT words used by Christ and is therefore enclosed in quotation marks. Notice that **inquit** does NOT stand before the quotation but is ALWAYS put after one or several words of the quotation.

RELATED ENGLISH WORDS

A *cogent* argument. The eternal *verities*. A *veracious* witness. We cannot question the *veracity* of St. John.

RELATED LATIN WORDS

Vēritās; agō.

EXERCISE 299
[Secondary Sequence]

1. Translate;
2. Explain the tense of the italicized words:

1. Lēgātus quaesīvit quantam aquae cōpiam mīlitēs *habērent.*
2. Lēgātus quaesīvit ubi hostēs *cōnstitissent.* 3. Barbarī quaesī-

vērunt quantam mīlitum cōpiam Rōmānī *coēgissent.* 4. Barbarī quaesīvērunt ubi Rōmānī castra *posuissent.* 5. Quaesīverat quae *esset* nātūra montis. 6. Quaesīverat quantum obsidum numerum lēgātus *coēgisset.* 7. Quaerēbat quī portūs *essent* in eīs locīs. 8. Quaerēbant num hostēs collēs *occupāvissent.* 9. Rōmānus, "Quaerō," inquit, "num Deus vester *sit* Deus vērus."

EXERCISE 300

Imitate the word order and structure of the model in translating:

MODEL: **Centuriō quaerēbat num cōpia frūmentī in castrīs esset.**

The centurion was asking whether there was a supply of grain in the camp.

1. The military tribune was asking whether there was an abundance of water in the winter quarters. 2. The lieutenant was asking whether there was a bridge on the river. 3. The barbarians were asking whether there were soldiers in the forest.

MODEL: **Lēgātus quaesīvit ubi Gallī cōnstitissent.**

The lieutenant asked where the Gauls had taken up a position.

1. The leader asked where the enemy had stationed the guards. 2. Caesar asked where the Gauls had prepared fortifications. 3. The barbarians asked where Caesar had drawn up the troops.

EXERCISE 301
[Essential]

1. Translate;
2. Parse the italicized words:

1. Lēgātus, "Quaerō," *inquit,* "*quī sint* sociī vestrī." 2. Tribūnus mīlitum quaesīvit quae hominum genera loca *incolerent.* 3. Rōmānī magnās mūnītiōnēs parāvērunt *quō* facilius hostēs

pellerent. 4. Barbarī impetum in agmen fēcērunt nē mīlitēs certum ōrdinem servārent. 5. Quaerō num Caesar *plūrimum* apud Rōmānōs valuerit. 6. Quaerit num amīcus vērus atque certus facile *cernātur*. 7. Nōnne Chrīstiānī Chrīstum *nōmine* rēgis appellant? 8. Quaerō num Chrīstum rēgem atque *Dominum* vocētis. 9. Rogāvit quō prīncipēs *convēnissent.* 10. Diū atque ācriter *pugnātum est* in locō angustō et difficilī nē hostēs agmen *flūmen* trādūcerent. 11. Lēgātum mīsit quī obsidēs clam ad castra *dēdūceret.* 12. Dux rogāvit quantam cōpiam aquae frūmentīque servī in hīberna *portāvissent.* 13. Eques *ducī* ostendit ubi cōpiae hostium cōnstitissent. 14. *Quō* prīncipēs cōpiās coēgērunt? 15. Eī custōdēs occīdērunt et usque *ad* castra nostra appropinquāvērunt. 16. Rōmānī collem *vallō* fossāque mūnīvērunt quō diūtius cōpiās hostium *sustinērent.* 17. Quaerit cūr gentēs barbarae obsidēs inter sē *dederint.* 18. Dux equitem celeriter mīsit quī auxilium *peteret.* 19. Imperātor quaesīvit num tribūnī mīlitum omnia comparāvissent. 20. Rogat unde equitātus *contenderit.*

EXERCISE 302
[Essential]
Translate:

1. I asked where the enemy was. 2. They asked whether the chief led the barbarians across the river. 3. They asked whom we called king and emperor. 4. We asked what chief was influential among them. 5. We asked where the barbarians had taken up a stand.[1] 6. They ask what races of men inhabit Gaul now. 7. We ask what kinds of arms they have. 8. The lieutenant asked how great fortifications they had prepared. 9. We asked why they were fighting without a sure hope. 10. We asked where they had led the allies. 11. He asked whence they had come. 12. They had secretly collected the hostages into a safe place. 13. He asked whether they had seen the column of the enemy. 14. He said, "Aren't you a brave and sure friend?" 15. He ad-

---

[1] *take up a stand = take a position.*

dressed the centurions by name, that they might fight longer.
16. He asked where there was an abundance of water.

EXERCISE 303
[Formal Review of Unit Seven]

1. How may direct questions be introduced in Latin? What mood is used?
2. What is the difference between **ubi** and **quō**?
3. What is the difference between **-ne, num,** and **nōnne**? Give Latin examples of each, and translate the examples of **num** and **nōnne** several ways into English.
4. Decline the interrogative pronoun. Why is it a pronoun?
5. Decline the interrogative adjective **quī**.
6. When is **quis** used as an adjective?
7. Is **quī** ever used for **quis**?
8. What construction do verbs of TRANSPORTING take?
9. What construction do verbs of CALLING, *etc.*, take?
10. What are the endings of the perfect and pluperfect subjunctive active? What stem is used?
11. What are indirect questions?
12. What mood is used in indirect questions? How are they introduced?
13. Can **-ne, nōnne,** and **num** be used in indirect questions?
14. Is **quī** ever used for **quis** in indirect questions?
15. Give the rules for sequence.
16. What does **inquit** mean and how is it used?
17. Give Latin examples illustrating the use of each subjunctive tense in an indirect question.

READING NO. 20

BATAAN!

Vōs omnēs cognōvistis quantās cōpiās nostrī mīlitēs in Bataan[1] diū sustinuissent. Japōnēs enim magnum et fortem impetum in

---

[1] Bataan, *indecl. noun: Bataan.*

MILITES AMERICANI FORTITER PUGNANT.

īnsulās[1] Philippīnās[2] fēcērunt. Omnia armōrum et tēlōrum genera quae nunc ad bellum ūtilia sunt habēbant. Etiam magnum numerum omnium generum mīlitum in īnsulās[1] trādūxerant. Quaesīverant quī portūs, quae locī nātūra, quae flūmina essent. Omnia quae ad bellum pertinēbant cognōverant. Itaque dux noster, vir magnus et fortis, omnēs cōpiās nostrās in loca difficilia et angusta quae Bataan vocant dēdūxit quō diūtius impetum hostium sustinēret. Mūnītiōnēs celeriter parāvit; custōdēs collocāvit; mīlitēs īnstrūxit; impetūs hostium exspectāvit. Undique nostrī ab hostibus et locī nātūrā continēbantur neque erant multī mīlitēs Americānī in Bataan; tamen diū et ācriter ibi pugnātum est. Nam nostrī fortēs erant et glōriae nōminis Americānī cupidī erant. Multōs impetūs fortiter sustinuērunt; saepe hostēs post magnam caedem pepulērunt.

Interim cognōvimus quantō in perīculō nostrae legiōnēs essent et quaerēbāmus cūr ducēs nostrī magnam armōrum et mīlitum cōpiam nōn mitterent. Eī tamen omnia perīcula cognōverant. Itaque auxilia nōn mīsērunt nē hostēs ea occīderent.

---

[1] īnsula, ae: *island.*
[2] Philippīnus, a, um: *Philippine.*

Tandem[1] nostrī, propter magnum hostium numerum, nōn diūtius sustinuērunt. Itaque hostibus sē dedērunt atque arma trādidērunt. Dux autem noster, "The President," inquit, "of the United
States ordered me to break through the Japanese lines and pro-
ceed from Corregidor to Australia for the purpose, as I understand
it, of organizing the American offensive against Japan. A primary
purpose of this is the relief of the Philippines. I came through
and I shall return."

Nōnne virtūtem mīlitum fortium semper laudābimus atque memoriā tenēbimus? Glōria enim eōrum glōria nostra est.

---

[1] tandem, *adv.: finally.*

UNIT EIGHT

LESSON 27: THE VOCATIVE;
IMPERATIVE MOOD

1. THE VOCATIVE

You, O Lord, I praise.
We shall not help you, Caesar!

In these sentences *O Lord* and *Caesar:*
1. Show the PERSON ADDRESSED OR SPOKEN TO.
2. Are therefore in the VOCATIVE case—the case of the PERSON ADDRESSED.
3. Are set off by commas because they are independent of the grammar of the rest of the sentence.

> Tē, Ō Domine, laudō.
> Tē, Caesar, nōn adjuvābimus.

ASSIGNMENT: Learn the rule for the formation of the vocative, GRAMMAR, No. 28.

VOCABULARY

avē! *interjection*	*hail!*
mora, ae	*delay*
doceō, docēre, docuī, doctus, *2, tr.*	*teach* *inform*
tollō, tollere, sustulī, sublātus, *3, tr.*	*raise (up)* *take away*
peccātum, ī	*mistake* *sin* (in Christian Latin)

NOTE

Doceō takes two accusatives when it means *teach someone something.*

Chrīstus nōs viam salūtis docet.
Christ teaches us the way of salvation.

However, doceō can also be used with other constructions:

Custōs Caesarem docuit ubi hostēs essent. *(Indirect question.)*
The guard informed Caesar where the enemy was.

Lēgātus eum dē omnibus rēbus docuit. (Dē *w. abl.*)
The lieutenant informed him about all the things (the whole matter).

RULE OF POSITION: THE VOCATIVE IN LATIN
GENERALLY DOES NOT STAND FIRST
IN THE SENTENCE.

EXERCISE 304

Give the vocative, singular and plural, for the following:

1. dux	12. eques	23. māter
2. lēgātus	13. Chrīstus[1]	24. puer
3. nuntius	14. frāter	25. Gallus
4. custōs	15. Chrīstiānus	26. senātus
5. Spīritus[1]	16. mīles	27. rēx magnus
6. barbarus	17. Rōmānus	28. amīcus bonus
7. socius	18. tribūnus mīlitum	29. frāter meus
8. Marīa[1]	19. vir	30. dominus nōbilis
9. Jēsūs[1]	20. homō	31. vir līber
10. centuriō	21. dominus	32. mīles fortis
11. amīcus	22. fīlius	33. fīlius meus

---

[1] Give the singular only.

EXERCISE 305
Translate:

1. Nōnne grātiās agēmus, frātrēs meī, Dominō nostrō Jēsū
Chrīstō, quī peccāta mundī sustulit et nōs vēritātem docuit?
2. Avē, Caesar! Docēbō tē ubi hostēs castra posuerint.
3. Vōs, mīlitēs, sine morā pontem occupābitis nē barbarī eum
occupent. 4. Tē, Fīlī Deī, laudāmus. 5. Centuriō, "Hostēs, lēgāte," inquit, "magnum clāmōrem sustulērunt et sē nōbīs sine
morā dedērunt." 6. In tē, Ō bone Jēsū, est spēs omnium. 7. Hostēs, rēx magne, virtūte et armīs vīcimus. 8. Tibi, Deus, grātiās
agō; tē, Deus, laudō; in tē, Ō Deus, est omnis spēs mea. 9. Tū,
Domine, servābis nōs. *(From the Roman Breviary.)* 10. Avē,
Caesar, imperātor et rēx noster es! 11. Avē, Jēsū Chrīste, quī prō
nōbīs multōs labōrēs atque mortem miseram sustinuistī.

EXERCISE 306
[Essential]
Translate:

1. O good Jesus, in You we place all our hope and faith.
2. Thou, O God, hast taught us Thy ways. 3. My son, God will
always defend you. 4. Soldiers, without delay we shall occupy
the bridges and the hills. 5. O noble king, we have come to seek
peace. 6. Hail, Mary! 7. The enemy raised up a shout on all
sides to terrify us. 8. Hail, Caesar! To you do we all give
thanks, for you have spared our lives. 9. Soldiers, we are held
in on all sides by the enemy, who is eager for victory and glory.
10. General, I shall inform you where the enemy has pitched
camp in order that you may attack it.

EXERCISE 307
[Review]

1. How are -ne, num, and nōnne used (1) in direct questions?
(2) in indirect questions?
2. What is the difference between ubi and quō?

2. PRESENT IMPERATIVE ACTIVE

The imperative mood is used in giving commands.

Praise God! **Laudā Deum!**

(Singular; addressed to ONE person.)

Fight bravely! **Pugnāte fortiter!**

(Plural; addressed to MORE THAN ONE.)

ASSIGNMENT: Study GRAMMAR, Nos. 208, 216-218. Note that the imperative is formed on the PRESENT STEM, that it has a SINGULAR and a PLURAL form.

RULE OF POSITION: THE IMPERATIVE MORE
FREQUENTLY STANDS FIRST IN
THE SENTENCE.

VOCABULARY

regō, regere, rēxī, rēctus, 3, tr.	*direct* *rule*
at, *conj.*	*but*
mēns, mentis	*mind*
dolor, dolōris	*pain* *sorrow*
miserēre nōbīs	*have mercy on us*
adōrō, 1, tr.	*adore*

RELATED ENGLISH WORDS

Congress *regulates* interstate commerce. A *regent* was appointed to govern for the boy king. Education produces *mental* habits. *Dolorous.*

RELATED LATIN WORDS

Miser; ōrō; rēx.

EXERCISE 308
Translate:

1. Praise God, Christians! 2. Help me! 3. Hold the hill, soldiers! 4. Slaves, prepare grain. 5. Hand over your arms. 6. Terrify the soldiers. 7. Wage war, O king. 8. Take away our sins. 9. Storm the town. 10. Fear God. 11. Seek help. 12. Carry the sword, slave. 13. Hear the leader. 14. Dismiss the chiefs. 15. Call upon God. 16. Wait for help.

MOMENTS AT MASS NO. 2

When the priest turns to the people at the Communion, he holds a host above the chalice and says:

Ecce[1] Agnus[2] Deī, Ecce[1] quī tollit peccāta mundī!

EXERCISE 309
[Essential]
Translate:

1. Rege, Domine, mentēs nostrās ut in Caelum contendāmus. 2. Tolle, Domine, peccāta nostra, tolle dolōrēs nostrōs! 3. Īnstrue, lēgāte, mīlitēs prō portā at equitēs mitte in silvās. 4. Deus, quī omnem mundum regis, rege etiam mentem et corpus meum. 5. Jēsū, quī dolōrēs gravēs prō nōbīs sustinuistī, miserēre nōbīs! 6. Adjuvā nōs, Domine, nē hostis nōs superet. 7. Dēfendite, lēgātī, agrōs nostrōs! 8. Ostende nōbīs, serve, ubi hostēs sint. 9. Sāncta Marīa, ōrā prō nōbīs. 10. Adōrāte, Chrīstiānī, Deum vestrum. 11. Docē mē, Domine, viās tuās ut grātiam tuam semper habeam. 12. Timēte Deum, Rēgem Caelī et terrae, Chrīstiānī! 13. Vocā, lēgāte, mīlitēs ad arma. 14. Colloca in prīmā aciē legiōnēs integrās quae equitēs pellant. 15. Portā, serve, frūmentum in castra nē inopia sit. 16. Incendite oppida, op-

---

[1] ecce: *behold.*
[2] agnus, ī: *lamb.*

pugnāte urbēs, pellite equitēs, occīdite mīlitēs, at vītās prīncipum cōnservāte! 17. Grātiās, frātrēs meī, Deō agite! 18. Chrīstus autem nōbīs, "Habēte," inquit, "pācem inter vōs." 19. "Timēte Dominum, omnēs sānctī ējus." *(From the Roman Breviary.)* 20. Chrīstus, "Date," inquit, "et dabitur vōbīs." 21. Chrīstus, "Petite," inquit, "et dabitur vōbīs." 22. Manē nōbīscum, Domine.

> AGE QUOD AGIS

EXERCISE 310
Translate:

1. Find out, lieutenant, what the plan of the enemy is. 2. Soldiers, wait for the arrival of Caesar lest the enemy conquer us. 3. Keep in memory the courage of our fathers. 4. Arrive, cavalry, at the bridge at dawn. 5. Lieutenant, lead away the legion. 6. Approach the enemy swiftly. 7. Soldiers, lay waste the fields of the barbarians. Burn their crops. Attack their towns. Kill their hostages. Seize their towns, hills, bridges! 8. Call Caesar king and general. 9. Address the centurions by name. 10. Be well. 11. Slave, show us where the enemy has stationed guards. 12. Centurion, lead the soldiers across the river and into the forest. 13. Ask the envoy why he has come. 14. Fight bravely for your king! 15. Inform us how large the army of the enemy is. 16. Raise up a shout and storm the city. 17. Guide, O Lord, my mind and my life. 18. Jesus Christ, have mercy on us. 19. Adore Jesus Christ, the Son of God.

EXERCISE 311
[Review]
Explain the italicized words:

1. Caesar *centuriōnēs nōmine* appellāvit.
2. Mīlitēs *Caesarem imperātōrem* appellāverant.

"VENĪTE AD MĒ."

(Ita Chrīstus omnēs hominēs ad sē vocat.)

READING NO. 21

A CHRISTIAN SERMON

Jēsūs Chrīstus, sīcut vōs, Chrīstiānī, cognōvistis, est et Fīlius Deī et frāter noster. Propter nōs enim et propter nostram salū- tem in mundum vēnit. Magnōs labōrēs et dolōrēs gravēs prō nōbīs sustinuit. Mortem etiam miseram prō nōbīs sustinuit. Deus est quī mundum regit, quī terram et caelum fēcit;[1] attamen[2] ad mortem prō nōbīs ductus est. Per ējus autem mortem vīta atque salūs nōbīs datae sunt. In mundum enim vēnit ut peccāta nostra misera tolleret.

Nōnne eum, fīliī meī, laudābimus atque adōrābimus? Nōnne eī grātiās agēmus? Nōnne eum Dominum et Rēgem appellābimus? Spem vestram, Ō Chrīstiānī, in eō pōnite nē hostis vōs per-

---

[1] **fēcit:** *(he) made.*

[2] When **at** and **tamen** are used together, they are written as one word.

turbet. Lēgem ējus sānctam cōnservāte ut grātiam Deī habeātis. Fidem servāte ut Deus mentēs vestrās regat et vōs viam salūtis doceat. Tenēte fortiter et semper vēritātem Chrīstī, quī est lūx mundī. Ōrāte et grātiam petite nē peccātum in vōbīs sit. Adjuvāte omnēs frātrēs vestrōs sīcut frāter noster, Chrīstus, nōs adjūvit. Sustinēte, frātrēs, sustinēte fortiter injūriās et dolōrēs ut similēs eī sītis quī mortem etiam prō vōbīs fortiter sustinuit. Is enim per dolōrem et mortem ad glōriam pervēnit; nōs etiam per dolōrem et mortem ad glōriam perveniēmus.

Itaque, Chrīstiānī, contendite in Caelum ut cum sānctīs Deī, cum Jōsēphō et Marīā, Patrem et Fīlium et Spīritum Sānctum laudētis in saecula saeculōrum. Āmēn.

3. THE SUBJUNCTIVE IN WISHES AND EXHORTATIONS

1. **Wishes.** In *wishes* the present subjunctive in main clauses is to be translated by a verb with the auxiliary verb *may*. **Utinam** is often used as the sign of wishes in Latin; it need not be translated. The negative is **nē**. Notice that the compound verb (e. g., *may . . . give*) can be separated in English.

> **Deus det nōbīs pācem.** *May God give us peace.*
>
> **Utinam veniat.** *May he come.*
>
> **Nē veniat.** *May he not come.*
>
> **Adjuvet nōs Deus.** *May God help us.*

2. **Exhortations.** In English we urge others to do something with us by using the auxiliary verb *let*, as "Let us give thanks." Latin uses the first person plural of the present subjunctive, called the HORTATORY SUBJUNCTIVE, for exhortations. In translating such verbs, use the English form *let us*.

> **Veniāmus.** *Let us come.*
> **Grātiās agāmus.** *Let us give thanks.*
> **Fortiter pugnēmus.** *Let us fight bravely.*

ASSIGNMENT: Learn the rules, GRAMMAR, Nos. 511, 518. Review the present subjunctive of all four conjugations and of sum, GRAMMAR, Nos. 186, 194-196, 352.

EXERCISE 312
Translate:

1. Utinam veniat. 2. Pugnēmus. 3. Comparēmus arma. 4. Dēfendāmus puerōs nostrōs. 5. Nē vincat. 6. Expugnet urbem. 7. Teneant collem. 8. Conveniāmus. 9. Incendāmus frūmenta. 10. Vincant! 11. Nē cēdāmus. 12. Nē eōs occīdat! 13. Mittāmus auxilium. 14. Nē exspectet.

EXERCISE 313
Translate:

1. May he fight bravely! 2. May they conquer the barbarians! 3. May God give us a reward! 4. Let us call the soldiers. 5. Let us pray. 6. May they fear God! 7. May they not hold the bridge! 8. Let us hasten and see the king. 9. Let us withstand the forces of the enemy. 10. May God defend us! 11. May Thy kingdom come! 12. May God lead us into the kingdom of heaven! 13. Let us not yield. 14. Let us send them help. 15. May Caesar conquer! 16. May they rout the barbarians! 17. Let us hear the speech of the chief. 18. May he be brave! 19. May Christ remain with us! 20. May God help us! 21. May God strengthen us! 22. May God preserve us! 23. Let us not wait for his coming. 24. Let us remember his courage. 25. May he arrive safe! 26. May they be well! 27. May you be well!

EXERCISE 314
Translate:

1. "Domine, exaudī[1] ōrātiōnem meam, et clāmor meus ad tē veniat." *(From the Mass.)* 2. "Deus autem pācis sit cum omnibus vōbīs. Āmēn." *(St. Paul.)* 3. "Ōrēmus." *(From the Mass.)*

---

[1] exaudiō, *4, tr.: hear.*

4. "Divīnum[1] auxilium maneat semper nōbīscum." *(From the Roman Breviary.)* 5. Rēgem martyrum[2] Dominum, venīte, adō-rēmus. *(From the Roman Breviary.)* 6. Sānctus Paulus: "Ipse[3] autem," inquit, "Dominus pācis det vōbīs pācem sempiternam[4] in omnī locō. Dominus sit cum omnibus vōbīs."

EXERCISE 315
Identify these forms:

1. veniam   3. laudet   5. regat
2. vincet   4. portent   6. conveniant

EXERCISE 316
1. Translate;
2. Explain the italicized forms:

1. *Veniat* celeriter. 2. *Vincat* Chrīstus Rēx! 3. *Valeāmus.*
4. *Valeās.* 5. *Veniāmus.* 6. *Venīte, adōrēmus.* 7. *Videāmus*
puerum. 8. *Valēte.* 9. Nē *pugnēmus.* 10. *Adjuvēmus* omnēs
hominēs. 11. *Petāmus* grātiam Deī. 12. *Vocāte* mīlitēs ad arma.
13. *Regat* Chrīstus mentēs nostrās. 14. Bonus *sīs.*

READING NO. 22

A SCENE FROM THE FIRST CHRISTMAS

SCENE: A country place in Judea. A group of country folk are gathered around a fire.

CHOIR *(softly in the distance).*

Adeste,[5] fidēlēs,[6]
Laetī,[7] triumphantēs,[8]

---

[1] divīnus, a, um: *divine.*
[2] martyr, martyris: *martyr.*
[3] Ipse . . . Dominus: *the Lord Himself.*
[4] sempiternus, a, um: *everlasting.*
[5] adeste: *be present.*
[6] fidēlis, e: *faithful.*
[7] laetus, a, um: *joyful.*
[8] triumphantēs: *triumphant.*

Venīte, venīte in Bethlehēm.
Nātum[1] vidēte Rēgem Angelōrum,[2]
Venīte, adōrēmus,
Venīte, adōrēmus,
Venīte adōrēmus Dominum.

(Enter the shepherds. Their faces are transformed and their eyes shining. The country folk look at them and speak.)

COUNTRY FOLK. Quās vōcēs audīmus?
SHEPHERDS. Audītis vōcēs angelōrum.[2] Audīte!
CHOIR *(strong and clear)*. Glōria in excelsīs[3] Deō, et in terrā pāx hominibus bonae voluntātis![4]
COUNTRY FOLK. Nōnne timuistis?
SHEPHERDS. Nōn timuimus. Angelī[2] enim Deī sunt et magnum nōbīs signum ostendērunt.
CHOIR *(softly)*. Nātum[1] vidēte . . . *to end.*
COUNTRY FOLK. Quid ostendērunt? Dīcite[5] nōbīs! Quid vīdistis?
SHEPHERDS. Exercitum angelōrum[2] cum lūce magnā in caelīs vīdimus. Rēgem rēgum et prīncipem pācis, Jēsūm Chrīstum, puerum cum Marīā mātre ējus vīdimus. Glōriam Fīliī Deī in terrā vīdimus.
COUNTRY FOLK *(excitedly)*. Fīlius Deī! in terrā! Deus homō? Cūr vēnit Deus in mundum?
SHEPHERDS. Chrīstus in mundō est ut peccāta nostra tollat, ut vītam victōriamque nōbīs det, ut in Caelum nōs miserōs hominēs dūcat. Glōria Deō sit! In nōmine Jēsū Chrīstī omnēs hominēs spem salūtis et pācis pōnent. Itaque nōmen ējus laudēmus et Deō grātiās agāmus. *(To audience.)* Et vōbīs, amīcī nostrī atque frātrēs, sit Deī pāx et grātia!

---

[1] nātus, a, um: *born.*
[2] angelus, ī: *angel.*
[3] in excelsīs: *in the highest.*
[4] voluntās, voluntātis: *will.*
[5] dīcite: *say, tell.*

EXERCITUM ANGELORUM VIDIMUS.

CHOIR *(full and loud)*.

Chrīstus nātus[1] est nōbīs;
Chrīstus datus est nōbīs;
Hodiē[2] vēnit Chrīstus in mundum;
Hodiē[2] vēnit salūs mundī.

(The scene and the songs fade out together.)

---

[1] nātus, a, um: *born.*
[2] hodiē, *adv.: today.*

LESSON 28: *SUUS* AND *SUI*

1. *SUUS* AND *SUĪ* AS DIRECT REFLEXIVES

We have seen that **suī** (**sibi, sē, sē**) is used for *himself (him)*, *herself (her)*, *itself (it)*, *themselves (them)*, when these words refer TO THE SUBJECT OF THEIR OWN CLAUSE. When so used, **suī** is called a DIRECT REFLEXIVE.

Sē laudat. *He praises himself.*

ASSIGNMENT: Review the declension and meanings of **suī**, GRAMMAR, No. 127. See also the previous lesson on reflexives, page 135.

Suus, a, um is the POSSESSIVE ADJECTIVE corresponding to **suī**. It is used to mean *his (his own), her (her own), its (its own), their (their own)*, ACCORDING TO THE WORD TO WHICH IT REFERS. Since **suus, a, um** is an adjective, it agrees in gender, number, and case with the word which it MODI-FIES. Like **suī, suus, a, um** is used to REFER TO THE SUBJECT OF ITS OWN CLAUSE (DIRECT REFLEXIVE).

Caesar suōs mīlitēs laudāvit.
Caesar praised his (own) soldiers.

Māter fīlium suum laudat.
A mother praises her (own) son.

Legiō signum suum dēfendit.
The legion defends its (own) standard.

Mīlitēs imperātōrem suum laudant.
The soldiers praise their (own) general.

When *his, her, its,* etc., do not refer to the subject of their own clause, **ējus** and **eōrum** (the possessive genitives of **is, ea, id**) are to be used (EXCEPT IN SOME CASES TO BE SEEN IN THE NEXT SECTION).

Centuriō fortiter pugnāvit. Itaque Caesar virtūtem ējus laudāvit.
The centurion fought bravely. And so Caesar praised his courage.

Caesar Gallōs vīcit atque eōrum ducēs occīdit.
Caesar conquered the Gauls and killed their leaders.

NOTE

Just as forms of **ego, nōs, tū, vōs** are used as reflexives of the first and second persons, so forms of **meus, noster, tuus, vester** are used as reflexives of the first and second persons. **Suī** and **suus** are used for the THIRD PERSON ONLY.

We defend our own lives. Vītās nostrās dēfendimus.

VOCABULARY

suus, a, um	his (own)
	her (own)
	its (own)
	their (own)
fuga, ae	flight
dēdō, dēdere, dēdidī, dēditus, 3, tr.[1]	give up
	surrender
rēs pūblica, reī pūblicae	state
	republic
dīligō, dīligere, dīlexī, dīlēctus, 3, tr.	love

NOTE

Where we say simply *surrender* in English, **dēdō** must always be used with an ACCUSATIVE REFLEXIVE PRONOUN.

The Gauls surrendered to the Romans. Gallī Rōmānīs sē dēdidērunt.

We surrendered to the Gauls. Gallīs nōs dēdidimus. (Nōs is accusative.)

Of course, **dēdō** may have other objects.

We surrendered the arms to the enemy. Arma hostibus dēdidimus.

RELATED ENGLISH WORDS

A *fugitive* from justice. We shall always defend our *republic*.

---

[1] Dēdō *always* takes an object in Latin.

Dō

RELATED LATIN WORD

EXERCISE 317
Distinguish:

1. dedistī   2. dēdidistī   3. dēdidērunt   4. dedērunt

EXERCISE 318
[Essential]

1. Translate;
2. Explain the use of the italicized words:

1. Agrōs atque urbēs *suās* dēfendēbant. 2. Fortiter *sē* dēfendunt. 3. Post Caesaris victōriam atque *suōrum* prīncipum caedem, hostēs *sē sua*que omnia *eī* dēdidērunt. 4. Barbarī post equitum *suōrum* caedem fugā salūtem petīvērunt. 5. Nōnne mātrēs fīliōs *suōs* dīligunt? 6. Barbarī fugā montēs petīvērunt, at magnus *eōrum* numerus in fugā ab equitibus Rōmānīs occīsus est. 7. Gallī lēgātōs ad Caesarem mīsērunt quī auxilium peterent. Itaque Caesar ad eōs mīsit equitēs quī fīnēs *eōrum* dēfenderent. 8. Dīligite, frātrēs meī, Deum. Deus enim pācem *suam* vōbīs dabit. 9. Laudāvitne Caesar virtūtem *suōrum?* 10. Etiam hostēs saepe fortiter pugnāvērunt. Itaque Caesar virtūtem *eōrum* laudāvit. 11. Gallī saepe equitēs ad Caesarem mīsērunt quī cum cōpiīs *ējus* pugnārent. 12. Lēgātus nuntium dē perīculō *suō* ad Caesarem mīsit. Itaque Caesar statim omnēs cōpiās *suās* in fīnēs barbarōrum clam et celeriter dēdūxit.

EXERCISE 319
[Essential]
Translate:

1. Did the Romans often rout the barbarians and kill a great number of them? 2. The tribes of Gaul were exchanging hostages in order to strengthen peace and friendship among themselves. 3. Caesar stationed guards at the bridge in order that he might more easily defend his (men). 4. The lieutenant asked the slaves

where their master was. 5. They fought long and bitterly because they were fighting for their lives. 6. They fortified the camp with a ditch and a rampart in order to defend themselves more easily. 7. Caesar was a great general. The Romans always kept his victories and courage in memory. 8. The general called the centurions and the military tribunes to him. 9. We will defend our own cities and our own fields.

> Chrīstus nōbīs, "Sīcut dīlēxit mē Pater,"
> inquit, "et ego dīlēxī vōs."

EXERCISE 320
[Review]
Parse the italicized words:

1. Lēgātus *exercitum flūmen* trādūxit.
2. Lēgātus trāns *flūmen exercitum* trādūxit.
3. *Veniāmus* ut Chrīstum *adōrēmus*.

READING NO. 23

A ROMAN LIEUTENANT ADDRESSES HIS MEN

Quantō in perīculō, mīlitēs, sīmus, vōs omnēs cognōvistis. In castrīs enim nostrīs est inopia frūmentī et omnium rērum. Undique autem ā barbarīs continēmur. Quantus sit numerus hostium, vōs doceō; quanta autem sit eōrum virtūs, vōs vidētis. Nam hostēs populī Rōmānī usque ad castra Rōmāna appropinquant. Cupidī victōriae et bellī glōriae neque equitēs neque legiōnēs nostrās timent. Litterās ad Caesarem mīsimus, at servus cui litterās dedimus ab hostibus vīsus est atque occīsus. Itaque neque auxilium exspectāmus neque sociōs habēmus.

Itaque quid, mīlitēs Rōmānī, agēmus? Num pācem petēmus? Num ad hostēs lēgātōs mittēmus quī dē salūte nostrā agant? Num nōs nostraque omnia hostibus populī Rōmānī trādēmus?

Pōnite, mīlitēs, spem in virtūte! Virtūtem patrum nostrōrum memoriā tenēte! Mūnīte castra! Impetūs hostium sustinēte! Cōpiās hostium pellite, vincite, occīdite! Pugnāte usque ad mortem! Imperātor Rōmānus propter glōriam nōminis Rōmānī vōs ad arma et mortem vocat!

2. *SUUS* AND *SUĪ* AS INDIRECT REFLEXIVES

When a personal pronoun of the THIRD person is in a SUBORDINATE PURPOSE clause or INDIRECT QUESTION and REFERS to the SUBJECT of the MAIN verb, suī and suus (not is, ea, id or ējus, eōrum) should be used. In this use suī and suus are called INDIRECT reflexives.

Caesar mīlitēs vocāvit quī sē dēfenderent.
Caesar called the soldiers to defend him.

Caesar equitēs mīsit quī lēgātōs suōs dēfenderent.
Caesar sent the cavalry to defend his envoys.

VOCABULARY

ante, *prep. w. acc.*   *before*

praesidium, ī $\begin{cases} garrison \\ protection \end{cases}$

vērō, *postpositive*[1] $\begin{cases} in\ truth \\ but \end{cases}$

RELATED ENGLISH WORDS

Verily. Caesar's wars *ante*date the birth of Christ.

IDIOM STUDY

1. Dō with in fugam means *put to flight.*

Caesar hostēs in fugam dedit. *Caesar put the enemy to flight.*

---

[1] Vērō is postpositive; *i. e.,* it never stands first in a clause.

2. With proper names the ablative nōmine, *by name*, is frequently used. Translate *named*.

Servus, nōmine Titus, in hībernīs erat.

A slave named (by name) Titus was in the winter quarters.

EXERCISE 321

[Essential]

1. Translate;
2. Explain the use of the italicized pronouns;
3. Diagram No. 1 (first sentence):

1. Centuriō servum, nōmine Titum, ad Caesarem mīsit quī *eum* docēret quantō in perīculō praesidia essent. Itaque Caesar statim exercitum *suum* dēdūxit atque equitēs mīsit quī *eum* dē adventū *suō* docērent. 2. Gallī, vērō, oppida *sua* ante Caesaris adventum incendērunt nē praesidia in *eīs* collocāret. 3. Lēgātus *eum* per nuntiōs ante proelium docuit quantō in perīculō esset legiō *sua*. 4. Rōmānī viās mūnīvērunt quō facilius cōpiās *suās* in prōvinciās dēdūcerent. 5. Caesar novās legiōnēs in Galliam mīsit nē barbarī *suōs* superārent. 6. Barbarī Rōmānōs proeliō pepulērunt nē *eī* per fīnēs *suōs* exercitum dūcerent. 7. Gallī praemia Caesarī mīsērunt ut grātiam apud *eum* habērent. 8. Caesar, vērō, mīlitēs *suōs* flūmen trādūxit ut reliqua oppida expugnāret atque incenderet.

EXERCISE 322

[Essential]

1. Translate;
2. Explain the translation of the italicized words:

1. The American people heard in how great danger *their* soldiers were in Bataan.[1] But they did not send arms and reinforcements because Bataan was far distant from *their* territory. 2. Caesar sent reinforcements into the first battle line in order

---

[1] *Bataan:* Bataan, *indecl. noun.*

that they might help *his* legions. 3. They routed the barbarians lest they should burn *their* crops. 4. He showed them what *his* plans were. 5. Did Caesar give rewards to the slaves who were in *his* camp?

EXERCISE 323
[Review]
Parse the italicized words:

1. Rogāvit *num* Chrīstus in mundum *vēnisset.*
2. *Num* bellum atque caedem laudāmus?

READING NO. 24

THE HAIL MARY

AVĒ MARĪA

GRĀTIĀ PLĒNA

DOMINUS TĒCUM

BENEDICTA[1] TŪ IN MULIERIBUS[2]

ET BENEDICTUS[1] FRŪCTUS[3] VENTRIS[4] TUĪ JĒSŪS

SĀNCTA MARĪA

MĀTER DEĪ

ŌRĀ PRŌ NŌBĪS PECCĀTŌRIBUS[5]

NUNC ET IN HŌRĀ[6] MORTIS NOSTRAE. ĀMĒN.

This beautiful prayer, which is known and loved by all Catholics, has its origin in the records of the New Testament. The first

---

[1] **benedictus, a, um:** *blessed.*
[2] **mulier, mulieris:** *woman.*
[3] **frūctus, ūs:** *fruit.*
[4] **venter, ventris:** *womb.*
[5] **peccātor, peccātōris:** *sinner.*
[6] **hōra, ae:** *hour.*

AVE GRATIA PLENA

words were spoken to Mary by the Angel Gabriel; the second section contains the greeting of St. Elizabeth. The following account is simplified from St. Luke.

Missus est angelus[1] Gabriēl ā Deō in cīvitātem Galilaeae cui nōmen [erat] Nazareth. Missus est ad Marīam. Marīa autem ōrābat. Angelus[1] eī,

"AVĒ GRĀTIĀ PLĒNA!"

inquit,

"DOMINUS TĒCUM!

BENEDICTA[2] TŪ IN MULIERIBUS!"[3]

---

[1] angelus, ī: *angel.*
[2] benedictus, a, um: *blessed.*
[3] mulier, mulieris: *woman.*

Mary was disturbed at the greeting, but the angel said:

"Do not be afraid, Mary, for thou hast found grace with God. The Holy Spirit shall come upon thee and the power of the Most High shall overshadow thee; and therefore the Holy One to be born shall be called the Son of God." Mary answered, "Behold the handmaid of the Lord; be it done to me according to thy word."

Then Mary went into the hill country to visit her cousin Elizabeth. Elizabeth autem Mariae,

"BENEDICTA,"[1] inquit, "TŪ INTER MULIERĒS[2]
ET BENEDICTUS[1] FRŪCTUS[3] VENTRIS[4] TUĪ."

Thus, the Angel Gabriel and St. Elizabeth composed the first part of the prayer. The word *Jēsūs* and the last part *(Sāncta Maria, etc.)* were added gradually by the devotion of Catholics. The Hail Mary, in the full form to which we are accustomed, appears first in the fifteenth or sixteenth century.

This beautiful scene of the Annunciation is commemorated also in the Angelus and in the first of the Joyful Mysteries of the Rosary.

---

[1] benedictus, a, um: *blessed.*
[2] mulier, mulieris: *woman.*
[3] fructus, ūs: *fruit.*
[4] venter, ventris: *womb.*

LESSON 29: THE PASSIVE SUBJUNCTIVE

1. PRESENT AND IMPERFECT SUBJUNCTIVE PASSIVE

ASSIGNMENT: Learn GRAMMAR, Nos. 267-274. Note that the passive subjunctive is formed by changing the final personal signs exactly as was done in the indicative.

Review the rules for purpose clauses, GRAMMAR, Nos. 546-547.

VOCABULARY

parvus, a, um	{ *small* *little*
mōs, mōris, *m.*	{ *custom* *habit*
manus, ūs, *f.*	{ *a band of men* *hand*
causa, ae	*cause*
causā, *preceded by gen.*	*for the sake of*

NOTE

1. The ablative of **causa** is used as a preposition. It governs the GENITIVE and always stands AFTER the word it governs.

> **aquae causā,** *for the sake of water*
> **pācis causā,** *for the sake of peace*

2. The ablative of **mōs** (**mōre**) may be translated *according to custom.*

RELATED ENGLISH WORDS

Manual labor; *manufactured* goods.

Sāncta Marīa, Māter Deī, ōrā prō nōbīs!

EXERCISE 324

1. Translate;
2. Explain the tenses in the subordinate clauses:

1. They came into the forest lest they be routed (seen; overcome; conquered; terrified; held; put to flight; heard). 2. He sent a small band to fortify (seize; hold; defend; burn; assault; storm) the winter quarters. 3. He is warning the soldiers lest they be overcome (conquered; routed; put to flight; terrified; seen; held; killed). 4. He is sending the cavalry that the town may be more easily seized (burned; fortified; defended; assaulted; stormed; held).

EXERCISE 325
[Essential]

1. Translate;
2. Diagram Sentence 1;
3. Parse the italicized words:

1. Caesar *suōs* nōmine appellābat atque signum legiōnis *manū* tenēbat nē *suī* ab hostibus in fugam darentur. 2. Caesar *aquae* causā ad flūmen castra posuit quō *facilius* atque diūtius impetus hostium ā *suīs* sustinērētur. 3. Imperātor legiōnēs clam in fīnēs hostium dēdūxit nē ab hostibus *vidērentur*. Statim impetum in Gallōs fēcērunt. Tum vērō prīncipēs Gallōrum *bellī* causā manūs cōgēbant, arma parābant, virtūtem *suōrum* ōrātiōnibus mōre *suō* cōnfirmābant. 4. Caesar cum parvā manū trāns montēs contendit nē ā mīlitibus *suīs* in *eōrum* perīculō abesset. 5. Gallī post proelium *sē sua*que omnia Caesarī dēdidērunt ut vītae obsidum suōrum ā Caesare cōnservārentur. 6. Nōnne nōs Americānī ante bellum exercitum cōgimus atque arma tēlaque parāmus nē ab hostibus vincāmur? 7. Portae incēnsae sunt, atque equitēs celeriter in oppidum missī sunt ut oppidum statim occupārētur. Tum barbarī mōre *suō* clāmōrem sustulērunt atque *sē sua*que omnia Rōmānīs salūtis causā dēdidērunt. Caesar vērō vītās *eōrum* nōn cōnservāvit nē lēgātī *suī* ā barbarīs occīderentur. Nam injūria atque caedēs lēgātōrum fuerant bellī causa.

EXERCISE 326

Translate:

1. May God be praised! 2. May the enemy be conquered!
3. May the town be burned! 4. May the leader be warned!
5. May we be spared! 6. May guards be stationed! 7. May
they be helped by God! 8. May the state be preserved! 9. May
my life be ruled by God! 10. May God be loved by all men!
11. May they be put to flight! 12. May our sins be taken away!
13. May we be taught by God! 14. May help be sent to us!
15. May he be always kept in memory! 16. May Mary be
praised by all men! 17. May the grace of God be given to you
all! 18. May rewards be given to brave men!

> In manūs tuās, Domine,
> Commendō[1] spīritum meum.

EXERCISE 327

Translate:

1. The barbarians according to their custom raised a shout lest
they be killed by the lieutenant. 2. Christ came into the world
that our sins might be taken away. 3. Let the state be preserved
for the sake of our peace and our common welfare. 4. The Gauls
burned their towns with their own hands lest they be seized by
the Romans. 5. God will give grace to those who sustain great
sorrows for the sake of peace. 6. Brave and free men will always
fight that our state may be preserved. 7. They pitched camp at
the river for the sake of water. 8. He waited for reinforcements
lest he be hard pressed by the enemy. 9. He stationed a small
band of men there lest the hill be seized by the barbarians.
10. Caesar informs us about the customs both of the Gauls and
of his own soldiers.

---

[1] commendō, *1, tr.: commend.*

EXERCISE 328
[Review]
Parse the italicized words:

1. Propter *quórum* salūtem vēnit Chrīstus in mundum?
2. *Quem* imperātōrem mīlitēs Rōmānī appellāvērunt?
3. *Quās* gentēs vīcit Caesar?

2. THE PERFECT SYSTEM OF THE PASSIVE SUBJUNCTIVE

The perfect tenses of the passive subjunctive OF ALL LATIN VERBS, REGULAR AND IRREGULAR, are formed in the same way. They are COMPOUND tenses just as in the indicative. To form these tenses:

1. Find the perfect participle passive.
2. Add, as a separate word, the proper form of the verb **sum**.

ASSIGNMENT: Study GRAMMAR, Nos. 275-282. Review in direct questions, GRAMMAR, Nos. 660-662 and FIRST YEAR LATIN, pages 281 and 286.

VOCABULARY

sciō, scīre, scīvī, scītus, *4, tr.*	*know*
pācō, *1, tr.*	*pacify*
subitō, *adv.*	*suddenly*
probō, *1, tr.*	*approve* / *prove*
relinquō, relinquere, relīquī, relictus, *3, tr.*	*leave* / *leave behind*

RELATED ENGLISH WORDS

Science. He is out on *probation.* He will not *relinquish* his rights. The story is not *probable.*

RELATED LATIN WORD

Pāx

CUM, *WHEN,* in secondary sequence usually takes the subjunctive. Use the imperfect or pluperfect according to the general rule, GRAMMAR, Nos. 531-533.

Cum equitēs in silvīs pugnārent, Caesar mīlitēs trāns flūmen trādūxit.

When the cavalry were fighting in the forest, Caesar led the soldiers across the river.

Caesar cum hostēs **vīdisset,** legiōnēs prō castrīs īnstrūxit.

When Caesar had seen the enemy, he drew up the legions in front of the camp.

EXERCISE 329

1. Translate;
2. Explain the tenses in the subordinate clauses:

1. He knew why they had been routed (praised; overcome; called; warned; killed; terrified; seen; held). 2. They knew where they had been led (sent; collected; called). 3. He knows who was sent (sought; killed; praised; warned; called; overcome; terrified). 4. He knew where they were being stationed (left; killed; drawn up). 5. He knows whether the fields are being laid waste (seized; defended). 6. He knows where they are being led (collected; called; moved; sent). 7. He knew why he was being praised (overcome; called; warned; feared; terrified; held; left).

EXERCISE 330
[Essential]
Translate:

1. Cum omnis Gallia pācāta esset, Caesar praesidia in hībernīs relīquit et in Italiam contendit. 2. Centuriō ante proelium rogāvit quae cōnsilia ā Caesare probāta essent. 3. Num scīs quō lēgātī missī sint? 4. Cum agmen per loca difficilia et angusta dūcerētur, subitō vīsa est aciēs barbarōrum. 5. Scītisne num legiō quae in castrīs fuerat ā lēgātō relicta sit? 6. Cum frūmenta

ab equitibus incenderentur, mīlitēs castra vallō fossāque mūniēbant. 7. Cum Chrīstus Jūdaeīs[1] ostēnsus ā Pīlātō[2] esset, Jūdaeī[1] magnum clāmōrem sustulērunt: "Nōn habēmus rēgem nisi[3] Caesarem. Tollite! Crucifīgātur!"[4]

EXERCISE 331

Translate:

When the legions had been left in winter quarters in Gaul and Caesar had hastened into Italy, the Gauls exchanged hostages and treated about war among themselves. When the plans had been approved in a common council, suddenly they attacked the winter quarters. The garrisons were in great danger. Therefore a messenger was sent to Caesar that help might be sent. Caesar knew how large the enemy forces were and where guards had been stationed. He immediately led his new legions into Gaul lest the winter quarters be taken (by storm). Suddenly his column was seen by the enemy. They were terrified and at once sent envoys to seek peace. Then they surrendered to him. Thus Gaul was pacified.

3. THE ABLATIVE OF CAUSE

We have seen that the CAUSE OR REASON may be expressed in Latin in various ways:

1. **Propter:**

   They were terrified on account of the arrival of Caesar.
   Propter adventum Caesaris territī sunt.

2. **Quod:**

   They were terrified because Caesar had arrived.
   Territī sunt **quod Caesar** advēnerat.

---

[1] Jūdaeus, ī: *Jew.*
[2] Pīlātus, ī: *Pilate.*
[3] nisi: *except.*
[4] crucifīgō, *3, tr.: crucify.*

3. **Nam; enim** (postpositive):

They were terrified, for Caesar had arrived.

Territī sunt, <u>nam Caesar</u> advēnerat.

The ablative without a preposition may also be used to express the CAUSE OR REASON (ABLATIVE OF CAUSE).

They were terrified <u>at (because of, on account of, by) the arrival</u> of Caesar.

Adventū Caesaris territī sunt.

ASSIGNMENT: Learn the rule, GRAMMAR, No. 781.

Note. The ablative of cause is frequently merely a special variety of the ablative of means. It is therefore sometimes very difficult to distinguish between these two types of ablatives.

```
┌─────────────────────────────────┐
│         Chrīste, audī nōs!      │
└─────────────────────────────────┘
```

EXERCISE 332

*All the italicized ablatives may be
classified as ablatives of cause.*

Translate:

1. Sociōrum *victōriīs* sublātī sunt. 2. *Adventū* Caesaris mōtī sunt. 3. *Metū* Caesaris territī sunt. 4. *Ōrātiōne* lēgātī perturbātī sunt. 5. *Litterīs* rēgis mōtus est.

EXERCISE 333

*All the italicized expressions are to be
translated by the ablative of cause.*

Translate:

1. They were violently disturbed *on account of the slaughter* of the leading men. 2. They were terrified *because of the arrival* of Caesar. 3. They were aroused *at the wrongs* of the Romans. 4. They were violently moved *by fear* of the lieutenant.

EXERCISE 334
[Essential Review]
Translate:

1. Hail, Jesus Christ, who for the sake of our salvation didst come into the world and through sorrow and toil didst take away our sins. Thou hast taught us the truth. Thou hast taught us the way of salvation. Rule our minds and our lives. Thou hast taught us where true peace is. Let us love Him and adore Him. Jesus Christ, our Lord, have mercy on us!

2. For the sake of peace Caesar left garrisons in the states which he had pacified. Then, however, Caesar hastened into Italy. When this[1] had been learned by the Gauls, new plans were approved by them and they exchanged hostages that peace and friendship might be strengthened among them. But Caesar, when he had learned what plans had been approved by the barbarians, left Rome and suddenly arrived in the territory of the Gauls with a small band of men. Meanwhile the Gauls had retained the envoys whom Caesar had sent to them and had assaulted the winter quarters. Caesar immediately hastened to the winter quarters lest they be stormed by the barbarians. He arrived with a small band of men. When his column had been seen by the enemy, they made[2] an attack on his men without delay. His men were hard pressed, but Caesar called upon them by name and held the standard of the legion with his hand lest they be routed. The enemy were put to flight. Caesar hastened with all his forces to their camp, but they, according to their custom, raised a shout and surrendered themselves and all their possessions to him. Caesar knew what had been the cause of the war. Therefore he killed the hostages of the Gauls, that his envoys might not afterwards be held and killed by them. Thus had he defended the state and, on account of his victory, the Roman Senate without delay praised him and gave thanks to him.

3. A lieutenant, by name Labienus, was often praised by Caesar.

---

[1] *this:* hoc.

[2] *they made:* fēcērunt.

4. May God give us His peace and always defend us!
5. Jesus Christ, Son of God, have mercy on us!
6. They were terrified at the arrival of Caesar.

EXERCISE 335
[Essential Formal Review]

1. Give the rules for the formation of the vocative. Give the vocative of: (a) Deus; (b) Jēsūs; (c) fīlius; (d) meus; (e) amīcus; (f) centuriō.
2. How is the present imperative active formed? Give examples.
3. Give the rule for the volitive subjunctive. Give examples.
4. Give the rule for the hortatory subjunctive. Give examples.
5. What is the rule for the use of suī and suus as direct reflexives?
6. What is the rule for the use of suī and suus as indirect reflexives?
7. What are the direct and indirect reflexives of the first and second persons? Give examples.
8. How do you translate: (a) surrender; (b) you surrender; (c) he surrenders; (d) we surrender; (e) they surrender?
9. What does the phrase **in fugam dare** mean?
10. Explain the use of the ablative **causā**.
11. Give the rule for **cum,** *when.*
12. Explain the ablative of cause. Give an example.

READING NO. 25

DAVĪD, RĒX

Davīd,[1] vir nōbilis et fortis, sīcut scītis, rēx erat Israēlītārum.[2] Israēlītae[2] autem bellum cum Philisthīnīs[3] gerēbant nē agrī suī ab eīs occupārentur. Philisthīnī[3] autem Bethlehēm[4] tenēbant. Cas-

---

[1] Davīd: *David.*
[2] Israēlītae, Israēlītārum: *the Israelites.*
[3] Philisthīnī, Philisthīnōrum: *the Philistines.*
[4] Bethlehēm: *Bethlehem.*

DAVID, REX

tra enim ibi posuerant. Davīd cum parvā hominum manū erat in praesidiō et nōn longē ab eōrum castrīs āfuit. Praesidium ibi collocātum erat ut Davīd et suōs dēfenderet et cognōsceret quae ab hostibus gererentur. In castrīs autem Israēlītārum[1] erat magna aquae inopia. Propter id magnum dolōrem et Davīd et mīlitēs sustinēbant. In Bethlehēm autem, quod ā Philisthīnīs tenēbātur, erat aquae cōpia. Itaque Davīd, "Sī habērem,"[2] inquit, "aquam dē[3] cisternā[4] quae est in Bethlehēm!"

Cum vērō ea ā mīlitibus audīta essent, trēs[5] fortēs virī clam ad

---

[1] Israēlītae, Israēlītārum: *the Israelites.*
[2] sī habērem: *if only I had.*
[3] dē, *prep. w. abl.,* here means *from.*
[4] cisterna, ae: *cistern.*
[5] trēs, tria: *three.*

castra hostium pervēnērunt ut aquam ad rēgem portārent. Magnum erat perīculum, tamen ā custōdibus hostium vīsī nōn sunt. Itaque aquam ad rēgem tūtī portāvērunt et eī dedērunt. Rēx vērō, cum aquam vīdisset, eōrum virtūte et amīcitiā vehementer mōtus est. Per loca enim perīculōrum plēna in castra hostium pervēnērunt ut ad eum aqua portārētur. Scīvit rēx quantō in perīculō propter sē fuissent. Itaque eīs grātiās ēgit sed aquam in terram Dominō lībāvit.[1]

Davīd enim, "The Lord," inquit, "be merciful to me that I may not do this; shall I drink the blood of these men that went at the peril of their lives?"

---

[1] lībō, *1, tr.: pour out as a sacrifice (to).*

UNIT NINE

LESSON 30: THE PERFECT PARTICIPLE
PASSIVE

A PARTICIPLE is a VERBAL ADJECTIVE.

The enemy, <u>having been</u> swiftly <u>repulsed</u>, hastened into the mountains.

In this sentence *HAVING BEEN REPULSED* is a participle.
It is an ADJECTIVE because it modifies the noun *enemy*.
It is a VERB because it expresses ACTION. Since it is a verb,
it may be modified by an adverb *(swiftly)*.

The fourth principal part of regular verbs in Latin is the PER-
FECT PARTICIPLE PASSIVE. It is declined like **magnus, a,
um.**

> laudō, laudāre, laudāvī, <u>laudātus, a, um</u>
>
> moneō, monēre, monuī, <u>monitus, a, um</u>
>
> mittō, mittere, mīsī, <u>missus, a, um</u>
>
> audiō, audīre, audīvī, <u>audītus, a, um</u>

EXERCISE 336
Decline in full:

1. laudātus, a, um
2. monitus, a, um

3. missus, a, um
4. audītus, a, um

The perfect participle passive may be translated into English
either by the long English form:

> **laudātus, a, um,** *having been praised*

or the shorter English form:

> **laudātus, a, um,** *praised*

Since the perfect participle passive is an adjective, it can modify
any noun or pronoun in a sentence according as the sense requires.

Caesar multīs nuntiīs perturbātus novās legiōnēs in Galliam dūxit.

Caesar, having been disturbed (disturbed) by many messages, led new legions into Gaul.

Caesar collem ab equitibus occupātum vallō mūnīvit.

Caesar fortified with a rampart the hill seized by the cavalry.

Propter lēgātōs occīsōs Caesar oppida barbarōrum incendit.

On account of the murdered envoys Caesar burned the towns of the barbarians.

Rōmānī Gallīs victīs frūmentum nōn dedērunt.

The Romans did not give grain to the conquered Gauls.

Spīritus Sāncte, Deus, miserēre nōbīs!

NOTE

1. When a verb is INTRANSITIVE, it can have only a NEUTER participle PASSIVE. In intransitive verbs, therefore, the fourth principal part is always given as neuter, as:

pugnō, pugnāre, pugnāvī, pugnātum, *1, intr.*

2. When a verb is DEFECTIVE and has no perfect participle passive at all, the FUTURE PARTICIPLE ACTIVE (which we shall study later) is given as the fourth principal part:

cēdō, cēdere, cessī, cessūrus, *3, intr.*

Cēdō has no perfect participle passive. The future participle active always ends in -ŪRUS (cess-ūrus).

3. When a verb has neither a perfect participle passive nor a future participle active, only three parts are given, as:

contendō, contendere, contendī, *3, intr.*

Review the ablative of cause, page 319.

VOCABULARY

addūcō, addūcere, addūxī, adductus, 3, tr.	*lead to* / *lead on*
commoveō, commovēre, commōvī, commōtus, 2, tr.	*alarm* / *arouse*
impediō, 4, tr.	*hinder* / *impede*
auctōritās, auctōritātis	*authority* / *influence*

NOTE

The perfect participle passive of **impediō, IMPEDĪTUS,** is used of soldiers *encumbered* by full packs, of an army *encumbered* by a baggage train, and of places in which it is *difficult* to maneuver. Hence it may frequently be translated, according to the context, as *encumbered* or *difficult*.

RELATED ENGLISH WORDS

There was a *commotion* in the hall. He had an *impediment* in his speech.

RELATED LATIN WORDS

Ad + dūcō; moveō.

EXERCISE 337

1. Give the perfect participle passive;

2. Give two English translations of the participle:

1. cognōscō	10. trādūcō	19. terreō
2. exspectō	11. ostendō	20. videō
3. dēdūcō	12. doceō	21. agō
4. addūcō	13. tollō	22. dēdō
5. commoveō	14. regō	23. dīligō
6. impediō	15. obtineō	24. pācō
7. vastō	16. retineō	25. adjuvō
8. quaerō	17. sustineō	26. administrō
9. rogō	18. teneō	27. appellō

28. colloco	41. īnstruō	53. contineō
29. comparō	42. mittō	54. habeō
30. cōnfirmō	43. occupō	55. moneō
31. cōnservō	44. oppugnō	56. moveō
32. dō	45. ōrō	57. occīdō
33. explōrō	46. parō	58. pellō
34. incitō	47. perturbō	59. petō
35. laudō	48. portō	60. pōnō
36. dēfendō	49. servō	61. premō
37. dīmittō	50. superō	62. trādō
38. dūcō	51. vocō	63. vincō
39. gerō	52. compleō	64. audiō
40. incendō		

EXERCISE 338
[Essential]

1. Translate;
2. Parse the italicized words;
3. Diagram Sentences 1 and 4:

1. Barbarī, *spē* commūnis salūtis *adductī*, equitēs in agmen Rōmānum mīsērunt. 2. Imperātor mīlitēs caede equitum *commōtōs* ōrātiōne cōnfirmāvit quō diūtius pugnārent. 3. Propter oppida *occupāta* atque agrōs vastātōs, Gallī frūmentum in hīberna Rōmānōrum nōn portābant. 4. Senātus Populusque Rōmānus, auctōritāte litterīsque Caesaris commōtus, legiōnēs novās in prōvinciam sine morā mīsit. 5. Tum barbarī servīque in agmen nostrum impedīmentīs *impedītum* subitō impetum undique fēcērunt. 6. Gallī, vērō, multīs proeliīs superātī atque ā sociīs relictī, in loca *impedīta* et angusta contendērunt. 7. Nuntius, "Mīlitēs nostrī," inquit, "*impedītī*, hostēs nōn statim in fugam dedērunt." 8. Centuriō ad hīberna ab *hostibus* oppugnāta auxilia dēdūxit. 9. Gallī, omnium rērum inopiā adductī atque *adventū* Caesaris *commōtī*, lēgātōs ad imperātōrem Rōmānum mīsērunt quī pācem *peterent*. 10. Britannī et Americānī, ā sociīs *suīs adjūtī*, magnās cōpiās in Galliam¹ trādūxērunt. 11. Gallī,

---

¹ Gallia, ae: *France.*

ā prīncipibus ad bellum *incitātī* atque *spē* victōriae *sublātī*, castra nostra vallō altō *mūnīta* oppugnāvērunt. 12. Interim mīlitēs, *praesidiī* causā in castrīs relictī, impetum hostium fortiter sustinēbant. 13. Hostēs autem cōpiās suās ad flūmen *ductās* īnstrūxērunt. 14. Multīs nuntiīs litterīsque *commōtus*, Caesar legiōnēs novās in Italiā coēgit et quī eās in Galliam *dēdūceret* lēgātum mīsit. 15. Rēx prīncipēs propter praemia ab eīs sibi *data* laudāvit.

Homō doctus in sē dīvitiās[1] **semper habet.**

—Phaedrus

EXERCISE 339

1. Translate;
2. Parse the italicized words:

1. Imperātor, vehementer *commōtus*, virtūtem mīlitum ōrātiōne cōnfirmāvit. 2. Mīlitēs, ā Caesare *laudātī* atque nōmine *appellātī*, impetum equitātūs sustinuērunt. 3. Ducēs Gallōrum, caede prīncipum vehementer *perturbātī*, arma ad bellum ā sē comparāta Rōmānīs trādidērunt. 4. Dux, vir fortis, collem ab equitibus *occupātum* et *vallō* et fossā mūnīvit. 5. Barbarī impetum in mīlitēs impedīmentīs *impedītōs* fēcērunt. 6. Caesar, perīculō lēgātōrum *perturbātus*, in fīnēs barbarōrum magnīs itineribus cum omnibus *cōpiīs* contendit. 7. Litterīs lēgātī *commōtus*, Caesar prīncipēs Gallōrum ad *sē vocāvit* atque quaesīvit quantae gentēs in armīs essent. 8. Equitēs ad flūmen *collocātī* hostēs in fugam dedērunt atque ita magnam eōrum partem tēlīs ac gladiīs occīdērunt. 9. Legiōnēs ad fīnēs hostium hībernōrum causā *collocātae* servum ad Caesarem mīsērunt quī auxilia peteret. 10. Centuriōnēs et tribūnī mīlitum ā Caesare nōmine *appellātī* diūtius cōpiās hostium sustinuērunt. 11. Hostēs, spē victōriae *cōnfirmātī, usque ad* prīmam aciem nostram celeriter appropin-

---

[1] dīvitiae, dīvitiārum: *riches, wealth.*

quāvērunt. 12. Nostrī, spē auxiliī *cōnfirmātī*, usque ad noctem pugnāvērunt. 13. Imperātor, vehementer *commōtus*, exercitum prō portīs statim īnstrūxit.

EXERCISE 340
[Essential]
Translate:

1. When the enemy, having been routed by the legions, fled to the mountains,[1] Caesar sent the cavalry to kill them. 2. The barbarians, alarmed by the arrival of Caesar, did not attack the hill seized by the Roman legion. 3. Led on by hope of victory and safety, the Gauls exchanged hostages and prepared arms to wage war with the Romans. 4. Moved by the authority and favor of Caesar, the Gauls carried grain into winter quarters. 5. They attacked our men, encumbered by the baggage train and held in by mountains. 6. The barbarians, having been overcome in many battles, surrendered themselves and all their possessions to the lieutenant. 7. Caesar, having been informed in how great danger the legions were, sent the cavalry to help them. 8. The general, having been informed what race of men dwelt there, led his army secretly across the river. 9. Men loved by God do not fear danger or death. 10. The town, having been taken by storm, was burned. 11. They left many bodies on the hill seized by the Romans. 12. On account of the devastated[2] fields there was a scarcity of grain. 13. Caesar learned the plans approved by the barbarians in council before his arrival.

EXERCISE 341
[Review]

1. What is the gender of **manus**?
2. What is the difference between **ubi** and **quō**?
3. Translate: The barbarians surrendered to Caesar.
4. Translate in two ways: They approached the camp.

---

[1] Translate *sought the mountains by flight.*
[2] *devastate:* **vastō,** *1, tr.*

LESSON 31: *HIC, HAEC, HOC*

1. THE DECLENSION OF *HIC, HAEC, HOC*

There are words in all languages that merely POINT OUT the person or thing about which we are talking:

> Which do you mean?
> I mean <u>that</u> one.
> I mean <u>this</u> one.

Such words as *THAT* (pl. *THOSE*), *THIS* (pl. *THESE*) are called DEMONSTRATIVE PRONOUNS, *i.e.*, "POINTING-OUT" words. (**Dēmōnstrō** in Latin means *I show, I point out*.)

ASSIGNMENT: Study the declension of **hic, haec, hoc,** *this* (pl. *these*), GRAMMAR, No. 133.

RULE FOR POSITION: *HIC, HAEC, HOC* GENER-
ALLY PRECEDES THE NOUN IT MODIFIES.

EXERCISE 342

1. Decline;
2. Give the meaning of each case:

1. hic homō
2. hic vir
3. haec via
4. haec legiō
5. hoc rēgnum
6. hoc flūmen

EXERCISE 343

1. Supply the correct form of hic;
2. Translate:

1. cum .... tribūnō mīlitum
2. per .... silvās
3. in .... flūmen
4. propter .... rem
5. prō .... oppidō
6. in .... ponte
7. trāns .... flūmen
8. in .... prōvinciā

9. in .... perīculō
10. post .... bellum
11. in .... collibus
12. propter .... vulnera
13. post .... montem
14. cum .... puerō
15. in .... agrīs
16. sine .... virō
17. post .... victōriam
18. propter .... victōriās
19. in .... montēs
20. cum .... servīs
21. propter .... metum

22. cum .... imperātōre
23. in .... mundum
24. in .... itinere
25. per .... agrōs
26. plēnus .... rērum
27. ad .... flūmen
28. ad .... castra
29. in .... mīlitēs
30. sine .... spē
31. propter .... causam
32. in .... proeliō
33. dē .... rē
34. in .... cīvitāte

Sāncte Jōsēph, ōrā prō nōbīs!

EXERCISE 344

1. Put these phrases in the genitive and dative;
2. Translate:

1. haec mora
2. hoc peccātum
3. haec rēs pūblica
4. haec manus
5. haec mēns

6. hic dolor
7. hoc praesidium
8. haec causa
9. haec fuga
10. hic mōs

---

2. USES OF *HIC, HAEC, HOC*

ASSIGNMENT: Study the uses of **hic, haec, hoc,** GRAMMAR, Nos. 793-794.

When **hic** is used as an adjective, the general rule for agreement, GRAMMAR, No. 477, applies.

When **hic** is used as a pronoun, the general rule for agreement, GRAMMAR, No. 479, applies.

VOCABULARY

contrā, *prep. w. acc.* { against / opposite

ā tergō { in the rear / from the rear

ā fronte { in the front / from the front

summus, a, um { highest / greatest / very great

RELATED ENGLISH WORDS
Contradiction; summit; contrary.

EXERCISE 345
[**Hic** as an Adjective]
1. *Translate;*
2. *Explain the agreement of the italicized words:*

1. *Haec* cīvitās lībera nostra est; *hī* agrī atque *hae* urbēs nostrae sunt. Itaque prō *hāc* cīvitāte līberā contrā hostēs fortiter pugnābimus atque *hōs* agrōs et *hās* urbēs semper sine morā dēfendēmus.
2. Multa et magna erant bella et victōriae patrum nostrōrum. Nōnne *haec* bella atque *hae* victōriae in *hāc* cīvitāte semper memoriā tenēbuntur?
3. Gallī, ā Caesare coāctī, multōs obsidēs ad *eum* mīserant. *Hōs* obsidēs Caesar, cum Gallī bellum gererent, occīdit. *Hāc* rē perturbātī, Gallī mīlitēs novōs celeriter coēgērunt ut Rōmānōs vincerent.
4. Prīmī mīlitēs trāns flūmen vēnerant; reliquī in flūmine erant. In *hōs* mīlitēs ita impedītōs barbarī subitō impetum ā tergō fortiter fēcērunt atque omnēs ferē occīdērunt.
5. Amīcī quī in rēbus difficilibus nōs adjuvant sunt vērī et certī amīcī. *Hōs* amīcōs dīligāmus.
6. Caesar, cum *hunc* nuntium audīvisset, litterās ad lēgātum

mīsit. Lēgātus vērō, *hīs* litterīs vehementer commōtus et impetū hostium territus, legiōnēs castrīs continuit, at equitēs ad Caesarem mīsit.

EXERCISE 346

[Hic as a Pronoun]

1. Translate;
2. Explain the agreement and reference of the
italicized words:

1. Erant in exercitū Caesaris equitēs aliēnī. *Hōs* Caesar propter fidem *eōrum* atque virtūtem vēram saepe laudāvit.
2. Ā tergō subitō cernēbantur equitēs hostium. Erant autem in prīmā aciē legiōnēs integrae. Itaque *hae* omnēs ferē impetūs hostium sustinuērunt.
3. Rōmānī multōs Chrīstiānōs propter lēgem et vēritātem Chrīstī occīdērunt. Nōnne *hōrum* memoriam semper laudābimus?
4. Germānī victōriae spē adductī rēgisque auctōritāte coāctī, omnēs cōpiās flūmen trādūxerant. Contrā Gallōs pugnābant; frūmenta et oppida occupāta incendēbant; prīncipēs atque rēgēs Gallōrum occīdēbant; omnēs agrōs vastābant. Gallī, vērō, vehementer commōtī et territī, lēgātōs ad Caesarem mīsērunt quī auxilium peterent. Caesar, cum *haec* omnia audīvisset, statim cum omnibus cōpiīs in fīnēs Gallōrum contendit ut Germānōs trāns flūmen ageret.

EXERCISE 347

[Hic as an Adjective and as a Pronoun]

Translate:

1. The enemy easily aroused the neighboring tribes to war, for these tribes were brave and eager for the glory of victory.
2. Caesar fought with many kings and chiefs. These he often killed.
3. The lieutenant pitched a camp in the fields of the barbarians. This camp, fortified by a ditch and a rampart, he bravely defended.

4. The centurion sent a letter to Caesar concerning this affair. Caesar, alarmed by this letter, sent new legions into the province. These legions defended the province and drove the enemy across the river into their own territory. 5. The barbarians suddenly made an attack on the legion from the rear. This legion easily withstood the attack.

"And they put above His head the
charge against Him, written,

HIC EST JĒSŪS RĒX JŪDAEŌRUM."[1]

—Matthew 27:37

EXERCISE 348
[Review]

1. Translate;
2. Parse the italicized words:

1. *Vōs amīcōs* appellō. 2. *Legiōnem flūmen* trādūxit. 3. Multī Rōmānī *amīcitiae causā* cum exercitū Caesaris erant. 4. *Barbarōs in fugam* dedit. 5. Fortiter *pugnātum est.*

---

[1] Jūdaeus, ī: *a Jew.*

LESSON 32: THE PREPOSITIONS
EX (Ē), AB (Ā), AND DĒ

In expressions of PLACE:

1. The prepositions **EX** (**Ē**) or **DĒ** with the ablative mean *OUT OF* or *FROM*.

When the motion begins, the person or thing moving is INSIDE THE PLACE:

> **Dē (ex) fīnibus hostium vēnit.**
> *He came from the territory of the enemy.*

2. The preposition **AB** (**Ā**) with the ablative means *AWAY FROM* or *FROM*.

When the motion begins, the person or thing moving is NOT INSIDE the place:

> **Ab hōc locō vēnit.**
> *He came away from (from) this place.*

3. The preposition **DĒ** with the ablative may also mean *DOWN FROM* or *FROM*.

The motion is DOWNWARDS.

> **Dē hōc monte vēnit.** *He came down from this mountain.*

AB Loco

De Monte

336

Ex Loco

STUDY THESE EXAMPLES:

dē mūrō, *down from (from) the wall*

ē castrīs, *out of (from) the camp*

ā castrīs, *away from the camp*

ex flūmine, *out of the river*

ā flūmine, *away from the river*

VOCABULARY

discēdō, discēdere, discessī, discessūrus, 3, intr.	*depart* / *withdraw*
nāvis, nāvis[1]	*ship*
ex (ē), prep. w. abl.	*out of* / *from*
ab (ā), prep. w. abl.	*away from* / *from*
dē, prep. w. abl.	*down from* / *from*
cadō, cadere, cecidī, cāsūrus, 3, intr.	*fall*

NOTE

The forms **ā** (for **ab**) and **ē** (for **ex**) are never used before words beginning with a vowel or *h*.

RELATED ENGLISH WORDS

The secretary of the *Navy* takes care of *naval* affairs. The song ended in a beautiful *cadence*.

EXERCISE 349
[Essential]
Translate:

1. This soldier fell from the wall. 2. Caesar hastened out of the territory of the enemy. 3. He departed from the province. 4. He

---

[1] The ablative may be either **nāvī** or **nāve.**

moved camp from this place.   5. The army came out of the
forest.   6. This sailor who had been killed by a dart fell from
the ship.   7. The cavalry were sent out of this camp.   8. The
legion hastened down from this hill.   9. These barbarians made
an attack from the hill.   10. They departed from this river.
11. This army was led out of winter quarters.   12. They came
out of this city.   13. The centurion fell from this bridge into
the river.   14. This centurion was carried out of the river.
15. This soldier came away from the river.   16. These were led
from the fields of the barbarians.   17. They were leading these
hostages out of the town.   18. Caesar hastened from this city to
Gaul.   19. This (man) hastened out of the territory of the Gauls.
20. These brave soldiers did not withdraw from the battle line.

EXERCISE 350
[Essential]

1. Translate;
2. Illustrate your translations with drawings or
   diagrams:

1. Multī nautae, tēlīs occīsī, dē nāvibus in aquam cecidērunt.
2. Exercitum ex hostium agrīs trāns flūmen in prōvinciam trā-
dūxerat.   3. Legiōnēs novās ex Italiā in Galliam dēdūxit.
4. Caesar, cum haec audīvisset, oppidum ex quō dux hostium
mīlitēs dūxerat oppugnāvit.   5. Ad flūmen diū atque ācriter
pugnātum est.   6. Omnēs ferē hostēs, tēlīs occīsī, dē mūrō cecidērunt.   7. Nōnne in hōc proeliō multī cecidērunt?   8. Prīmā
lūce hic lēgātus, nōmine Labiēnus, castra ab hōc locō in collem
mōvit.   9. Hī barbarī dē montibus in agmen impedītum subitō
impetum fēcērunt.   10. Virtūtem atque fidem hōrum mīlitum
nostrōrum quī in hīs proeliīs cecidērunt semper memoriā tenēbimus.   11. Caesar auxilia ex castrīs in prīmam aciem mīsit.
12. Hīs litterīs commōtus, Caesar, cum agrī barbarōrum vastātī
essent et frūmenta omnia incēnsa essent, exercitum ex fīnibus
hostium per loca difficilia et impedīta trāns flūmen in prōvinciam
salūtis causā dēdūxit.

MOMENTS AT MASS NO. 3

At the most solemn moment of the Mass—when all are silent and waiting—the priest, bowing low over the altar, unites himself with the Eternal High Priest Christ and speaks, in His name, these sacred words:

HOC EST ENIM CORPUS MEUM

—and the Lord Jesus Christ is present on the altar.

EXERCISE 351
[Review]

1. Translate;
2. Explain the use of the italicized pronouns:

1. Mīles fugā silvās petīvit nē hostēs *sē* occīderent. 2. Hostēs mōre *suō* clāmōrem sustulērunt. 3. Barbarī impetum in hīberna fēcērunt. Itaque Caesar obsidēs *eōrum* interfēcit. 4. Gallī obsidēs inter *sē* dant.

Sāncta Agnēs, ōrā prō nōbīs!

LESSON 33: *ILLE* AND *IS*

ASSIGNMENT: Study GRAMMAR, Nos. 134-135 and 795-798.
You have already learned the declension of **is, ea, id.**

VOCABULARY

is, ea, id
: *that* (as a demonstrative)
: *he, she, it* (as a personal pronoun)

ille, illa, illud
: *that* (as a demonstrative)
: *he, she, it* (as a personal pronoun)

numquam, *adv.* never

praetereā, *adv.*
: *besides*
: *furthermore*

ratiō, ratiōnis
: *reason*
: *manner*

NOTE

Ratiō is used in a great number of meanings; the vocabulary gives only the most general idea of them. Be sure to translate **ratiō** into good English as the sense and context demand.

RELATED ENGLISH WORD

A *rational* explanation.

EXERCISE 352

1. *Supply the proper forms of: (a)* **ille,** *(b)* **is;**
2. *Translate:*

1. cum .... nautīs
2. prō .... portā
3. in .... prōvinciā
4. ex .... silvīs
5. propter .... victōriam
6. cum .... amīcō
7. prō .... Chrīstiānīs
8. contrā .... dominum
9. cum .... fīliīs
10. per .... Gallōs
11. sine .... gladiīs
12. in .... mūrō

341

13. apud .... servōs	21. trāns .... flūmen
14. in .... oppidō	22. propter .... vulnera
15. dē .... colle	23. propter salūtem .... Rōmānōrum
16. in .... ponte	24. propter inopiam .... rērum
17. ex .... portū	25. dē causā .... bellī
18. .... reī causā	26. propter .... lēgem
19. .... virīs	27. dē .... montibus
20. .... hominum	28. .... hominī

> Omnēs Sānctī discipulī[1] Dominī, ōrāte prō nōbīs!

EXERCISE 353
[Essential]

1. Translate;
2. Explain the use of the italicized pronouns:

1. Omnēs Gallī inter *sē* obsidēs dabant et dē bellī ratiōne agēbant. *Hāc* rē commōtus Caesar legiōnēs novās ex Italiā in Galliam statim dēdūxit. *Illī* vērō subitō lēgātōs ad *eum* mīsērunt quī amīcitiam cum *eō* cōnfirmārent.

2. Apud Americānōs Lincoln et Washingtonius plūrimum laudantur. *Hic* enim rem pūblicam īnstituit;[2] *ille* vērō *eam* nōn sine labōre cōnservāvit.

3. Et Hannibal et Caesar magnās cōpiās per Alpēs dūxērunt. *Hic* mīlitēs ex Italiā dēdūxit ut Galliam pācāret, *ille* vērō in Italiam exercitum dūxit ut Rōmānōs vinceret et Rōmam occupāret.

4. *Eī* quī sine spē pugnant, numquam fortiter pugnant.

5. *Eum* quī rem pūblicam nostram īnstituit[2] memoriā semper tenēbimus.

6. Et Hitler et Caesar exercitum in Galliam dūxērunt ut Gallōs vincerent. *Ille* cōpiās ex Germāniā in Galliam mīsit quae *eam*

---

[1] discipulus, ī: *disciple.*
[2] īnstituō, īnstituere, īnstituī, īnstitūtus, 3, *tr.: found, establish.*

vastārent et vincerent, *hic* exercitum ex Italiā per montēs in Galliam dūxit ut *eam* pācāret atque occupāret. *Ille* ā Gallīs *eōrum*que sociīs victus est, *hic* vērō imperium Galliae diū obtinuit.

7. Caesar, "Germānī et Gallī," inquit, "saepe inter *sē* proeliīs contendēbant. Aut enim Gallī fīnēs *suōs* dēfendēbant aut in *illōrum* fīnēs cōpiās *suās* trādūcēbant."

8. Gallōrum dux suīs, "Ego vōs," inquit, "in *hunc* locum vocāvī ut dē bellī ratiōne agam. *Illī* *(he points towards the distant Roman camp)* enim in fīnēs nostrōs vēnērunt ut *hōs* agrōs et *haec* oppida occupārent atque incenderent. Praetereā *illī* fortēs et victōriae cupidī sunt. Ad omnia parātī sunt. Dē vītīs nostrīs atque dē commūnī Galliae salūte cum *eīs* contendimus. Itaque *eōs* quī fortiter contrā *illōs* nōn pugnābunt meā manū occīdam. Pugnāte usque ad mortem! Dēfendite *hōs* agrōs, *haec* oppida, *hōs* puerōs nostrōs ab *eīs*. Hostēs pellāmus, vincāmus, occīdāmus!"

EXERCISE 354
[Essential]
Translate:

1. That manner of battle was praised by the Romans. 2. Besides, those tribes have never given hostages to the Romans. 3. On account of those reasons, Caesar pitched camp at the river. 4. Besides, those tribes have always fought against the Roman legions. 5. Led on by those reasons they fought against us, but they will never conquer us. 6. These they repulsed but those they killed. 7. He who loves God will never leave the Christian faith. 8. These men came down from the mountains; but those remained in the mountains. 9. The camp was assaulted by these, but the soldiers encumbered in the river were attacked by those. 10. The cavalry were put to flight, but the soldiers took up a position on that hill and did not yield. To these, therefore, the general gave thanks, but to those rewards were not given. 11. Those chiefs, moved by the authority of Caesar, gave him hostages.

12. He asked where those tribes dwelt.　13. They will never seize this hill, but we shall seize that camp.　14. That sailor, having been killed by a dart, fell from the ship.　15. Let us love God and all men.

EXERCISE 355
[Review]

Explain the mood and tense of the italicized verbs:

1. Rogō num Chrīstus *sit* Deus.　2. Rogō num Caesar barbarōs *vīcerit*.　3. Caesar, cum in Galliā *esset,* cum Gallīs bellum gessit. 4. Caesar, cum haec *vīdisset,* auxilia ad mīlitēs suōs mīsit.

Nunc aut numquam!

LESSON 34: ABLATIVE CONSTRUCTIONS

1. THE ABLATIVE OF SEPARATION

ASSIGNMENT: Study Grammar, No. 766.

VOCABULARY

These words may take an ablative of separation :[1]

līberō, *1, tr.; abl. of separation*	*free (from)*
vacuus, a, um; *abl. of separation*	*empty (of)*
līber, lībera, līberum; *abl. of separation*	*free (from)*
prohibeō, *2, tr.; abl. of separation*	$\left\{\begin{array}{l}\textit{ward off (from)}\\\textit{prevent}\end{array}\right.$

These words MAY have **ab** (**ā**) with THINGS. They regularly have **ab** (**ā**) with PERSONS:

tūtus, a, um	*safe (from)*
dēfendō, dēfendere, dēfendī, dēfēnsus, *3, tr.*	*defend (from)*

RELATED ENGLISH WORDS

A *vacuum*. We fought to *liberate* the conquered countries. We tried *prohibition* once. Smoking is *prohibited* in streetcars. *"Liberty"* is the battle cry of Americans.

EXERCISE 356
[Essential]
Translate:

1. Bonōrum vīta vacua est metū. 2. Rēgēs metū līberī numquam sunt. 3. Caesar vērō, "Tē," inquit, "ab hostibus dēfendam." 4. Līberā mē, Domine, ab eīs quī vītam meam petunt. 5. Castra, nātūrā locī mūnīta, ab omnī perīculō tūta erant. 6. Rogāvit num mūrus ā mīlitibus vacuus esset. 7. Gallī saepe cum Ger-

---

[1] The words in this vocabulary, of course, take an ablative of separation *only* when the sense requires it.

mānīs quī trāns flūmen Rhēnum incolunt proeliīs contendunt. Aut enim suīs fīnibus eōs prohibent aut in eōrum fīnibus bellum gerunt. 8. Caesar in Galliam missus est ut prōvinciam ab hostibus dēfenderet. 9. Post adventum Caesaris prōvincia tūta ab hostibus erat. 10. Lincoln, vir magnus et nōbilis, servōs in nostrā cīvitāte līberāvit.

MOMENTS AT MASS NO. 4

THE AGNUS DEI

Shortly before the Communion the priest bows before the altar and says:

Agnus[1] Deī, quī tollis peccāta mundī, miserēre nōbīs.

Agnus[1] Deī, quī tollis peccāta mundī, miserēre nōbīs.

Agnus[1] Deī, quī tollis peccāta mundī, dōnā[2] nōbīs pācem.

EXERCISE 357

[Essential]

Translate:

We are free from fear and the power of foreign nations. In the beginning we were freed by brave men from the power of a foreign people. In 1812[3] the attacks of our enemies were warded off from our territory by our soldiers and sailors. In 1861[4] we waged war among ourselves, but in that war the slaves were freed from their masters and the republic preserved. Besides, after that war, peace and friendship were established[5] among us and have always been preserved.

The Japanese,[6] led on by the influence of their chiefs and

---

[1] agnus, ī: *lamb.*
[2] dōnō, *1, tr.: give.*
[3] *in 1812:* annō millēsimō octingentēsimō duodecimō.
[4] *in 1861:* annō millēsimō octingentēsimō sexāgēsimō prīmō.
[5] *establish:* cōnfirmō, *1, tr.*
[6] *Japanese:* Japō, Japōnis.

PEARL HARBOR

leaders and eager for glory and empire, made an attack on our
harbors and fields. But we have been defended against them by
brave men. The nations which they have conquered were freed
from their power; the peoples against whom they have waged
war will be safe from slaughter and death; their fields shall be
cleared[1] of foreign armies. Let us thank the brave men who have
defended us from our enemies. Let us praise them and help them.
Let us always hold in memory their brave deeds,[2] and, prepared
for death and glory, let us always preserve the republic which
they have freed from fear and the dangers of war. Besides, let us
always give thanks to God our Father.

2. REVIEW OF ABLATIVE CONSTRUCTIONS

STUDY: Ablative of agent, GRAMMAR, No. 764.

               Ablative of means, GRAMMAR, No. 765.

---

[1] *cleared of = empty (of).*
[2] *deed:* **factum, ī;** or *deeds:* **rēs gestae.**

Ablative of accompaniment, GRAMMAR, No. 772.
Ablative of place, GRAMMAR, Nos. 915-916.
Ablative of cause, GRAMMAR, No. 781.
Ablative of separation, GRAMMAR, No. 766.

REVIEW VOCABULARY

plēnus, a, um; *w. gen. or abl.*	*full*
cum, *prep. w. abl.*	*with*
in, *prep. w. abl.*	*in* *on*
prō, *prep. w. abl.*	*in front of (before)* *on behalf of (for)*
ab (ā), *prep. w. abl.*	*by* *from*
dē, *prep. w. abl.*	*concerning (about)* *down from* *from*
sine, *prep. w. abl.*	*without*
absum, abesse, āfuī, āfutūrus, *intr.;* ab (ā) *w. abl.*	*am away* *am distant*

NOTE

1. In the expression **mūrum hominibus complet, hominibus,** though meaning *persons,* is an ablative of means.

2. When **locō** is modified by an adjective, **in** is often omitted.

3. **Proeliō** is generally used without a preposition: **proeliō,** *in battle.*

EXERCISE 358

1. Translate;

2. Explain the italicized constructions:

1. Legiō *ex Italiā* in Galliam *ā Caesare* missa est. 2. Imperātor *cum omnibus cōpiīs* suīs in prōvinciam contendit. 3. Hīberna, *nātūrā* locī atque *vallō* mūnīta, ab omnī hostium *impetū* tūta erant. 4. Nōnne flūmen *aquae* plēnum est? 5. Hostēs, hāc

caede vehementer commōtī, dē *bellō* in commūnī Galliae conciliō agēbant. 6. Prō commūnī *salūte* nostrā ad arma vōs vocō. 7. Marīa, Māter Jēsū Chrīstī, *grātiā* erat plēna. 8. Hostēs, multīs *proeliīs* victī, sē suaque omnia lēgātō dēdidērunt. 9. Ille lēgātus, nōmine Labiēnus, *impetū* hostium perturbātus mūrum *hominibus* complēvit. 10. Num lēgātus castra *locō* aliēnō posuit? 11. Sine *morā* mīlitēs prō *portā* īnstrūctī sunt. 12. Hīs *litterīs* commōtus, lēgātus in fīnēs barbarōrum contendit nē *ā castrīs* abesset. 13. Barbarī, hāc *victōriā* sublātī, *dē montibus* impetum in agmen nostrum impedītum fēcērunt. 14. Prīmā lūce *ex eō locō* castra movet. 15. *Ā flūmine* in montēs celeriter contendit. 16. Multī, *tēlīs* occīsī, *dē mūrō* in hostēs cecidērunt.

Ab omnī malō
Līberā nōs, Domine!

EXERCISE 359
[Essential Review of Unit Nine]
Translate:

1. The Japanese, having been driven out of the fortifications, sought the forest in flight. 2. They departed from this river that they might be safe from attack. 3. Led on by the influence of their leaders, the Japanese suddenly made an attack on our harbors. 4. These nations were our allies, but against those nations we waged war. 5. The enemy came secretly out of the forest and were suddenly seen in the rear. Besides, the cavalry of the enemy made an attack from the front. 6. Having been killed by a dart, he fell from the ship into the water. 7. We were freed by brave men from foreign power. 8. He was praised by Caesar on account of his very great courage and faithfulness. 9. The encumbered soldiers were being killed by the cavalry of the enemy. 10. The soldiers, hindered by the nature of the place, withdrew. 11. The camp was empty. For the soldiers, alarmed by the speech of the chief, had withdrawn

into the province. 12. We shall ward off the enemy from these cities and fields. They shall never seize these fields and these cities. 13. The cavalry of the enemy were hindering our column. The leaders of the enemy therefore approved this manner of war. But we warded off their attacks.

EXERCISE 360
[Essential Formal Review of Unit Nine]

1. How do you find the perfect participle passive?
2. Explain the meaning of these phrases: **mīlitēs impedītī; agmen impedītum; loca impedīta.**
3. How may **hic, haec, hoc** be used?
4. Explain the difference between **ex, dē, ab.**
5. When are **ā** and **ē** used for **ab** and **ex**?
6. Explain the uses of **ille** and **is.**
7. Give the rule for the ablative of separation. Give examples.

Vēritās vōs līberābit.
—John 8:32

UNIT TEN

LESSON 35: *POSSUM;* THE INFINITIVE IN NOUN CONSTRUCTIONS

1. INDICATIVE OF *POSSUM*

POSSUM, *I am able, I can,* is a compound of **pote,** *able,* and **sum,** *I am.* The present tenses of the indicative are formed:

1. By prefixing **pos-** to any form of **sum** which begins with an **s** (*e. g.,* **pos** + **sum** = **possum**).

2. By prefixing **pot** to all other forms of **sum** (*e. g.,* **pot** + **eram** = **poteram**).

Now, without looking in the GRAMMAR, complete the conjugation of **possum:**

PRESENT

possum, *I am able, I can*
potes, *you are able, you can*
etc.

IMPERFECT

poteram, *I was able, I could*
etc.

FUTURE

poterō, *I shall be able*
etc.

The perfect tenses are formed with the usual endings on the perfect stem, **potu-.**

ASSIGNMENT: Study GRAMMAR, Nos. 399-401.

VOCABULARY

possum, posse, potuī, *irreg., intr.* $\left\{ \begin{array}{l} \textit{am able} \\ \textit{can} \end{array} \right.$

NOTE

I am unable, etc., is **nōn possum,** *etc.*

351

EXERCISE 361

Translate:

1. Potest. 2. Poteram. 3. Num possunt? 4. Nōn possum.
5. Potueram. 6. Poterit. 7. Poterunt. 8. Potuērunt. 9. Nōn
poterant. 10. Quis poterat? 11. Potesne? 12. Possumus.
13. Potuistis. 14. Nōn potestis. 15. Nōnne potuit?

Glōria tibi, Domine!

EXERCISE 362

Translate:

1. I can. 2. He was unable. 3. They could. 4. Who was able?
5. He will be able. 6. They were unable. 7. Were they able?
8. We can. 9. I am unable. 10. They had been able. 11. We
can't, can we? 12. We have been able. 13. They were able.
14. You are able, aren't you? 15. Why can't they? 16. He had
been able. 17. Why was he unable? 18. You can't, can you?

2. THE INFINITIVE AS SUBJECT, PREDICATE NOUN, AND OBJECT

The PRESENT INFINITIVE ACTIVE is the SECOND
principal part of regular active verbs (see GRAMMAR, Nos. 209,
219-221). Thus:

Laudō, <u>laudāre,</u> laudāvī, laudātus, *1, tr.* *praise*

Present Infinitive Active: LAUD-ĀRE *to praise*

The PRESENT INFINITIVE PASSIVE is formed on the
present stem. For the endings study GRAMMAR, Nos. 284, 292-294.

Present Infinitive Passive: LAUD-ĀRĪ *to be praised*

The infinitive is a NEUTER VERBAL NOUN.
As a NOUN it is used as SUBJECT, PREDICATE NOUN,
or OBJECT. The infinitive is always NEUTER.

As subject: **Ōrāre est bonum.**

> *To pray is good (is a good thing).*

As predicate noun: **Labōrāre est ōrāre.**

> *To work is to pray.*

As object: **Venīre parant.**

> *They prepare to come.*

As a VERB the infinitive has TENSE, takes OBJECTS, and is modified by ADVERBS and ADVERBIAL PHRASES.

Infinitive with object: **Mōs est fortēs laudāre.**

> *It is a custom to praise the brave.*

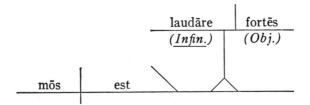

Adverbial modifier: **Fortiter pugnāre possunt.**

> *They can fight bravely.*

Passive voice: **Oppidum expugnārī nōn potuit.**

> *The town could not be taken by storm.*

The PRESENT INFINITIVE, denoting another action of the same subject, COMPLETES the meaning of such verbs as **possum,** *am able, can;* **contendō,** *strive, hasten;* **cōnsuēvī,** *have become accustomed.*

> **Redīre contendunt.**
>
> *They hasten to return.*

> **Gallī sē dēfendere nōn potuērunt.**
>
> *The Gauls were unable to defend themselves.*

Notice that in most cases the Latin construction is just like the English. After *can* the *to* of the English infinitive is not used. The infinitive, when used as subject or predicate noun, may also be translated by the English verbal noun in *-ing* or by a noun.

Ōrāre est bonum. *To pray (prayer, praying) is good.*

VOCABULARY

possum, posse, potuī, *irreg.; w. infin.*	$\begin{cases} am\ able \\ can \end{cases}$
adversus, a, um; *w. dat.*	$\begin{cases} facing\ (towards) \\ unfavorable \end{cases}$
proximus, a, um; *w. dat.*	$\begin{cases} nearest \\ next \end{cases}$
jam, *adv.*	$\begin{cases} already \\ now\ (at\ that\ time) \end{cases}$
prīmum, *adv.*	*first*

RELATED ENGLISH WORDS

Is it *possible* to fly to the moon? Penicillin is a *potent* drug. Meet your *adversary* fairly. Do men pray more in *adversity?* We must avoid *proximate* occasions of sin.

RELATED LATIN WORDS

Prīmus; ad (versus means *having been turned*).

REVIEW VOCABULARY

parō, *1, tr.; w. infin.*	$\begin{cases} prepare \\ get\ ready \end{cases}$
timeō, timēre, timuī, *2, tr.; w. infin.*	$\begin{cases} fear \\ am\ afraid \end{cases}$
parātus, a, um; *w.* ad *or infin.*	$\begin{cases} prepared\ (for \\ ready \end{cases}$
contendō, contendere, contendī, *3, intr.; w. infin.*	$\begin{cases} strive \\ contend \\ hasten \end{cases}$

NOTE

1. The *w. infin.* in the vocabularies indicates that these verbs and **parātus** MAY, when the SENSE requires it, take an infinitive to complete their meaning. They may also take other constructions. For example, note the various uses of **parātus**:

Ad mortem parātī sunt. *They are ready for death.*
Pugnāre parātī sunt. *They are prepared to fight.*
Parātī sunt. *They are prepared.*

2. **Adversus, a, um** is frequently used with the plural of **rēs** to mean *adversity* (literally, *unfavorable things*).

in rēbus adversīs, *in adversity*

EXERCISE 363

1. Give the present infinitive active;
2. Give the present infinitive passive:

1. ōrō	5. audiō	9. timeō
2. retineō	6. dēfendō	10. agō
3. compleō	7. vocō	11. trādō
4. incendō	8. videō	12. mūniō

EXERCISE 364

Translate:

1. Venīre parant. 2. Peccātum est mātrem nōn dīligere. 3. Manēre possunt. 4. Arma parāre ūtile est. 5. Exspectāre timuērunt. 6. Pervenīre poterunt. 7. Rōma dēfendī nōn potest. 8. Agrōs vastāre parant. 9. Deum laudāre sānctum est. 10. Castra dēfendere parātī erant. 11. Gallī pācārī possunt. 12. Hīberna mūnīre nōn potuērunt. 13. Impedīrī nōn potest. 14. Tūtum est in castrīs manēre. 15. Nōn est mōs populī Rōmānī obsidēs dare.

EXERCISE 365

Translate:

1. They are prepared to yield. 2. It is difficult to storm a camp. 3. They cannot be freed. 4. It is easy to incite the Gauls

to war. 5. They are preparing to go away. 6. It is a sin not to love one's[1] father. 7. They are afraid to fight. 8. He strives to conquer the barbarians. 9. They are afraid to be seen. 10. It is difficult to fight in the mountains.

WARNING!

THE INFINITIVE IS NOT USED IN CLASSICAL LATIN
TO EXPRESS PURPOSE

They prepare to wage war.
(Infinitive as object)
Bellum gerere parant.

BUT: *They prepare arms to wage war.*
(Purpose!)
Arma parant ut bellum gerant.

EXERCISE 366
[Essential]

1. Translate;
2. Diagram Sentences 3, 6, and 9:

1. Nōnne omnēs hominēs ōrāre possunt? 2. Amīcus certus in rēbus adversīs facile cernī potest. 3. Peccātum est contrā amīcōs pugnāre. 4. Propter locī nātūram hostēs adversī nōbīs cōnsistere nōn potuērunt. 5. Hannibal, Caesar, Napoleon, magnās cōpiās per montēs difficilēs et altōs dūcere potuērunt. 6. Galliam pācāre difficile fuit. 7. Mīlitēs Americānī quī in Bataan erant, propter omnium rērum inopiam, impetūs hostium diūtius sustinēre nōn jam poterant. 8. Caesar prīmum cum eīs gentibus quae prōvinciae proximae erant bellum gessit, tum in omnēs partēs Galliae lēgātōs legiōnēsque mīsit ut eās etiam partēs explōrāret, cognōsceret, vinceret. 9. In rēbus adversīs nōn facile est fortiter pugnāre. 10. Possumusne nōs Americānī fīnēs nostrōs ab omnibus

---

[1] Do not translate *one's.*

hostibus dēfendere et eōs ex fīnibus nostrīs pellere? 11. Caesar diū in fīnēs hostium contendit, tum cōnstitit ut novās exspectāret cōpiās. 12. Americānī et Britannī in eam partem Galliae quae adversa Britanniae est magnum exercitum trādūcere potuērunt. 13. Sānctum est Deum laudāre atque dīligere. 14. Prīmum Japōnēs Americānōs propter inopiam eārum rērum quae ad bellum pertinent premere atque proeliō pellere potuērunt. 15. Germānī Gallīs proximī erant, nam trāns flūmen Rhēnum incolēbant. Itaque agrōs Gallōrum facile vastāre poterant.

EXERCISE 367
[Essential]
Translate:

The Americans and British were first able to lead a large army across into Sicily. The Germans had taken up positions opposite them. There was bitter fighting there. But the Germans were not able to withstand the attacks of the Americans and their allies. The Germans had not been able to learn what plan and what manner of battle had been approved by the Allies. And so they were unable to station troops and prepare fortifications. They yielded; and the Allies conquered them. Then the Allies quickly led their forces across into Italy. They made an attack on the Germans both from the front and from the rear. They were able to seize a large part of Italy. After many battles they were able to take Rome. The Germans were now unable to withstand the forces of the Allies and they sought safety in flight. They hastened to those parts of Italy which are nearest the Alps. These places they fortified and there awaited the attack of the Allies.

SENTENTIAE SĒLECTAE

1. Habēre nōn potest Deum patrem quī ecclēsiam[1] nōn habet mātrem. *(St. Cyprian.)*
2. Amīcī probantur rēbus adversīs. *(Proverb.)*
3. Sine virtūte amīcitia esse nōn potest. *(Cicero.)*

---

[1] ecclēsia, ae: *church.*

4. Sine virtūte nihil laudārī potest. *(Adapted from Cicero.)*

5. Malum est cōnsilium quod mūtārī[1] nōn potest. *(Publilius Syrus.)*

6. Fortis cadere potest, cēdere nōn potest. *(Proverb.)*

7. Sānctus Jōannēs, "Quī enim," inquit, "nōn dīligit frātrem suum quem videt, Deum, quem nōn videt, quōmodo[2] potest dīligere? Et hoc mandātum[3] habēmus ā Deō: ut[4] quī dīligit Deum, dīligat et[5] frātrem suum."

READING NO. 26

DĒ RĒGIBUS SĀNCTĪS

Possuntne etiam rēgēs sānctī esse? Rēgēs quī imperium et rēgnum obtinent saepe agrōrum aliēnōrum cupidī sunt; saepe glōriā bellī incitātī magnōs exercitūs contrā gentēs et rēgēs proximōs dūcunt. Saepe etiam frātrēs suōs timent atque occīdunt nē rēgnum suum armīs occupent. Rēgēs tamen sānctī esse possunt. Potuit enim Sānctus Stephanus[6] et rēgnum obtinēre et bella gerere et tamen Deum dīligere. Stephanus rēx fuit Hungariae et populum suum fidem Chrīstiānam docuit.

Ōlim[7] vēnit homō quīdam[8] ad Stephanum ut eum occīderet. Nox erat et Stephanus dormiēbat.[9] Cum ille ad rēgem appropinquāret, gladius subitō ex manū cecidit. Stephanus, cum cōnsilium illīus cognōvisset, neque commōtus neque perturbātus, "Sī[10] Deus mēcum est," inquit, "quis contrā mē erit?"

Praetereā Wenceslāus,[11] Rēx Bohemiae, et sānctus et rēx esse potuit. Ōlim[7] Ratislāus, dux gentis fīnitimae, bellum contrā

---

[1] mūtō, *1, tr.: change* (cf. *mutability*).

[2] quōmodo, *adv.: how.*

[3] mandātum, ī: *command* (cf. *mandate*).

[4] Translate ut by *that . . . should.*

[5] Et here means *also.*

[6] The Feast of St. Stephen of Hungary is celebrated on September 2.

[7] ōlim, *adv.: once.*

[8] quīdam (modifies homō): *a certain.*

[9] dormiō, *4, intr.: sleep.*

[10] sī: *if.*

[11] The Feast of St. Wenceslaus of Bohemia is celebrated on September 28.

GLADIUS EX MANU CECIDIT.

Wenceslāum gerēbat. Cupidus enim erat rēgnī Bohemiae. Wenceslāus lēgātōs ad eum mīsit quī dē pāce et amīcitiā agerent. Tamen amīcitiam cōnfirmāre nōn potuit. Itaque contrā illum cum omnibus cōpiīs contendit. Cum jam hostibus appropinquāret, Wenceslāus, nē caedēs esset, dē novā bellī ratiōne agēbat. *(Here Wenceslaus proposed that the two kings settle the war by single combat in order to save their soldiers' lives. Ratislaus accepted.)* Itaque rēgēs inter exercitūs cōnstitērunt ut inter sē pugnārent. Sed Ratislāus tēlum in sānctum Wenceslāum mittere nōn potuit. Itaque, grātiā Deī victus, amīcitiam cum eō cōnfirmāvit. Ita servātae sunt et mīlitum vītae et rēgnum Bohemiae.

3. SUBJUNCTIVE OF *POSSUM*

ASSIGNMENT: Learn the present and imperfect subjunctive of **possum** in GRAMMAR, Nos. 411-412. Note that the present subjunctive follows the rule given on page 351 of FIRST YEAR LATIN, while the imperfect subjunctive follows the rule given in Lesson 23, page 235.

The perfect and pluperfect subjunctive of **possum** are formed regularly on the perfect stem, **potu-**.

VOCABULARY

cōnstituō, cōnstituere, cōnstituī, cōnstitūtus, *3, tr.; w. infin.*

- place
- set up
- decide
- determine

cōnsuēvī, cōnsuētus, *3, tr. and intr.;*
w. infin.

- have accustomed
- have become accustomed
- am accustomed

sententia, ae

- opinion
- vote

regiō, regiōnis — region

omnīnō, *adv.*

- at all (with negatives like **nōn**)
- altogether
- in all (with numerals)

NOTE

1. **Cōnstituō,** of course, takes an infinitive only when the SENSE requires it.

In montēs contendere cōnstituit. *He determined to hasten into the mountains.*

Mīlitēs in colle cōnstituit. *He placed the soldiers on the hill.*

2. The present tenses of **cōnsuēvī** are not common. Hence only the perfect indicative active and the perfect participle passive are given. But note that the perfect can have a PRESENT meaning and the pluperfect can have a PERFECT meaning:

cōnsuēvī	intransitive	*I have become accustomed =* *I am accustomed*
	transitive	*I have accustomed*
cōnsuēveram	intransitive	*I had become accustomed =* *I was accustomed*
	transitive	*I had accustomed*

RELATED ENGLISH WORDS

Let us defend the *Constitution* of the United States. The judge passes *sentence;* the jury merely determines the fact of the crime. Webster was a *sententious* writer.

> Ab omnī peccātō,
> Līberā nōs, Domine!

EXERCISE 368
[Drill on Forms of **Possum**]
Change the persons in each sentence and translate:

1. Arma parō ut hostēs vincere possim.
   Arma parās ut hostēs vincere possīs, *etc.*
2. Arma parāvī ut hostēs vincere possem, *etc.*
3. Quaerō num hostēs vincere possim, *etc.*
4. Quaerō num hostēs vincere potuerim, *etc.*
5. Quaesīvī num hostēs vincere possem, *etc.*
6. Quaesīvī num hostēs vincere potuissem, *etc.*

EXERCISE 369
Translate:

1. Caesar mīlitēs ad flūmen cōnstituit quō facilius pontem dēfendere possent. 2. Rogāvit quantās cōpiās ex eīs regiōnibus cōgere posset. 3. Rēx sententiam suam lēgātīs ostendere cōnstituit. 4. Lēgātus cōpiās novās exspectāre cōnstituit nē barbarī sē superāre possent. 5. Rogō num Caesar Gallōs vincere potuerit.

6. Gallī, cum per prōvinciam cōpiās suās dūcere nōn potuissent, per loca impedīta atque angusta eās dūcere cōnstituērunt. 7. Caesar, cum illās regiōnēs vastāre nōn potuisset, legiōnēs trāns flūmen in prōvinciam dēdūcere cōnstituit. 8. Rogō quis hoc bellum fortiter administrāre possit. 9. Rogāvit num equitēs eās regiōnēs cognōscere possent. 10. Rōmānī obsidēs dare nōn cōnsuēverant. 11. Mīlitēs Rōmānī sē suaque signa hostibus dēdere nōn cōnsuēverant. 12. Mīlitēs Americānī omnēs hostēs vincere cōnsuēvērunt. 13. Lēgātus custōdēs ibi cōnstituet nē hostēs eās regiōnēs explōrāre possint.

EXERCISE 370
[Essential]
Translate:

1. He asked whether Columbus was able to get ready three ships in all. 2. The lieutenant placed guards there lest the barbarians might be able to reconnoiter those regions. 3. In all there are ten[1] commandments[2] of God. 4. Americans were asking why we were not at all able to send help to our soldiers then. 5. "We," said the Roman leader, "are not at all accustomed to give hostages." 6. We often ask why the Gauls were not at all able to withstand the attack of the Romans. 7. He asked whether they were able to learn the opinion of the Senate. "For," he said, "I have decided not to wage this war against the authority of the Senate." 8. He asked whether this man had been freed by many votes. 9. Saints were accustomed to pray often that they might be able more easily to keep the faith and to love God. 10. Caesar had determined to reconnoiter and conquer all the regions of Gaul. First therefore he waged war with those tribes which are next to the Roman province lest they might be able to make[3] an attack upon him from the rear. Then he waged war with the rest of the tribes, and, after many battles and great slaughter, he was able to pacify and hold all Gaul.

---

[1] *ten:* decem, *indecl. adj.*
[2] *commandment:* mandātum, ī.
[3] *to make:* facere.

4. THE INFINITIVE WITH SUBJECT ACCUSATIVE

Since the infinitive is a VERB it may also have a subject.

> **THE SUBJECT OF AN INFINITIVE IS IN THE ACCUSATIVE CASE.**

When the sense requires it, the infinitive as object, subject, and predicate noun may have a subject accusative:

> **Malum est hominēs inter sē pugnāre.**
> *It is a bad thing that men fight among themselves.*
> *It is bad for men to fight among themselves.*

An infinitive with accusative subject is regularly used with certain verbs; for example:

1. **Jubeō,** *I order, I command* is often followed by an infinitive with subject in the accusative case:

> **Caesar mīlitēs in castrīs manēre jussit.**
> *Caesar ordered the soldiers to remain in the camp.*

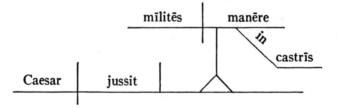

2. **Oportet,** *it behooves* may be followed by an infinitive:

> **Oportet tē Deum dīligere.**
> *It behooves you to love God.*
> In better English, *It is necessary that you love God.*

> **Oportet nōs bonōs esse.**
> *It is necessary that we be good.*
> *We ought to be good.*

VOCABULARY

jubeō, jubēre, jussī, jussus, *2, tr.; acc. w. infin.*	$\begin{cases} order \\ command \end{cases}$
oportet, oportēre, oportuit, *2, intr.; acc. w. infin.*[1]	*it behooves*
timor, timōris	*fear*

NOTE

1. It is very difficult to translate **oportet** into good English. Various English idioms may be used:

> *You ought to love God.*
> *It is proper for you to love God.*
> *You should love God.*

In translating **oportet** always try to find a *good* English expression for the IDEA or MEANING of the Latin sentence.

2. **Jubeō,** in the passive, is used just as in English.

> **Lēgātī <u>convenīre</u> jussī sunt.**
> *The lieutenants were ordered to come together.*

> **Lēgātus mīlitēs dūcere jussus est.**
> *The lieutenant was ordered to lead the soldiers.*

3. A predicate adjective after the INFINITIVE agrees with the word, expressed or understood, to which it REFERS.

> **Oportet <u>mīlitēs</u> esse <u>parātōs</u>.**
> *It behooves soldiers to be prepared.*

> **Dux <u>mīlitem</u> esse <u>parātum</u> jussit.**
> *The leader ordered the soldier to be prepared.*

> **<u>Puerī</u> <u>bonī</u> esse jussī sunt.**
> *The boys were commanded to be good.*

> **<u>Māter</u> esse <u>fortis</u> potest.**
> *A mother can be brave.*

---

[1] In translating use *it is proper; should; it is necessary*, etc.

RELATED ENGLISH WORDS

We have studied the *jussive* subjunctive. A *timorous* person will not be a good soldier.

RELATED LATIN WORD

Timeō

EXERCISE 371

Translate:

(First translate literally; then into *good* English.)
1. Oportet tē mātrem dēfendere. 2. Oportet tē ōrāre. 3. Oportet vōs omnēs Deum dīligere. 4. Oportet nōs lēgem Chrīstī servāre. 5. Oportet omnēs hominēs Chrīstum dīligere.

In hōrā mortis meae vocā mē,
Et jubē mē venīre ad tē,
Ut cum sānctīs tuīs laudem tē
In saecula saeculōrum. Āmēn.

—From the *Anima Chrīstī*

EXERCISE 372

Translate:

1. Caesar lēgātum manēre jussit. 2. Lēgātus mīlitēs convenīre jussit. 3. Caesar obsidēs occīdī jussit. 4. Gallī Caesarem excēdere[1] jussērunt. 5. Imperātor mīlitēs sē dēfendere jussit. 6. Tribūnī mīlitum in aciē manēre jussī sunt. 7. Hostēs sē dēdere jussī sunt. 8. Nōs sānctī esse ā Chrīstō jussī sumus. 9. Puerī mātrēs dīligere ā Deō jussī sunt. 10. Fortis esse jussus sum.

EXERCISE 373

Translate:

1. It behooves us to help our friends. 2. Christ commanded us to pray always. 3. It behooves us to preserve our lives. 4. Caesar ordered the soldiers to burn the crops. 5. It behooves

---

[1] excēdō, excēdere, excessī, excessum, 3, *intr.: depart.*

us to call upon God. 6. He ordered them to reconnoiter the forest. 7. The slave was commanded to be good. 8. We were commanded by Christ to pray always. 9. The soldiers were ordered to burn the crops. 10. They were ordered to reconnoiter the forest. 11. It behooves us to love our mothers. 12. It behooves Americans to defend their republic. 13. Lincoln ordered the Americans to free their slaves. 14. The chiefs were ordered to depart. 15. The barbarians were ordered to surrender.

EXERCISE 374
[Essential]
Translate:

1. Mīlitēs Rōmānī, timōre perturbātī, nōn saepe salūtem fugā petīvērunt, attamen[1] Caesar semper eōs in aciē manēre jussit. Oportuit enim eōs semper virtūtem Rōmānam memoriā tenēre.

2. Chrīstus nōs et Deum dīligere et omnēs hominēs adjuvāre jussit. Itaque oportet nōs omnēs hanc lēgem servāre.

3. Americānī numquam bellī cupidī erant sed, cum propter injūriās gravēs pugnāre atque rem pūblicam dēfendere jussī essent, sine timōre aut morā fortiter bellum cum Japōnibus gessērunt. Oportet nōs virtūtem mīlitum nostrōrum et rēs ab eīs gestās memoriā semper tenēre.

4. Dux, cum in agrōs aliēnōs mīlitēs dēdūceret, prīmum equitēs omnia loca explōrāre jussit nē in loca impedīta atque angusta legiōnēs dūceret. Oportuit enim ducem vītās mīlitum suōrum dēfendere atque cōnservāre.

EXERCISE 375
Translate:
(Use **oportet** in each sentence.)

1. We should all love God. 2. It is proper for soldiers to fight without fear. 3. It is necessary for you to pray often. 4. We must remember the victories of our fathers. 5. It is right for Americans to defend their state.

---

[1] **attamen**: *but nevertheless.*

READING NO. 27

DĒ LEGIŌNE THĒBAIĀ

This is the story of a heroic band of Christian Roman soldiers who were put to death for the faith by their own commander, the Emperor Maximian.[1] They had been recruited in northern Egypt around the city of Thebes (hence they were called the Theban Legion), but were martyred in Gaul near Lake Geneva, probably about A. D. 287.

Tum in exercitū Rōmānō erat legiō quae Thēbaia vocābātur. In hāc legiōne omnēs mīlitēs centuriōnēsque Chrīstiānī erant. Erat autem eō tempore[2] bellum in Galliā. Itaque Maximiānus, quī cum Dioclētiānō imperium obtinēbat, legiōnēs ex omnibus prōvinciīs in Galliam mīsit ut contrā eās gentēs quae cum Rōmānīs bellum gerēbant pugnārent. Maximiānus autem vir bonus nōn erat atque multōs Chrīstiānōs propter nōmen fidemque Chrīstī occīderat. Itaque, cum ea legiō in Galliam vēnisset, Maximiānus eam etiam Chrīstiānōs occīdere jussit. Mīlitēs vērō ējus legiōnis, Chrīstiānī fortēs et nōbilēs, quae imperātor jusserat nōn fēcērunt. Itaque Maximiānus, vehementer hāc rē commōtus, decimum quemque[3] mīlitem occīdī jussit. Post hanc caedem autem mīlitēs imperia imperātōris nōn fēcērunt neque tamen contrā eum pugnāvērunt. Parātī enim erant prō fidē Chrīstiānā et prō Chrīstō Rēge occīdī, at mīlitēs Rōmānī erant quī contrā Imperātōrem Rōmānum armīs nōn pugnābant. Maximiānus autem rūrsus[4] decimum quemque[3] mīlitem occīdī jussit. Post hanc alteram[5] caedem, Sānctus Mauricius, quī in eā legiōne centuriō erat, litterās ad Maximiānum mīsit:

---

[1] This account is based on the record left by St. Eucherius, Bishop of Lyons. Two reasons are given for the martyrdom of these Christian soldiers. St. Eucherius says that they were martyred for refusing to execute condemned Christians; another account relates that they refused to offer sacrifice before battle. The number of those martyred has been doubted.

[2] eō tempore: *at that time.*

[3] decimum quemque: *every tenth* (agrees with mīlitem).

[4] rūrsus, *adv.: again.*

[5] alter, altera, alterum: *other, second.*

"Mīlitēs sumus, imperātor, tuī, sed servī tamen Deī vērī. Prō tē pugnāmus, tē dēfendimus; nam imperātor es noster, et tū nōbīs et frūmentum et praemia perīculōrum nostrōrum dās. Deus autem nōbīs grātiam dat atque vītam aeternam. Itaque Deum, et nostrum et, imperātor, tuum relinquere nōn possumus. In hāc rē gravī imperia tua nōn faciēmus. Fidēs nostra enim prohibet. Sī[1] contrā hostēs pugnāre jusseris, sī[1] labōrēs atque dolōrēs, sī[1] impetum barbarōrum sustinēre jusseris, sī[1] urbēs hostium oppugnāre et agrōs vastāre jusseris, pugnābimus, sustinēbimus, oppugnābimus, vastābimus. Chrīstiānōs autem, etiam ā tē, imperātor, jussī, occīdere nōn possumus. Jam ex nōbīs multōs virōs bonōs et fortēs propter Chrīstum occīdistī, tamen contrā tē nōn pugnāvimus. Ecce[2] enim arma tenēmus et nōn nōs dēfendimus. Parātī sumus omnēs ad mortem, neque propter metum mortis Chrīstum relinquēmus. Deum Patrem, rēgem omnium, et Fīlium ejus, Jēsūm Chrīstum, Deum adōrāmus. Chrīstiānōs gladiīs occīdere nōn possumus!"

Maximiānus vērō, cum haec audīvisset, vehementer commōtus, illōs omnēs statim occīdere cōnstituit. Itaque omnēs ējus legiōnis mīlitēs centuriōnēsque ad mortem dūcī jussit. Reliquī mīlitēs, quī Chrīstiānī nōn erant, eōs gladiīs occīdērunt atque ita eōs sānctōs Deī in Caelum ad Deum mīsērunt. Posteā omnēs Chrīstiānī eōrum mortem memoriā tenēbant et semper tenēbunt. Nōnne nōs etiam eōs laudāmus? Nam et mīlitēs fortēs et Chrīstiānī fortēs erant.

Omnēs sānctī martyrēs,[3] ōrāte prō nōbīs.

---

[1] sī, *conj.: if.*
[2] ecce: *behold.*
[3] martyr, martyris: *martyr* (one who has died for the faith).

MOMENTS AT MASS NO. 5

At the Sanctus

After reciting the "secret" prayers, the priest says in a loud voice: " . . . per omnia saecula saeculōrum."

SERVER. Āmēn.

PRIEST. Dominus vōbīscum.

SERVER. Et cum spīritū tuō.

PRIEST. Sursum corda.[1]

SERVER. Habēmus ad Dominum.

PRIEST. Grātiās agāmus Dominō Deō nostrō.

SERVER. Dignum[2] et justum[3] est.

(The priest then reads the Preface *and, bowing, says:)*

PRIEST. Sānctus, sānctus, sānctus *(the bells ring),* Dominus Deus Sabaoth.[4] Plēnī sunt caelī[5] et terra glōriā tuā. Hosanna[6] in excelsīs.[7] Benedictus[8] quī venit in nōmine Dominī. Hosanna[6] in excelsīs.[7]

---

[1] Sursum corda: *Lift up your hearts.*
[2] dignus, a, um: *worthy.*
[3] justus, a, um: *right.*
[4] Sabaoth: a Hebrew word meaning *of Hosts.*
[5] In Christian Latin the plural of caelum is caelī, caelōrum.
[6] Hosanna: a Hebrew cry of joy and exultation.
[7] in excelsīs: *in the highest.*
[8] benedictus, a, um: *blessed.*

LESSON 36: NUMERALS; IRREGULAR ADJECTIVES

1. NUMERALS

ASSIGNMENT: Learn the cardinal numerals from **ūnus,** *one,* to **decem,** *ten,* and **centum,** *one hundred,* GRAMMAR, No. 112. Learn the declension of **ūnus, duo,** and **trēs,** GRAMMAR, Nos. 114-116. Notice that **ūnus** is declined like **magnus** except in the GENITIVE and DATIVE. **Trēs** is declined like the plural of **gravis,** on the stem **tr-.**

VOCABULARY

quot, *indecl. adj.*	*how many?*
aeternus, a, um	$\begin{cases} eternal \\ everlasting \end{cases}$
caput, capitis	*head*

NOTE

Indecl. means that the adjective **quot** never changes its form, no matter what form the noun may be with which it agrees.

Quot hominēs? *How many men?*

In quot urbibus? *In how many cities?*

Rogāvit quot mīlitēs in castrīs essent.

He asked how many soldiers were in the camp.

RELATED ENGLISH WORDS

Washington is the *capital* of the United States. In arithmetical division which number is called the *quotient?* Many men were *decapitated* during the French Revolution.

> Fīlī Deī, tē rogāmus, audī nōs!

EXERCISE 376
[Drill on Forms]
Translate:

1. With three legions. 2. After two battles. 3. In five cities.
4. Without ten legions. 5. Into two cities. 6. With one general.
7. After three victories. 8. After the slaughter of a hundred
hostages. 9. Across two rivers. 10. After the death of these
three men. 11. On behalf of one king. 12. By one man. 13. By
means of five darts. 14. On account of the courage of one man.
15. Concerning the safety of three hostages. 16. Through two
provinces. 17. Out of three cities. 18. On account of one sin.
19. To one man *(dative)*. 20. To two chiefs *(dative)*.

Rōma—Caput Mundī

EXERCISE 377
Respondē Latīnē:

1. Quot sunt quīnque et quattuor?
2. Quot sunt ūnum et quattuor?
3. Quot sunt sex et ūnum?
4. Quot sunt quīnque et ūnum?
5. Quot sunt quattuor et quattuor?
6. Quot sunt sex et quattuor?
7. Quot sunt duo et ūnum?
8. Quot capita habet homō?
9. Quot manūs habet homō?
10. Quot corpora habet homō?
11. Quot mentēs habet homō?

EXERCISE 378
Translate:

1. "Audī, Israēl, Deus tuus Deus ūnus est." *(From the Old Testament.)* 2. Ūnī Deō sit glōria aeterna. 3. Virtūte ūnīus virī fortis

rēs pūblica saepe cōnservātur. 4. In ūnō virō salūs commūnis saepe posita est. 5. Per ūnum hominem, Jēsūm Chrīstum, salūtem et vītam aeternam habēmus. 6. Duo sānctī, Petrus et Paulus, eōs quī urbem Rōmam incolēbant fidem Chrīstiānam docuērunt. 7. Chrīstus cum duōbus hominibus malīs ad mortem ductus est. 8. Nōmina duōrum virōrum, Washingtoniī quī rem pūblicam nostram cōnstituit atque Lincoln quī eam cōnstitūtam cōnservāvit, memoriā semper tenēbuntur. 9. Trēs Persōnās,[1] Patrem et Fīlium et Spīritum Sānctum, in ūnō Deō adōrāmus. 10. Chrīstiānus vērus hīs tribus virtūtibus, fidē, spē, cāritāte,[2] cernī potest. 11. Homō ūnum caput sed duās manūs habet.

EXERCISE 379
[Essential]
Translate:

1. Through the death of one man, Jesus Christ, we have been freed from the danger of eternal death. 2. In what great and renowned city were there seven hills? 3. We Christians adore the five wounds of Jesus Christ, our Lord and God. 4. A centurion is so called because he leads a hundred men. 5. How many are four and six? 6. There are ten commandments[3] of God. 7. There are eight beatitudes.[4] 8. There are seven gifts[5] of the Holy Spirit.

SENTENTIA SĀNCTĪ PAULĪ

"Ūnus Dominus, ūna fidēs, ūnum baptisma,[6] ūnus Deus et Pater omnium, quī est super[7] omnēs et per omnia et in omnibus nōbīs."

---

[1] persōna, ae: *person.*
[2] cāritās, cāritātis: *charity.*
[3] *commandment:* mandātum, ī.
[4] *beatitude:* beātitūdō, beātitūdinis.
[5] *gift:* dōnum, ī.
[6] baptisma, baptismatis, *n.: baptism.*
[7] super, *prep. w. acc.: above.*

MOMENTS AT MASS NO. 6

THE LAST BLESSING

Benedīcat[1] vōs omnipotēns[2] Deus, Pater et Fīlius et Spīritus
Sānctus. Āmēn.

---

[1] benedīcō, benedīcere, benedīxī, benedictus, 3, *tr.: bless.*
[2] omnipotēns (an adjective modifying Deus): *almighty.*

2. ADJECTIVES WITH IRREGULAR ENDINGS IN THE GENITIVE AND DATIVE SINGULAR

All the adjectives in the vocabulary are like **ūnus** in the genitive and dative singular.

VOCABULARY

alius, alia, aliud	*other* *another* (of more than two)
alter, altera, alterum[1]	*the one* *the other* (of two)
uter, utra, utrum[2]	*which?* (of two)
neuter, neutra, neutrum[2]	*neither* (of two)
ūllus, a, um[3]	*any*
nūllus, a, um[3]	*no* *none*
sōlus, a, um[3]	*alone* *only* (as adjective)
tōtus, a, um[3]	*whole* *all of* *the whole of*

NOTE

When **tōtus** modifies the ablative of a noun indicating *place where,* **in** is not used.

> tōtā urbe, *in the whole city*
> tōtīs castrīs, *in the whole camp*
> tōtā aciē, *in the whole battle line*

The only forms you have to learn for these adjectives are the genitive and dative singular, and for **alius,** that the nominative and accusative neuter singular is **aliud.** All the rest you know already.

---

[1] Like **līber** except in genitive and dative singular.
[2] Like **integer** except in genitive and dative singular.
[3] Like **magnus** except in genitive and dative singular.

RELATED ENGLISH WORDS

A marriage performed for Catholics by a justice of the peace is *null* and void. What do you mean by *total* war? The *total* number of conversions each year in the United States has been steadily growing. An infinitive in Latin is always *neuter*. Circumstances *alter* cases. There have been many saints who lived as *solitaries*.

ASSIGNMENT: Study GRAMMAR, Nos. 84-88, 822-828.

> MĀTER BONĪ CŌNSILIĪ,
> ŌRĀ PRŌ NŌBĪS!

EXERCISE 380
[Drill]
Translate:
(Use the dative for all *to*-phrases.)

1. Of another king. 2. Of the other centurion. 3. To another tribe. 4. To all Italy. 5. Of God alone. 6. To no men. 7. Not of any kingdom. 8. To this republic alone. 9. Of only this man. 10. To no mother. 11. Of no soldier. 12. Of all Gaul. 13. To the whole army. 14. Of another victory. 15. Of this boy alone. 16. Of the whole people.

EXERCISE 381
[Essential]
Translate:

1. Aliam viam habēmus nūllam. 2. Sōlī Deō, Rēgī Caelī et terrae, sit glōria. 3. Gallīs, cum per prōvinciam cōpiās dūcere parārent, Caesar respondit: "Mōre populī Rōmānī iter per prōvinciam nūllī dare possum." 4. Neque ūllus metus neque ūllum perīculum mīlitēs nostrōs terret. 5. Cum hīberna oppugnāta essent, Caesar, litterīs dē eā rē doctus, sine ūllā morā mīlitēs

statim dēdūxit ut suōs adjuvāret. 6. Barbarī eōs sōlōs laudant quī fortiter pugnāre possunt. 7. Washingtonium et Lincoln omnēs Americānī memoriā tenent. Alter enim rem pūblicam nostram cōnstituit, alter eam in bellī perīculīs cōnservāvit. 8. Caesar et cum Gallīs et cum Germānīs bellum gessit. Alterī enim sē contrā eum dēfendēbant, alterī autem agrōs aliēnōs vastāre cōnsuēverant. 9. In proeliō aliī tēlīs, aliī autem gladiīs occīduntur. 10. Aliī glōriae causā bellum gerunt, aliī vērō salūtis causā. 11. Aliī aliōs imperātōrēs laudant. 12. Aliī aliās sententiās probant. 13. Impedīmenta tōtīus exercitūs in ūnum locum mittī jussit. 14. Tōtum montem hominibus complērī jussit. 15. Caesar imperium tōtīus Galliae obtinēbat. 16. Cum hostium clāmor audītus esset, mīlitēs tōtīs castrīs perturbātī sunt atque alius ex aliō causam clāmōris quaesīvit.

EXERCISE 382
[Essential]
Translate:

1. The bodies of some were in the camp; the bodies of others were in the forest. 2. Some praised Caesar; others praised Hannibal. 3. Two men taught those who inhabited Rome the Christian faith. The one was Peter; the other was Paul. 4. Caesar and Hannibal were very great generals. The one conquered the whole of Gaul; the other was conquered by the Romans. 5. Caesar alone conquered all Gaul. 6. They determined to attack the town without any delay. 7. Some are eager for war; others are eager for peace. 8. No soldiers were left in the camp. 9. We praise America; others praise other nations. 10. Caesar often thanked his whole army. 11. Lee and Grant were very great generals. The one conquered; the other was conquered. 12. Isn't Rome the glory of all Italy? 13. Let us surrender to no enemy. 14. Christ alone is the King of all men. 15. There were two leading men in this tribe. The one was a friend of Caesar and the Roman Senate; the other was not. 16. Caesar was not accustomed to give hostages to any chief. 17. Some are afraid

to fight; others are always ready to fight. 18. He seized the fields of another man. 19. The chiefs of all Gaul were conquered by Caesar. 20. Some approve one plan; others another. 21. There were two Ciceros, of whom one was in Caesar's army, the other was in the Senate. 22. Some praise one nation; others another.

MOMENTS AT MASS NO. 7

As the priest places the Host on the tongue of the communicant, he prays:

Corpus Dominī nostrī Jēsū Chrīstī custōdiat[1] animam[2] tuam in vītam aeternam.

READING NO. 28

DĒ SĀNCTĀ TRĪNITĀTE[3]

Alia est enim persōna[4] Patris, alia Fīliī, alia Spīritūs Sānctī, sed Patris et Fīliī et Spīritūs Sānctī ūna est divīnitās.[5] . . . Aeternus Pater, aeternus Fīlius, aeternus Spīritus Sānctus; et tamen nōn trēs aeternī sed ūnus aeternus. . . . Ita Deus Pater, Deus Fīlius, Deus Spīritus Sānctus, et tamen nōn trēs Deī sed ūnus est Deus. Ita Dominus Pater, Dominus Fīlius, Dominus Spīritus Sānctus; et tamen nōn trēs Dominī sed ūnus est Dominus. . . . Ūnus ergō[6] Pater, nōn trēs Patrēs; ūnus Fīlius, nōn trēs Fīliī; ūnus Spīritus Sānctus, nōn trēs Spīritūs Sānctī. *(From the Creed "Quīcumque," called the Athanasian Creed; composed in the fifth century, possibly in Spain.)*

---

[1] custōdiō, *4, tr.: guard, keep* (cf. **custōs**).
[2] anima, ae: *soul.*
[3] Trīnitās, Trīnitātis: *Trinity.*
[4] persōna, ae: *person.*
[5] divīnitās, divīnitātis: *divinity.*
[6] ergō, *adv.: therefore.*

SENTENTIA CHRĪSTĪ

Chrīstus, "Ūnus," inquit, "est enim Pater vester, quī in caelīs est."

NOTE ON TRANSLATION

Rēs, as is clear from its meaning, is a very general word. It is used in Latin in many contexts where we would use in English a more specific or definite word. For example:

Illud ad rem nōn pertinet. *That does not pertain to the subject.*

Avoid, as much as possible, translating **rēs** by *thing*. Try to find a good English word that fits the context. In this exercise choose from the list given the best English word to translate the italicized word or words in each Latin sentence:

ENGLISH WORDS: *matter; reason; new deal* or *revolution; circumstance; affair, subject.*

EXAMPLE: **Illud ad rem nōn pertinent.** *That does not pertain to the subject.*

1. Quā *rē* (*abl. of cause*) eum occīdistī?
2. Gallī *rērum novārum* cupidī erant.
3. Sī[1] *rēs* cōgit, oportet hominem sē etiam armīs dēfendere.
4. Lēgātus Caesarem dē tōtā *rē* docuit.
5. Prīncipēs dē *rē* gravī agēbant.

READING NO. 29

DĒ PĀCE AC BELLŌ

Pācem omnēs hominēs laudant et petunt, at tamen nūlla est pāx.

Hannibal per Galliam trāns flūmina lāta et montēs altōs cōpiās dūxit ut in Italiā cum Rōmānīs bellum gereret. Mīlitēs ējus labōrēs atque dolōrēs gravēs sustinēbant; multī ex eīs in montibus difficilibus cadēbant, multī ex eīs occīsī sunt. Ille tamen

---

[1] **sī**: *if.*

NAPOLEON

neque cōnstitit neque pācis causā lēgātōs ad Rōmānōs mīsit, nam cōnstituerat et Rōmānōs vincere et Rōmam occupāre. Diū cum Rōmānīs proeliīs contendit, tandem vērō proeliō pulsus est atque victus. Posteā Rōmānī cum Gallīs et omnibus ferē gentibus fīnitimīs bella gessērunt. Illī, bellī glōriā adductī, hōs virtūte et armīs superāvērunt atque vīcērunt. Itaque diū imperium tōtīus Italiae atque multārum gentium aliārum obtinēbant.

Tum barbarī, victōriae spē adductī, in urbēs et prōvinciās Rōmānās vēnērunt ut omnia vastārent atque occupārent. Post id multa alia bella in Eurōpā gerēbantur.

Napoleon, vir magnus et fortis, quī rēgnum in Galliā occupāverat, imperiī atque glōriae spē adductus, tōtam Eurōpam vincere atque tenēre cōnstituit. Itaque ille in omnēs gentēs et cīvitātēs Galliae fīnitimās exercitūs dūxit ut eōrum imperium obtinēret. Diū omnēs proeliīs pepulit et bellīs vīcit. Magnus

hominum numerus occīsus est; gravēs dolōrēs ab omnibus susti-
nēbantur. Ille vērō etiam virtūte et armīs victus est.

Post illud imperātor alius, nōmine Hitler, vir glōriae et rēgnī
cupidus, tōtam Eurōpam vastāvit atque armīs vīcit. Ille diū
tōtīus ferē Eurōpae imperium tenuit sed nunc victus est cum
omnibus sociīs ējus. Nūlla est pāx. Omnēs tamen hominēs bonī pācem petunt atque
laudant. Bella tamen, "horrida¹ bella," semper geruntur. Cūr
nōn possumus amīcitiam et pācem et fidem inter omnēs populōs
cōnfirmāre? Nōnne bonum est in pāce esse? Nōnne sānctum est
aliōs adjuvāre? Nōnne Chrīstiānum est omnēs hominēs inter sē
dīligere? Chrīstus enim, "Vōs omnēs," inquit, "frātrēs estis." At
malum est frātrēs frātrēs occīdere. Et rūrsus Chrīstus, "Dīlige,"
inquit, "Deum ex tōtō animō tuō et proximum tuum sīcut
tēipsum."² Illī autem quī omnēs dīligunt neque cum aliīs pugnant
neque aliōs occīdunt. Deus, Rēx Caelī et terrae, "Dīligite," inquit, "pācem et vēritātem." Bonum et sānctum est pācem et
dīligere et servāre. Sānctus Paulus, "Alter," inquit, "alterīus
onera³ portāte." Chrīstiānum est enim aliōs adjuvāre. Tamen,
sīcut cognōvistis, nūlla est pāx.

Cūr hominēs, timōre mortis et bellī perīculīs vehementer commōtī, bellum tamen gerunt, agrōs vastant, hostēs occīdunt, urbēs
expugnant incenduntque? Aliī agrōrum lātōrum aliēnōrum cupidī
sunt. Aliī spē glōriae ad bellum incitātī sunt. Aliī gentēs fīnitimās
timent. Itaque bellum gerere' cōnstituērunt nē vincerentur. Aliī,
injūriīs commōtī, mīlitēs propter glōriam nōminis suī ad arma
vocant.

Itaque, quod lēgēs Deī atque Chrīstī nōn erant servātae, bella
semper fuērunt, undique nunc sunt et semper erunt. Nōs tamen
Chrīstiānī pācem cōnfirmēmus, petāmus, dīligāmus, cōnservēmus.

> Sōlus omnīnō est quī sine amīcō est.

---

¹ **horridus, a, um**: *savage, wild.*
² **tēipsum**: *thyself.*
³ **onus, oneris, n.**: *burden.*

UNIT ELEVEN

LESSON 37: *-IŌ* VERBS; RULES FOR TIME

1. INDICATIVE ACTIVE OF *-IŌ* VERBS

There is a group of important verbs which have some forms like the third conjugation and some forms like the fourth conjugation. These verbs are called -IŌ VERBS OF THE THIRD CONJUGATION.

They can be distinguished by the endings of the first and second principal parts, which are always **-iō** and **-ere**. Thus:

$$\text{cap-}\underline{\textbf{IŌ}}, \text{ cap-}\underline{\textbf{ERE}}, \text{ cēpī, captus, } 3, \textit{ tr.} \quad \begin{cases} \textit{take} \\ \textit{capture} \end{cases}$$

They follow a simple rule:

WHENEVER THE <u>ENDING</u> OF THE FOURTH CONJUGATION BEGINS WITH TWO VOWELS, -IŌ VERBS USE THE ENDINGS OF THE FOURTH CONJUGATION; OTHERWISE THEY USE THE ENDINGS OF THE THIRD CONJUGATION.

ASSIGNMENT: Study GRAMMAR, Nos. 311-314 (present system indicative). Note·that the entire imperfect and future has the endings of the fourth conjugation.

The perfect tenses are formed, just like all the other verbs, on the perfect stem, *e. g.,* **cēp-,** with the regular endings.

VOCABULARY

capiō, capere, cēpī, captus, *3, tr.*	$\begin{cases} \textit{take} \\ \textit{capture} \end{cases}$
fugiō, fugere, fūgī, fugitūrus, *3, tr.*	*flee*
faciō, facere, fēcī, factus, *3, tr.*	$\begin{cases} \textit{do} \\ \textit{make} \end{cases}$
voluntās, voluntātis	$\begin{cases} \textit{good will} \\ \textit{will} \end{cases}$

NOTE

1. Learn these special idioms:
   a. **Iter facere,** *to march.*

   Iter fēcērunt. *They marched* (literally, *made a journey.*)

   b **Cōnsilium capere,** *to make a plan.*

   Cōnsilium novum cēpērunt. *They made a new plan.*

2. Remember that verbs of MAKING *may* take a direct object and a predicate accusative.

   Tē rēgem fēcimus. *We made you king.*

3. With **fidēs, voluntās,** and similar words, **in** with the accusative means *towards.*

   Tua in mē voluntās, *your good will towards me.*

RELATED ENGLISH WORDS

The *fugitive* hours. *Voluntary* contributions. We are impressed by *facts. Manufactured* goods. *Captives.*

RELATED LATIN WORD

Fuga

> **Jēsū, rēx glōriae, miserēre nōbīs!**

EXERCISE 383
[Drill]
Translate:

1. Whom did they make king? 2. How great fortifications are they making? 3. Where did he march with all his forces? 4. Did he flee? 5. Who fled? 6. What plans will they make? 7. Where will they march from that place? 8. Why does he flee? 9. Did they take the city? 10. You won't flee before the battle, will you? 11. Has he made the bridge? 12. They didn't take Rome, did they? 13. Who will take that hill? 14. Hannibal, you will

never take Rome. 15. After the battle they fled in all directions.[1]
16. The leaders fled for the sake of safety. 17. Did they make
him leader? 18. They fled to the mountains, didn't they? 19. The
hostages also were fleeing. 20. Roman soldiers do not flee.

EXERCISE 384
[Essential]
Translate:

1. Dē Mīlitibus
[Drill on the Present Tense]

Oportet mīlitēs fortēs et victōriae cupidōs esse. Nam multōs
labōrēs et dolōrēs gravēs sustinent. Mīlitēs, ā duce ex castrīs
dēductī, longa itinera faciunt. Castra pōnunt. In fīnēs hostium
dēductī, magnās mūnītiōnēs celeriter faciunt. Mīlitēs, ā centuriōnibus in aciē īnstrūctī, impetum in hostēs faciunt. Ā duce
jussī, collēs et pontēs capiunt. Mīlitēs quī fortēs sunt, ab hoste
pressī, nōn fugiunt. Hostēs vērō in fugam dant et cōpiam frūmentī et armōrum capiunt.

2. Dē Mīlitibus Rōmānīs
[Drill on the Imperfect Tense]

Mīlitēs Rōmānī fortēs erant. Nōn saepe, timōre mōtī, fugiē-
bant. Castra mūnīta capiēbant; urbēs et mūrīs et locī nātūrā
mūnītās capiēbant. Capiēbant etiam multōs mīlitēs. Impetūs
fortiter et in aciēs et in equitēs faciēbant. Longās magnāsque
mūnītiōnēs faciēbant. Mīlitēs Rōmānī, ab imperātōre nōmine
appellātī, propter suam in eum voluntātem ācriter et diū pugnābant. Itinera longa et per prōvinciās et per fīnēs hostium
faciēbant. Mīlitēs Rōmānī saepe ducēs suōs rēgēs Rōmānōs
fēcērunt.

3. Dē Caesare Duce
[Drill on the Perfect Tense]

Caesar, dux fortis, bella fortiter administrāvit. Cōnsilia bona
cēpit et magnās rēs gessit. Urbēs Gallōrum cēpit; magnās mūnī-

---
[1] *directions:* use **partēs.**

MĪLITĒS AMERICĀNĪ

tiōnēs fēcit; longa itinera et per silvās et per montēs fēcit. Numquam, aut tēlīs aut clāmōre territus, fūgit. Bonam in mīlitēs voluntātem habēbat. Itaque ex mīlitum suōrum caede saepe magnum dolōrem cēpit. Mīlitēs ab eō ductī propter ējus in sē voluntātem fortiter pugnāvērunt. Mīlitēs propter suam in Caesarem voluntātem eum imperātōrem appellāvērunt.

4. Dē Mīlitibus Americānīs
[Drill on the Future Tense]

Mīlitēs Americānī etiam fortēs sunt at bellī nōn sunt cupidī. Pācem enim dīligunt. Tamen, injūriīs incitātī, et ācriter et fortiter bellum gerent. Itinera longa sine morā facient; cōpiam armōrum et tēlōrum parābunt. Urbēs et portūs et oppida capient et capta tenēbunt. Magnās mūnītiōnēs facient et mūnītiōnēs ab hostibus factās capient. Impetūs sine morā et sine metū in hostēs facient. Cōnsilium ā ducibus captum laudābunt. Perīcula mortis nōn timēbunt. Timōre et tēlīs āctī, nōn fugient. Summam voluntātem in rem pūblicam ostendent, sīcut patrēs nostrī in cīvitātem nostram līberam semper voluntātem ostendērunt. Numquam mīlitēs Americānī ducēs rēgēs facient, nam summam in rem pūblicam habēbunt voluntātem.

Nōnne mīlitēs et Rōmānōs et Americānōs semper laudābimus et memoriā tenēbimus?

SENTENTIAE SĒLECTAE

1. Chrīstus, "Nōn quaerō," inquit, "voluntātem meam sed voluntātem ējus quī mīsit mē."
2. Domine, tū es quī fēcistī caelum et terram, mare[1] et omnia quae in eīs sunt. *(From the Acts of the Apostles.)*
3. Chrīstus, "Māter mea et frātrēs meī," inquit, "hī sunt quī verbum[2] Deī audiunt et faciunt."

EXERCISE 385
[Essential]
Translate:

1. The Japanese made a plan of war. Then suddenly they made an attack on a great harbor of the Americans.
2. The soldiers marched a long time through the territory of the Gauls. Then suddenly these were seen on a hill. The Gauls had made fortifications on that hill lest the Romans might seize it. The Romans made an attack on the hill from the front. The Gauls, terrified by the darts and swords, raised (up) a shout and fled.
3. The Gauls had stationed cavalry in the forest and soldiers at the river. These the Romans captured, but those they put to flight.
4. The chief of the Gauls said to Caesar: "On account of your good will towards my tribe, I shall make an attack on your enemies; I shall capture their fields and towns; I shall also capture those soldiers who will not have fled."
5. The general said: "How great is the number of the enemy? How large fortifications have they made? Have they captured a supply of grain? Will they flee after the attack?"
6. Napoleon made himself king and emperor of France.[3]
7. The leader of the allies said to Caesar: "You have stationed me and my men on this hill to hold it. On account of your

---

[1] mare, maris, *n.: sea.*
[2] verbum, ī: *word.*
[3] *France:* Gallia, ae.

good will towards me, I shall hold it and I shall not flee. I shall make fortifications and prepare darts. They[1] will never take this hill."

2. TIME WHEN

ASSIGNMENT: Study GRAMMAR, Nos. 920-921.

VOCABULARY

annus, ī	*year*
vigilia, ae	*watch*
tempus, temporis, *n.*	*time*
diēs, diēī, *m. (f.)*	*day*
hōra, ae	*hour*
prīmus, a, um	*first*
secundus, a, um ⎫ alter, altera, alterum ⎭	*second*
tertius, a, um	*third*

RELATED ENGLISH WORDS

An *annual* celebration. The school *annual*. St. Ignatius kept *vigil* at the shrine of Our Lady. The Saints do not allow *temporal* things to worry them. *Secondary*. A *tertiary* of St. Francis.

A. D. 1776

A. D.—Annō Dominī

EXERCISE 386

Answer in English:

1. Quō annō Columbus ad novās terrās quās Americam vocāmus pervēnit?

2. Quō diē Deō propter nostram līberam cīvitātem grātiās agimus?

---

[1] The speaker here points to the distant camp of the enemy. What pronoun would be the best to use?

3. Quō annō Lincoln servōs ā dominīs eōrum līberāvit?
4. Quō diē Chrīstus occīsus est?
5. Quō diē hominēs prīmum Chrīstum puerum vīdērunt?
6. Quō diē Chrīstus in Caelum sublātus est?

EXERCISE 387
Translate:

1. at the third watch
2. in the second hour
3. on the third day

4. in the first year
5. at that time
6. on that day

TEMPUS FUGIT

EXERCISE 388
Translate:

1. Caesar diem cōnstituit quō diē omnēs prīncipēs Gallōrum ad sē convenīrent. Eō diē omnēs convēnērunt. 2. Prīmā vigiliā clāmor custōdum audiēbātur. 3. Eō tempore bellum cum Gallīs gerēbātur. 4. Tertiā diē omnia frūmenta quae in agrīs erant incendērunt. 5. Eō annō Rōmānī Gallōs multīs proeliīs vīcērunt. 6. Eō diē multī proeliō cecidērunt. 7. Eō tempore custōdēs in mūrō nōn erant. 8. Proximō diē frūmentum mīlitibus dabātur. 9. Prīmā vigiliā legiōnem clam ē castrīs dēdūxit. 10. Tertiō diē nuntius ad Caesarem ā lēgātō mittēbātur quī auxilium peteret. 11. Et in bellō et in pāce Rōmānī fortēs erant. 12. Eō annō multa proelia adversa fēcērunt. 13. Tertiā vigiliā servus clam ē castrīs ad Caesarem missus est.

EXERCISE 389
[Forms of -iō Verbs and Time When]
Translate:

1. At the third hour they fled. 2. At that time they captured the hill. 3. On the second day they marched into the mountains.

4. At the third hour they pitched camp. 5. In that year they made fortifications in the province. 6. They captured the king on the third day. 7. In the next year they captured the city. 8. At the third watch the enemy made an attack.

SENTENTIA CICERŌNIS

Cicerō, "Historia,"[1] inquit, "[est] testis[2] temporum, lūx vēritātis, vīta memoriae."

READING NO. 30

THE "OUR FATHER"

And the Lord said: "Thus therefore shall you pray:

PATER NOSTER

QUĪ ES IN CAELĪS

SĀNCTIFICĒTUR[3] NŌMEN TUUM

ADVENIAT[4] RĒGNUM TUUM

FĪAT[5] VOLUNTĀS TUA SĪCUT IN CAELŌ ET[6] IN TERRĀ

PANEM[7] NOSTRUM COTĪDIĀNUM[8] DĀ NŌBĪS HODIĒ[9]

ET DĪMITTE NŌBĪS DĒBITA[10] NOSTRA

SĪCUT ET[6] NŌS DĪMITTIMUS DĒBITŌRIBUS[11] NOSTRĪS

---

[1] historia, ae: *history.*
[2] testis, testis, *m.: witness.*
[3] sānctificētur: *hallowed be.*
[4] adveniat: *(may)* . . . *come.*
[5] fīat: *(may)* . . . *be done.*
[6] et here means *also.* It may be left untranslated.
[7] panis, panis, *m.: bread.*
[8] cotīdiānus, a, um: *daily.*
[9] hodiē, *adv.: today.*
[10] dēbitum, ī: *debt, trespass.*
[11] dēbitor, dēbitōris: *debtor, one who trespasses.*

CHRISTUS HOMINES DOCET.

ET NĒ[1] NŌS INDŪCĀS[1] IN TENTĀTIŌNEM[2]
SED LĪBERĀ NŌS Ā MALŌ. ĀMĒN."

3. SUBJUNCTIVE ACTIVE OF -IŌ VERBS

ASSIGNMENT: Learn GRAMMAR, Nos. 315-316.

The perfect and pluperfect subjunctive of -iō verbs are formed regularly on the perfect stem.

---

[1] nē . . . indūcās: *lead . . . not.*
[2] tentātiō, tentātiōnis: *temptation.*

VOCABULARY

conjiciō, conjicere, conjēcī, conjectus, 3, tr. $\begin{cases} throw \\ hurl \end{cases}$

recipiō, recipere, recēpī, receptus, 3, tr. $\begin{cases} receive \\ accept \\ recover \end{cases}$

(with a reflexive pronoun mē, tē, sē, *etc.)*   *withdraw*

cupiō, cupere, cupīvī, cupītus, 3, tr.; w. infin.   *desire*

rūrsus, *adv.*   *again*

NOTE

1. Notice this special use of **conjiciō**:

   In fugam hostēs conjēcit. *He threw the enemy into flight.*

2. **Recipiō** with the proper reflexive pronoun means *withdraw*:

   Ad castra sē recēpērunt. *They withdrew to the camp.*

   In silvās nōs recipiēmus. *We shall withdraw into the forest.*

RELATED ENGLISH WORD

The *cupidity* of misers is proverbial.

RELATED LATIN WORDS

Cupidus; capiō.

Jēsū, Deus pācis, miserēre nōbīs!

EXERCISE 390
[Drill on the Present Subjunctive]
Translate:

1. Grātiam Deī cupiāmus.   2. Capiat urbem.   3. Fugiant hostēs.   4. Fugiāmus.   5. Capiāmus cōnsilium.   6. Fugiat rēx. 7. Faciāmus rūrsus impetum in illōs.

EXERCISE 391
[Drill on the Present Subjunctive]
Translate:

1. Let us desire to see God. 2. Let us march into the mountains. 3. May they take the town! 4. May they flee! 5. Let us make a plan. 6. May they make an attack again! 7. May they capture the king! 8. Let us flee.

EXERCISE 392

1. Write a main clause for each of these sentences;
2. Complete the verbs in the subordinate clauses by adding imperfect endings:

(The main clause should make sense and should demand the imperfect subjunctive in sequence. The first sentence shows how the exercise is to be done.)

1. .... quō facilius tēla in hostēs conjic............
[Mūnītiōnēs fēcērunt quō facilius tēla in hostēs conjicerent.]
2. .... nē hostēs collem cap.............
3. .... nē mīlitēs sē in castra recip.............
4. .... quō facilius mīlitēs ē timōrē sē recip.............
5. .... nē dux hostium impetum facere cup.............
6. .... nē hostēs impetum fac.............
7. .... nē mīlitēs suī fug.............
8. .... nē hostēs in loca tūta sē recip.............
9. .... ut mīlitēs victōriam cup.............

EXERCISE 393
[Essential]
Translate:

Dux Rōmānus, hīs nuntiīs commōtus, lēgātōs et tribūnōs mīlitum ad sē vocāvit ut cōnsilium caperet. Equitem mīserat quī cognōsceret quae hostēs facerent. Prīmum in conciliō hunc equitem rogat quō diē hostēs pervēnerint, ubi castra posuerint, quantās mūnītiōnēs fēcerint, quantās cōpiās habeant, num cōpiam frūmentī et aquae habeant, quōs collēs cēperint. Tum ā centuriōnibus quaesīvit num mīlitēs suī victōriam cuperent, num ad proelium parātī essent, num in sē bonam voluntātem habērent, num cōpiam tēlōrum habērent. Post haec cōnsilium cēpit atque lēgātōs tribūnōsque mīlitum dīmīsit.

Proximō diē dux cum omnibus cōpiīs suīs prīmā lūce per silvās iter fēcit ut collem nātūrā locī mūnītum caperet. Dux vērō hostium, cum agmen Rōmānum vīdisset, cōpiās ex castrīs dūxit atque īnstrūxit. Tum Rōmānīs appropinquāvērunt ut in eōs impetum facerent. Rōmānī, cum hostēs nōn longē abessent, tēla in eōs conjēcērunt. Statim multī ex hostibus, timōre mōtī, cessērunt atque fūgērunt. Reliquī tamen rūrsus impetum fēcērunt. Tum Rōmānī exspectāvērunt quō facilius tēla rūrsus conjicerent. Itaque, Rōmānī cum rūrsus tēla in hostēs conjēcissent, clāmōrem sustulērunt et impetum in hostēs fēcērunt. Rem gladiīs[1] gessērunt. Magna fuit caedēs. Hostēs aliī celeriter fūgērunt, aliī mōre suō clāmōrem sustulērunt atque sē suaque omnia Rōmānīs dēdidērunt. Ita Rōmānī et castra cēpērunt et magnam omnium rērum cōpiam cēpērunt. Itaque Rōmānī in castra sē recēpērunt.

EXERCISE 394

Translate:

1. The Romans stationed men on the walls to hurl darts against the enemy. 2. The Romans made fortifications lest the enemy should easily hurl darts against them. 3. The general asked whether the men desired the signal to be given. 4. Caesar shows us how great sorrow the Gauls take from the slaughter of their hostages. 5. The general asked the soldiers whether they desired glory and rewards. Then said he: "Fight bravely. The enemy will flee and we shall take their camp. It is full of all these things which you desire." 6. When the soldiers had hurled the darts, he sent the cavalry against the enemy lest

---

[1] This was the equivalent of the modern bayonet charge.

they should recover from their fear and again make an attack. According to their. custom, the barbarians then raised (up) a shout and fled in all directions.[1]

4. EXTENT OF TIME AND SPACE

ASSIGNMENT: Study GRAMMAR, No. 761.

VOCABULARY

pēs, pedis, *m.*	*foot* (part of body or measure of distance)
passus, ūs	*pace* (a measure of distance = 5 Roman feet [pedēs])
mīlle, *indecl. adj.*	*thousand*
mīlia, mīlium, *neuter noun*	*thousands*
mīlle passūs	*a mile* (literally, *a thousand paces* = 1,618 English yards)
mīlia passuum	*miles* (literally, *thousands of paces*)
quam, *interrogative adv. of degree*	*how?*

NOTE

1. For **mīlle** and **mīlia**, study GRAMMAR, No. 117.

2. **Quam** does NOT mean ˙ *how* in the sense of *in what way, by what means.* It CANNOT translate: *"How* did you do it?" It means *how* in the sense of *to what degree,* as in *"how* high," *"how* long," *"how* violently," *etc.*

Quam longum est illud flūmen? *How long is that river?*

RELATED ENGLISH WORDS

A *pedestrian* should be careful at crossings. A *mill* is one-thousandth part of a dollar. A *pedometer* measures the number of steps taken by a walker or runner. The *pedals* of a bicycle.

---

[1] *directions:* use **partēs.**

TO A DOCTOR TURNED UNDERTAKER

"Nūper[1] erat medicus,[2] nunc est vispillō[3] Diaulus,[4]
Quod vispillō[3] facit, fēcerat et[5] medicus[2]" *(Martial)*.

EXERCISE 395
[Drill]

1. Translate;
2. Parse the italicized words:

1. Quīnque *diēs* iter fēcērunt.　2. Quīnque *mīlia passuum* iter fēcērunt.　3. Castra *mīlle passūs* ab montibus āfuērunt.　4. Castra *duo mīlia passuum* ab montibus āfuērunt.　5. Eō *diē tria mīlia hominum* in proeliō cecidērunt.　6. Montem *tribus mīlibus hominum* complēvit.　7. Corpora *trium mīlium hominum* in agrīs vīsa sunt.　8. *Mīlle diēs* in montibus erat.　9. *Duo mīlia diērum* in montibus erat.　10. Dux duōbus *mīlibus* hominum praemia dedit.　11. *Duo mīlia* ferē annōrum fidēs Chrīstī in terrā jam est.[6]　12. Septem *annōs* Caesar in Galliā cum barbarīs bellum gessit.

---

[1] nūper, *adv.: formerly.*
[2] medicus, ī: *doctor.*
[3] vispillō, vispillōnis, *m.: undertaker.*
[4] Diaulus, ī: a proper name.
[5] et here means *also.*
[6] est: translate by *has been.*

13. Hostēs quattuor *diēs* celeriter fūgērunt. 14. *Quam* lāta fuit illa fossa? 15. Quam altus est hic mūrus? 16. Mīlitēs fossam decem *passūs* lātam fēcērunt. 17. Vallum erat decem *pedēs* altum.

> Chrīstum Deī Fīlium,
> Quī suō nōs redēmit[1] sanguine,[2]
> Venīte, adōrēmus!

EXERCISE 396
[Drill]
Translate:

1. They marched three days. 2. They marched five miles. 3. The city was two miles distant from the river. 4. They fled for three days. 5. They held the hill five hours; then the Romans captured it. 6. They gave swords to three thousand men. 7. The hill was taken by two thousand men. 8. He marched into the province with a thousand men. 9. How high is this mountain? 10. The river was a mile away. 11. They fought for two hours. 12. This river is many feet wide. 13. He waited nine days. 14. The Saints were often able to pray for two or three hours. 15. The Americans defended Bataan for many days. 16. Shall we be able to preserve peace for many years? 17. Our state has been free many years. 18. They waged war for three years.

EXERCISE 397
Answer in English:

1. Quot mīlia passuum longum est illud flūmen quod Mississippi vocātur?
2. Quam lātum est illud flūmen?
3. Quam longē abest urbs Rōma ā fīnibus nostrīs?

---

[1] redēmit: *redeemed.*
[2] sanguis, sanguinis, *m.: blood.*

4. Quot diēs Chrīstus post mortem suam in terrā fuit?
5. Quot annōs Chrīstus in terrā hominēs viam salūtis docuit?
6. Quot annōs Americānī illud bellum quod Civil vocātur inter sē gessērunt?
7. Quot annōs Americānī cum Germānīs proeliīs contendērunt?

SENTENTIA CHRĪSTĪ

Chrīstus apostolīs[1] suīs, "Quī recipit vōs," inquit, "mē recipit; et quī mē recipit, recipit eum quī mīsit mē."

EXERCISE 398
[Essential]
Translate:

1. Christ was not seen for three days after His death, but then He showed Himself to His friends. For many days He remained on the earth to teach His friends and to encourage them. Then He was raised up into heaven, and there He will remain in the glory of the Father forever.

2. Let us establish and preserve peace that for many years we may be free from the fears and sorrows of war.

3. Those who first came to our land often marched many miles for many days through narrow places, through forests full of dangers, through difficult and high mountains, in order to arrive at good fields and to have an abundance of water.

4. It is a bad thing for men to fight among themselves. In all those wars which have been waged during thousands of years, many thousands of men have been killed and captured. It is a good thing to remain in peace; it is a good thing to love peace and to preserve it.

5. The Romans pitched and fortified a camp daily.[2] They often fortified it with a rampart ten feet high and a ditch five feet wide. Thus daily[2] they marched many miles and prepared fortifications for many hours.

---

[1] apostolus, ī: *apostle.*
[2] *daily:* cotīdiē, *adv.*

READING NO. 31

DĒ SĀNCTŌ PETRŌ CLAVER, SERVŌRUM APOSTOLŌ

Sānctus Petrus Claver erat Jēsuīta. Ad portum Carthāginem,[1] quae urbs in Americā est, pervēnit ut servōs ibi adjuvāret. Nam eīs temporibus hominēs malī ad Africam nāvigābant[2] ut illōs miserōs hominēs quī illās regiōnēs incolēbant caperent atque servōs facerent. Tum eōs servōs in Americam trādūcēbant atque ibi vēndidērunt.[3] Illī servī nāvibus malīs et parvīs ex Africā trāductī sunt. In hīs nāvibus nōn erat cōpia aquae frūmentīque neque ūllārum rērum quae ad vītam ūtilēs sunt. Itaque Sānctus Petrus, cum nāvēs in portum pervēnissent, in nāvēs sine morā contendēbat ut servōs miserōs adjuvāret. Et corpora et animās[4] eōrum adjuvābat. Difficile vērō est ostendere quā virtūte rēs gesserit. Nam multōs quī propter dolōrem et vulnera in nāvibus cecidērunt, manibus suīs ex nāvibus portābat. Eōs aquā et frū-mentō adjuvābat. Ita vītās multōrum servōrum cōnservābat. Praetereā omnēs fidem Chrīstiānam docuit. Docuit eōs et ōrāre et Deum dīligere. Nēminem[5] ā sē prohibuit; omnēs vērō ad sē recipiēbat. Servīs miserīs sē tōtum dedit. Itaque servī eum et patrem et amīcum appellāvērunt.

Sānctus Petrus autem multōs dolōrēs servōrum salūtis causā sustinuit. Nam multī dominī malam in eum voluntātem habē-bant. Itaque eum impediēbant. Tamen Sānctus Petrus, hīs injūriīs neque commōtus neque perturbātus, omnia sustinuit ut servōs, frātrēs suōs dīlēctōs, Chrīstiānōs faceret. Multōs annōs[6] haec

---

[1] The Port of Cartagena, on the northeast coast of South America, was a notorious slave market. Fifty per cent of the slaves are estimated to have died in the foul holds of the slave ships during the Atlantic crossing, yet 10,000 slaves were sold annually in Cartagena. The slave trade was vigorously con-demned by Pope Pius III.

[2] nāvigō, 1, intr.: sail.

[3] vēndō, vēndere, vēndidī, vēnditus, 3, tr.: sell.

[4] anima, ae: soul.

[5] nēminem: no one (accusative).

[6] He spent about thirty-five years in this work. He died September 8, 1654, and was canonized in 1888. His feast is celebrated on September 9. Pope Leo XIII made him special patron of all missions among all African peoples.

SANCTUS PETRUS CLAVER

agēbat, et tandem[1] labōribus cōnfectus[2] ad caelī praemium pervēnit. Post multōs annōs sānctus factus est et nunc ab omnibus
Chrīstiānīs laudātur.

5. INDICATIVE PASSIVE OF *-IŌ* VERBS

ASSIGNMENT: Study GRAMMAR, Nos. 311, 322-324.

The perfect tenses are formed regularly by using the perfect
participle passive with the proper forms of the verb **sum.**

Review GRAMMAR, Nos. 312-314.

---

[1] tandem, *adv.: at last.*
[2] cōnfectus, a, um: *worn out.*

VOCABULARY

interficiō, interficere, interfēcī, interfectus, *3, tr.*   *kill*

ēripiō, ēripere, ēripuī, ēreptus, *3, tr.* $\begin{cases} take\ away \\ save\ (from) \end{cases}$

nihil, *indecl. noun*   *nothing*

NOTE

1. The present system passive of **faciō** is irregular, but almost all the compounds of **faciō**, such as **interficiō**, are regular.

2. After **ēripiō** *from* is translated as ex (ē) *w. abl.*

Ē perīculō ēreptus sum.
I was saved from danger.

EXERCISE 399
Translate:

1. We were being killed by the enemy. 2. They were being captured. 3. The town has been taken. 4. Rome has often been captured. 5. He was saved from the hands of the enemy. 6. Many thousand soldiers were killed. 7. Darts were hurled against the enemy. 8. Two thousand of them were killed. 9. A thousand men were captured. 10. The swords were taken away. 11. Nothing was captured. 12. That town will be taken. 13. I was saved from death by a friend.

> Sāncte Petre Claver, Apostole Servōrum,
> Ōrā prō nōbīs!

EXERCISE 400
[Essential]
Translate:

1. Cīvitās nostra ē magnō perīculō ā Washingtoniō ērepta est. 2. Japōnēs, saepe in loca impedīta et angusta coāctī, tēlīs gladiīsque interficiēbantur. 3. Dux mīlitibus, "Quid," inquit, "timent

mīlitēs Rōmānī?" Centuriō vērō eī, "Nihil," inquit, "timēmus."
4. Centuriō ab equitibus ē manibus hostium ēreptus est. 5. Ā quō
capta est urbs Rōma? 6. Lēgātī quī frūmentī causā ad cīvitātēs
Gallōrum missī erant saepe ā Gallīs aut captī aut interfectī sunt.
Haec caedēs saepe fuit bellī causa. Nam Caesar multa mīlia
Gallōrum interficere cōnstituit nē aliī lēgātī suī ab eīs occīderentur. 7. Multī, tēlīs interfectī, dē mūrō cecidērunt. 8. Sānctī
ā Deō saepe ē perīculīs ēripiuntur. 9. Nihil dē hāc rē audīvī.
Audīvistīne tū dē hāc rē? 10. Propter Gallōrum injūriās obsidēs
ā Rōmānīs saepe interficiēbantur. 11. Nihil cupitur ab eō quī
cōpiam omnium rērum habet. 12. Multa ab hominibus cupiuntur,
at maximē[1] cupitur salūs.

EXERCISE 401
Translate:

1. Who were being killed by Caesar? 2. Nothing was taken
away from the town. 3. The grace of God is taken away from
us by sin. 4. We were saved from eternal death by the Son of
God. 5. That man was saved from death by a brave centurion.
6. Many are now being killed by wicked men. 7. Men are often
saved from death by their friends. 8. What is desired by the
Saints? 9. The enemy was often thrown into flight by the Romans. 10. This city was often captured by the enemy. 11. Two
thousand men were captured. 12. Was Rome captured by the
Gauls? 13. All the others were either captured or killed.

READING NO. 32

THE LAZY SLAVE

Dominus servum malum castīgābat.[2] Servus clāmāvit,[3] "Cūr,
domine, mē percutis?[4] Nihil fēcī." Dominus, autem, "Propter id,"
inquit, "tē percutiō[4] quod nihil fēcistī."

---

[1] maximē, adv.: most of all.
[2] castīgō, 1, tr.: punish.
[3] clāmō, 1, intr.: shout, cry.
[4] percutiō, percutere, percussī, percussus, 3, tr.: beat.

6. TIME WITHIN WHICH

ASSIGNMENT: Study GRAMMAR, No. 922.

VOCABULARY

cōnspiciō, cōnspicere, cōnspexī, cōnspectus, *3, tr.* | see
| catch sight of

accipiō, accipere, accēpī, acceptus, *3, tr.* | receive
| accept

cōnficiō, cōnficere, cōnfēcī, cōnfectus, *3, tr.* | finish
| wear out

nēmō, nēminis, *m.*[1] no one

RELATED ENGLISH WORDS

A *conspicuous* appearance. A speech of *acceptance*. He *accepted* the nomination.

EXERCISE 402

THE FRIENDLESS MAN

Translate:

He who loves no one, praises no one, helps no one, gives thanks to no one, is alone and without friends. Within a short time he will be worn out with sorrows and toil. Help will be received from no one. He will be unable to carry on great affairs, for he will have no allies and no friends. He will be a wretched man, for life without friends and without virtue is wretched.

EXERCISE 403

Translate:

1. They will arrive within three days. 2. Within two hours the column of the enemy will be seen. 3. The letter will be received within two days. 4. In two days the war will be finished. 5. Within two days the ships were caught sight of. 6. Within three hours the soldiers will be worn out with the journey and toil. 7. No one worn out with wounds can fight long and bravely.

---

[1] nūllīus, nūllō, and nūllā are usually used for nēminis and nēmine.

EXERCISE 404
[Essential]

Translate:

1. Sex diēbus omnēs mūnītiōnēs cōnfectae sunt. 2. Mīlitēs, vulneribus cōnfactī, labōrem diūtius sustinēre nōn potuērunt. 3. Legiō clam per silvās iter fēcit neque ē castrīs hostium cōnspecta est. 4. Tribus diēbus ad flūmen perventum est. 5. Tertiā diē ad castra perventum est. 6. In omnibus partibus barbarī cōnspiciuntur. 7. Dux Rōmānus barbarīs, "Rōmānī," inquit, "obsidēs accipere, nōn dare, cōnsuēvērunt." 8. Rōmānī illam bellī glōriam quae ā patribus accepta erat semper cōnservāvērunt. 9. Litterae ā Caesare acceptae sunt quibus lēgātus doctus est quantō in perīculō legiōnēs essent. 10. Apud Rōmānōs servī ā dominīs malīs saepe injūriās accēpērunt. 11. Multa vulnera in eō proeliō accepta sunt.

READING NO. 33

THE VIATICUM[1]

When Holy Communion is given to the dying, the priest recites this prayer:

Accipe, frāter, viāticum[1] Corporis Dominī nostrī Jēsū Chrīstī, quī tē custōdiat[2] ab hoste malignō[3] et perdūcat[4] in vītam aeternam. Āmēn.

SENTENTIAE SĒLECTAE

1. Chrīstus, "Ego," inquit, "sum via, et vēritās, et vīta: nēmō venit ad Patrem, nisi[5] per mē."

---

[1] **viāticum, ī:** *viaticum* (the word was originally used of *provision for a journey*).

[2] **custōdiō, 4,** *tr.: guard* (cf. **custōs**).

[3] **malignus, a, um:** *evil.*

[4] **perdūcō, perdūcere, perdūxī, perductus, 3,** *tr.: lead to.*

[5] **nisi:** *except.*

2. Sānctus Paulus, "Fundāmentum,"[1] inquit, "enim aliud nēmō potest pōnere, praeter[2] id quod positum est, quod est Chrīstus Jēsūs."

3. Seneca, "Bonus vērō vir," inquit, "sine Deō nēmō est."

7. SUBJUNCTIVE PASSIVE OF -IŌ VERBS

ASSIGNMENT: Study GRAMMAR, Nos. 325-326.

The perfect tenses are formed regularly by using the perfect participle passive with the forms of the verb **sum.**

VOCABULARY

magnitūdō, magnitūdinis	*size* *greatness*
satis, *adv.*	*enough* *sufficiently*
animus, ī	*mind* *soul*
satis, *indecl. noun w. gen.*	*enough*

RELATED ENGLISH WORDS

The *magnitude* of the sun astounds us. The arrangement is *satisfactory.* An *animist* believes that *inanimate* objects have souls.

RELATED LATIN WORD

Magnus

EXERCISE 405

Translate:

1. May the fortifications be finished! 2. May the town be taken! 3. May we be saved from this danger! 4. May letters

---

[1] **fundāmentum, ī:** *foundation.*

[2] **praeter,** *prep. w. acc.: besides.*

be received! 5. May they be captured! 6. May the bridge be finished! 7. May they flee! 8. May enough water be captured! 9. May the king be taken!

EXERCISE 406

Translate:

1. Benedictus Arnold, quī fidem in nostram rem pūblicam nōn servāverat, ē castrīs Americānīs sē ēripuit et in aliās partēs fūgit nē ab eīs interficerētur. 2. Chrīstus interfectus est ut hominēs ē morte et peccātō ēriperentur. 3. Castra ad flūmen posita erant ut satis aquae ex flūmine caperētur. 4. Vītās obsidum cōnservāvit nē ex eōrum caede magnus dolor ā Gallīs caperētur. 5. Nōn satis tūtum erat in eō locō pugnāre. Itaque in castra contendērunt nē ab hostibus caperentur et interficerentur. 6. Ab centuriōnibus quaesīvit num mīlitēs magnitūdine itineris et vulneribus cōnfectī essent. 7. Arma parēmus nē mīlitēs nostrī ab hostibus capiantur et interficiantur. 8. Omnēs ducēs mūnītiōnēs parant nē urbēs et oppida ab hostibus capiantur et mūniantur. 9. Legiōnēs clam per silvās ad collem dēdūxit nē ā barbarīs cōnspicerentur. 10. Dux ā tribūnīs mīlitum quaesīvit num agmen hostium cōnspectum esset. 11. Lēgātus ā centuriōnibus quaesīvit num post urbem captam satis frūmentī habērent. 12. Ibi multōs diēs mānsit nē mīlitēs magnitūdine labōris et itineris cōnficerentur.

EXERCISE 407

AN ASSIGNMENT FOR THE INTELLIGENCE DEPARTMENT

You are a Gaul who has been sent into the Roman camp as a spy. You have managed to get into the tent of the *lēgātus* and there you have found the torn pieces of an official message of great importance. When you fit it together, it looks something like what you see on page 405. Can you supply the missing letters and discover the plan of the Roman general staff? Draw a diagram of the battle plan contained in this message.

LITTERAE TUAE ME HORA PRIMA ACCEPTAE SUNT.
AGMEN HOSTIUM AB EQUITIBUS MEIS HORA SE-
CUNDA CONSPECTUM EST. HORA TERTIA CASTRA
EORUM POSITA SUNT IN COLLE QUI CENTUM PEDES
A FLUMINE ABEST. CASTRA IBI POSUERUNT UT SATIS
AQUAE EX FLUMINE CAPERETUR. QUAESIVI NUM
SATIS FRUMENTI ETIAM ACCEPISSENT. SATIS AC-
CEPERUNT. ITAQUE OPORTET NOS STATIM IN EOS
IMPETUM FACERE NE EX TIMORE ET LABORE SE
RECIPIANT. ITAQUE COPIAS MEAS PER SILVAS ILLI
COLLI PROXIMAS CLAM DEDUCAM NE A CUSTODIIS
CONSPICIAMUR. ALTERAM PARTEM COPIARUM A
TERGO IN SILVIS COLLOCABO. NE HOSTES IN SILVAS
SE RECIPIANT; ALTERAM AUTEM PARTEM A FRONTE
IN HOSTES MITTAM. TE JUBEO LEGIONEM TERTIAM
PER MONTES CLAM DEDUCERE NE EX CASTRIS
CONSPICIANTUR. HANC LEGIONEM TRANS FLUMEN
COLLOCA NE HOSTES TRANS FLUMEN IN MONTES SE
RECIPIANT. ITER ERIT SATIS LONGUM ET DIFFICILE.
ITAQUE DIU EXSPECTABO ET HORA TERTIA SIGNUM
DABO. PRIMUM ALTERA PARS COPIARUM MANEBIT
IN SILVIS, AT ALTERA PARS IMPETUM IN CASTRA A
FRONTE FACIET. HOSTES, TIMORE MOTI, CONTRA
HOS MILITES PUGNABUNT. TUM EI QUI IN SILVIS
SUNT, POST SIGNUM DATUM, IMPETUM A TERGO
FACIENT ET TELA CONJICIENT. SI[1] AUXILIUM A TE
CUPIAM, MITTAM NUNTIUM QUI JUBEAT TE LEGIO-
NEM TERTIAM TRANS FLUMEN TRADUCERE. VALE.

---

[1] sī, *conj.: if.*

SENTENTIAE SĒLECTAE

1. DĒ ELEPHANTŌ

Why has an elephant a trunk? Here is Cicero's explanation:
Manus data elephantō est quia,[1] propter magnitūdinem corporis, difficilēs aditūs[2] habēbat ad pastum.[3]

2. DĒ SPĒ

Thalēs,[4] rogātus quid maximē commūne esset hominibus, "Spēs," inquit, "hanc enim illī etiam habent quī nihil habent aliud."

3. SENTENTIA EPICTĒTĪ[5]

Epictētus, rogātus quis esset dīves,[6] "Cui," inquit, "satis est quod habet."

---

[1] quia: *because* (like quod).
[2] aditus, ūs: *approach (to), access (to).*
[3] pastus, ūs: *forage, food.*
[4] Thalēs, Thalis: *Thales* (one of the seven Wise Men of Greece).
[5] Epictētus, ī: *Epictetus* (an ancient philosopher).
[6] dīves, dīvitis: *rich, wealthy.*

LESSON 38: DATIVE VERBS; THE PASSIVE OF VERBS OF CALLING

1. Many verbs in Latin take cases other than the accusative. The dative is used after some intransitive verbs, especially compounds of prepositions. (GRAMMAR, Nos. 739 and 746-747.)

Legiōnī praeest. *He is in command of the legion.*

Reī pūblicae nocet. *He does harm to the state.*

Tibi nōn cēdam. *I will not yield to you.*

2. We have seen that verbs of *calling, naming, etc.,* take a direct object and a predicate accusative. In the passive these verbs take a predicate NOMINATIVE.

Caesar imperātor appellātur. *Caesar is called commander in chief.*

Imperātor refers back to the subject of the sentence and is therefore in the NOMINATIVE CASE.

VOCABULARY

noceō, nocēre, nocuī, nocitūrus, 2, *intr.; w. dat.*   { *do harm to* / *injure*

praesum, praeesse, praefuī, praefutūrus, *intr.; w. dat.*   { *am in command of* / *am in charge of*

mare, maris[1]   *sea*

ventus, ī   *wind*

nāvigō, *1, intr.*   *sail*

RELATED ENGLISH WORDS

A *mariner; marine* animals; the Merchant *Marine;* the American *Marines;* a *noxious* weed; a *navigator.*

RELATED LATIN WORDS

Nāvis; sum.

---

[1] **Mare** is declined like the neuter of **gravis, grave,** and NOT like **flūmen.**

MAGNAE COPIAE IN GALLIAM TRADUCTAE SUNT.

EXERCISE 408

D-DAY

Translate:

Cum diēs cōnstitūta advēnisset,[1] ducēs Americānī propter magnitūdinem ventī ad Galliam[2] nāvigāre nōn potuērunt. Nam magnitūdō ventōrum nāvibus nocet. Itaque in Britanniā diūtius mānsērunt nē ventī et mare nāvibus nocērent. Posteā[3] vērō magnās cōpiās trāns mare in Galliam[2] ūnō diē trādūxērunt ut hostibus nocērent. Hostēs magnās mūnītiōnēs fēcerant. Tamen Americānī eōrumque sociī, et ad mortem et ad victōriam parātī, illās mūnītiōnēs cēpērunt et hostēs in fugam conjēcērunt.

Dux fortis et magnus, nōmine Bradley, praefuit exercituī Americānō.

Nōnne et ducem nostrum et mīlitēs nostrōs propter virtūtem semper laudābimus?

---

[1] advēnisset: *had arrived.*
[2] Gallia, ae: *France.*
[3] posteā, *adv.: afterwards.*

EXERCISE 409
[Essential]
Translate:

1. A centurion was in charge of a hundred men; a lieutenant was often in charge of two or three legions; the general was in charge of the whole army.

2. MacArthur, a great and brave leader, was in charge of that American army which was in Australia and the neighboring regions. He did harm to the Japanese ships and soldiers.

3. Sailors are brave men, for the sea is full of dangers but they do not fear to sail. The greatness of the winds injures their ships and they are often in danger of death. Therefore I praise sailors very much.

4. For many years peoples and states have contended with one another on land and sea. But in these times they have filled the sky with soldiers and arms.

5. Bad men injure the state most. It behooves us to make good men leaders and chiefs. For men without faithfulness and without virtue cannot preserve a free state. Are good men in charge of our nation now?

READING NO. 34

DĒ COLUMBŌ

Columbus, nauta fortis et bonus, cōnstituit novīs viīs ad Indiam nāvigāre. Tamen propter inopiam omnium rērum neque nāvēs parāre neque omnia quae ūtilia erant comparāre potuit. Itaque ad castra rēgis Hispāniae pervēnit ut auxilium peteret. Ille autem prīmum eum nōn adjūvit; tum vērō ā Rēgīnā Isabellā adductus omnia quae cupiēbat dedit. Itaque trēs nāvēs parātae atque īnstrūctae sunt. Prīma nāvis in quā fuit Columbus, *Santa Maria* vocābātur, altera nāvis *Pinta* vocābātur; tertia nāvis *Niña* vocābātur. Hīs tribus nāvibus Columbus praeerat. Centum et vīgintī[1] nautae etiam coāctī sunt. Itaque cum omnia jam essent parāta ex

---

[1] vīgintī: *twenty.*

COLUMBUS

portū illae trēs parvae nāvēs nāvigābant. Mare magnum erat. Nēmō ante id tempus trāns illud mare nāvigāverat. Quod nāvēs parvae erant, mare perīculōrum plēnum fuit. Nōn saepe, autem, propter magnitūdinem ventōrum difficile fuit nāvigāre.

Cum multōs diēs nāvigāvissent, terram vīdērunt. Omnēs nautae vehementer commōtī sunt. Ē nāvibus contendērunt atque illam terram in nōmine rēgis Hispānicī occupāvērunt. Ita Columbus ad Americam pervēnit.

HOW GOOD IS YOUR IMAGINATION?

A newspaper reporter is rushed by plane from the front lines in the island fighting in the Pacific to San Francisco. He arrives in a dying condition. All you can get from him before he dies is this:

"Soldiers . . . sailors . . . ships . . . wind for days . . . wind! Got there . . . terrible . . . no water . . . days on fortifications . . . no water . . . rations low . . . bombarded us . . . days . . .

and days . . . no help . . . men killed . . . then they . . . attack
. . . bombardment . . . thousands of Japs . . . shooting . . . bayonets . . . they got . . . in . . . our camp. At last . . . routed . . .
fled . . . days . . . help came . . . we attack . . . terrible fighting . . . they . . . sur . . . sur . . . "

Now your job is to write up the story here in simple Latin for
a Latin newspaper. What kind of a story can you make out of
it? Use simple Latin and the words and constructions you are
sure of. Here are some hints:

For *rations* use **frūmentum.**

For *low* use **inopia.**

For *bombardment* use **tēla conjicere.**

For *shooting, etc.,* use **tēla conjicere.**

For *bayonets* use **gladiī.**

For *Japs* use **Japōnēs.**

> **Per adventum tuum,**
> **Līberā nōs, Jēsū!**

UNIT TWELVE

LESSON 39: THE ACCUSATIVE WITH THE INFINITIVE

1. PERFECT AND FUTURE INFINITIVES ACTIVE

The PERFECT INFINITIVE ACTIVE of ALL LATIN VERBS, REGULAR AND IRREGULAR, is formed by adding -isse to the PERFECT stem.

> laudāvī (perfect indicative)   STEM: laudāv-
> Perfect Infinitive Active: LAUDĀVISSE, *to have loved*

The FUTURE INFINITIVE ACTIVE of ALL LATIN VERBS is a COMPOUND tense made up of the FUTURE PARTICIPLE ACTIVE and esse.

The FUTURE PARTICIPLE ACTIVE is formed by dropping the -us of the perfect participle passive and adding -ūrus.

> laudātus (perfect participle passive)   STEM: laudāt-
> Future Participle Active: laudātūrus, a, um
> Future Infinitive Active: LAUDĀTŪRUS, A, UM ESSE

ASSIGNMENT: Study Grammar, Nos. 210, 222-224; 215, 237-239; 211, 225-227.

EXERCISE 410

1. Give the principal parts and the meaning;
2. Give the present infinitive active;
3. Give the perfect infinitive active;
4. Give the perfect participle passive;
5. Give the future participle active;
6. Give the future infinitive active:

1. laudō	3. superō	5. sustineō
2. parō	4. habeō	6. audiō

7. dēfendō	16. pugnō	25. comparō
8. collocō	17. oppugnō	26. addūcō
9. accipiō	18. īnstruō	27. obtineō
10. retineō	19. moneō	28. trādō
11. premō	20. terreō	29. cōnstituō
12. mittō	21. recipiō	30. dō
13. dīmittō	22. cognōscō	31. trādūcō
14. occīdō	23. expugnō	32. ostendō
15. compleō	24. capiō	33. vastō

Note. Remember that, when a verb is intransitive, the perfect participle passive is always given in the neuter, as **perveniō, pervenīre, pervēnī, perventum,** *4, intr.* This is because the passive of intransitive verbs can be used only IMPERSONALLY (as we shall see), and so will always be in the NEUTER.

When, however, a verb has no perfect participle passive, the future participle active is given as the fourth principal part, as **maneō, manēre, mānsī, mānsūrus,** *2, intr.*

ASSIGNMENT: Review GRAMMAR, No. 332 and FIRST YEAR LATIN, page 326.

EXERCISE 411

Here is a complete list of intransitive verbs which you have had. Study them and give their future infinitive active.

appropinquō, *1, intr.*
nāvigō, *1, intr.*
perveniō, pervenīre, pervēnī, perventum, *4, intr.*
conveniō, convenīre, convēnī, conventum, *4, intr.*
veniō, venīre, vēnī, ventum, *4, intr.*
noceō, nocēre, nocuī, nocitūrus, *2, intr.*
discēdō, discēdere, discessī, discessūrus, *3, intr.*
maneō, manēre, mānsī, mānsūrus, *2, intr.*
cēdō, cēdere, cessī, cessūrus, *3, intr.*
absum, abesse, āfuī, āfutūrus, *intr.*
sum, esse, fuī, futūrus, *intr.*
valeō, valēre, valuī, valitūrus, *2, intr.*

> Ostende nōbīs, Domine,
> Misericordiam[1] tuam!

2. ACCUSATIVE WITH THE INFINITIVE AFTER VERBS OF *SAYING, THINKING, SEEING,* AND THE LIKE

We know that God loves all men.

We know that Caesar conquered the Gauls.

We know that God will give rewards to good men.

These are complex sentences. The MAIN clause is: *WE KNOW.* The *THAT* clauses are SUBORDINATE NOUN CLAUSES because they are used as the object of *WE KNOW. What* do we know? THAT GOD LOVES ALL MEN, *etc.*

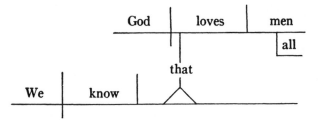

Noun clauses after verbs of *SAYING, THINKING, SEEING, KNOWING,* AND THE LIKE are, in Latin, put in the ACCUSATIVE WITH THE INFINITIVE.

In this construction:

1. The VERB is always an INFINITIVE.

2. The SUBJECT is always in the ACCUSATIVE CASE.

3. The TENSE of the INFINITIVE is determined by the RULE: TENSE BY RELATION.

ASSIGNMENT: Study GRAMMAR, Nos. 897-898.

---

[1] misericordia, ae: *mercy.*

Scīmus Deum dīligere omnēs hominēs.
Literally, *We know God to love all men.*

Scīmus Caesarem vīcisse Gallōs.
Literally, *We know Caesar to have conquered the Gauls.*

Scīmus Deum hominibus bonīs praemia datūrum esse.
Literally, *We know God to be about to give rewards to good men.*

NOTE

1. The *that* is NOT translated in Latin.
2. Since the future participle active is used like an adjective in a compound tense, it will agree with the accusative subject.

Dīcō hanc cīvitātem semper futūram esse līberam.
I say that this state will always be free.

Dīcō sānctōs Deum vīsūrōs esse.
I say that the saints will see God.

ASSIGNMENT: Review the rules for the indirect reflexive, GRAMMAR, No. 804.

VOCABULARY

(Verbs which may take the accusative with
the infinitive; tense by relation)

dīcō, dīcere, dīxī, dictus, 3, tr.	say tell
respondeō, respondēre, respondī, respōnsus, 2, tr.	answer
putō, 1, tr.	think
sciō, 4, tr.	know
audiō, 4, tr.	hear

RELATED ENGLISH WORDS

His *diction* is excellent. The *response* was prompt.

Jēsū, Deus noster,
Miserēre nōbīs!

EXERCISE 412
[Essential]

1. *Point out the main clause;*
2. *Point out the accusative with the infinitive;*
3. *Explain the tense of the infinitive;*
4. *Translate:*

A. The Present Infinitive

1. Putō omnēs sānctōs Deum dīligere. 2. Sciō Americānōs fortiter pugnāre. 3. Putō omnēs hominēs amīcitiam quaerere. 4. Lēgātus dīxit Caesarem Gallōs vincere. 5. Centuriō dīxit mīlitēs ācriter pugnāre. 6. Nuntius dīxit Gallōs oppugnāre urbem.

B. The Perfect Infinitive

1. Scīmus Caesarem vīcisse Gallōs. 2. Scīmus Columbum ad Americam pervēnisse. 3. Scīmus Rōmānōs occīdisse Chrīstum. 4. Caesar audīvit Gallōs occīdisse lēgātum. 5. Caesar putāvit equitēs ad castra pervēnisse. 6. Lēgātus putāvit Caesarem hostēs vīcisse.

C. The Future Infinitive

Warning. Remember that the future participle is declined like **magnus, a, um** and must agree with the SUBJECT ACCUSATIVE.

1. Putō Americānōs fortiter pugnātūrōs esse. 2. Sciō hominēs bonōs Deum vīsūrōs esse. 3. Putō Americānōs semper hostēs victūrōs esse. 4. Sciō Marīam semper Deum vīsūram esse. 5. Putō Deum omnibus hominibus grātiam datūrum esse. 6. Caesar putāvit Gallōs cessūrōs esse.

D. Reflexives after Infinitives
Explain the italicized words:

1. Dīcō *mē* esse Chrīstiānum, fuisse Chrīstiānum, semper futūrum Chrīstiānum. 2. Putāsne *tē* esse sānctum? 3. Caesar dīxit *sē* victūrum esse Gallōs. 4. Dīcimus *nōs* esse līberōs. 5. Dīcitisne *vōs* obsidēs datūrōs nōbīs esse? 6. Rōmānī dīxērunt

sē imperium tōtīus Galliae obtinēre. 7. Dīcō *mē* agrōs *meōs* dēfēnsūrum esse. 8. Hic Americānus ostendit nūllum rēgem in cīvitāte *suā* rēgnum tenēre. 9. Chrīstus dīxit *nōs* esse frātrēs *suōs*. 10. Caesar putāvit *suōs* fortiter esse pugnātūrōs. 11. Marīa scīvit *sē* Fīlium suum adōrāre posse.

E. Agreement after Infinitives

Warning. Remember that ACCORDING TO THE GENERAL RULE a linking verb takes the same case after it as before it. Therefore a predicate adjective or noun in the accusative with the infinitive will agree with the subject accusative.

Explain the agreement of the italicized words:

1. Dīcit Chrīstum esse *Fīlium* Deī. 2. Dīcō omnes ferē hominēs glōriae *cupidōs* esse. 3. Sciō nostram cīvitātem *līberam* esse. 4. Vir sānctus Rōmānīs respondit Chrīstum esse Fīlium Deī. 5. Rōmānī scīvērunt Caesarem esse summum *imperātōrem*. 6. Rōmānī scīvērunt Rōmam esse *magnam*.

EXERCISE 413

Translate:

A.

1. The American says that Americans fight bravely. 2. The American says that Washington was a very great general. 3. The American says that his soldiers will fight bravely.

B.

1. The lieutenant said that Caesar was conquering the Gauls. 2. The lieutenant said that Caesar had conquered the Gauls. 3. The lieutenant said that his men would conquer the enemy.

C.

1. We shall know that God loves us. 2. We shall know that God took away our sins. 3. We shall know that our men will conquer.

D.

1. I was saying that our state was free. 2. I was saying that the Roman state had been free. 3. I was saying that our state would always be free.

E.

1. He said that he would see God. 2. I said that I would see Rome. 3. She said that she would see Gaul. 4. They said that they would fight bravely. 5. You said that you would send hostages to us. 6. He said that Caesar would give him a reward.

F.

1. He had heard that they were in arms. 2. He had heard that the Gauls had fled. 3. They had heard that the Gauls would send hostages.

EXERCISE 414
[Essential]
Translate:

A. Present Infinitive

1. I say that Americans fight bravely. 2. He says that God defends good men. 3. They say that our soldiers are conquering the enemy. 4. He said that Caesar was conquering the Gauls. 5. They said that the Senate was praising Caesar. 6. They said that the Gauls were sending hostages.

B. Perfect Infinitive

1. I say that the Romans fought bravely. 2. He says that the Americans were conquering the enemy. 3. We say that Caesar had conquered Gaul. 4. They said that the Gauls had attacked the winter quarters. 5. They said that Caesar had hastened into Gaul. 6. He said that the Senate had given thanks to Caesar.

C. Future Infinitive

1. I say that the Americans will fight bravely. 2. He says that we shall conquer the enemy. 3. They will know that we will send help. 4. He said that he would conquer the barbarians.

PYRRHUS ET CINEAS

READING NO. 35

DĒ PYRRHŌ, ĒPĪRĪ RĒGE

Pyrrhus erat rēx Ēpīrī. Potesne hoc rēgnum in tabulā[1] vidēre?
Pyrrhus nōn erat Rōmānus. Neque in Italiā neque in Galliā
incolēbat. Erat Graecus. Erat autem rēx fortis et glōriae cupidus.
Multās aliās gentēs vincere cōnstituit. Erat cum exercitū ējus
amīcus, nōmine Cīneas. Hic vērō vir bonus fuit neque cōnsilia
Pyrrhī probāvit. Quod Pyrrhī amīcus fuit, eum fortiter monēre

---

[1] tabula, ae: *map*. (See the map on page 30.)

nōn timēbat. Ōlim[1] Pyrrhus, glōriā sublātus, eī dīxit sē exercitum in Italiam ductūrum esse et Rōmānōs victūrum esse. Putāvit enim sē eōs facile superāre posse.

Cīneas autem, "Post illam victōriam, Rēx magne," inquit, "quid cōnstituistī facere?"

Pyrrhus, "Īnsula[2] Sicilia, bona et magna," inquit, "Italiae fīnitima est. In illam trādūcam mīlitēs meōs ut eam vincam atque obtineam. Facile erit eam īnsulam[2] armīs et virtūte occupāre."

Tum Cīneas, "Post illam victōriam," inquit, "quid dīcis tē factūrum esse?"

Eī Pyrrhus respondit sē mīlitēs suōs trāns mare in Africam ductūrum esse atque eās etiam regiōnēs victūrum esse.

Cīneas, "Post haec proelia atque hās victōriās, quid cōnstituistī facere?"

Respondit Pyrrhus, "Post hās victōriās pācem cōnfirmābō."

Statim autem Cīneas, "Cūr, Ō Rēx bone," inquit, "nōn nunc pācem cōnfirmās? Quid tē impedit?"

3. ACCUSATIVE WITH THE INFINITIVE AFTER VERBS OF *SAYING, THINKING, SEEING,* AND THE LIKE (CONTINUED)

We have seen that when a verb is used impersonally in Latin:

1. It has no definite subject (English *it,* as in "It rains").
2. It is in the third person singular.
3. In a compound tense the participle is always neuter singular.

An impersonal verb is used in the accusative with the infinitive construction:

1. In the infinitive;
2. Without a subject expressed (English, *it*).
3. In a compound infinitive the participle is always NEUTER.

---

[1] ōlim, *adv.: once.*
[2] īnsula, ae: *island.*

It behooves us to love God.
Oportet nōs Deum dīligere.

I say that it behooves us to love God.
Dīcō oportēre nōs Deum dīligere.

It was bitterly fought (i. e., there was bitter fighting).
Ācriter pugnātum est.

I say that it was bitterly fought (i. e., that there was bitter fighting).
Dīcō ācriter pugnātum esse.

We have seen that verbs like **jubeō** and **oportet** take the accusative with the infinitive. Note this difference: IN THE ACCUSATIVE WITH THE INFINITIVE AFTER VERBS OF *SAYING*, ETC., THE TENSE OF THE INFINITIVE IS DETERMINED BY RELATION. When the accusative with the infinitive is used AFTER OTHER VERBS AND EXPRESSIONS the tense is generally PRESENT.

VOCABULARY
(More verbs that may take the accusative
with the infinitive; tense by relation)

scrībō, scrībere, scrīpsī, scrīptus, *3, tr.*	*write*
reperiō, reperīre, repperī, repertus, *4, tr.*	*find (out)*
negō, *1, tr.*	*deny* *say . . . not*
nuntiō, *1, tr.*	*announce* *report*
dēmōnstrō, *1, tr.*	*show* *point out*

NOTE
Verbs which may take an accusative with the infinitive do not always do so. When the sense requires, they also govern indirect questions, accusative objects, *etc.*

Haec nuntiāvit. *He reported these things.*
Nuntiāvit quot essent hostēs. *He reported how many the enemy were.*

RELATED ENGLISH WORDS

Some people's *script* is illegible. He *described* the *inscriptions* found on ancient monuments. They gave a *negative* answer. He was *demonstrating* the use of a tank.

RELATED LATIN WORD

Caesar **nuntium** ā lēgātō suō accēpit.

REVIEW VOCABULARY

cernō, cernere, 3, tr.	{ *distinguish* / *see*
cognōscō, cognōscere, cognōvī, cognitus, 3, tr.	{ *learn* / *find out*
cōnfirmō, 1, tr.	*affirm*
cōnspiciō, cōnspicere, cōnspexī, cōnspectus, 3, tr.	{ *see* / *catch sight of*
ostendō, ostendere, ostendī, ostentus, 3, tr.	*show*
probō, 1, tr.	{ *approve* / *prove*
moneō, 2, tr.	{ *warn* / *advise*
videō, vidēre, vīdī, vīsus, 2, tr.	*see*

EXERCISE 415
[Essential]
Translate:

1. Probat sē Chrīstiānum esse. 2. Dīcimus virōs bonōs vēritātem virtūtemque semper quaerere. 3. Vōs moneō vītam esse brevem. 4. Puer respondit sē rēs ā Washingtoniō gestās memoriā tenēre. 5. Tē moneō Deum hominibus malīs praemia nōn esse datūrum. 6. Sciō Americānōs sē posse dēfendere. 7. Cōnfirmāmus mīlitēs nostrōs fortiter pugnāre. 8. Nōs Chrīstiānī cōnfirmāmus Deum, Patrem nostrum, omnēs gentēs dīligere. 9. Nautae dīcunt ventōs magnōs nāvibus nocēre. 10. Scīmus omnēs hominēs, perīculō mortis perturbātōs, ōrāre atque grātiam ā Deō petere.

11. Scīmus memoriam esse custōdem rērum cognitārum. 12. Vōs, puerī, moneō bonam memoriam ad vītam esse ūtilem. 13. Columbus repperit barbarōs incolere Americam. 14. Cicerō, vir bonus atque nōbilis, scrīpsit sē semper virtūtem laudātūrum esse. 15. Sānctus Paulus scrīpsit Chrīstum sē dē rēbus quae ad fidem pertinent docuisse. 16. Scrīptum est Sānctum Paulum Chrīstum in viā subitō vīdisse. 17. Washingtonius, cum audīvisset Benedictum Arnold ad hostēs fūgisse, repperit ea omnia esse vēra. 18. Chrīstus dīxit omnēs sānctōs sēcum in Caelō Deum vīsūrōs esse. 19. Nōnne, amīce mī, audīvistī omnēs nōs esse frātrēs? 20. Chrīstus jussit nōs omnēs hominēs dīligere. 21. Chrīstus, cum ā Pīlātō rogātus esset, respondit sē esse rēgem. 22. Chrīstus negāvit sē armīs et legiōnibus rēgnum tenēre. 23. Thōmas More, cum ad mortem dūcerētur, negāvit sē ā fidē Chrīstiānā discessūrum esse. 24. Apostolī omnibus hominibus nuntiāvērunt Chrīstum esse Fīlium Deī atque prō nōbīs interfectum esse. 25. Pīlātus putāvit Chrīstum esse virum bonum at timuit eum dīmittere. Jūdaeī enim dīxērunt Chrīstum sē rēgem vocāre. Itaque dīxērunt, "Quī sē rēgem facit, contrādīcit[1] Caesarī." 26. Columbus putāvit sē nōn ad novās terrās sed ad Indiam pervēnisse. 27. Imperātōrēs Rōmānī reppererunt Chrīstiānōs in Italiā et in omnibus prōvinciīs esse. Itaque multōs ex eīs ad mortem dūcī jussērunt. Tamen nōn potuērunt fidem Chrīstī vincere.

EXERCISE 416
[Imitation]
Imitate the construction of the model
in translating these sentences:

MODEL: **Negāvit sē ventūrum esse.**
He said that he would not come.

1. They said that they would not give hostages to him.
2. He said that he would not surrender the arms.
3. They said that they would not flee.

---

[1] contrādīcō, contrādīcere, contrādīxī, contrādictum, 3, *intr.; w. dat.: speak against.*

EXERCISE 417
Translate:

Warning. In some of these sentences the main verb of SAY-
ING, *etc.*, governs the accusative with the infinitive, in some it
governs an indirect question or an accusative object.

1. I found that those things were true. 2. We found out where
the enemy had stationed guards. 3. We saw that the enemy had
prepared fortifications. 4. We saw where the enemy had pitched
camp. 5. They said that the greatness of the winds had injured
the ship. 6. I said that Caesar was in charge of the legion. 7. He
said that he would not hand over the slaves. 8. He showed that
he was a brave man. 9. They reported the slaughter of the
hostages. 10. They knew how large the Roman camp was.
11. They were saying that the Gauls were afraid to fight. 12. He
saw that the barbarians had come out of the forest. 13. He had
seen that the barbarians had prepared fortifications. 14. He knew
the names of the centurions. 15. He said that the plans were not
useful.

EXERCISE 418
[Essential]
Translate:

Warning. Remember that after verbs of SAYING, *etc.*, the tense
of the infinitive is TENSE BY RELATION; after **jubeō** and
other expressions it is generally PRESENT.

1. I am able to fight. 2. I said that I was able to fight. 3. I
say that I was able to fight. 4. I shall prove that I was able to
fight. 5. He said he would fight. 6. He was ordered to fight.
7. They ordered him to fight. 8. It is good to fight bravely.
9. They determined to fight at once. 10. It behooved us to fight
bravely. 11. We are prepared to sail. 12. They said they were
prepared to sail. 13. They said that they had been prepared to
sail for five days. 14. He said he would be prepared to sail within
two days. 15. On the third day he was able to sail. 16. It be-

hooves us to sail at once. 17. They are accustomed to sail from
this harbor. 18. They said they were accustomed to sail from
that harbor. 19. They said there was not sufficient water.
20. It is not difficult to pray. 21. He said that the enemy had fled
five miles. 22. On account of the greatness of the winds he said
he would not sail. 23. He ordered them to defend the hill until
night. 24. They said that they would defend the hill for three
days. 25. He did not know whether they had attacked the
column. 26. Christ said that He would help and defend all
men.

READING NO. 36

DĒ RĒGE FORTĪ

Leōnidās quī Lacedaemoniōrum[1] rēx erat, et cui Xerxēs, Per-
sārum[2] rēx, scrīpserat, "Mitte arma," eī respondit, "Venī et ea
cape."

> Chrīstum Rēgem adōrēmus.

READING NO. 37

PILATE'S REPLY

Posuērunt in cruce[3] Jēsū signum in quō scrīptum erat: *"Hic est
Jēsūs Rēx Jūdaeōrum."*[4] Itaque prīncipēs Jūdaeōrum[4] cum hoc
signum vīdissent, vehementer mōtī, ad Pīlātum vēnērunt. "Nōlī[5]
scrībere: *Rēx Jūdaeōrum,"*[4] inquiunt,[6] "sed: *'Hic dīxit sē esse
rēgem Jūdaeōrum.'* "[4]

---

[1] **Lacedaemoniī, ōrum:** *the Spartans,* who were famous for their courage and
their brevity of speech.
[2] **Persae, ārum:** *the Persians.*
[3] **crux, crucis:** *cross.*
[4] **Jūdaeī, Jūdaeōrum:** *the Jews.*
[5] **nōlī scrībere:** *do not write* (literally, *be unwilling to write*).
[6] **inquiunt:** *they said.*

"QUOD SCRIPSI, SCRIPSI."

Respondit Pīlātus: "Quod scrīpsī, scrīpsī!" *(Adapted from the account of St. John.)*

A LATIN RIDDLE

Can you solve it?

Quis est quī nōn est et tamen nōmen habet et quaerentī[1] respondet?

---

[1] **quaerentī:** *to one asking.*

O bone Jēsū, miserēre nōbīs!

READING NO. 38

DĒ BELLŌ CUM PYRRHŌ GESTŌ

Jam dēmōnstrāvimus Rōmānōs multās Italiae gentēs vīcisse atque imperium magnae partis Italiae obtinēre. Cum gentēs sibi proximās vīcissent, bellum cum aliīs gentibus gerēbant. Itaque Tarentīnī, quī Rōmānōs t'mēbant, contrā eōs pugnābant nē ab eīs vincerentur. Tarentīnī, quod Rōmānōs pellere sōlī nōn potuērunt, lēgātōs ad Pyrrhum, rēgem Ēpīrī, mīsērunt quī auxilium ab eō peterent. Pyrrhus, glōriae cupidus, dīxit sē exercitum in Italiam auxiliī causā ductūrum esse.

Interim Rōmānī omnia quae ad bellum pertinēbant parābant. Itaque Pyrrhus, cum exercitum in Italiam trādūxisset, repperit Rōmānōs ad bellum parātōs esse. Itaque cum omnibus cōpiīs contrā eōs contendit. Rōmānī aciem īnstrūxērunt et impetum Pyrrhī exspectābant. Pyrrhus autem sēcum multōs elephantōs habēbat. Hōs prīmum in equitēs Rōmānōs mīsit; tum, cum equitēs in fugam datī essent, in aciem mīlitum mīsit. Rōmānī autem numquam ante id elephantōs in proeliīs vīderant. Itaque, ōrdinēs eōrum ab elephantīs perturbātī sunt atque multī mīlitēs occīsī sunt. Tamen Rōmānī fortiter pugnābant. Sed magnitūdine corporis elephantōrum territī hostēs vincere nōn potuērunt. Post magnam caedem Rōmānī in castra sē recēpērunt nē omnēs omnīnō occiderentur.

Septem mīlia mīlitum Rōmānōrum in hōc proeliō cecidērunt. Agrī corporum plēnī erant, sed Pyrrhus, cum corpora Rōmānōrum interfectōrum vulnera in fronte[1] habēre vīdisset, dīxit sē cum hīs mīlitibus Rōmānīs omnēs omnīnō terrās vincere posse. Ex mīlitibus Pyrrhī quattuor mīlia occīsa sunt. Rōmānī facile aliōs mīlitēs cōgere potuērunt sed difficile fuit novās cōpiās ex Ēpīrō comparāre. Itaque Pyrrhus propter magnum occīsōrum

---

[1] in fronte: *in front.*

numerum vīdit hanc victōriam nōn satis ūtilem esse. "If I conquer again in this same manner," inquit, "I shall have no soldiers left."

Ever since then a victory won at the cost of disastrous losses has been called a "Pyrrhic victory."

4. PASSIVE INFINITIVES

ASSIGNMENT: Review the present infinitive passive, GRAMMAR, Nos. 284, 292-294.

The perfect infinitive passive is a COMPOUND tense formed by using the perfect participle passive with **esse.**

Since the participle in a compound tense is declined like an adjective, the participle will agree with the SUBJECT ACCUSATIVE.

> *I say that the Gauls were conquered.*
> Dīcō Gallōs <u>victōs</u> esse.

The future infinitive passive is very rare; hence you need not learn it now.

ASSIGNMENT: Study GRAMMAR, Nos. 285, 295-297.

VOCABULARY

(Words that may take the accusative with the infinitive; tense by relation.)

exīstimō, *1, tr.*	*think*
sentiō, sentīre, sēnsī, sēnsus, *4, tr.*	$\left\{\begin{array}{l}\textit{feel}\\\textit{perceive}\\\textit{think}\end{array}\right.$

RELATED ENGLISH WORDS

We cannot perceive God with our *senses.* He *sensed* that something was wrong. The *sensation* caused by extreme heat.

ASSIGNMENT: Write out the present and perfect infinitives passive of the verbs in Exercise 410.

EXERCISE 419

[Essential]

Translate:

1. Dīcō omnēs hominēs ā Deō dīligī. 2. Dīcō Gallōs ā Caesare victōs esse. 3. Dīxit Caesarem ā senātū laudārī. 4. Dīxit Gallōs ā Caesare pulsōs esse. 5. Caesar dīxit sē ā Gallīs nōn laudārī. 6. Dīcō mē ā Deō dēfendī. 7. Dīxistī tē ā senātū laudārī. 8. Dīcit sē ā barbarīs adjuvārī. 9. Dīcimus nōs ab hostibus vidērī. 10. Dīcitis vōs ā Deō adjuvārī. 11. Dīcunt sē ā duce appellārī. 12. Dīxī mē ā barbarīs captum esse. 13. Negāvit tē ā barbarīs captum esse. 14. Dīxit sē ā Caesare laudātum esse. 15. Dīcimus nōs ā virīs fortibus līberātōs esse. 16. Dīxērunt sē in castra ā Caesare vocātōs esse. 17. Lēgātus negāverat Caesarem ā Gallīs victum esse. 18. Lēgātus negāverat Caesarem ā Gallīs vincī. 19. Negō mē ibi collocātum esse.

Dominus nōs benedīcat[1] et ab omnī malō dēfendat et in vītam perdūcat[2] aeternam.

EXERCISE 420

[Essential]

Translate:

1. I think that Lincoln was killed by a bad man. 2. I perceive that the hill has been seized. 3. He thought that Rome was being attacked. 4. He denied that Rome had been seized. 5. I think that Lincoln is praised by all good men. 6. We said that we had been freed by a brave man. 7. You know that our slaves were freed by Lincoln. 8. You heard that America was found by Columbus. 9. We know that grace is being given to all men. 10. We knew that fortifications were being prepared by the enemy.

---

[1] benedīcō, benedīcere, benedīxī, benedictus, 3, *tr.: bless.*
[2] perdūcō, perdūcere, perdūxī, perductus, 3, *tr.: lead to.*

11. We knew that the enemy were being aroused to war by their leaders. 12. We knew that arms were not being prepared by our own leaders. 13. You know that all men are loved by God. 14. Do you think that God has always been adored? 15. We think that God is being adored and praised by good Christians.

EXERCISE 421

1. Translate;
2. Parse the italicized words:

1. Scīmus Washingtonium *virum* fortem ab omnibus vocātum esse. 2. Dīximus obsidēs ā Caesare propter injūriās Gallōrum saepe *occīsōs* esse. 3. Jam dēmōnstrāvimus Chrīstum ā *Rōmānīs* interfectum esse. 4. Dīcimus in bellō mātrēs saepe *interficī*. 5. Americānī, cum audīvissent *suōs* in Bataan captōs esse, vehementer perturbātī sunt. 6. Gallī audīvērunt obsidēs suōs ā Caesare occīsōs esse. Praetereā scīvērunt omnia frūmenta ab *eō* incēnsa esse; urbēs et oppida aut expugnāta esse aut expugnārī; arma et servōs captōs esse; exercitūs victōs esse; tōtam Galliam vastātam esse neque *sē* ab eō dēfendī posse. Itaque miserī ad eum lēgātōs mittere coāctī sunt quī pācem ab eō peterent. 7. Germānī, cum *nuntiātum esset* magnās cōpiās ab Americānīs eōrumque sociīs in Galliam *esse trāductās*, vehementer *mōtī* atque perturbātī sunt.

READING NO. 39

DĒ PYRRHŌ ET FABRICIŌ

Post illud proelium dē quō jam dēmōnstrāvimus Rōmānī dē pāce nōn ēgērunt. Cōpiās novās coēgērunt; arma ac tēla comparābant. Pyrrhum enim atque ējus elephantōs vincere et ex Italiā pellere jam cōnstituerant.

Fabricius imperātor factus est et contrā Pyrrhum missus est. Cum ad castra Pyrrhī appropinquāvisset atque castra posuisset, medicus[1] ex castrīs Pyrrhī ad Fabricium vēnit. Hic dīxit sē

---

[1] medicus, ī: *doctor* (cf. *medical*).

Pyrrhum rēgem occīsūrum esse, et ita Rōmānōs ab eō līberātūrum esse. Praemia autem rogāvit. Fabricius vērō eum cēpit et jussit eum ligātum¹ ad Pyrrhum dūcī. Praetereā ad Pyrrhum scrīpsit Rōmānōs gladiīs nōn perfidiā² pugnāre. Pyrrhus, ita ab hoste dē perīculō suō monitus, vehementer mōtus est. "It is easier," inquit, "to move the sun from its course, than Fabricius from the path of honesty."

Rōmānī autem Fabricium, virum fortem, ad Pyrrhum mīsērunt quī dē captīvīs commūtandīs³ ageret. Pyrrhus, cum dē hāc rē cum Fabriciō ēgisset, vīdit eum esse virum fortem atque nōbilem. Itaque eī praemia dabat ut sēcum pugnāret. Fabricius autem haec praemia nōn accēpit. Ita ostendit sē esse vērum Rōmānum. Tum Pyrrhus, "Cūr nōn mēcum in Ēpīrum veniēs?" inquit; "tibi magnam rēgnī meī partem dabō." Rūrsus Fabricius negāvit sē rēgnum acceptūrum esse dīxitque sē semper in rē pūblicā līberā mānsūrum.

Post hoc Pyrrhus lēgātōs ad senātum Rōmānum mīsit quī dē pāce agerent. Itaque in senātum ductī sunt atque dēmōnstrāvērunt quae essent pācis condiciōnēs.⁴ In senātū aliī pācem cōnfirmāre cupīvērunt, aliī vērō negāvērunt sē condiciōnēs⁴ acceptūrōs. Praetereā hī ostendērunt exercitum Rōmānum victum esse; agrōs sociōrum vastātōs esse; glōriam nōminis Rōmānī nōn cōnservātam esse. Diū dē hāc rē agēbant. At ūnus ex eīs, vir summus, nōmine Appius Claudius, vehementer commōtus, "The Roman people," inquit, "will not discuss terms of peace while an armed and victorious foe yet stands on the soil of Italy." Itaque senātus condiciōnēs⁴ nōn probāvit et bellum rūrsus gerere cōnstituit.

> Vir fortis neque armīs neque praemiīs vincī potest.

---

¹ ligō, *1, tr.: bind.*
² perfidia, ae: *treachery.*
³ dē captīvīs commūtandīs: *concerning an exchange of prisoners.*
⁴ condiciō, condiciōnis: *condition, term(s).*

READING NO. 40

THE POLITE FLY

In dorsō[1] taurī[2] musca[3] parva erat. Musca,[3] "Sī[4] tē premō," inquit, "statim discēdam." Taurus[2] autem eī respondit, "Ubi es? Nihil enim sentiō."

EXERCISE 422
[Formal Review of Unit Twelve]

1. Explain the formation of: (a) the present infinitive active; (b) the perfect infinitive active; (c) the future participle active; (d) the future infinitive active; (e) the present infinitive passive; (f) the perfect infinitive passive.

2. Give the rules for the accusative with the infinitive after verbs of *saying, etc.*

3. Explain the rule, "Tense by Relation."

4. With what does a predicate noun or adjective in the accusative with the infinitive agree?

5. How is a verb used IMPERSONALLY in the accusative with the infinitive?

---

[1] dorsum, ī: *back.*
[2] taurus, ī: *bull.*
[3] musca, ae: *fly.*
[4] sī, *conj.: if.*

6. Is there any important difference between the use of the accusative with the infinitive after verbs of *saying, etc.*, and after other verbs?

7. Must verbs of *saying, etc.*, ALWAYS take an accusative with the infinitive? Name some other constructions they MAY take and give examples.

EXERCISE 423
[Functional Review of Unit Twelve]

1. Translate;
2. Explain the italicized constructions:

1. Dīcō *Deum esse bonum.* 2. Respondit *sē* fidem Chrīstiānam nōn *negātūrum esse.* 3. Caesar putāvit omnem Galliam *esse pācātam.* 4. Sānctī scrīpsērunt Deum omnēs hominēs *dīligere.* 5. Columbus repperit multās gentēs Americam *incolere.* 6. Negāvit *sē* ventūrum esse. 7. Nuntiātum est ācriter *pugnātum esse.* 8. Dēmōnstrāvit *oportēre* eōs *sē* dēdere. 9. Exīstimō nōs Americānōs līberōs semper *futūrōs esse.* 10. Sēnsit *sē* in magnō perīculō esse. 11. Dīxit sē eō annō in Galliā *fuisse.*

UNIT THIRTEEN

LESSON 40: THE COMPARISON OF ADJECTIVES

1. REGULAR COMPARISON OF ADJECTIVES

POSITIVE DEGREE. An adjective may simply describe a noun, as:

The Gaul is <u>brave.</u> **Gallus est <u>fortis.</u>**

This is called the POSITIVE DEGREE of the adjective.

COMPARATIVE DEGREE. An adjective may COMPARE a noun with some other noun either expressed or understood. In this case the COMPARATIVE DEGREE of the adjective is used. In English the comparative degree is formed either by adding *-er* to the positive or by using the adverb *more* with the positive.

The Roman is <u>braver</u> than the Gaul.

Braver is the COMPARATIVE DEGREE of *brave.* The "other noun" *(Gaul)* is EXPRESSED.

This thing is <u>more useful.</u>

More useful is the COMPARATIVE DEGREE of *useful.* Another noun is here UNDERSTOOD. "This thing is more useful than *some other thing.*"

SUPERLATIVE DEGREE. An adjective may show that a noun has a quality in the HIGHEST DEGREE. In this case the SUPERLATIVE DEGREE of the adjective is used. In English the superlative degree is formed either by adding *-est* to the positive or by using the adverb *most* with the positive.

The Belgians are the <u>bravest</u> of all the Gauls.

Bravest is the SUPERLATIVE DEGREE of *brave.*

This thing is <u>most useful</u>.

Most useful is the SUPERLATIVE DEGREE of *useful*.

ASSIGNMENT: Study GRAMMAR, Nos. 91-98. Memorize the rules for comparison. To COMPARE an adjective means to give the positive, comparative, and superlative degrees, *e. g.*:

COMPARISON OF FORTIS AND ŪTILIS

Positive	*Comparative*	*Superlative*
fortis, e	fortior, fortius	fortissimus, a, um
brave	*braver*	*bravest*
ūtilis, e	ūtilior, ūtilius	ūtilissimus, a, um
useful	*more useful*	*most useful*

EXERCISE 424

Compare these adjectives:

1.	aliēnus	6.	commūnis	11.	sānctus
2.	altus	7.	longus	12.	vērus
3.	angustus	8.	gravis	13.	tūtus
4.	brevis	9.	plēnus	14.	lātus
5.	cupidus	10.	nōbilis	15.	certus

EXERCISE 425

Compare these adjectives:

1.	facilis	3.	līber	5.	miser
2.	difficilis	4.	integer	6.	similis

2. DECLENSION OF COMPARATIVE AND SUPERLATIVE ADJECTIVES

VOCABULARY

aestimō, *1, tr.; acc. w. infin.*	*think*
jūdicō, *1, tr.; acc. w. infin.*	*judge*
quam, *adv.*	*than*
certiōrem (-ēs) facere; *acc. w. infin.; dē w. abl.,* or an indirect question	*to inform*

NOTE

1. **Quam,** *than,* takes the same case after as before it.

   They are braver than the Gauls.

   Eī fortiōrēs sunt quam Gallī (nominative).

   He said that they were braver than the Gauls.

   Dīxit eōs fortiōrēs esse quam Gallōs.

2. **Certiōrem (-ēs)** is the comparative of **certus.** Literally the phrase **certiōrem facere** means *to make (someone) more certain.* **Certiōrem (-ēs)** will therefore always agree with the DIRECT OBJECT of **faciō.**

   They informed Caesar.

   Caesarem certiōrem fēcērunt.

   (Literally: *They made Caesar more certain.*)

   He informed the Gauls.

   Gallōs certiōrēs fēcit.

Certiōrem (-ēs) facere may take either: (1) **dē** with the ablative, (2) the accusative with the infinitive (tense by relation), or (3) an indirect question, since the phrase is like a verb of *saying.*

1. *He informed Caesar about this matter.*

   Caesarem dē hāc rē certiōrem fēcit.

2. *He informed Caesar that Gaul had been pacified.*

   Caesarem certiōrem fēcit Galliam pācātam esse.

3. *He informed Caesar how large the fortifications were.*

   Caesarem certiōrem fēcit quantae mūnītiōnēs essent.

ASSIGNMENT: Study Grammar, Nos. 101-102.

EXERCISE 426

Decline:

1. servus miserior
2. via difficilior
3. flūmen lātius

4. mōns altissimus
5. cīvitās līberrima
6. agmen longissimum

EXERCISE 427
Translate:

1. On account of a more wretched life. 2. On a higher wall.
3. On account of a truer friendship. 4. Across a wider ditch.
5. With braver military tribunes. 6. With a most holy man.
7. Without a most difficult plan. 8. With a braver lieutenant.
9. On account of most serious effort. 10. In a longer rank.
11. On behalf of the most wretched hostages. 12. Into a safer
place. 13. On the higher mountains. 14. On a longer journey.
15. Through most difficult places. 16. Across the widest river.
17. With the truest friends. 18. On account of most serious affairs. 19. For a nobler leader. 20. In a freer state.

EXERCISE 428
[Essential]
Translate:

1. Mēns est pars hominis nōbilissima. 2. Marīa est omnium
sānctōrum sānctissima. 3. Haec via brevior est quam illa.
4. Quid vērius esse potest quam fidēs nostra? 5. Caesar glōriae
cupidissimus erat. 6. Jūdicāsne Lincoln fortiōrem et nōbiliōrem
fuisse quam Washingtonium? 7. Aestimāsne Americānōs līberi-
ōrēs esse quam aliōs? 8. Nōnne arma et tēla ad bellum ūtilissima
sunt? 9. Is quī nōs in rēbus adversīs sine morā adjuvat est
amīcus certissimus et vērissimus. 10. Nōnne jūdicās sānctōs
similiōrēs Chrīstō esse quam aliōs Chrīstiānōs? 11. Marīa est
grātiā plēnissima. 12. Tūtius est in castrīs manēre quam in aciē
pugnāre. Tamen oportet omnēs mīlitēs fortissimōs, ā duce jussōs,
in aciē pugnāre. 13. Difficillimum est per montēs iter facere.

EXERCISE 429
Answer in English:

1. Fuitne Lincoln fortior quam Washingtonius?
2. Estne flūmen Mississippi omnium flūminum longissimum?
3. Estne flūmen Mississippi longius quam flūmen Missouri?

4. Quod flūmen longissimum omnium flūminus est?
5. Quī montēs in nostrīs fīnibus altissimī sunt?
6. Estne mōns Pike's Peak altior quam mōns Wilson?

EXERCISE 430

Translate:

1. Quae sunt ūtilissima ad bellum? Nōnne arma et tēla sunt ūtilissima ad bellum? Nōnne cōpia frūmentī et exercitus magnus ūtilissima etiam sunt? Sumusne nōs ad bellum parātī? Sumusne parātiōrēs ad bellum quam aliī populī et gentēs? Jūdicāsne oportēre nōs omnium populōrum parātissimōs ad bellum semper esse? Num timēs hostēs? Num putās bellum rūrsus futūrum esse?

2. Quī vir amīcus vērissimus et certissimus esse potest? Vērissimus amīcus summam in nōs fidem atque summam in nōs voluntātem habet. Vir fortis et sānctus vērissimus amīcus esse potest, nam etiam Cicerō, quī Chrīstiānus nōn fuit, dīcit nūllam posse esse amīcitiam sine virtūte et fidē. Nōnne jūdicāmus oportēre vērissimum et certissimum amīcum nōs semper adjūvāre atque dīligere? Nōnne in rēbus adversīs ab eō auxilium petimus atque exspectāmus? Vērus amīcus etiam post longissimum tempus in fidē amīcitiāque manet. Itaque quis amīcus vērior esse potest quam Chrīstus? Nam prō nōbīs dolōrēs gravēs sustinuit atque ad mortem ductus est. Quis certior amīcus esse potest quam Chrīstus? Nam semper nōs dīligit et adjuvat. Nēmō nōbīs amīcior[1] est quam Chrīstus. Nōnne eum dīligēmus? In fidē et amīcitiā cum eō semper maneāmus.

3. In nostrīs fīnibus sunt multī montēs et altī et magnī. Scīsne quī mōns altissimus sit omnium montium quī in nostrīs fīnibus sunt? Estne mōns Pike's Peak altior quam mōns Wilson? Estne altissimus omnium nostrōrum montium?

4. In nostrīs fīnibus etiam sunt multa flūmina longa et lāta. Cognōvistīne quae sint flūmina longissima? Estne flūmen Mississippi longius quam flūmen Missouri? Estne flūmen Mississippi longissimum omnium flūminum quae in nostrīs fīnibus sunt?

---

[1] amīcus, a, um: *friendly.*

Quod flūmen lātissimum est? Estne flūmen Missouri aut flūmen Ohio lātius quam flūmen Mississippi? Estne flūmen Mississippi lātissimum omnium nostrōrum flūminum?

Venī, Sāncte Spīritus!

EXERCISE 431
[Essential]

Translate:

1. Was Caesar the bravest of all the Romans? 2. Do you think that Caesar was braver than all other generals? 3. This way is easier than that. 4. Do you judge that this way is easier than that? 5. Who informed you that this way is safest? 6. This mountain is higher. 7. It is safer to withdraw from the first battle line, but it is braver to withstand the attack of the enemy. 8. Hope is the most common of all things. 9. Generals often lead their troops across the widest rivers and through the highest mountains. 10. The Roman slaves were often most wretched. 11. Which state is freest of all? 12. The chiefs informed Caesar that this tribe was the bravest of all the Gauls. 13. Was Caesar more eager for victory than Napoleon? 14. Don't you think that Christ is the truest of all friends?

3. THE ABLATIVE OF COMPARISON

ASSIGNMENT: Study GRAMMAR, Nos. 777-780.

EXERCISE 432

Translate:

1. Nihil fidē nostrā vērius est. 2. Caesar aliīs ducibus fortior erat. 3. Quid est in homine mente nōbilius? 4. Quis Caesare fortior erat? 5. Quem jūdicās nostrō Washingtoniō nōbiliōrem fuisse? 6. Nēmō Chrīstō sānctior esse potest. 7. Num ille mōns est hōc monte altior? 8. Saepe tūtius est pugnāre quam fugere.

EXERCISE 433

Translate:

(Use the ablative of comparison whenever possible.)

1. What river is longer than this river? 2. What is more common than hope? 3. What mountain is higher than that mountain? 4. One way is more narrow; the other, however, is safer. 5. This ditch is wider than that. 6. No one is more holy than Christ. 7. The way through the mountains is shorter than the other way. 8. What is more certain than the friendship of Christ? 9. Who was braver than Caesar? 10. Who was more wretched than a Roman slave?

4. IRREGULAR COMPARATIVES AND SUPERLATIVES

ASSIGNMENT: Learn the irregular comparatives and superlatives in GRAMMAR, Nos. 99, 1-6, 11; 100, 2 and 7-8. Study GRAMMAR, page 22, footnote 2.

SENTENTIA CICERONIS

Nihil est vēritātis lūce dulcius.[1]

NOTE ON IDIOM

The Latin superlative may often be translated by *very* with the English positive (GRAMMAR, No. 93).

Haec via optima est. *This way is very good.*

EXERCISE 434

Translate:

1. With greater forces. 2. Towards the greatest city. 3. With the best men. 4. In a smaller camp. 5. In the greatest danger. 6. On account of more rewards. 7. For the sake of greater glory. 8. With the worst men. 9. After the greatest slaughter. 10. After

---

[1] **dulcis, e:** *sweet, delightful.*

the smallest things. 11. On account of very great danger. 12. For
the sake of very great rewards.

EXERCISE 435
[Essential]
Translate:

1. Quid virtūte melius est? 2. Jūdicāsne amīcitiam meliōrem
esse quam virtūtem? 3. Aestimō nihil virtūte melius esse.
4. Nōnne plūrimī hominēs aestimant glōriam aut imperium
melius esse quam virtūtem? 5. Eī tamen pessimī sunt hominēs
quī, glōriae causā, omnia loca maximā caede et summō dolōre
complent. 6. Itaque dīcimus virtūtem esse rem optimam et
summam. 7. Quid peccātō pējus est? 8. Jūdicātisne mortem
pējōrem esse quam peccātum? 9. Nōnne peccātum pessimum est
Chrīstum relinquere et fidem negāre? 10. Itaque aestimāmus
nihil peccātō pējus esse, nam Deus nōs docet peccātum esse rem
omnium rērum pessimam. 11. Sed difficile est ad summam virtūtem pervenīre, nam per maximōs labōrēs et summum dolōrem
ad summam virtūtem pervenīmus. 12. Deō Optimō Maximō
grātiās agāmus. 13. Salūs populī sit suprēma lēx. 14. Cicerō,
"Summus dolor," inquit, "plūrēs diēs manēre nōn potest."
15. Nihil pējus est quam ex aciē fugere. 16. Peccāta et maxima
et minima relinquāmus. 17. Melius est ā rēgibus et dominīs
līberum esse. 18. Sunt plūrimàe et maximae urbēs in nostrīs
fīnibus. 19. Melior et facilior est via brevissima quam via longissima. 20. Lēgātus pessimus plūs frūmentī petīvit, sed Gallī plūs
frūmentī dare nōn potuērunt. 21. Scīmus Rōmam minōrem esse
quam multās aliās cīvitātēs. 22. Sunt plūrēs hominēs in nostrīs
fīnibus quam in Galliā. 23. Quem jūdicās esse omnium hominum
pessimum? 24. Rōmānī castra locīs superiōribus semper pōnēbant. 25. Rōma propior est Galliae quam nostrae urbēs. 26. Is
quī mājōribus cōpiīs impetum in hostēs facit, saepe vincit.
27. In Bataan nostrae cōpiae minōrēs erant quam Japōnum.
28. Caesar legiōnēs ex aliīs hībernīs ad sē vocāvit quō mājōrēs
cōpiās sēcum habēret.

SENTENTIAE SĒLECTAE

1. Īracundiam[1] quī vincit, hostem superat maximum. *(Publilius Syrus.)*
2. Virtūs praemium est optimum. *(Plautus.)*
3. Nihil est virtūte melius. *(Adapted from Cicero.)*
4. Ad mājōrem Deī glōriam. *(Motto of the Jesuits.)*

Ē plūribus ūnum

(Inscription on coins of the United States)

EXERCISE 436
[Essential]

Translate:

1. Caesar took up a stand on a higher place and waited for larger forces. 2. Very many men praise virtue, but of these many are very bad men. 3. It behooves the best men to be in charge of the state. 4. Was not Judas[2] worse than Benedict[3] Arnold? The latter helped the enemies of his own state, but the former gave Jesus Christ into the hands of the worst men. 5. Do you judge that Lincoln was a better man than Washington? 6. Brave men with a smaller supply of arms often conquer a larger band of the enemy. 7. Don't you think that sailors and soldiers are often in the greatest danger? Let us pray for them. 8. MacArthur with a very small band of men long withstood the strongest attacks of the enemy. 9. We were not able to send MacArthur more arms and provisions[4] because he was many miles away and the ships of the enemy were on all sides. 10. More men have been killed in this war than in any other war. 11. The highest law is the law of Christ.

---

[1] īracundia, ae: *anger.*
[2] *Judas:* Jūdas, ae.
[3] *Benedict:* Benedictus, ī.
[4] *provisions:* frūmentum, ī.

NATHAN HALE

READING NO. 41

NATHAN HALE

Rōmānī virtūtem virōrum optimōrum memoriā semper tenuērunt. Nōs Americānī etiam multōs optimōs virōs quī prō hāc nostrā rē pūblicā maximās rēs gessērunt laudāmus atque memoriā tenēmus.

Ōlim[1] nostrī cum Britannīs maximum bellum gerēbant ut rem pūblicam nostram ab eōrum imperiō līberārent. Imperātor Americānus fuit Washingtonius, vir optimus et fortissimus, quī diū prō cīvitāte suā et rēs magnās gessit et gravissimōs sustinuit dolōrēs.

Cum dux Britannōrum cōpiās suās in Manhattan trādūxisset, Washingtonius cum omnibus suīs cōpiīs adversus eī cōnstitit. Cōnsilium autem capere nōn potuit, nam nōn cognōverat ubi imperātor hostium mīlitēs suōs collocāvisset. Erat autem in exercitū

---

[1] ōlim, *adv.: once.*

Americānō centuriō fortissimus, nōmine Nathan Hale. Hic parātus erat in castra hostium contendere atque omnia loca explōrāre ut cognōsceret quibus in locīs hostēs custōdēs collocāvissent quantaeque essent eōrum mūnītiōnēs. Hunc Washingtonius in hostium castra mīsit.

Sine morā Hale in hostium castra contendit. Clam pervēnit. Omnia loca explōrāvit. Custōdēs, armōrum cōpiam, mūnītiōnēs vīdit—at hostēs tandem[1] intellēxērunt[2] quid ageret. Itaque eum captum ad ducem dūxērunt. Dux, dē rē certior factus, eum ad mortem dūcī jussit. Cum autem fortissimus ille Nathan Hale ad mortem dūcerētur, "I regret," inquit, "that I have but one life to give for my country."

Nōnne virtūte maximā hūjus virī incitātī cōnfirmātīque rem pūblicam nostram dīligere atque dēfendere parātiōrēs sumus?

READING NO. 42

THE ANSWER OF THE SPARTAN KING

Lacedaemoniī[3] magnam glōriam bellī et virtūtis habēbant. Ōlim[4] bellum gerēbant. Vēnit nuntius ad rēgem Lacedaemoniōrum.[3] "Magnus," inquit, "est numerus hostium." Rēx, vir fortissimus, eī respondit, "Tantō[5] mājor erit glōria nostra."

---

[1] tandem, *adv.*: *at last.*
[2] intellegō, intellegere, intellēxī, intellectus, *3, tr.*: *understand.*
[3] Lacedaemoniī, Lacedaemoniōrum: *the Lacedaemonians, the Spartans.*
[4] ōlim, *adv.*: *once.*
[5] tantō: lit., *by so much;* translate *so much the* . . .

LESSON 41: DEPONENT VERBS

1. INDICATIVE OF DEPONENT VERBS

In Latin some verbs have PASSIVE FORMS but ACTIVE MEANINGS. Such verbs are called DEPONENTS. They are conjugated like the passive of the regular conjugations but each PASSIVE FORM has the corresponding ACTIVE MEANING.

> Cōnor. *I try.*
>
> Ducem sequētur. *He will follow the leader.*
>
> Hannibal Rōmānōs vincere cōnātus est.
> *Hannibal tried to conquer the Romans.*

ASSIGNMENT: Study GRAMMAR, Nos. 334-335.

VOCABULARY

cōnor, cōnārī, cōnātus sum, *1, tr.; w. infin.*	{ *try* *attempt*
vereor, verērī, veritus sum, *2, tr.; w. infin.*	*fear*
sequor, sequī, secūtus sum, *3, tr.*	*follow*
patior, patī, passus sum, *3, tr.; acc. w. infin.*	{ *suffer* *allow*
orior, orīrī, ortus sum, *4, intr.*	{ *rise* *arise*

RELATED ENGLISH WORDS

The *Orient.* We have learned the rules for the *sequence* of tenses. We have been saved by the *Passion* and death of Christ. The Saints were very *patient.*

EXERCISE 437

Write out the third person, singular and plural, of the present, imperfect, future, perfect, and pluperfect indicative of the words in the vocabulary and give the English meanings.

EXERCISE 438
Translate:

1. cōnābātur	10. oriētur	18. sequuntur
2. verēbantur	11. cōnāta est	19. patior
3. sequēbar	12. ortum est	20. oriuntur
4. patiēbāmur	13. passus est	21. ortum erat
5. oriēbātur	14. veritī sumus	22. passī erant
6. cōnābuntur	15. secūtī estis	23. secūta erat
7. verēbitur	16. cōnāris	24. veritī estis
8. sequar	17. verētur	25. cōnāta es
9. patiēmur		

EXERCISE 439
Translate:

1. We were trying. 2. They were following the centurion.
3. He fears the military tribune. 4. They were following the
ships. 5. He is trying to flee. 6. He had feared the allies.
7. They fear severe wounds. 8. He will follow no leader. 9. They
will not allow it. 10. A shout arose. 11. They fear God alone.
12. He had tried to capture the king. 13. A band of men followed
them. 14. Will he allow us to lead our troops across the river?
15. They will try to capture the fortifications and to burn the
town.

EXERCISE 440
Translate:

1. Hostēs nōn vereor. 2. Chrīstiānī Chrīstum sequuntur.
3. Chrīstus multa passus est. 4. Bellum novum ortum est. 5. Eōs
interficere nōn veritus est. 6. Chrīstiānī plūrima patiēbantur.
7. Ōrāre nōn cōnātus es. 8. Quī sequitur Chrīstum, ducem optimum sequitur. 9. Rōmānī Deum vērum nōn verēbantur.
10. Eōs per prōvinciam contendere nōn passus est. 11. Tē,
Chrīste, sequar. 12. Fugere cōnābantur. 13. Cūr eum sequē-
bantur? 14. Marīa dolōrēs gravissimōs passa est. 15. Equitēs
hostēs secūtī sunt. 16. Maximus clāmor undique ortus est.

17. Timor inter mīlitēs subitō ortus est. 18. Jūdaeī Deum vehementer verēbantur. 19. Illam urbem capere cōnābātur. 20. Eōs interficere cōnātī sumus.

EXERCISE 441
[Essential]
Translate:

1. Nōn patiar maximās cōpiās per prōvinciam dūcī. 2. Cum Caesar tōtam Galliam pācātam esse putāvisset, subitō novum et difficillimum bellum ortum est. 3. Pīlātus Chrīstum verēbātur et adjuvāre cōnātus est. Veritus est tamen etiam Jūdaeōs et Rōmānōs. Itaque eōs passus est Chrīstum ad mortem dūcere. 4. Plūrimae gentēs Rōmānōs vincere cōnātae sunt, at nūlla gēns eōs vīcit. 5. Omnēs sānctī, grātiā Deī incitātī, Chrīstum secūtī sunt. 6. Chrīstus prō salūte nostrā gravissimōs dolōrēs passus est. 7. Plūrimī mīlitēs Napoleon, propter ējus magnitūdinem animī, secūtī sunt. 8. Plūrimae gentēs deōs nōn vērōs verēbantur. 9. Tē, dux, nōn sequar, nam glōriae cupidus, omnia loca caede atque dolōre complēbis. 10. Cum legiōnēs ad oppidī mūrōs appropinquāvissent, maximus clāmor ortus est, nam Gallī mōre suō clāmāvērunt[1] sē omnia Rōmānīs dēditūrōs esse.

SENTENTIA OVIDII

" . . . Videō meliōra probōque;
Dēteriōra[2] sequor."

EXERCISE 442
[Essential]
Translate:

1. I am following Caesar. 2. You fear God. 3. He is suffering pain. 4. We do not allow him to come. 5. You (pl.) are trying

---

[1] clāmō, *1, intr.: shout.*
[2] dēterior, ius: *worse.*

to fight. 6. Wars arise on account of injustices done. 7. They were trying to flee. 8. You (pl.) were fearing Caesar. 9. We were allowing them to flee. 10. A war was arising. 11. You were following the commander in chief. 12. I was fearing death. 13. Wars will always arise. 14. He will not allow us to fight. 15. He tried to capture Rome. 16. The Romans swiftly followed the enemy. 17. They had allowed the hostages to depart. 18. A new war had arisen. 19. You have followed Christ for a long time. 20. We have not feared to fight.

2. SUBJUNCTIVE OF DEPONENT VERBS

ASSIGNMENT: Study GRAMMAR, Nos. 334-335. Review GRAMMAR, Nos. 267-282, 518, 561, 660-662, and FIRST YEAR LATIN, page 300.

EXERCISE 443
[Subjunctive in Wishes]
Translate:

1. Nē patiātur eōs fugere. 2. Nē oriātur novum bellum. 3. Sequātur ducem. 4. Vereantur Deum. 5. Patiantur nōs in castra venīre.

Rēgem quī fēcit nōs,
Venīte adōrēmus!

EXERCISE 444
[Hortatory Subjunctive]
Translate:

1. Sequāmur Chrīstum etiam ad mortem. 2. Prō Chrīstō patiāmur. 3. Sānctī esse cōnēmur. 4. Patiāmur omnēs in pāce esse. 5. Nē vereāmur mortem. 6. Deum vereāmur. 7. Cōnēmur pācem servāre. 8. Nē sequāmur ducēs malōs.

EXERCISE 445
[Indirect Questions]
Translate:

1. Rogāvit num novum bellum ortum esset. 2. Mīlitēs rogāvit num mortem vehementer vererentur. 3. Quaesīvit num sānctī Chrīstum secūtī essent. 4. Eōs certiōrēs fēcit quis sē secūtus esset. 5. Rogō quae gentēs Rōmānōs vincere cōnātae sint. 6. Senātus Caesarem rogāvit num Gallōs maximās cōpiās per prōvinciam dūcere passus esset. 7. Dux tribūnum mīlitum rogāvit quantae cōpiae sē secūtae essent. 8. Rogō cūr omnēs hominēs Deum vērum et ūnum nōn vereantur.

EXERCISE 446
[Cum-Clauses]
Translate:

1. Hostēs, cum maximās cōpiās trāns flūmen lātissimum dūcere cōnārentur, ā Caesare in fugam conjectī sunt. 2. Caesar, cum hostēs difficillimā viā secūtus esset, eōs in fugam dedit. 3. Chrīstus, cum gravissimōs dolōrēs paterētur, nōbīs mātrem suam dedit. 4. Lincoln, cum bellum in nostrā cīvitāte ortum esset, omnēs servōs ā dominīs līberāvit. 5. Caesar, cum Gallōs per prōvinciam iter facere omnīnō nōn passus esset, fīnēs prōvinciae armīs dēfendit.

EXERCISE 447
[Essential]
Translate:

1. Jesus Christ, the Son of God, allowed Himself to be led to death for our salvation. Let us therefore also follow Him without delay and without fear. Let us not fear the greatest danger. Let us not fear the worst death. Let us place our hope in God that He may not allow us to be overcome in adversity by the enemy.
2. Our soldiers, when they were following the bravest leaders

and the best generals, did not fear the attacks of the enemies or the dangers of sea and forest. When the enemy tried to drive them out of their fortifications, when the enemy tried to withstand their attacks, they did not leave the battle line nor did they flee. Our leader, Christians, is the bravest and best of all. Let us try always to do the things He orders that we may follow Him to certain victory and to the greatest glory.

3. You ask how great things Christ suffered. He suffered the greatest and worst. You ask why He suffered the greatest pains. He suffered the greatest pains that we, moved by His sorrow, might follow Him, that we might try always to remain in His friendship.

4. They always asked why wars arose. Now in these times they are again asking why wars arise. Wars arise because kings and those who are in charge of nations do not follow Christ.

3. PERFECT PARTICIPLE OF DEPONENT VERBS

The perfect participle of deponent verbs has an ACTIVE meaning:

secūtus, *having followed* (NOT: *having been followed*)
passus, *having allowed*
cōnātus, *having tried*
veritus, *having feared*
ortus, *having arisen*

VOCABULARY

polliceor, pollicērī, pollicitus sum, 2, tr.; *acc. w. future infinitive*	*promise*
loquor, loquī, locūtus sum, 3, tr.	*speak* / *talk*
proficīscor, proficīscī, profectus sum, 3, intr.; *ad w. acc.*	*set out*
nactus, a, um	*having obtained* / *having found*

NOTE

Nactus, a, um is the perfect participle of a deponent verb.
The other forms of this verb are not common.

EXERCISE 448
[Essential]

Translate:

1. Caesar, ad Galliam profectus, tribus diēbus ad castra Rōmāna pervēnit. 2. Chrīstus, multa cum amīcīs suīs locūtus, in Caelum sublātus est. 3. Rōmānī, locum ad castra idōneum[1] nactī, cōnstitērunt. 4. Equitēs, hostēs celeriter secūtī, plūrimōs ex eīs occīdērunt. 5. Chrīstus, gravissimōs dolōrēs et mortem pessimam prō nōbīs passus, ad glōriam suam pervēnit. 6. Barbarī, Caesarem veritī, fugā montēs petīvērunt. 7. Caesar Gallōs castra expugnāre cōnātōs in silvās pepulit. 8. Caesar, ad urbem profectus, tertiā diē pervēnit. 9. Barbarī, hominēs fortissimī, in Rōmānōs ē castrīs profectōs impetum fēcērunt. 10. Propter novum bellum ortum, Caesar in Galliam profectus erat.

DE CHRISTO

Numquam locūtus est homō sīcut hic homō.

EXERCISE 449
[Essential]

Translate:

1. Christ, having spoken with His friends for many days and having promised to send them the Holy Spirit, was raised up into heaven.

2. Saint Polycarp,[2] having been asked whether he was a Christian, answered that, having followed Christ very many years and having always feared God, he would not deny Him.

---

[1] idōneus, a, um: *suitable.*
[2] *Polycarp:* Polycarpus, ī.

3. Columbus, having promised to give his sailors the greatest and best rewards, collected a small band of brave men and prepared three ships. Having obtained a good wind, he set out. 4. The leaders of the Jews,[1] having often tried to injure Christ, at last[2] captured and killed Him. Then His friends, having followed Him for two or three years, fled and, having feared the Jews,[1] withdrew into a safe place. When, however, the Holy Spirit had been sent to them, they set out from the city and announced to all men that Christ was the Son of God.

READING NO. 43

DĒ PRAEMIŌ TARPĒIAE

Sabīnī,[3] quī Rōmānīs proximī erant, bellum cum eīs gerēbant. Ex suīs fīnibus cum maximīs cōpiīs profectī, in agrōs Rōmānōrum vēnērunt. Rōmānī, cōpiās eōrum veritī, sē in urbem Rōmam recēpērunt. Itaque Sabīnī, celeriter secūtī, omnēs agrōs vastāvērunt atque occupāvērunt. Etiam in urbem Rōmam brevī tempore cōpiās dūxērunt, nam Rōmānī impetūs eōrum sustinēre nōn potuērunt. Capitōlium[4] autem, mūnītiōnibus et locī nātūrā mūnītum, Sabīnī capere nōn potuērunt.

Sabīnī, cum nōn longē ā Capitōliō[4] abessent, Tarpēiam,[5] fīliam[6] ducis Rōmānī, quae aquam in Capitōlium[4] portābat, vīdērunt. Itaque eam captam ad ducem dūxērunt. Dux vērō putāvit eam exercitum suum in Capitōlium[4] dūcere posse. Itaque pollicitus est sē eī maxima praemia datūrum esse. Tarpēiam[5] autem rogāvit quod praemium cuperet. Ea dīxit sē cupere eās rēs quās Sabīnī in sinistrīs[7] manibus gererent. Itaque dux pollicitus est sē eās rēs

---

[1] *Jews:* Jūdaeī, Jūdaeōrum.
[2] *at last:* tandem, *adv.*
[3] Sabīnī, ōrum: *the Sabines* (an ancient Italian tribe).
[4] Capitōlium, ī: *the Capitoline* (one of the seven hills of Rome).
[5] Tarpēia, ae: *Tarpeia* (a feminine proper name).
[6] fīlia, ae: *daughter.*
[7] sinister, sinistra, sinistrum: *left.* (The Sabines wore gold rings and bracelets on their left hands.)

TARPEIA ET SABINUS

Tarpēiae[1] trāditūrum esse. Sabīnī, eam secūtī, brevī tempore Capitōlium occupāvērunt.

Tarpēia,[1] neque Deum neque patrem suum verita, populum suum et urbem suam in manūs hostium praemiī causā trādiderat. Ecce[2] praemium ējus. Sabīnī, cum in Capitōliō cōnstitissent, subitō scūta[3] in Tarpēiam omnēs conjēcērunt. Fidem tamen ita cōnservāvērunt et quae pollicitī sunt dedērunt, nam Sabīnī etiam scūta[3] in sinistrīs[4] manibus gerēbant. Ita illa miserrima interfecta est.

**Auxilium Chrīstiānōrum,
Ōrā prō nōbīs!**

---

4. INFINITIVES OF DEPONENT VERBS

The present and perfect infinitives of deponent verbs are formed just like the regular passive infinitives of the four conjugations.

BUT THE FUTURE INFINITIVE is ACTIVE both in form and meaning.

Dīxit sē **profectūrum esse.** *He said that he would set out.*

ASSIGNMENT: Study GRAMMAR, Nos. 336-338. Review all infinitive constructions, pages 352, 363, 414, 420.

---

[1] Tarpēia, ae: *Tarpeia.*
[2] ecce: *behold.*
[3] scūtum, ī: *shield.*
[4] sinister, sinistra, sinistrum: *left.*

VOCABULARY

ēgredior, ēgredī, ēgressus sum, *3, intr.*   *go out*

prōgredior, prōgredī, prōgressus sum, *3, intr.*   *advance*

arbitror, arbitrārī, arbitrātus sum, *1, tr.; acc. w. infin.* $\begin{cases} \textit{think} \\ \textit{consider} \end{cases}$

hortor, hortārī, hortātus sum, *1, tr.* $\begin{cases} \textit{urge} \\ \textit{encourage} \end{cases}$

NOTE
Arbitror takes the accusative with the infinitive (tense by relation) because it is a verb of *thinking*.

EXERCISE 450
Form the three infinitives of all the words in the vocabulary.

Divīnum¹ auxilium maneat
semper nōbīscum. Āmēn.

EXERCISE 451
[Present Infinitive of Deponents]
Translate:

1. Post difficillimum proelium Caesar suōs prōgredī jussit.
2. Ex difficillimīs locīs ēgredī nōn potuērunt. 3. Caesar saepe tribūnōs mīlitum suōs hortārī atque cōnfirmāre jussit. 4. Nōnne oportet nōs prīmā lūce proficīscī? 5. Oportet hominēs pessimōs Deum vehementer verērī. 6. Oportet Chrīstiānōs sānctōs esse semper cōnārī. 7. Caesar jussit lēgātum cum ducibus hostium loquī. 8. Optimum est Chrīstum sequī sed difficillimum etiam est. 9. Oportet nōs multa et gravissima patī. 10. Ēgredī nōn possumus; tamen, ā tē jussī, cōnābimur. 11. Oportet nōs omnēs Chrīstum sequī, plūrimōs dolōrēs patī et ita ad glōriam nostram pervenīre.

---

¹ divīnus, a, um: *divine.*

EXERCISE 452
[Present and Perfect Infinitives of Deponents]
Translate:

1. Nuntius dīxit hostēs prīmā lūce ēgressōs esse. 2. Dīxērunt sē ex difficillimō locō ēgressōs nōn esse. 3. Arbitrātus est tribūnōs mīlitum suōs hortātōs esse. 4. Dīxit oportēre nōs prīmā lūce proficīscī. 5. Nōs certiōrēs fēcit hostēs profectōs esse. 6. Cōnfirmāvit legiōnem esse ēgressam. 7. Audīvimus Gallōs cōpiās maximās trāns flūmen dūcere cōnātōs esse. 8. Chrīstiānī putant optimum esse Chrīstum sequī.

EXERCISE 453
[Future Infinitive of Deponents]
Translate:

1. Caesar dīxit sē tribus diēbus profectūrum esse. 2. Pollicitus est sē haec omnia duōbus diēbus factūrum esse. 3. Lēgātus Rōmānus dīxit sē numquam cum hoste locūtūrum esse. 4. Putāvimus eōs quīnque diēbus ēgressūrōs esse. 5. Dīxit sē nōn passūrum eōs hāc viā maximās cōpiās dūcere. 6. Scīmus ducem, virum fortissimum et optimum, suōs hortātūrum esse. 7. Apostolī pollicitī sunt sē Chrīstum semper secūtūros esse. 8. Rēx dīxit sē in locum tūtissimum prōgressūrum esse.

SENTENTIA LIVII

Et facere et patī fortiter Rōmānum est.

EXERCISE 454
Translate:

1. I think that the enemy has advanced two miles. 2. He announced that the cavalry had suddenly gone out of the camp. 3. We saw that the military tribunes and centurions were encouraging the soldiers. 4. The hostages promised that they would not go out of the camp. 5. They thought that they would not set

out at dawn. 6. They feared to speak the truth. 7. Having set out, they followed the enemy three miles. 8. He said that, having set out, they had followed the enemy four miles. 9. He said that, having obtained a good wind, the ships had set out on the third day. 10. He said he would set out within three days. 11. The soldiers said they would not follow that leader. 12. He said he would not allow them to march through the province. 13. They affirmed that they would suffer the worst pains. 14. He tried to set out but was captured by the cavalry. 15. The horseman announced that the enemy, having advanced three miles into the province, was trying to come across the river. 16. They informed Caesar that the enemy were trying to seize the hill.

UNIT FOURTEEN

LESSON 42: THE IRREGULAR VERB *EŌ*

1. INDICATIVE OF *EŌ*

ASSIGNMENT: Learn the present, imperfect, and future of eō, GRAMMAR, Nos. 363-365. The perfect tenses are formed regularly on the stem īv- or i-. Review GRAMMAR, Nos. 761, 915-924, and the lesson on dē, ex, and ab, FIRST YEAR LATIN, page 336.

VOCABULARY

eō, īre, īvī (iī), itum, *irreg., intr.*	*go*
exeō, exīre, exiī, exitum, *irreg., intr.*	*go out*
ineō, inīre, iniī, initus, *irreg., tr.*	*go into* *enter upon*

NOTE

Compounds of eō like exeō and ineō are conjugated like eō, but note that the v is regularly dropped in the perfect stem of compounds.

EXERCISE 455

Give the third person, singular and plural, of the present, imperfect, future, perfect, and pluperfect indicative of the words in the vocabulary.

EXERCISE 456

1. Translate;
2. Explain the italicized words:

1. Tōtam *noctem* īvērunt. 2. Secundā *vigiliā* exiit. 3. Duo *mīlia* passuum iit. 4. Tribus *diēbus* exībit. 5. Centum *pedēs* ierat. 6. Quā *hōrā,* amīce mī,[1] exībis? 7. Novum *cōnsilium* iniērunt. 8. Quot *diēs* iērunt? 9. *Altera* legiō ē *castrīs* exiit; *altera*

---

[1] See GRAMMAR, No. 28.

in castrīs mānsit. 10. *Salūtis* causā in *oppida* iniērunt.
11. Omnēs ferē exeunt. 12. Dē *fīnibus suīs* exībant. 13. Ad
flūmen it. 14. Tertiā *diē* exībat. 15. Centuriō cum centum
hominibus exībit. 16. Legiō sine ūllā morā exiit. 17. *Quam* diū
ierat? 18. *Quō*, fīlī mī, ībis? 19. Per *loca* impedīta et difficillima
ierat. 20. Chrīstus, "Ad Patrem," inquit, "ībō."

EXERCISE 457
Translate:

1. They went five miles. 2. He went out to the camp on the
second day. 3. Others were going out of the camp. 4. Within
three days he will enter the city. 5. Will we all go to heaven?
6. He is going through a very large forest. 7. Where did you go?
8. Caesar went into the province. 9. They came into the winter
quarters. 10. They entered upon a new method of war. 11. They
will go within five days. 12. They went out of the camp.
13. They entered the province on the third day. 14. Having set
out on that day, they went four miles. 15. They entered a very
deep river. 16. Having obtained a good wind, they went out
of the harbor. 17. They went into Gaul by the shortest way.
18. For two days they went through the highest mountains.
19. In the first watch he went secretly out of the town. 20. When
they had set out, they went three miles and pitched camp.

EXERCISE 458

1. Translate;
2. Answer the questions in complete Latin sentences:

A. Mīlitēs Americānī ex nostrīs fīnibus trāns mare lātissimum
in Galliam iērunt ut contrā hostēs pugnārent.

QUESTION. Quō iērunt?

ANSWER. Ē nostrīs fīnibus trāns mare lātissimum in Galliam
iērunt.

1. Ex quō locō iērunt?
2. Iēruntne trāns mare lātissimum?
3. Cūr in Galliam iērunt?

B. Chrīstus, multōs diēs cum amīcīs suīs locūtus, in Caelum ad Patrem suum īvit.
1. Cum quibus locūtus est Chrīstus?
2. Quam diū cum eīs locūtus est?
3. Quō īvit?
4. Ad quem īvit?

C. Omnēs sānctī, Chrīstum fortiter secūtī, in Caelum ībunt.
1. Quī Chrīstum sunt secūtī?
2. Quō ībunt?

D. Marquette, vir optimus et fortissimus, multōs diēs per silvās perīculōrum plēnās et per loca impedīta et difficillima ierat. Tum audīvit nōn longē abesse flūmen lātissimum et longissimum. Hoc flūmen ab eīs quī eās regiōnēs incolēbant Pater Aquārum vocābātur. Itaque nāve parvā rūrsus profectus, plūrimōs diēs iit et tandem¹ flūmen quod nunc ā nōbīs Mississippi vocātur prīmus iniit.
1. Quot diēs ierat Marquette?
2. Per quae loca ierat?
3. Num per silvās ierat?
4. Quid tum audīvit?
5. Quid illud flūmen vocābātur?
6. Quī id Patrem Aquārum vocābant?
7. Estne Marquette rūrsus profectus?
8. Ad quod flūmen pervēnit?
9. Cognōvistīne quō locō Marquette hoc flūmen prīmum cōn-spexerit?
10. Scīsne quis socius Patris Marquette fuerit?
11. Fuitne Marquette Jēsuīta?

E. Jam dēmōnstrāvimus mīlitēs nostrōs nōn potuisse diūtius in Bataan impetum hostium sustinēre. Nam, sīcut cognōvistis, Japōnēs mājōribus cōpiīs et plūribus armīs in nostrōs impetūs faciēbant. MacArthur, quī praesidiō nostrō praeerat, jussus est

¹ tandem. *adv.: at last.*

mīlitēs relinquere et ex eō locō quī Corregidor vocātur exīre.
Itaque sine morā nāve parvā cum paucīs sociīs exiit. Plūrimās
noctēs per maria perīculōrum plēna iērunt. Saepe portūs nātūrā
locī mūnītōs iniērunt atque ibi per diem mānsērunt nē ab hostibus
cōnspicerentur. Nocte rūrsus profectī celeriter iērunt. Ita ē
manibus hostium sē ēripuērunt et tandem[1] portum ā nostrīs occupātum iniērunt.

1. Cūr nostrī impetūs Japōnum sustinēre nōn potuērunt?
2. Cui praesidiō praeerat MacArthur?
3. Quid facere jussus est?
4. Exiitne statim?
5. Quibuscum exiit?
6. Ubi saepe mānsērunt?
7. Cūr ibi mānsērunt?
8. Cōnspexēruntne eōs hostēs?
9. Quō tandem[1] pervēnērunt?

> Ā malā morte,
> Līberā eum, Domine!
> —From the Prayers for the Dying

2. SUBJUNCTIVE OF *EŌ*

ASSIGNMENT: Study Grammar, Nos. 375-376. Review
Grammar, Nos. 518, 546-549, 561, 660-662.

VOCABULARY

trānseō, trānsīre, trānsiī, trānsitus, *irreg., tr.*	go across / cross
redeō, redīre, rediī, reditum, *irreg., intr.*	*return*
adeō, adīre, adiī, aditus, *irreg., tr.*	go to / approach / visit

---

[1] **tandem,** *adv.: at last.*

EXERCISE 459
1. Translate;
2. Explain the mood and tense of the italicized verbs:

1. Columbus, cum mare lātissimum *trānsīret*, in perīculō maximō saepe erat. 2. Columbus, cum ex portū ēgressus mare *trānsiisset*, ad Americam pervēnit. 3. Caesar, cum omnēs Galliae gentēs *adiisset*, in Italiam rediit. 4. Legiōnēs, cum tōtam noctem *iissent*, cōnstitērunt et castra posuērunt. 5. Dux, cum optimam bellī ratiōnem *iniisset*, hostēs facilius vīcit. 6. Equitēs, cum ā duce jussī ex castrīs *exiissent*, hostēs celeriter secūtī sunt.

EXERCISE 460
1. Translate;
2. Explain the italicized constructions:

1. *Eāmus.* 2. *Nē* ex prīmā aciē *exeāmus.* 3. In hīberna *redeāmus.* 4. Omnēs Italiae cīvitātēs *adeāmus.* 5. *Nē eat.* 6. Celeriter *redeant.*

EXERCISE 461
1. Translate;
2. Explain the italicized constructions:

1. Rogat *quantae* cōpiae flūmen *trānseant.* 2. Dux rogāvit *quā* hōrā hostēs ex castrīs *exiissent.* 3. Rogō *num* in castra *ierīs.* 4. Caesarem certiōrem fēcit *quot* hostēs flūmen *trānsiissent.* 5. Rogō *quā* viā per montēs *ierint.*

EXERCISE 462
1. Translate;
2. Explain the italicized constructions:

1. Caesar pontem in flūmine lātissimō fēcit *quō* facilius equitēs *redīrent.* 2. Custōdēs undique collocat *nē* barbarī ē silvīs *exeant.* 3. Mīlitēs Americānī multōs portūs occupāvērunt *nē* nāvēs hostium in eōs *redīrent.* 4. Equitēs celeriter mīsit *quī* flūmen *trānsīrent.* 5. Imperātor centuriōnēs ad sē vocāvit *ut* novum

cōnsilium *inīret.* 6. Mūnītiōnēs in portū fēcērunt *nē* nāvēs eum *inīrent.*

> Ā cūnctīs[1] nōs, quaesumus,[2] Domine,
> mentis et corporis dēfende perīculīs.

EXERCISE 463
Translate:

Cum novum bellum in Eurōpā ortum esset et omnēs illīus regiōnis gentēs terrā marīque inter sē armīs contenderent, nōs prīmum Gallōs et Britannōs cōpiā armōrum et frūmentī adjuvābāmus, tum bellum cum eīs contrā hostēs gerēbāmus. Itaque plūrimās nāvēs parāvimus ut nostrī mīlitēs mare trānsīrent; maximam tēlōrum et armōrum cōpiam parāvimus ut, cum nostrī in Eurōpam trānsiissent, fortiter contrā hostēs et diū pugnāre possent. In hōc bellō mīlitēs Americānī multa loca adiērunt. Nam aliī in Africam trānsiērunt; aliī prīmum in Britanniam, tum in Galliam trānsiērunt; aliī etiam in aliās regiōnēs trānsiērunt. Scīmus nostrōs in omnibus hīs locīs fortiter pugnāre et fortiter pugnātūrōs esse. Multōs dolōrēs et plūrima vulnera passī post victōriam ad nōs redībunt. Eōs eōrumque rēs gestās semper memoriā teneāmus.

Answer in complete Latin sentences:

1. Ubi erat novum bellum ortum?
2. Quae gentēs inter sē armīs contendēbant?
3. Quibus rēbus sociōs nostrōs prīmum adjūvimus?
4. Bellumne cum eīs gessimus?
5. Quō iērunt mīlitēs nostrī?
6. Nōnne aliī in Britanniam, aliī autem in Africam trānsiērunt?
7. Arbitrārisne nostrōs mīlitēs fortiter pugnāre?
8. Quō tempore ad nōs redībunt?

---

[1] cūnctus, a, um: *all.*
[2] quaesumus: *we beseech.*

EXERCISE 464

Translate:

1. The Japanese, when they had gone out of the fortifications, sought the forest in flight. 2. They returned from this river that they might be safe from attack. 3. The ships of the Japanese crossed the sea secretly that they might make an attack on our harbors. 4. These soldiers are returning from the camp, but those are going to the camp. 5. The enemy went secretly out of the forest and were suddenly seen in the rear. 6. When he had returned to the ship, he was killed by a dart and fell into the water. 7. These brave soldiers went to France to free the French from a foreign power. 8. The cavalry drove back the enemy that the encumbered soldiers might go across the river. 9. The soldiers, hindered by the nature of the place, returned to the camp. 10. The camp was empty, for, when the soldiers had gone into the province, none returned. 11. We shall ward off the enemy from these fields and these cities, that those who dwelt in them may return. 12. The leaders of the enemy entered upon a new manner of war. Their cavalry went out of the towns to hinder our columns. 13. We warded off the attack of the cavalry in order that the legion might return into the winter quarters. 14. The lieutenant said, "I ask where your allies have gone." 15. The leader asked the envoys what races of men they had visited. 16. The Romans constructed roads that they might more easily visit the provinces. 17. The cavalry made an attack from the rear lest the enemy return to their camp. 18. He went to the chiefs to ask who was most influential among them. 19. When the leaders of the Jews had gone to Pilate, they said that Christ had called Himself by the name of king. 20. Christ asked the Apostles by what name He was called. 21. The chief men assembled to enter on new plans. 22. There was bitter fighting there and very many did not return. 23. He sent envoys to visit the leading men of those tribes. 24. The leader asked with how great forces the enemy had gone into the province. 25. When they had gone down from the hill, they there took up

a position. 26. When Caesar had gone out of the camp, the enemy approached the rampart. 27. When the Romans had gone into the territory of the enemy, they pitched camp and fortified it with a ditch and a rampart. 28. He asked whether the hostages had gone secretly out of the camp. 29. When Caesar returned from Italy, he asked whether everything useful for war had been prepared. 30. They asked where he had returned from. 31. Terrified by the arrival of Caesar, the barbarians went into their own territory. 32. When Caesar returned to the winter quarters, he found that a new war had arisen in Gaul.

3. INFINITIVES OF *EŌ*

ASSIGNMENT: Study Grammar, No. 378. Form the perfect and future infinitive active of eō according to the general rules. Review all infinitive constructions, pages 352, 363, 414, 420.

EXERCISE 465
1. Translate;
2. Explain the italicized constructions:

1. Chrīstus dīxit *sē* paucīs diēbus in Caelum *itūrum esse*. 2. Oportet *nōs redīre*. 3. Pessimum est ad sociōs malōs jam relictōs *redīre*. 4. Respondit *equitēs* nōn jam *rediisse*. 5. Chrīstus pollicitus est *sē reditūrum esse*. 6. Equitēs reppererunt *barbarōs* jam flūmen *trānsiisse*. 7. Caesar *obsidēs* ē castrīs ad suōs *exīre* nōn passus est. 8. Dux scrīpsit *sē* duōbus diēbus *reditūrum esse*. 9. Nuntius ostendit quot hominēs castra iniissent. 10. Pilātus dīxit *Jūdaeōs* nōn *probāvisse Chrīstum esse* hominem *pessimum*. 11. Putō plūrimōs *hominēs* in Caelum *itūrōs esse*. 12. Dux arbitrātus est *optimum esse* flūmen statim trānsīre. 13. Caesarem certiōrem fēcit *barbarōs* tria mīlia passuum *iisse*. 14. Equitēs sine morā flūmen *trānsīre* jussit. 15. Lēgātus cōnstituit *oportēre sē* statim cum omnibus cōpiīs ad Caesarem *īre* ut eum contrā barbarōs adjuvāret. 16. Equitēs reppererunt hostēs jam in castra rediisse. 17. Tribūnus mīlitum scrīpsit sē in agrōs hostium

trānsitūrum esse. 18. Jūdaeī cōnstituērunt Pīlātum *adīre* ut Chrīstus occīderētur. 19. Chrīstus, dolōribus atque vulneribus *cōnfectus,* per viās ductus est. 20. Chrīstus sē ā manibus eōrum *ēripere* potuit, nam Deus erat. 21. Jūdaeī, cum Pīlātum Chrīstum *adjuvāre cōnārī* sēnsissent, eī dīxērunt Chrīstum sē rēgem *fēcisse.*

EXERCISE 466
Translate:

1. They were unable to go. 2. Caesar will not allow the Helvetians to go. 3. He said he would go within three days. 4. The centurion announced that the enemy had returned. 5. It behooved Caesar to visit Gaul. 6. They were ordered to go out of the camp. 7. They said they would return with greater forces. 8. He did not allow them to cross the river. 9. It is good to enter upon this plan. 10. They informed Caesar that the Gauls had gone three miles. 11. On account of the Roman soldiers they were unable to cross the river. 12. He determined to return on the third day.

EXERCISE 467
Translate:

Caesar, cum in Galliam pervēnisset, audīvit Helvētiōs per prōvinciam īre cōnstituisse ut in novōs agrōs pervenīrent. Helvētiī erant gēns Gallōrum quae prōvinciae proxima erat. Hī omnia quae ad iter pertinēbant parāverant quō facilius ex suīs fīnibus exīrent. Caesar vērō arbitrātus est oportēre sē eōs prohibēre. Itaque negāvit sē passūrum eōs per prōvinciam īre. Custōdēs collocāvit nē flūmen quod inter prōvinciam et agrōs eōrum erat trānsīrent. Eī autem cum omnibus suīs cōpiīs trānsīre multōs diēs cōnābantur. Caesar armīs eōs prohibēbat. Itaque, cum flūmen trānsīre et prōvinciam inīre nōn potuissent, alterā viā, difficiliōre et angustiōre, īre cōnstituērunt. Caesar, cum nuntiātum est eōs dē fīnibus suīs exiisse ut hāc viā in novōs agrōs īrent, statim cum omnibus suīs cōpiīs ē castrīs exiit et eōs secūtus est. Multōs diēs eōs secūtus est; tandem proeliīs eōs vīcit. Gallī, ā Caesare omnīnō superātī, sē suaque omnia eī dēdidērunt. Eōs in suōs fīnēs redīre jussit. Itaque rediērunt. Numquam enim Caesar passus est gentēs Galliae ex suīs fīnibus in aliōs trānsīre.

Answer in English:

1. Quid audīvit Caesar post adventum suum?
2. Ubi incolēbant Helvētiī?
3. Cūr per prōvinciam īre cōnstituērunt?
4. Nōnne omnia quae ad iter ūtilia sunt comparāvērunt?
5. Estne Caesar passus eōs ē fīnibus suīs exīre?
6. Quod flūmen trānsīre cōnātī sunt?
7. Potuēruntne id flūmen trānsīre?
8. Cūr nōn potuērunt flūmen trānsīre?
9. Quid tum fēcērunt?
10. Audīvitne Caesar eōs ē fīnibus suīs exiisse?
11. Estne Caesar eōs secūtus?
12. Putāsne Caesarem flūmen dē quō jam dēmōnstrāvimus trānsiisse?
13. Quibuscum profectus est Caesar?
14. Quot diēs eōs secūtus est?
15. Vīcitne eōs Caesar?
16. Rediēruntne Helvētiī in suōs agrōs, cum redīre ā Caesare jussī essent?
17. Num Caesar passus est aliās gentēs ex suīs fīnibus exīre?

READING NO. 44

THE CONDEMNATION OF CHRIST

Duōs aut trēs annōs Chrīstus Jūdaeōs[1] viam salūtis docuerat. Dē rēgnō caelōrum et dē voluntāte Patris suī eīs locūtus erat. Sē esse Fīlium Deī atque omnium hominum rēgem ostenderat. Bonam in omnēs hominēs voluntātem semper ostenderat. Omnēs ad sē vocāverat nam "Venīte," inquit, "ad mē." Omnēs recēperat; omnēs adjūverat. Tamen plūrimī prīncipēs Jūdaeōrum,[1] hominēs

---

[1] Jūdaeī, ōrum: the Jews.

pessimī, eum timēbant. Arbitrātī enim sunt eum rēgnum Jūdae-
ōrum¹ occupātūrum esse atque suum imperium sublātūrum esse.
Itaque hī cōnsilia capiēbant ut Chrīstum caperent et occīderent.
Ad eōs, cum cōnsilium caperent, vēnit ūnus dē discipulīs² Chrīstī,
nōmine Jūdas.³ Hic pollicitus est sē Chrīstum in manūs eōrum
trāditūrum esse. "Quid," inquit, "dabitis mihi et ego vōbīs eum
trādam?" At illī cōnstituērunt eī trīgintā⁴ argenteōs.⁵ Ex hōc
tempore Jūdas³ parātus erat Chrīstum trādere.

Chrīstus vērō post illam coenam⁶ in quā sacrāmentum⁷ sānctis-
simum nōbīs relīquit, ex urbe exīvit. Ēgressus, trāns flūmen quod
Cedron vocābātur trānsiit et in locum quod Gethsemani vocābātur
īvit. Cōnsuēverat enim in hunc locum cum amīcīs suīs sē recipere
ut ōrāret. Itaque hāc nocte, paucōs⁸ pedēs ab amīcīs prōgressus,
in terram cecidit et vehementer ōrāvit. Scīvit enim sē maximōs
dolōrēs prō nōbīs passūrum esse. Diū ōrāvit. "Nōn mea voluntās,"
inquit, "sed tua fīat."⁹ Post haec ad discipulōs² vēnit et illīs,
"Ecce,"¹⁰ inquit, "appropinquāvit hōra et Fīlius hominis trādētur
in manūs peccātōrum.¹¹ Eāmus; ecce appropinquāvit quī mē
trādet." Cum jam loquerētur, Jūdas,³ ūnus dē duodecim,¹² vēnit.
Cum eō autem erat manus mīlitum ā prīncipibus Jūdaeōrum
missa. Jūdas ad Chrīstum vēnit et eum osculātus¹³ est. Hoc autem
signum eīs dederat ut scīrent quis Chrīstus esset. Illī autem
Jēsūs, "Amīce," inquit, "ad quid vēnistī? Jūda, osculō¹⁴ Fīlium
hominis trādis?" Tum Jēsūs prōgressus ad eōs quī missī sunt.

---

¹ Jūdaeī, ōrum: *the Jews.*
² discipulus, ī: *disciple.*
³ Jūdas, ae: *Judas.* (Jūda is the vocative.)
⁴ trīgintā: *thirty.*
⁵ argenteus, ī: *piece of silver.*
⁶ coena, ae: *supper.*
⁷ sacrāmentum, ī: *sacrament.*
⁸ paucī, ae, a: *few.*
⁹ fīat: *be done.*
¹⁰ ecce: *behold.*
¹¹ peccātor, peccātōris: *sinner.*
¹² duodecim: *"the Twelve"* (i. e., *the twelve Apostles*).
¹³ osculor, 1, tr.: *kiss.*
¹⁴ osculum, ī: *a kiss.*

"Quem," inquit, "quaeritis?" Respondērunt eī, "Jēsūm Nazarēnum."[1] Eīs Jēsūs, "Ego," inquit, "sum." Cum dīxisset eīs, "Ego
sum," illī in terram cecidērunt. Rūrsus eōs rogāvit, "Quem
quaeritis?" Illī autem respondērunt, "Jēsūm Nazarēnum."[1] Respondit Jēsūs, "Dīxī vōbīs quia[2] ego sum. Sī[3] ergō[4] mē quaeritis,
sinite[5] hōs abīre."[6] Illī Chrīstum cēpērunt et ad concilium dūxērunt. Pontifex[7] eum
interrogāvit[8] dē discipulīs[9] ējus et dē doctrīnā[10] ējus. Respondit eī
Jēsūs: "Ego palam[11] locūtus sum mundō. Ego semper docuī in
synagōgā[12] et in templō,[13] quō omnēs Jūdaeī conveniunt; et in
occultō[14] locūtus sum nihil. Cūr mē interrogās?[8] Interrogā[8] eōs
quī audīvērunt quid locūtus sim. Ecce[15] hī sciunt quae dīxerim
ego."

Pontifex[7] interrogābat[8] eum: "Tū es Chrīstus Fīlius Deī bene-
dictī?"[16] Jēsūs autem illī, "Ego," inquit, "sum." Et omnēs clāmāvērunt[17] eum esse reum[18] mortis.

Itaque mane[19] Chrīstum ad Pīlātum dūxērunt. Exiit Pīlātus
ad eōs et rogāvit cūr Chrīstum ad sē dūxissent. Respondērunt
Chrīstum pessimum hominem esse. Pīlātus autem eīs, "Accipite,"
inquit, "vōs, et secundum[20] lēgem vestram jūdicāte eum." Dīxērunt

[1] Nazarēnus, a, um: *of Nazareth.*
[2] quia: *that* (introducing a noun clause as in English).
[3] sī, conj.: *if.*
[4] ergō, adv.: *therefore.*
[5] sinō, sinere, sīvī, situs, 3, tr.; acc. w. infin.: *allow, permit.*
[6] abeō, abīre, abiī, abitum, irreg., intr.: *go away.*
[7] pontifex, pontificis: *priest, high priest.*
[8] interrogō, 1, tr.: *question.*
[9] discipulus, ī: *disciple.*
[10] doctrīna, ae: *teaching.*
[11] palam, adv.: *openly.*
[12] synagōga, ae: *synagogue.*
[13] templum, ī: *temple.*
[14] in occultō: *in secret.*
[15] ecce: *behold.*
[16] benedictus, a, um: *blessed.*
[17] clāmō, 1, intr.: *shout.*
[18] reus, a, um: *guilty of.*
[19] mane, adv.: *in the morning.*
[20] secundum, prep. w. acc.: *according to.*

autem Jūdaeī sē nōn posse eum ad mortem dūcere. Itaque iniit Pīlātus et vocāvit Jēsūm et dīxit eī, "Tū es Rēx Jūdaeōrum?" Respondit Jēsūs, "Ā tēmetipsō¹ hoc dīcis an² aliī dīxērunt tibi dē mē?" Respondit Pīlātus: "Numquid³ ego Jūdaeus sum? Gēns tua et pontificēs⁴ trādidērunt tē mihi. Quid fēcistī?" Respondit Jēsūs: "Rēgnum meum nōn est dē hōc mundō; sī⁵ ex hōc mundō esset rēgnum meum, ministrī⁶ meī utique⁷ dēcertārent⁸ ut nōn trāderer Jūdaeīs: nunc autem rēgnum meum nōn est hinc."⁹ Itaque eī Pīlātus, "Ergō,"¹⁰ inquit, "rēx es tū?" Respondit Jēsūs: "Tū dīcis quia¹¹ rēx sum ego. Ego in hoc nātus¹² sum et ad hoc vēnī in mundum, ut testimōnium¹³ perhibeam¹⁴ vēritātī; omnis quī est ex vēritāte audit vōcem meam." Eī Pīlātus, "Quid," inquit, "est vēritās?" Et cum hoc dīxisset, rūrsus exiit ad Jūdaeōs et dīxit eīs sē nūllam causam in eō reperīre. Erat autem mōs dīmittere ūnum vinctum¹⁵ tempore Paschae.¹⁶ Itaque Pīlātus Jūdaeīs, "Dīmittamne vōbīs rēgem Jūdaeōrum?" Clāmāvērunt¹⁷ omnēs: "Nōn hunc, sed Barabbam.¹⁸ Tolle hunc! Et dīmitte nōbīs Barabbam."¹⁸ Erat autem Barabbas¹⁸ latrō.¹⁹

Illīs Pīlātus, "Quid," inquit, "faciam dē Jēsū quī vocātur

---

¹ tēmetipsō: *yourself* (an emphatic form).
² an: *or.*
³ numquid: an emphatic form of num.
⁴ pontifex, pontificis: *priest, high priest.*
⁵ sī, *conj.: if.*
⁶ minister, ministrī: *servant.*
⁷ utique, *adv.: certainly.*
⁸ dēcertō, *1, tr.: strive.*
⁹ hinc, *adv.: hence, from here.*
¹⁰ ergō, *adv.: therefore.*
¹¹ quia, *conj.: that* (introducing a noun clause as in English).
¹² nātus sum: *(I) was born.*
¹³ testimōnium, ī: *testimony.*
¹⁴ perhibeō, *2, tr.: give.*
¹⁵ vinctus, a, um: *bound* (i. e., *a prisoner*).
¹⁶ Pascha, ae: *the festival of the Pasch.*
¹⁷ clāmō, *1, intr.: shout.*
¹⁸ Barabbas, ae: *Barabbas.*
¹⁹ latrō, latrōnis: *a robber.*

CHRISTUS REX

Chrīstus?" Clāmābant¹ omnēs, "Crucifīgātur."² Illīs Pīlātus,
"Quid enim malī," inquit, "fēcit?" At illī rūrsus clāmābant,¹
"Crucifīgātur."²
Tum Pīlātus Chrīstum flagellārī³ jussit. Mīlitēs vērō, plectentēs⁴
corōnam⁵ spineam,⁶ imposuērunt⁷ capitī ējus et veste⁸ purpureā⁹
circumdedērunt¹⁰ eum. Et veniēbant ad eum et dīcēbant, "Avē,
Rēx Jūdaeōrum." Et dabant eī alapās.¹¹
Rūrsus exiit Pīlātus et dīxit Jūdaeīs: "Ecce addūcō vōbīs eum
ut cognōscātis mē nūllam causam in eō reperīre." Exiit Jēsūs.
Portābat autem corōnam⁵ spineam⁶ et purpuream⁹ vestem.⁸ Pīlātus
autem eīs, "Ecce,"¹² inquit, "homō!"
Prīncipēs Jūdaeōrum autem, cum eum vīdissent, clāmābant,¹
"Crucifīge,² crucifīge eum." Eīs Pīlātus: "Accipite," inquit, "vōs
et crucifīgite.² Ego enim nōn reperiō in eō causam." Respondērunt
eī Jūdaeī: "Nōs lēgem habēmus, et secundum¹³ lēgem oportet eum
interficī, quod Fīlium Deī sē fēcit." Haec Pīlātus cum audīvisset,
vehementer timuit. Rūrsus iniit et Jēsū, "Unde es," inquit, "tū?"
Jēsūs autem nihil respondit. Dīcit eī Pīlātus: "Mihi nōn loqueris?
Nescīs¹⁴ quia¹⁵ potestātem¹⁶ habeō crucifīgere² tē et potestātem¹⁶
habeō dīmittere tē?" Respondit Jēsūs: "Nōn habērēs¹⁷ potestātem¹⁶

---

¹ clāmō, *1, intr.: shout.*
² crucifīgō, crucifigere, crucifīxī, crucifīxus, *3, tr.: crucify.*
³ flagellō, *1, tr.: scourge.*
⁴ plectentēs: *platting.*
⁵ corōna, ae: *crown.*
⁶ spineus, a, um: *of thorns.*
⁷ impōnō, impōnere, imposuī, impositus, *3, tr.; w. dat.: put upon.*
⁸ vestis, vestis: *garment.*
⁹ purpureus, a, um: *purple.*
¹⁰ circumdō, circumdare, circumdedī, circumdatus, *1, tr.: clothe.*
¹¹ alapa, ae: *blow, slap.*
¹² ecce: *behold.*
¹³ secundum, *prep. w. acc.: according to.*
¹⁴ nesciō, nescīrī, nescīvī, *4, tr.: not know.*
¹⁵ quia: *that* (introducing a noun clause as in English).
¹⁶ potestās, potestātis: *power.*
¹⁷ nōn habērēs: *you would not have.*

adversum[1] mē ūllam, nisi tibi datum esset dēsuper.[2] Prŏptereā[3] quī mē trādidit tibi, mājus peccātum habet."

Ex hōc tempore cōnābātur Pīlātus eum dīmittere. Jūdaeī autem clāmābant:[4] "Sī[5] hunc dīmittis, nōn es amīcus Caesaris; omnis enim quī sē rēgem facit, contrādīcit[6] Caesarī." Pīlātus autem cum haec audīvisset, dīxit Jūdaeīs, "Ecce rēx vester." Illī autem clāmābant,[4] "Tolle! Tolle! Crucifīge[7] eum!" Pīlātus eīs, "Rēgem," inquit, "vestrum crucifīgam?"[7] Respondērunt prīncipēs Jūdaeōrum, "Nōn habēmus rēgem, nisi Caesarem." Itaque Pīlātus, Caesarem atque Jūdaeōs veritus, Jēsūm eīs trādidit. Eum autem in locum quī Golgotha vocābātur dūxērunt atque ibi Jēsūm Chrīstum, Fīlium Deī, crucifīxērunt.[7]

---

[1] adversum, *prep. w. acc.: against.*
[2] dēsuper, *adv.: from above.*
[3] prŏptereā: *therefore.*
[4] clāmō, *1, intr.: shout.*
[5] sī, *conj.: if.*
[6] contrādīcō, contrādīcere, contrādīxī, contrādictum, *3, intr.; w. dat.: speak against.*
[7] crucifīgō, crucifīgere, crucifīxī, crucifīxus, *3, tr.: crucify.*

MASTERY REVIEW VOCABULARY NO. 3

[Units Six-Fourteen]

VERBS OF THE FIRST CONJUGATION

adōrō, *1, tr.*	*adore*
aestimō, *1, tr.; acc. w. infin.*	*think*
appellō, *1, tr.; two accs.*	*call* *call upon* *address*
appropinquō, *1, intr.; w. ad or dat.*	*draw near to* *approach*
cōnfirmō, *1, tr.; acc. w. infin.*	*encourage* *strengthen* *affirm*
dēmōnstrō, *1, tr.; acc. w. infin.*	*show* *point out*
exīstimō, *1, tr.; acc. w. infin.*	*think*
expugnō, *1, tr.*	*storm* *take by storm*
exspectō, *1, tr.*	*wait for* *wait*
jūdicō, *1, tr.; acc. w. infin.*	*judge*
līberō, *1, tr.; abl. of separation*	*free (from)*
nāvigō, *1, intr.*	*sail*
negō, *1, tr.; acc. w. infin.*	*deny* *say . . . not*
nuntiō, *1, tr.; acc. w. infin.*	*announce* *report*
pācō, *1, tr.*	*pacify*
probō, *1, tr.*	*approve* *prove*
putō, *1, tr.; acc. w. infin.*	*think*
rogō, *1, tr.*	*ask*

vastō, *1, tr.*	*lay waste* *ravage*
vocō, *1, tr.; two accs.*	*call*

VERBS OF THE SECOND CONJUGATION

commoveō, commovēre, commōvī, commōtus, 2, *tr.*	*alarm* *arouse*
doceō, docēre, docuī, doctus, 2, *tr.*[1]	*teach* *inform*
jubeō, jubēre, jussī, jussus, 2, *tr.; acc. w. infin.*	*order* *command*
moveō, movēre, mōvī, mōtus, 2, *tr.*	*move*
noceō, nocēre, nocuī, nocitūrus, 2, *intr.; w. dat.*	*do harm to* *injure*
pertineō, pertinēre, pertinuī, 2, *intr.; ad w. acc.*	*pertain to* *stretch to*
prohibeō, 2, *tr.; abl. of separation*	*ward off (from)* *prevent*
respondeō, respondēre, respondī, respōnsus, 2, *tr.; acc. w. infin.*	*answer*
valeō, valēre, valuī, valitūrus, 2, *intr.*	*am strong* *am well* *am influential*

VERBS OF THE THIRD CONJUGATION

addūcō, addūcere, addūxī, adductus, 3, *tr.*	*lead to* *lead on*
cadō, cadere, cecidī, cāsūrus, 3, *intr.*	*fall*
cernō, cernere, 3, *tr.*	*distinguish* *see*

---

[1] Doceō takes two accusatives when it means "teach *someone something*."

cognōscō, cognōscere, cognōvī, cognitus, 3, tr. — { *learn* / *find out* }

cōgō, cōgere, coēgī, coāctus, 3, tr. — { *collect* / *force* }

cōnsistō, cōnsistere, cōnstitī, 3, intr. — { *halt* / *take a position* }

cōnstituō, cōnstituere, cōnstituī, cōnstitūtus, 3, tr.; w. infin. — { *place* / *set up* / *decide* / *determine* }

cōnsuēvī, cōnsuētus, 3, tr. and intr.; w. infin.¹ — { *have accustomed* / *have become accustomed* / *am accustomed* }

contendō, contendere, contendī, 3, intr.; w. infin. — { *strive* / *contend* / *hasten* }

dēdō, dēdere, dēdidī, dēditus, 3, tr.² — { *give up* / *surrender* }

dēdūcō, dēdūcere, dēdūxī, dēductus, 3, tr. — { *lead* / *lead away* }

dēfendō, dēfendere, dēfendī, dēfēnsus, 3, tr.; abl. of separation — *defend*

dīcō, dīcere, dīxī, dictus, 3, tr.; acc. w. infin. — { *say* / *tell* }

dīligō, dīligere, dīlēxī, dīlēctus, 3, tr. — *love*

discēdō, discēdere, discessī, discessūrus, 3, intr. — { *depart* / *withdraw* }

incolō, incolere, incoluī, 3, tr. — { *inhabit* / *dwell in* }

ostendō, ostendere, ostendī, ostentus, 3, tr. — *show*

---

¹ The present tenses of cōnsuēvī are not common. Hence only the perfect indicative active and the perfect participle passive are given. BUT note that the perfect can have a PRESENT meaning and the pluperfect can have a PERFECT meaning.

² Dēdō *always* takes an object in Latin.

quaerō, quaerere, quaesīvī, quaesītus, 3, tr.	*seek* *ask*
regō, regere, rēxī, rēctus, 3, tr.	*direct* *rule*
relinquō, relinquere, relīquī, relictus, 3, tr.	*leave* *leave behind*
scrībō, scrībere, scrīpsī, scrīptus, 3, tr.; acc. w. infin.	*write*
tollō, tollere, sustulī, sublātus, 3, tr.	*raise (up)* *take away*
trādūcō, trādūcere, trādūxī, trāductus, 3, tr.; two accs. or acc. and trāns w. acc.[1]	*lead across*

VERBS OF THE FOURTH CONJUGATION

audiō, 4, tr.; acc. w. infin.	*hear*
impediō, 4, tr.	*hinder* *impede*
perveniō, pervenīre, pervēnī, perventum, 4, intr.; in or ad w. acc.	*arrive*
reperiō, reperīre, repperī, repertus, 4, tr.; acc. w. infin.	*find (out)*
sciō, 4, tr.; acc. w. infin.	*know*
sentiō, sentīre, sēnsī, sēnsus, 4, tr.; acc. w. infin.	*feel* *perceive* *think*

-IŌ VERBS OF THE THIRD CONJUGATION

accipiō, accipere, accēpī, acceptus, 3, tr.	*receive* *accept*
capiō, capere, cēpī, captus, 3, tr.	*take* *capture*

---

[1] With **trādūcō** the thing OVER WHICH the direct object is led, is put either (1) in the accusative, or (2) with **trāns** in the accusative.

cōnficiō, cōnficere, cōnfēcī, cōnfectus, *3, tr.* — *finish / wear out*

conjiciō, conjicere, conjēcī, conjectus, *3, tr.* — *throw / hurl*

cōnspiciō, cōnspicere, cōnspexī, cōnspectus, *3, tr.* — *see / catch sight of*

cupiō, cupere, cupīvī, cupītus, *3, tr.; w. infin.* — *desire*

ēripiō, ēripere, ēripuī, ēreptus, *3, tr.;* ex (ē) *w.*
abl. — *take away / save (from)*

faciō, facere, fēcī, factus, *3, tr.* — *do / make*

fugiō, fugere, fūgī, fugitūrus, *3, tr.* — *flee*

interficiō, interficere, interfēcī, interfectus, *3, tr.*[1] — *kill*

recipiō, recipere, recēpī, receptus, *3, tr.* — *receive / accept / recover*

(with a reflexive pronoun mē, tē, sē, *etc.)* — *withdraw*

DEPONENT VERBS OF THE FIRST CONJUGATION

arbitror, arbitrārī, arbitrātus sum, *1, tr.; acc.*
w. infin.[2] — *think / consider*

cōnor, cōnārī, cōnātus sum, *1, tr.; w. infin.* — *try / attempt*

hortor, hortārī, hortātus sum, *1, tr.* — *urge / encourage*

DEPONENT VERBS OF THE SECOND CONJUGATION

polliceor, pollicērī, pollicitus sum, *2, tr.; acc.*
w. future infinitive — *promise*

vereor, verērī, veritus sum, *2, tr.; w. infin.* — *fear*

---

[1] The present system passive of **faciō** is irregular but almost all the compounds of **faciō**, such as **interficiō**, are regular.

[2] **Arbitror** takes the accusative with the infinitive (tense by relation) because it is a verb of *thinking*.

DEPONENT VERBS OF THE THIRD CONJUGATION

loquor, loquī, locūtus sum, *3, tr.*   *talk* / *speak*

proficīscor, proficīscī, profectus sum, *3, intr.;*   *set out*
    ad *w. acc.*

sequor, sequī, secūtus sum, *3, tr.*   *follow*

DEPONENT VERBS OF THE FOURTH CONJUGATION

orior, orīrī, ortus sum, *4, intr.*   *rise* / *arise*

DEPONENT -*IŌ* VERBS OF THE THIRD CONJUGATION

ēgredior, ēgredī, ēgressus sum, *3, intr.*   *go out*

patior, patī, passus sum, *3, tr.; acc. w. infin.*   *suffer* / *allow*

prōgredior, prōgredī, prōgressus sum, *3, intr.*   *advance*

VERBS LIKE *EŌ*

adeō, adīre, adiī, aditus, *irreg., tr.*   *go to* / *approach* / *visit*

eō, īre, īvī (iī), itum, *irreg., intr.*[1]   *go*

exeō, exīre, exiī, exitum, *irreg., intr.*   *go out*

ineō, inīre, iniī, initus, *irreg., tr.*   *go into* / *enter upon*

redeō, redīre, rediī, reditum, *irreg., intr.*   *return*

trānseō, trānsīre, trānsiī, trānsitus, *irreg., tr.*   *go across* / *cross*

---

[1] Compounds of eō like exeō and ineō are conjugated like eō, but note that the v is regularly dropped in the perfect stem of compounds.

IRREGULAR VERBS AND IDIOMS

absum, abesse, āfuī, āfutūrus, *intr.;* ab (ā) *w.*
abl.

$\left\{\begin{array}{l}am\ distant\\am\ away\end{array}\right.$

certiōrem (-ēs) facere; *acc. w. infin.;* dē *w.*
abl., *or an indirect question*[1]

to inform

inquit[2]

$\left\{\begin{array}{l}he\ says\\he\ said\end{array}\right.$

memoriā teneō, tenēre, tenuī, tentus, *2, tr.*

$\left\{\begin{array}{l}keep\ in\ memory\\remember\end{array}\right.$

miserēre nōbīs

have mercy on us

nactus, a, um[3]

$\left\{\begin{array}{l}having\ obtained\\having\ found\end{array}\right.$

oportet, oportēre, oportuit, *2, intr.; acc. w.*
infin.

it behooves[4]

possum, posse, potuī, *irreg.; w. infin.*

$\left\{\begin{array}{l}am\ able\\can\end{array}\right.$

praesum, praeesse, praefuī, praefutūrus, *intr.;*
w. dat.

$\left\{\begin{array}{l}am\ in\ command\ of\\am\ in\ charge\ of\end{array}\right.$

---

[1] Certiōrem (-ēs) is the comparative of certus. Literally the phrase certiōrem facere means *to make (someone) more certain.* Certiōrem (-ēs) will therefore always agree with the direct object of faciō.

[2] Inquit is always used with DIRECT quotations; that is, with quotations enclosed in QUOTATION MARKS.

[3] Nactus, a, um is the perfect participle of a deponent verb. Since, however, the other forms of this verb are not common, it is sufficient to learn only the participle, which is frequently used.

[4] In translating use *it is proper; should; it is necessary,* etc.

NOUNS OF THE FIRST DECLENSION

amīcitia, ae	*friendship*
aqua, ae	*water*
causa, ae	*cause*
fossa, ae	*ditch*
fuga, ae	*flight*
hōra, ae	*hour*
injūria, ae	{ *injustice* *wrong*
memoria, ae	*memory*
mora, ae	*delay*
nātūra, ae	*nature*
sententia, ae	{ *opinion* *vote*
vigilia, ae	*watch*
vīta, ae	*life*

MASCULINE NOUNS OF THE SECOND DECLENSION

animus, ī	{ *mind* *soul*
annus, ī	*year*
lēgātus, ī	{ *envoy* *lieutenant*
nuntius, ī	{ *messenger* *message*
socius, ī	*ally*
tribūnus, ī	*tribune*
ventus, ī	*wind*

NEUTER NOUNS OF THE SECOND DECLENSION

auxilia, auxiliōrum	*reinforcements*
auxilium, ī	$\begin{cases} help \\ aid \end{cases}$
concilium, ī	*council*
cōnsilium, ī	$\begin{cases} plan \\ counsel \end{cases}$
peccātum, ī	$\begin{cases} mistake \\ sin \ (\text{in Christian Latin}) \end{cases}$
praesidium, ī	$\begin{cases} garrison \\ protection \end{cases}$
vallum, ī	$\begin{cases} wall \\ rampart \end{cases}$

MASCULINE AND FEMININE NOUNS OF THE THIRD DECLENSION LIKE *LĒX*

auctōritās, auctōritātis	$\begin{cases} authority \\ influence \end{cases}$
custōs, custōdis	*guard*
dolor, dolōris	$\begin{cases} pain \\ sorrow \end{cases}$
labor, labōris	$\begin{cases} effort \\ toil \end{cases}$
magnitūdō, magnitūdinis	$\begin{cases} size \\ greatness \end{cases}$
mōs, mōris, *m.*[1]	$\begin{cases} custom \\ habit \end{cases}$
mūnītiō, mūnītiōnis	*fortification*
nēmō, nēminis, *m.*	*no one*
obses, obsidis, *c.*[2]	*hostage*

---

[1] The ablative of **mōs**, **mōre**, may be translated *according to custom*.

[2] **Obses** is marked *c* = common gender; that is, it may be either masculine or feminine, as hostages were men and women. However, use it as masculine unless it clearly refers to women.

ōrdō, ōrdinis, *m.*	*rank* (of soldiers)
pēs, pedis, *m.*	*foot* (part of body or measure of distance)
ratiō, ratiōnis[1]	{ *reason* *manner*
regiō, regiōnis	*region*
timor, timōris	*fear*
voluntās, voluntātis	{ *good will* *will*

NOUNS OF THE THIRD DECLENSION LIKE *PARS*

mēns, mentis	*mind*
nāvis, nāvis[2]	*ship*
nox, noctis	*night*

NEUTER NOUNS OF THE THIRD DECLENSION

caput, capitis	*head*
genus, generis, *n.*	{ *kind* *race*
tempus, temporis, *n.*	*time*

OTHER NOUNS

diēs, diēī, *m. (f.)*	*day*
manus, ūs, *f.*	{ *a band of men* *hand*
mare, maris[3]	*sea*
mīlia, mīlium, *neuter noun*	*thousands*

---

[1] **Ratiō** is used in a great number of meanings; the vocabulary gives only the most general idea of them. Be sure to translate **ratiō** into good English as the sense and context demand.

[2] The ablative may be either **nāvī** or **nāve**.

[3] **Mare** is declined like the neuter of **gravis, grave,** and NOT like **flūmen.**

mīlia passuum	*miles* (literally, *thousands of paces*)
mīlle passūs	*a mile* (literally, *a thousand paces*)
nihil, *indecl. noun*	*nothing*
passus, ūs	*pace* (a measure of distance)
rēs pūblica, reī pūblicae	$\begin{cases} state \\ republic \end{cases}$
satis, *indecl. noun w. gen.*	*enough*

PRONOUNS

hic, haec, hoc	*this* (pl., *these*)
ille, illa, illud	$\begin{cases} that \text{ (as a demonstrative)} \\ he, she, it \text{ (as a personal pronoun)} \end{cases}$
is, ea, id	$\begin{cases} that \text{ (as a demonstrative)} \\ he, she, it \text{ (as a personal pronoun)} \end{cases}$
quī, quae, quod	$\begin{cases} who \text{ } (whose, whom) \\ which \\ that \end{cases}$
quī, quae, quod	$\begin{cases} which? \\ what? \end{cases}$
quis, quid	$\begin{cases} who? \\ what? \end{cases}$
suus, a, um	$\begin{cases} his \text{ } (own) \\ her \text{ } (own) \\ its \text{ } (own) \\ their \text{ } (own) \end{cases}$

ADJECTIVES OF THE FIRST AND SECOND DECLENSION

adversus, a, um; *w. dat.*	*facing (towards)* *unfavorable*
aeternus, a, um	*eternal* *everlasting*
barbarus, a, um[1]	*barbarian*
certus, a, um	*certain* *sure*
lātus, a, um	*wide*
līber, lībera, līberum; *abl. of separation*	*free (from)*
novus, a, um	*new*
parātus, a, um; *w.* ad *or infin.*	*prepared (for)* *ready*
parvus, a, um	*small* *little*
prīmus, a, um	*first*
proximus, a, um; *w. dat.*	*nearest* *next*
quantus, a, um, *interrogative adj.*	*how large?* *how great?*
summus, a, um	*highest* *greatest* *very great*
tertius, a, um	*third*
tūtus, a, um; *abl. of separation*	*safe (from)*
vacuus, a, um; *abl. of separation*	*empty (of)*
vērus, a, um	*true*

---

[1] Barbarus can, of course, be used as a noun to mean *barbarian.*

OTHER ADJECTIVES

alius, alia, aliud	$\begin{cases} other \\ another \text{ (of more than two)} \end{cases}$
alter, altera, alterum	$\begin{cases} the\ one \\ the\ other \text{ (of two)} \end{cases}$
alter, altera, alterum ⎱ secundus, a, um ⎰	second
mīlle, *indecl. adj.*	thousand
neuter, neutra, neutrum	neither (of two)
nūllus, a, um	$\begin{cases} no \\ none \end{cases}$
quot, *indecl. adj.*[1]	how many?
sōlus, a, um	$\begin{cases} alone \\ only \text{ (as adjective)} \end{cases}$
tōtus, a, um	$\begin{cases} whole \\ all\ of \\ the\ whole\ of \end{cases}$
ūllus, a, um	any
uter, utra, utrum	which? (of two)
ūtilis, e; *w.* ad	useful (for)

ADVERBS

ācriter, *adv.*	$\begin{cases} bitterly \\ eagerly \end{cases}$
celeriter, *adv.*	swiftly
clam, *adv.*	secretly
cūr, *interrogative adv.*	why?
diū, *adv.*	$\begin{cases} a\ long\ time \\ long \end{cases}$
diūtius, *comparative adv.*	longer
facile, *adv.*	easily

---

[1] *Indecl.* means that the adjective quot never changes its form, no matter what form the noun may be with which it agrees.

facilius, *comparative adv.*	*more easily*
jam, *adv.*	$\begin{cases} \textit{already} \\ \textit{now (at that time)} \end{cases}$
numquam, *adv.*	*never*
omnīnō, *adv.*	$\begin{cases} \textit{at all} \text{ (with negatives like } \textbf{nōn}) \\ \textit{altogether} \\ \textit{in all} \text{ (with numerals)} \end{cases}$
plūrimum, *adv.*	$\begin{cases} \textit{very much} \\ \textit{very} \end{cases}$
praetereā, *adv.*	$\begin{cases} \textit{besides} \\ \textit{furthermore} \end{cases}$
prīmum, *adv.*	*first*
quam, *adv.*[1]	*than*
quam, *interrogative adv. of degree*	*how?*
quō, *interrogative adv.*[2]	$\begin{cases} \textit{whither?} \\ \textit{where} \ldots \textit{(to)?} \\ \textit{to what place?} \end{cases}$
rūrsus, *adv.*	*again*
satis, *adv.*	$\begin{cases} \textit{enough} \\ \textit{sufficiently} \end{cases}$
statim, *adv.*	$\begin{cases} \textit{at once} \\ \textit{immediately} \end{cases}$
subitō, *adv.*	*suddenly*
ubi, *interrogative adv.*[2]	*where?*
unde, *interrogative adv.*[2]	$\begin{cases} \textit{whence?} \\ \textit{from what place?} \\ \textit{where} \ldots \textit{from?} \end{cases}$
usque, *adv.*	*all the way*
vērō, *postpositive*[3]	$\begin{cases} \textit{in truth} \\ \textit{but} \end{cases}$

---

[1] Quam, *than*, takes the same case after as before it.

[2] Ubi, quō, and unde can all translate the English *where*. Ubi can be used only when the *where* refers to place IN WHICH and implies REST; quō can be used only when the *where* refers to place TO WHICH and implies MOTION or direction; unde can be used only when the *where* refers to place FROM WHICH and implies MOTION or direction.

[3] Vērō is postpositive, *i.e.*, it never stands first in a clause.

PREPOSITIONS

ab (ā), *prep. w. abl.*[1]	*from* *away from* *by* (agency)
ad, *prep. w. acc.*	*to* *until* *at* *for* (with adjectives)
ante, *prep. w. acc.*	*before*
apud, *prep. w. acc.*	*among* *in the presence of*
contrā, *prep. w. acc.*	*against* *opposite*
causā, *preceded by gen.*[2]	*for the sake of*
dē, *prep. w. abl.*	*concerning* *about* *down from* *from*
ex (ē), *prep. w. abl.*[3]	*out of* *from*
in, *prep. w. abl.*	*in* *on*
in, *prep. w. acc.*	*into* *in* *against* *upon* *onto* *on*
inter, *prep. w. acc.*	*between* *among*
sine, *prep. w. abl.*	*without*

---

[1] The form ā is never used before words beginning with a vowel or *h*.

[2] The ablative of causa is used as a preposition. It governs the GENITIVE and always stands AFTER the word it governs.

[3] The form ē is never used before words beginning with a vowel or *h*.

CONJUNCTIONS

at, *conj.*   *but*
cum, *conj.*   *when*
-que, *conj.*   *and*

OTHER WORDS AND IDIOMS

ā fronte $\begin{cases} in\ the\ front \\ from\ the\ front \end{cases}$

ā tergō $\begin{cases} in\ the\ rear \\ from\ the\ rear \end{cases}$

avē! *interjection*   *hail!*

LATIN-ENGLISH VOCABULARY

ā. *See* **ab.**

ā fronte, in the front, from the front.

ā tergō, in the rear, from the rear.

ab (ā), *prep. w. abl.,* by, from, away from.

absum, abesse, āfuī, āfutūrus, *intr.; ab (ā) w. abl.,* am away, am distant.

ac. *See* **atque.**

accipiō, accipere, accēpī, acceptus, *3, tr.,* receive, accept.

aciēs, aciēī, battle line.

ācriter, *adv.,* bitterly, eagerly.

ad, *prep. w. acc.,* to, until, at, for.

addūcō, addūcere, addūxī, adductus, *3, tr.,* lead to, lead on.

adeō, adīre, adiī, aditus, *irreg., tr.,* go to, approach, visit.

adjuvō, adjuvāre, adjūvī, adjūtus, *1, tr.,* help, aid.

administrō, *1, tr.,* manage, attend to.

adōrō, *1, tr.,* adore.

adventus, ūs, arrival, coming.

adversus, a, um; *w. dat.,* facing (towards), unfavorable; **rēs adversae, rērum adversārum,** adversity.

aestimō, *1, tr.; acc. w. infin.,* think.

aeternus, a, um, eternal, everlasting.

Africa, ae, Africa.

ager, agrī, field.

agmen, agminis, column (of soldiers), army (on the march).

Agnēs, Agnētis, Agnes.

agō, agere, ēgī, āctus, *3, tr.,* drive, do, act, treat; **grātiās agere,** to give thanks, to thank.

aliēnus, a, um, unfavorable, another's, foreign.

alius, alia, aliud, other, another (of more than two).

Alpēs, Alpium, *m.,* the Alps.

alter, altera, alterum, the one, the other (of two), second.

altus, a, um, high, deep.

Ambiorīx, Ambiorīgis, Ambiorix.

America, ae, America.

Americānus, a, um, American.

Americānus, ī, an American.

amīcitia, ae, friendship.

amīcus, ī, friend.

angustus, a, um, narrow.

animus, ī, mind, soul.

annus, ī, year.

ante, *prep. w. acc.,* before.

appellō, *1, tr.; two accs.,* call (upon), address.

Appius (ī) Claudius (ī), Appius Claudius (a Roman senator).

appropinquō, *1, intr.; w. ad or dat.,* draw near to, approach.

apud, *prep. w. acc.,* among, in the presence of.

aqua, ae, water.

arbitror, arbitrārī, arbitrātus sum, *1, tr.; acc. w. infin.,* think, consider.

arma, armōrum, arms.

at, *conj.,* but.

atque (ac), *conj.,* and.

auctōritās, auctōritātis, authority, influence.

audiō, *4, tr.; acc. w. infin.,* hear.

Augustus, ī, Augustus.

aut, *conj.,* or.

aut . . . aut, *conjs.,* either . . . or.

autem, *conj., postp.,* however.

auxilia, auxiliōrum, reinforcements.

auxilium, ī, help, aid.

avē! *interjection,* hail!

barbarus, a, um, barbarian.

barbarus, ī, a barbarian.

bellum, ī, war.

Benedictus, ī, Benedict.

Bethlehēm, *indecl. n.,* Bethlehem.

bonus, a, um, good.

brevis, e, short.

489

Britannia, ae, Great Britain.

Britannus, ī, a Briton.

cadō, cadere, cecidī, cāsūrus, *3, intr.,* fall.

caedēs, caedis, slaughter.

caelum, ī, sky, heaven.

Caesar, Caesaris, Caesar.

capiō, capere, cēpī, captus, *3, tr.,* take, capture; **cōnsilium capere,** to make a plan.

caput, capitis, head.

Carthāginiēnsēs, Carthāginiēnsium, the Carthaginians.

castra, castrōrum, camp.

causa, ae, cause; **causā,** *w. gen.,* for the sake of.

cēdō, cēdere, cessī, cessūrus, *3, intr.,* give way, yield.

Cedron, *indecl. n.,* Cedron.

celeriter, *adv.,* swiftly.

centum, one hundred.

centuriō, centuriōnis, a centurion.

cernō, cernere, *3, tr.,* distinguish, see.

certiōrem (-ēs) facere; *acc. w. infin.; dē w. abl.,* to inform.

certus, a, um, certain, sure; **certiōrem (-ēs) facere;** *acc. w. infin.; dē w. abl.,* to inform.

Chrīstiānus, a, um, Christian.

Chrīstiānus, ī, a Christian.

Chrīstus, ī, Christ.

Cicerō, Cicerōnis, Cicero.

Cīneas, Cīneae, *m.,* Cineas.

cīvitās, cīvitātis, state.

clam, *adv.,* secretly.

clāmor, clāmōris, shouting, shout.

cognōscō, cognōscere, cognōvī, cognitus, *3, tr.,* learn, find out.

cōgō, cōgere, coēgī, coāctus, *3, tr.,* collect, force.

collis, collis, *m.,* hill.

collocō, *1, tr.,* place, station.

Columbus, ī, Columbus.

commoveō, commovēre, commōvī, commōtus, *2, tr.,* alarm, arouse.

commūnis, e, common.

comparō, *1, tr.,* get, prepare.

compleō, complēre, complēvī, complētus, *2, tr.; w. abl.,* fill (with).

concilium, ī, council.

cōnficiō, cōnficere, cōnfēcī, cōnfectus, *3, tr.,* finish, wear out.

cōnfirmō, *1, tr.; acc. w. infin.,* affirm, encourage, strengthen.

conjiciō, conjicere, conjēcī, conjectus, *3, tr.,* throw, hurl; **in fugam conjicere,** to throw into flight.

cōnor, cōnārī, cōnātus sum, *1, tr.; w. infin.,* try, attempt.

cōnservō, *1, tr.,* preserve, spare.

cōnsilium, ī, plan, counsel; **cōnsilium capere,** to make a plan.

cōnsistō, cōnsistere, cōnstitī, *3, intr.,* halt, take a position.

cōnspiciō, cōnspicere, cōnspexī, cōnspectus, *3, tr.,* see, catch sight of.

cōnstituō, cōnstituere, cōnstituī, cōnstitūtus, *3, tr.; w. infin.,* place, set up, decide, determine.

cōnsuēvī, cōnsuētus, *3, tr. and intr.; w. infin.,* have accustomed, have become accustomed, am accustomed. (The present tenses of **cōnsuēvī** are not common. Hence only the perfect indicative active and the perfect participle passive are given. BUT note that the perfect CAN have a PRESENT meaning and the pluperfect can have a PERFECT meaning.)

contendō, contendere, contendī, *3, intr.; w. infin.,* strive, contend, hasten.

contineō, continēre, continuī, contentus, *2, tr.,* restrain, hold in.

contrā, *prep. w. acc.,* against, opposite.

conveniō, convenīre, convēnī, conventum, *4, intr.,* come together, assemble.

cōpia, ae, supply, abundance.

cōpiae, cōpiārum, *f.,* troops, forces.

corpus, corporis, *n.,* body.

Corregidor, *indecl. n.,* Corregidor.

cum, *conj.*, when.
cum, *prep. w. abl.*, with.
cupidus, a, um; *w. gen.*, eager, desirous.
cupiō, cupere, cupīvī, cupītus, *3, tr.; w. infin.*, desire.
cūr, *adv.*, why?
custōs, custōdis, guard.

dē, *prep. w. abl.*, concerning, about, down from, from.
decem, ten.
dēdō, dēdere, dēdidī, dēditus, *3, tr.*, give up, surrender.
dēdūcō, dēdūcere, dēdūxī, dēductus, *3, tr.*, lead, lead away.
dēfendō, dēfendere, dēfendī, dēfēnsus, *3, tr.*, defend.
dēmōnstrō, *1, tr.; acc. w. infin.*, show, point out.
Deus, Deī, God.
dīcō, dīcere, dīxī, dictus, *3, tr.; acc. w. infin.*, say, tell.
diēs, diēī, *m. (f.)*, day.
difficilis, e, difficult.
dīligō, dīligere, dīlēxī, dīlēctus, *3, tr.*, love.
dīmittō, dīmittere, dīmīsī, dīmissus, *3, tr.*, send away, dismiss.
Dioclētiānus, ī, Diocletian.
discēdō, discēdere, discessī, discessūrus, *3, intr.*, depart, withdraw.
diū, *adv.*, for a long time, long.
diūtius, *comparative adv.*, longer.
dō, dare, dedī, datus, *1, tr.*, give; in fugam dare, to put to flight; inter sē dare, to exchange.
doceō, docēre, docuī, doctus, *2, tr.; two accs.; acc. w. infin.*, teach, inform.
dolor, dolōris, pain, sorrow.
dominus, ī, master, Lord (in Christian Latin used of God or Christ).
dūcō, dūcere, dūxī, ductus, *3, tr.*, lead, guide.
duo, ae, o, two.
dux, ducis, leader.

ē. *See* ex.
ego, meī, I.
ēgredior, ēgredī, ēgressus sum, *3, intr.*, go out.
elephantus, ī, elephant.
enim, *conj., postp.*, for.
eō, īre, īvī (iī), itum, *irreg., intr.*, go.
Ēpīrus, ī, Epirus.
eques, equitis, horseman (*pl.*, cavalry).
equitātus, ūs, cavalry.
ēripiō, ēripere, ēripuī, ēreptus, *3, tr.; ex w. abl.*, take away, save (from).
et, *conj.*, and.
et . . . et, both . . . and.
etiam, *adv.*, also.
Eurōpa, ae, Europe.
ex (ē), *prep. w. abl.*, out of, from.
exeō, exīre, exiī, exitum, *irreg., intr.*, go out.
exercitus, ūs, army.
exīstimō, *1, tr.; acc. w. infin.*, think.
explōrō, *1, tr.*, reconnoiter, find out.
expugnō, *1, tr.*, storm, take by storm.
exspectō, *1, tr.*, wait for, wait.
exterior, ius, outer.
extrēmus, a, um, outermost.

Fabricius, ī, Fabricius.
facile, *adv.*, easily.
facilis, e, *easy.*
facilius, *comparative adv.*, more easily.
faciō, facere, fēcī, factus, *3, tr.*, do, make; iter facere, to march; certiōrem (-ēs) facere; *acc. w. infin.; dē w. abl.*, to inform.
ferē, *adv.*, almost.
fidēs, fideī, faith, reliability, faithfulness.
fīlius, ī, son.
fīnēs, fīnium, *m.*, territory.
fīnitimus, a, um; *w. dat.*, neighboring, next.
flūmen, flūminis, river.
fortis, e, brave, strong.
fortiter, *adv.*, bravely, strongly.
fortūna, ae, fortune.

fossa, ae, ditch.

frāter, frātris (frātrum), brother.

frūmentum, ī, grain (pl., crops).

fuga, ae, flight; in fugam conjicere, to throw into flight; in fugam dare, to put to flight.

fugiō, fugere, fūgī, fugitūrus, 3, tr., flee.

Gabriēl, Gabriēlis, Gabriel.

Galilaea, ae, Galilee.

Gallia, ae, Gaul.

Gallus, ī, a Gaul.

gēns, gentis, tribe.

genus, generis, n., kind, race.

Germānia, ae, Germany.

Germānus, ī, a German.

gerō, gerere, gessī, gestus, 3, tr., carry, carry on, wage (w. bellum).

Gethsemani, indecl. n., Gethsemani.

gladius, ī, sword.

glōria, ae, fame, glory.

Graecus, ī, a Greek.

grātia, ae, favor, influence, grace.

grātiae, grātiārum, thanks; grātiās agere, to give thanks, to thank.

gravis, e, heavy, severe, serious.

habeō, 2, tr., have.

Hannibal, Hannibalis, m., Hannibal (a great Carthaginian general who fought against the Romans).

Helvētiī, Helvētiōrum, the Helvetians.

hīberna, hībernōrum, winter quarters.

hic, haec, hoc, this.

Hispānia, ae, Spain.

Hispānicus, a, um, Spanish.

homō, hominis, man.

hōra, ae, hour.

hortor, hortārī, hortātus sum, 1, tr., urge, encourage.

hostis, hostis, enemy (in war).

ibi, adv., there.

ille, illa, illud, that, he, she, it.

impedīmenta, impedīmentōrum, baggage, baggage train.

impediō, 4, tr., hinder, impede.

impedītus, a, um, encumbered, difficult.

imperātor, imperātōris, commander in chief, general, emperor.

imperium, ī, command, power, empire.

impetus, ūs, attack.

in, prep. w. abl., in, on; prep. w. acc., in, into, against, upon, onto, on, towards.

in fugam conjicere, to throw into flight.

in fugam dare, to put to flight.

in prīncipiō, in the beginning.

in saecula saeculōrum, world without end, forever.

incendō, incendere, incendī, incēnsus, 3, tr., set fire to, burn.

incitō, 1, tr., incite, arouse.

incolō, incolere, incoluī, 3, tr., inhabit, dwell in.

India, ae, India.

ineō, inīre, iniī, initus, irreg., tr., go into, enter upon.

injūria, ae, injustice, wrong.

inopia, ae, scarcity, want.

inquit, he says, he said.

īnstruō, īnstruere, īnstrūxī, īnstrúc-tus, 3, tr., draw up, equip.

integer, integra, integrum, fresh, un-injured, whole.

inter, prep. w. acc., between, among.

inter sē dare, to exchange.

interficiō, interficere, interfēcī, inter-fectus, 3, tr., kill.

interim, adv., meanwhile.

is, ea, id, that, he, she, it.

Isabella, ae, Isabella.

Israēl, Israēlis, Israel.

ita, adv., so, thus.

Italia, ae, Italy.

itaque, conj., therefore, and so.

iter, itineris, n., journey, march, route; iter facere, to march.

jam, adv., already, now (at that time).

Japō, Japōnis, a Japanese.

Japōnia, ae, Japan.

Jēsuīta, ae, *m.*, a Jesuit.

Jēsūs, ū (declined: Jēsūs, Jēsū, Jēsū, Jēsūm, Jēsū), Jesus.

Jōannēs, is, John.

Jōsēphus, ī, Joseph.

jubeō, jubēre, jussī, jussus, 2, *tr.; acc. w. infin.*, order, command.

Jūdaeus, ī, a Jew.

jūdicō, *1, tr.; acc. w. infin.*, judge.

Labiēnus, ī, Labienus.

labor, labōris, effort, toil.

Latīnē, *adv.*, in Latin.

lātus, a, um, wide.

laudō, *1, tr.*, praise.

lēgātus, ī, envoy, lieutenant.

legiō, legiōnis, *f.*, legion.

Leōnidās, Leōnidae, *m.*, Leonidas.

lēx, lēgis, law.

līber, lībera, līberum; *abl. of separ.*, free, free (from).

līberō, *1, tr.; abl. of separ.*, free (from).

litterae, litterārum, letter (an epistle), dispatch.

locus, ī (*pl.*, loca, locōrum), place.

longē, *adv.*, far, by far.

longus, a, um, long.

loquor, loquī, locūtus sum, *3, tr.*, talk, speak.

lūx, lūcis, light; prīmā lūce, at dawn.

magnitūdō, magnitūdinis, size, greatness.

magnus, a, um, great, large.

mājor, mājus, greater.

malus, a, um, bad.

maneō, manēre, mānsī, mānsūrus, 2, *intr.*, remain.

manus, ūs, *f.*, a band of men. hand.

Mārcus, ī, Marcus (a Roman name).

mare, maris, sea. (Mare is declined like the neuter of gravis, grave, and NOT like flūmen.)

Marīa, ae, Mary.

māter, mātris (mātrum), mother.

Mauricius, ī, Maurice.

Maximiānus, ī, Maximian.

maximus, a, um, greatest.

melior, ius, better.

memoria, ae, memory; memoriā tenēre, to keep in memory, to remember.

mēns, mentis, mind.

metus, ūs, fear.

meus, a, um, my, mine.

mīles, mīlitis, soldier; tribūnus (-ī) mīlitum, military tribune.

mīlia, mīlium, *neuter noun*, thousands; mīlia passuum, miles (literally, thousands of paces).

mīlle, *indecl. adj.* (*pl.*, mīlia, mīlium, *n.*), thousand; mīlle passūs, a mile (literally, a thousand paces).

minimus, a, um, smallest.

minor, minus, smaller.

miser, misera, miserum, wretched.

miserēre nōbīs, have mercy on us.

mittō, mittere, mīsī, missus, *3, tr.*, send.

moneō, *2, tr.*, warn, advise.

mōns, montis, *m.*, mountain.

mora, ae, delay.

mōre, according to custom.

mors, mortis, death.

mōs, mōris, *m.*, custom, habit; mōre, according to custom.

moveō, movēre, mōvī, mōtus, *2, tr.*, move.

multus, a, um, much (*pl.*, many).

mundus, ī, world.

mūniō, *4, tr.*, fortify, construct (*w. viam or viās*).

mūnītiō, mūnītiōnis, fortification.

mūrus, ī, wall.

nactus, a, um, having obtained, having found.

nam, *conj.*, for (when *for* means *because* and introduces a REASON).

nātūra, ae, nature.

nauta, ae, sailor.

nāvigō, *1, intr.*, sail.

nāvis, nāvis, ship.

nē, *conj. (in negative purpose clauses),* lest, in order that not, that not.

-ne, *particle used in questions.*

negō, *1, tr.; acc. w. infin.,* deny, say . . . not.

nēmō, nēminis, *m.,* no one.

neque, *conj.,* nor, and . . . not.

neque . . . neque, *conjs.,* neither . . . nor.

neuter, neutra, neutrum, neither (of two).

nihil, *indecl. noun,* nothing.

nōbilis, e, noble, renowned.

noceō, nocēre, nocuī, nocitūrus, *2, intr.; w. dat.,* do harm to, injure.

nōmen, nōminis, name; **nōmine,** named (by name).

nōn, *adv.,* not.

nōn possum, posse, potuī, *irreg., intr.; w. infin.,* am unable.

nōnne, *particle used in questions expecting an affirmative answer.*

nōs, nostrī, we.

noster, nostra, nostrum, our, ours.

novem, nine.

novus, a, um, new.

nox, noctis, night.

nūllus, a, um, no, none.

num, *particle used in questions expecting a negative answer.*

numerus, ī, number.

numquam, *adv.,* never.

nunc, *adv.,* now.

nuntiō, *1, tr.; acc. w. infin.,* announce, report.

nuntius, ī, messenger, message.

obses, obsidis, *c.,* hostage.

obtineō, obtinēre, obtinuī, obtentus, *2, tr.,* hold, occupy.

occīdō, occīdere, occīdī, occīsus, *3, tr.,* kill.

occupō, *1, tr.,* seize.

octō, eight.

omnīnō, *adv.,* at all *(w. negatives like nōn);* altogether, in all *(w. numerals).*

omnis, e, all, every.

oportet, oportēre, oportuit, *2, intr.; acc. w. infin.,* it behooves *(in translating use:* it is proper, should, it is necessary, *etc.).*

oppidum, ī, town.

oppugnō, *1, tr.,* attack, assault, storm.

optimus, a, um, best.

ōrātiō, ōrātiōnis, speech, prayer.

ōrdō, ōrdinis, *m.,* rank (of soldiers).

orior, orīrī, ortus sum, *4, intr.,* arise, rise.

ōrō, *1, tr.,* beg, pray.

ostendō, ostendere, ostendī, ostentus, *3, tr.,* show.

pācō, *1, tr.,* pacify.

parātus, a, um; *w. ad or infin.,* prepared (for), ready.

parō, *1, tr.; w. infin.,* prepare, get ready.

pars, partis, part.

parvus, a, um, small, little.

passus, ūs, pace (a measure of distance); **mīlle passūs,** a mile (literally, a thousand paces); **mīlia passuum,** miles (thousand of paces).

pater, patris (patrum), father.

patior, patī, passus sum, *3, tr.; acc. w. infin.,* suffer, allow.

Paulus, ī, Paul.

pāx, pācis, peace.

peccātum, ī, mistake, sin (in Christian Latin).

pējor, pējus, worse.

pellō, pellere, pepulī, pulsus, *3, tr.,* drive, repulse, rout.

per, *prep. w. acc.,* through.

perīculum, ī, danger.

pertineō, pertinēre, pertinuī, *2, intr.; ad w. acc.,* pertain to, stretch to.

perturbō, *1, tr.,* confuse, disturb.

perveniō, pervenīre, pervēnī, perventum, *4, intr.; in or ad w. acc.,* arrive.

pēs, pedis, *m.,* foot (part of body or measure of distance).

pessimus, a, um, worst.
petō, petere, petīvī, petītus, 3, tr.,
    seek, beg, request.
Petrus, ī, Peter.
Philippīnus, a, um, Philippine.
Pīlātus, ī, Pilate.
Pīsō (Pīsōnis) Aquītānus (ī), Piso
    Aquitanus.
plēnus, a, um; w. gen. or abl., full.
plūrēs, a, more.
plūrimī, ae, a, very many.
plūrimum, adv., very much, very.
plūrimus, a, um, most.
plūs, plūris, n.; w. gen., more.
polliceor, pollicērī, pollicitus sum, 2,
    tr.; acc. w. future infinitive, promise.
pōnō, pōnere, posuī, positus, 3, tr.,
    put, place, set, pitch (w. castra).
pōns, pontis, m., bridge.
populus, ī, people, nation.
porta, ae, gate.
portō, 1, tr., carry.
portus, ūs, harbor.
possum, posse, potuī, irreg., intr.; w.
    infin., am able, can.
post, prep. w. acc., after, behind.
posteā, adv., afterwards.
praemium, ī, reward.
praesidium, ī, garrison, protection.
praesum, praeesse, praefuī, praefu-
    tūrus, intr.; w. dat., am in com-
    mand of, am in charge of.
praetereā, adv., besides, furthermore.
premō, premere, pressī, pressus, 3,
    tr., press, press hard.
prīmā lūce, at dawn.
prīmum, adv., first.
prīmus, a, um, first.
prīnceps, prīncipis, chief, leading man.
prō, prep. w. abl., in front of (before),
    on behalf of (for).
probō, 1, tr., approve, prove.
proelium, ī, battle.
proficīscor, proficīscī, profectus sum,
    3, intr.; ad w. acc., set out.
prōgredior, prōgredī, prōgressus sum,
    3, intr., advance.

prohibeō, 2, tr.; abl. of separ., ward
    off (from), prevent.
propinquus, a, um, near.
propior, ius, nearer.
propter, prep. w. acc., on account of.
prōvincia, ae, province.
proximus, a, um; w. dat., nearest, next.
puer, puerī, boy.
pugnō, 1, intr., fight.
putō, 1, tr.; acc. w. infin., think.
Pyrrhus, ī, Pyrrhus.

quaerō, quaerere, quaesīvī, quaesītus,
    3, tr., seek, ask.
quam, adv., than (same case after as
    before); interrogative adv. of de-
    gree, how?
quantus, a, um, interrogative adj.,
    how large? how great?
quattuor, four.
-que, conj., and.
quī, quae, quod, relative pronoun,
    who (whose, whom), which, that;
    interrogative adj., which? what?
quīnque, five.
quis, quid, interrogative pronoun,
    who? what?
quō, interrogative adv., whither? to
    what place? where . . . (to) ?; conj.,
    in order that, that (before compara-
    tives in purpose clauses).
quod, conj., because.
quot, indecl. adj., how many?

ratiō, ratiōnis, reason, manner. Be
    sure to translate ratiō into good
    English as the sense and context
    demand. The vocabulary gives only
    the most general idea of the great
    number of meanings.
Ratislāus, Ratislāī, Ratislaus.
recipiō, recipere, recēpī, receptus, 3,
    tr., receive, accept, recover; w. a
    reflexive pronoun (mē, tē, sē, etc.),
    withdraw.
redeō, redīre, rediī, reditum, irreg.,
    intr., return.

rēgīna, ae, queen.

regiō, regiōnis, region.

rēgnum, ī, kingdom, royal power.

regō, regere, rēxī, rēctus, *3, tr.*, direct, rule.

relinquō, relinquere, relīquī, relictus, *3, tr.*, leave, leave behind.

reliquus, a, um, remaining, the rest of.

reperiō, reperīre, repperī, repertus, *4, tr.; acc. w. infin.*, find (out).

rēs, reī, thing, affair.

rēs adversae, rērum adversārum, adversity.

rēs pūblica, reī pūblicae, state, republic.

respondeō, respondēre, respondī, respōnsus, *2, tr.; acc. w. infin.*, answer.

retineō, retinēre, retinuī, retentus, *2, tr.*, hold back, keep.

rēx, rēgis, king.

Rhēnus, ī, the Rhine (a river).

rogō, *1, tr.*, ask.

Rōma, ae, Rome.

Rōmānus, a, um, Roman.

Rōmānus, ī, a Roman.

rūrsus, *adv.*, again.

saepe, *adv.*, often.

salūs, salūtis, safety, welfare, salvation.

sānctus, a, um, holy.

sānctus, ī; sāncta, ae, a saint.

satis, *adv.*, enough, sufficiently; *indecl. noun w. gen.*, enough.

sciō, *4, tr.; acc. w. infin.*, know.

Scīpiō, Scīpiōnis, Scipio (the name of several great Roman generals).

scrībō, scrībere, scrīpsī, scrīptus, *3, tr.; acc. w. infin.*, write.

secundus, a, um, second.

sed, *conj.*, but.

semper, *adv.*, always.

senātus, ūs, senate.

sententia, ae, opinion, vote.

sentiō, sentīre, sēnsī, sēnsus, *4, tr.; acc. w. infin.*, feel, perceive, think.

septem, seven.

sequor, sequī, secūtus sum, *3, tr.*, follow.

servō, *1, tr.*, guard, keep.

servus, ī, slave, servant.

sex, six.

Sicilia, ae, Sicily.

sīcut, *conj.*, as.

signum, ī, standard, signal, sign.

silva, ae, forest.

similis, e; *w. gen. or dat.*, like, similar.

sine, *prep. w. abl.*, without.

socius, ī, ally.

sōlus, a, um, alone, only (as adj.).

spēs, speī, hope.

spīritus, ūs, breath, spirit.

statim, *adv.*, at once, immediately.

subitō, *adv.*, suddenly.

suī (*third personal reflexive pronoun*, GR., No. 127), himself, herself, itself, themselves.

sum, esse, fuī, futūrus, *intr.*, am.

summus, a, um, highest, greatest, very great.

superior, ius, higher.

superō, *1, tr.*, overcome, conquer, surpass.

suprēmus, a, um, highest.

sustineō, sustinēre, sustinuī, sustentus, *2, tr.*, sustain, withstand.

suus, a, um, his (own), her (own), its (own), their (own).

tamen, *adv.*, nevertheless.

Tarentīnus, ī, an inhabitant of Tarentum, a Tarentine.

tēlum, ī, dart.

tempus, temporis, *n.*, time.

teneō, tenēre, tenuī, tentus, *2, tr.*, hold; memoriā tenēre, to keep in memory, to remember.

terra, ae, earth. land.

terreō, *2, tr.*, terrify.

tertius, a, um, third.

Thēbaius, a, um, Theban.

Thōmas, Thōmae, *m.*, Thomas.

Tiberis, is, *m.*, the Tiber (a river).

timeō, timēre, timuī, 2, tr.; w. infin.,
fear, am afraid.
timor, timōris, fear.
Titus, ī, Titus (a Roman name).
tollō, tollere, sustulī, sublātus, 3, tr.,
raise (up), take away.
tōtus, a, um, whole, all of, the whole
of.
trādō, trādere, trādidī, trāditus, 3,
tr., hand over.
trādūcō, trādūcere, trādūxī, trāductus, 3, tr.; two accs. or acc. and
trāns w. acc., lead across.
trāns, prep. w. acc., across.
trānseō, trānsīre, trānsiī, trānsitus,
irreg., tr., go across, cross.
trēs, tria, three.
tribūnus, ī, tribune; tribūnus (-ī)
mīlitum, military tribune.
tū, tuī, you (sing.).
tum, adv., then, at that time.
tūtus, a, um, safe (from).
tuus, a, um, your, yours (when referring to one person).

ubi, adv., where?
ūllus, a, um, any.
ulterior, ius, farther.
ultimus, a, um, farthest.
unde, adv., whence? from what place?
where . . . from?
undique, adv., from all sides, on all
sides.
ūnus, a, um, one.
urbs, urbis, city.
usque, adv., all the way.
ut, conj., in order that, that (in purpose clauses).
uter, utra, utrum, which? (of two).
ūtilis, e; w. ad, useful (for).

utinam, may, would that (used with
the subjunctive in wishes).

vacuus, a, um; abl. of separ., empty
(of).
valeō, valēre, valuī, valitūrus, 2, intr.,
am strong, am well, am influential.
vallum, ī, wall, rampart.
vastō, 1, tr., lay waste, ravage.
vehementer, adv., greatly, violently.
veniō, venīre, vēnī, ventum, 4, intr.,
come.
ventus, ī, wind.
vereor, verērī, veritus sum, 2, tr.; w.
infin., fear.
vēritās, vēritātis, truth.
vērō, adv., postp., in truth, but.
vērus, a, um, true.
vester, vestra, vestrum, your, yours
(when referring to more than one).
via, ae, road, way.
victōria, ae, victory.
videō, vidēre, vīdī, vīsus, 2, tr., see.
vigilia, ae, watch.
vincō, vincere, vīcī, victus, 3, tr., conquer.
vir, virī, man.
virtūs, virtūtis, courage, virtue.
vīta, ae, life.
vocō, 1, tr.; two accs., call.
voluntās, voluntātis, good will, will.
vōs, vestrī, you (pl.).
vōx, vōcis, voice, cry.
vulnus, vulneris, n., wound.

Washington, Washington (the city).
Washingtonius, ī, Washington
(George).

Xerxēs, Xerxis, Xerxes.

ENGLISH-LATIN VOCABULARY

able, am, possum, posse, potuī, *irreg.,*
intr.; w. infin.
about, dē, *prep. w. abl.*
abundance, cōpia, ae.
accept, accipiō, accipere, accēpī, acceptus, *3, tr.;* recipiō, recipere, recēpī, receptus, *3, tr.*
according to custom, mōre.
account of, on, propter, *prep. w. acc.*
accustomed, am, or have accustomed, cōnsuēvī, cōnsuētus, *3, tr. and intr.;*
w. infin.
across, trāns, *prep. w. acc.*
across, go, trānseō, trānsīre, trānsiī, trānsitus, *irreg., tr.*
across, lead, trādūcō, trādūcere, trādūxī, trāductus, *3, tr.; two accs. or acc. and trāns w. acc.*
act, agō, agere, ēgī, āctus, *3, tr.*
address, appellō, *1, tr.; two accs.*
adore, adōrō, *1, tr.*
advance, prōgredior, prōgredī, prōgressus sum, *3, intr.*
adversity, rēs adversae, rērum adversārum.
advise, moneō, *2, tr.*
affair, rēs, reī.
affirm, cōnfirmō, *1, tr.; acc. w. infin.*
afraid, am, timeō, timēre, timuī, *2, tr.;*
w. infin.
after, post, *prep. w. acc.*
afterwards, posteā, *adv.*
again, rūrsus, *adv.*
against, contrā, *prep. w. acc.;* in, *prep. w. acc.*
aid, auxilium, ī.
aid, adjuvō, adjuvāre, adjūvī, adjūtus, *1, tr.*
alarm, commoveō, commovēre, commōvī, commōtus, *2, tr.*
all, omnis, e.
all of, tōtus, a, um (GR., No. 84).
all the way, usque, *adv.*

allow, patior, patī, passus sum, *3, tr.;*
acc. w. infin.
ally, socius, ī.
almost, ferē, *adv.*
alone, sōlus, a, um (GR., No. 84).
Alps, Alpēs, Alpium, *m.*
already, jam, *adv.*
also, etiam, *adv.*
altogether, omnīnō, *adv.*
always, semper, *adv.*
am, sum, esse, fuī, futūrus, *intr.*
am able, possum, posse, potuī, *irreg.,*
intr.; w. infin.
am accustomed, cōnsuēvī, cōnsuētus,
3, intr.; w. infin.
am afraid, timeō, timēre, timuī, *2, tr.;*
w. infin.
am away, absum, abesse, āfuī, āfutūrus, *intr.; ab (ā) w. abl.*
am distant, absum, abesse, āfuī, āfutūrus, *intr.; ab (ā) w. abl.*
am in charge of, praesum, praeesse,
praefuī, praefutūrus, *intr.; w. dat.*
am in command of, praesum, praeesse,
praefuī, praefutūrus, *intr.; w. dat.*
am influential, valeō, valēre, valuī,
valitūrus, *2, intr.*
am strong, valeō, valēre, valuī, valitūrus, *2, intr.*
am well, valeō, valēre, valuī, valitūrus,
2, intr.
America, America, ae.
American, Americānus, a, um.
Americans, Americānī, Americānōrum.
among, apud, *prep. w. acc.;* inter,
prep. w. acc.
and, atque (ac) ; et ; -que, *conjs.*
and . . . not, neque, *conj.*
and so, itaque, *conj.*
announce, nuntiō, *1, tr.; acc. w. infin.*
another *(of more than two),* alius,
alia, aliud (GR., Nos. 85-86).
another's, aliēnus, a, um.

answer, respondeō, respondēre, respondī, respōnsus, 2, *tr.; acc. w. infin.*
any, ūllus, a, um (GR., No. 84).
apostle, apostolus, ī.
approach, adeō, adīre, adiī, aditus, *irreg., tr.;* appropinquō, 1, *intr.; w. ad or dat.*
approve, probō, 1, *tr.*
arise, orior, orīrī, ortus sum, 4, *intr.*
arms, arma, armōrum.
army, exercitus, ūs; (on the march), agmen, agminis.
arouse, commoveō, commovēre, commōvī, commōtus, 2, *tr.;* incitō, 1, *tr.*
arrival, adventus, ūs.
arrive, perveniō, pervenīre, pervēnī, perventum, 4, *intr.; in or ad w. acc.*
as, sīcut, *conj.*
ask, quaerō, quaerere, quaesīvī, quaesītus, 3, *tr.;* rogō, 1, *tr.*
assault, oppugnō, 1, *tr.*
assemble, conveniō, convenīre, convēnī, conventum, 4, *intr.*
at, ad, *prep. w. acc.*
at all *(w. negatives)*, omnīnō, *adv.*
at dawn, prīmā lūce.
at once, statim, *adv.*
at that time, tum, *adv.*
attack, impetus, ūs.
attack, oppugnō, 1, *tr.*
attempt, cōnor, cōnārī, cōnātus sum, 1, *tr.; w. infin.*
attend to, administrō, 1, *tr.*
Augustine, Augustīnus, ī.
Australia, Austrālia, ae.
authority, auctōritās, auctōritātis.
away, am, absum, abesse, āfuī, āfutūrus, *intr.; ab (ā) w. abl.*
away, lead, dēdūcō, dēdūcere, dēdūxī, dēductus, 3, *tr.*
away, send, dīmittō, dīmittere, dīmīsī, dīmissus, 3, *tr.*
away, take, ēripiō, ēripere, ēripuī, ēreptus, 3, *tr.;* tollō, tollere, sustulī, sublātus, 3, *tr.*
away from, ab (ā), *prep. w. abl.*

back, hold, retineō, retinēre, retinuī, retentus, 2, *tr.*
bad, malus, a, um.
baggage, impedīmenta, impedīmentōrum.
baggage train, impedīmenta, impedīmentōrum.
band of men, manus, ūs, *f.*
barbarian *(adj.)*, barbarus, a, um; *(noun)*, barbarus, ī.
Bataan. *Use the English form unchanged in Latin.*
battle, proelium, ī.
battle line, aciēs, aciēī.
be. *See* am.
because, quod, *conj.*
become accustomed, have, cōnsuēvī, cōnsuētus, 3, *tr. and intr.; w. infin.*
before *(time)*, ante, *prep. w. acc.; (place)*, prō, *prep. w. abl.*
beg, ōrō, 1, *tr.;* petō, petere, petīvī, petītus, 3, *tr.*
beginning, in the, in prīncipiō.
behalf of, on, prō, *prep. w. abl.*
behind, post, *prep. w. acc.;* **leave behind**, relinquō, relinquere, relīquī, relictus, 3, *tr.*
behooves, it, oportet, oportēre, oportuit, 2, *intr.; acc. w. infin.*
besides, praetereā, *adv.*
best, optimus, a, um.
better, melior, ius.
between, inter, *prep. w. acc.*
bitterly, ācriter, *adv.*
body, corpus, corporis, *n.*
both . . . and, et . . . et.
boy, puer, puerī.
brave, fortis, e.
bravely, fortiter, *adv.*
breath, spīritus, ūs.
bridge, pōns, pontis, *m.*
British, Britannī, Britannōrum.
brother, frāter, frātris (frātrum).
burn, incendō, incendere, incendī, incēnsus, 3, *tr.*
but, at, *conj.;* sed, *conj.;* vērō, *adv., postp.*

by, ab (ā), *prep. w. abl.*
by far, longē, *adv.*
by name, nōmine.

Caesar, Caesar, Caesaris.
call, vocō, *1, tr.; two accs.*
call (upon), appellō, *1, tr.; two accs.*
camp, castra, castrōrum; to pitch camp, castra pōnere.
can, possum, posse, potuī, *irreg., intr.; w. infin.*
capture, capiō, capere, cēpī, captus, *3, tr.*
carry, gerō, gerere, gessī, gestus, *3, tr.;* portō, *1, tr.*
carry on, gerō, gerere, gessī, gestus, *3, tr.*
Carthaginians, Carthāginiēnsēs, Carthāginiēnsium.
catch sight of, cōnspiciō, cōnspicere, cōnspexī, cōnspectus, *3, tr.*
cause, causa, ae.
cavalry, equitātus, ūs; equitēs, equitum.
centurion, centuriō, centuriōnis.
certain, certus, a, um.
charge of, am in, praesum, praeesse, praefuī, praefutūrus, *intr.; w. dat.*
chief, prīnceps, prīncipis.
Christ, Chrīstus, ī.
Christian *(adj.)*, Chrīstiānus, a, um; *(noun)*, Chrīstiānus, ī.
Cicero, Cicerō, Cicerōnis.
city, urbs, urbis.
collect, cōgō, cōgere, coēgī, coāctus, *3, tr.*
Columbus, Columbus, ī.
column (of soldiers), agmen, agminis.
come, veniō, venīre, vēnī, ventum, *4, intr.*
come together, conveniō, convenīre, convēnī, conventum, *4, intr.*
coming, adventus, ūs.
command, imperium, ī.
command, jubeō, jubēre, jussī, jussus, *2, tr.; acc. w. infin.*
command of, am in, praesum, prae-

esse, praefuī, praefutūrus, *intr.; w. dat.*
commander in chief, imperātor, imperātōris.
common, commūnis, e.
concerning, dē, *prep. w. abl.*
confuse, perturbō, *1, tr.*
conquer, superō, *1, tr.;* vincō, vincere, vīcī, victus, *3, tr.*
consider, arbitror, arbitrārī, arbitrātus sum, *1, tr.; acc. w. infin.*
construct, mūniō, *4, tr. (w. viam or viās).*
contend, contendō, contendere, contendī, *3, intr.; w. infin.*
council, concilium, ī.
counsel, cōnsilium, ī.
courage, virtūs, virtūtis.
crops, frūmenta, frūmentōrum.
cross, trānseō, trānsīre, trānsiī, trānsitus, *irreg., tr.*
cry, vōx, vōcis.
custom, mōs, mōris, *m.;* according to custom, mōre.

danger, perīculum, ī.
dart, tēlum, ī.
dawn, at, prīmā lūce.
day, diēs, diēī, *m. (f.).*
death, mors, mortis.
decide, cōnstituō, cōnstituere, cōnstituī, cōnstitūtus, *3, tr.; w. infin.*
deep, altus, a, um.
defend, dēfendō, dēfendere, dēfendī, dēfēnsus, *3, tr.; abl. of separ.*
delay, mora, ae.
deny, negō, *1, tr.; acc. w. infin.*
depart, discēdō, discēdere, discessī, discessūrus, *3, intr.*
desire, cupiō, cupere, cupīvī, cupītus, *3, tr.; w. infin.*
desirous, cupidus, a, um; *w. gen.*
determine, cōnstituō, cōnstituere, cōnstituī, cōnstitūtus, *3, tr.; w. infin.*
difficult, difficilis, e; impedītus, a, um.
direct, regō, regere, rēxī, rēctus, *3, tr.*

dismiss, dīmittō, dīmittere, dīmīsī, dīmissus, *3, tr.*

dispatch, litterae, litterārum.

distant, am, absum, abesse, āfuī, āfutūrus, *intr.; ab (ā) w. abl.*

distinguish, cernō, cernere, *3, tr.*

disturb, perturbō, *1, tr.*

ditch, fossa, ae.

do, agō, agere, ēgī, āctus, *3, tr.;* faciō, facere, fēcī, factus, *3, tr.*

do harm to, noceō, nocēre, nocuī, nocitūrus, *2, intr.; w. dat.*

down from, dē, *prep. w. abl.*

draw near to, appropinquō, *1, intr.; w. ad or dat.*

draw up, īnstruō, īnstruere, īnstrūxī, īnstrūctus, *3, tr.*

drive, agō, agere, ēgī, āctus, *3, tr.;* pellō, pellere, pepulī, pulsus, *3, tr.*

dwell in, incolō, incolere, incoluī, *3, tr.*

eager, cupidus, a, um; *w. gen.*

eagerly, ācriter, *adv.*

earth, terra, ae.

easily, facile, *adv.; more easily,* facilius, *comparative adv.*

easy, facilis, e.

effort, labor, labōris.

eight, octō.

either . . . or, aut . . . aut, *conjs.*

elephant, elephantus, ī.

emperor, imperātor, imperātōris.

empire, imperium, ī.

empty (of), vacuus, a, um; *abl. of separ.*

encourage, cōnfirmō, *1, tr.; acc. w. infin.;* hortor, hortārī, hortātus sum, *1, tr.*

encumbered, impedītus, a, um.

enemy (in war), hostis, hostis, *m.*

enough, satis, *adv. and indecl. noun w. gen.*

enter upon, ineō, inīre, iniī, initus, *irreg., tr.*

envoy, lēgātus, ī.

equip, īnstruō, īnstruere, īnstrūxī, īnstrūctus, *3, tr.*

eternal, aeternus, a, um.

everlasting, aeternus, a, um.

every, omnis, e.

exchange, inter sē dō, dare, dedī, datus, *1, tr.*

facing (towards), adversus, a, um; *w. dat.*

faith, fidēs, fideī.

faithfulness, fidēs, fideī.

fall, cadō, cadere, cecidī, cāsūrus, *3, intr.*

fame, glōria, ae.

far, longē, *adv.; by far,* longē, *adv.*

farther, ulterior, ius.

farthest, ultimus, a, um.

father, pater, patris (patrum).

favor, grātia, ae.

fear, metus, ūs; timor, timōris.

fear, timeō, timēre, timuī, *2, tr.; w. infin.;* vereor, verērī, veritus sum, *2, tr.; w. infin.*

feel, sentiō, sentīre, sēnsī, sēnsus, *4, tr.; acc. w. infin.*

field, ager, agrī.

fight, pugnō, *1, intr.*

fill (with), compleō, complēre, complēvī, complētus, *2, tr.; w. abl.*

find, reperiō, reperīre, repperī, repertus, *4, tr.; acc. w. infin.; having found,* nactus, a, um.

find out, cognōscō, cognōscere, cognōvī, cognitus, *3, tr.;* explōrō, *1, tr.;* reperiō, reperīre, repperī, repertus, *4, tr.; acc. w. infin.*

finish, cōnficiō, cōnficere, cōnfēcī, cōnfectus, *3, tr.*

fire to, set, incendō, incendere, incendī, incēnsus, *3, tr.*

first, prīmus, a, um; prīmum, *adv.*

five, quīnque.

flee, fugiō, fugere, fūgī, fugitūrus, *3, tr.*

flight, fuga, ae; *to put to flight, in* fugam dare; *to throw into flight,* in fugam conicere.

follow, sequor, sequī, secūtus sum, *3, tr.*

foot *(part of body or measure of distance)*, pēs, pedis, *m.*

for *(conj.)*, enim, *postp.;* nam *(when meaning is because and introduces a reason).*

for *(prep.)*, prō, *prep. w. abl.;* ad, *prep. w. acc. (w. adj.).*

for the sake of, causā *w. gen.*

force, cōgō, cōgere, coēgī, coāctus, *3, tr.*

forces *(a military term)*, cōpiae, cōpiārum, *f.*

foreign, aliēnus, a, um.

forest, silva, ae.

forever, in saecula saeculōrum.

fortification, mūnītiō, mūnītiōnis.

fortify, mūniō, *4, tr.*

fortune, fortūna, ae.

found, having, nactus, a, um.

four, quattuor.

France. *Use* Gallia, ae.

free, līber, lībera, līberum; free (from), līber, lībera, līberum; *abl. of separ.*

free (from), līberō, *1, tr.; abl. of separ.*

French. *Use* Gallī, Gallōrum.

fresh, integer, integra, integrum.

friend, amīcus, ī.

friendship, amīcitia, ae.

from, ab (ā), *prep. w. abl.;* dē, *prep. w. abl.;* ex (ē), *prep. w. abl.*

from all sides, undique, *adv.*

from the front, ā fronte.

from the rear, ā tergō.

from what place, unde.

front, from the, ā fronte.

front, in the, ā fronte.

front of, in, prō, *prep. w. abl.*

full, plēnus, a, um; *w. gen. or abl.*

furthermore, prabtereā, *adv.*

garrison, praesidium, ī.

gate, porta, ae.

Gaul *(the country)*, Gallia, ae.

Gaul *(an inhabitant of Gaul)*, Gallus, ī.

general, imperātor, imperātōris.

get, comparō, *1, tr.*

get ready, parō, *1, tr.; w. infin.*

give, dō, dare, dedī, datus, *1, tr.*

give thanks, grātiās agō, agere, ēgī, āctus, *3, tr.*

give up, dēdō, dēdere, dēdidī, dēditus, *3, tr.*

give way, cēdō, cēdere, cessī, cessūrus, *3, intr.*

glory, glōria, ae.

go, eō, īre, īvī (iī), itum, *irreg., intr.*

go across, trānseō, trānsīre, trānsiī, trānsitus, *irreg., tr.*

go into, ineō, inīre, iniī, initus, *irreg., tr.*

go out, ēgredior, ēgredī, ēgressus sum, *3, intr.;* exeō, exīre, exiī, exitum, *irreg., intr.*

go to, adeō, adīre, adiī, aditus, *irreg., tr.*

God, Deus, Deī.

good, bonus, a, um.

good will, voluntās, voluntātis.

grace *(in Christian Latin)*, grātia, ae.

grain *(pl., crops)*, frūmentum, ī.

Grant. *Use the English form unchanged in Latin.*

great, magnus, a, um; how great, quantus, a, um, *interrogative adj.*

greater, mājor, mājus.

greatest, maximus, a, um; summus, a, um.

greatly, vehementer, *adv.*

greatness, magnitūdō, magnitūdinis.

guard, custōs, custōdis.

guard, servō, *1, tr.*

guide, dūcō, dūcere, dūxī, ductus, *3, tr.*

habit, mōs, mōris, *m.*

hail, avē! *interjection.*

halt, cōnsistō, cōnsistere, cōnstitī, *3, intr.*

hand, manus, ūs, *f.*

hand over, trādō, trādere, trādidī, trāditus, *3, tr.*

Hannibal, Hannibal, Hannibalis, *m.*

harbor, portus, ūs.

harm to, do, noceō, nocēre, nocuī, nocitūrus, *2, intr.; w. dat.*

hasten, contendō, contendere, contendī, *3, intr.; w. infin.*
have, habeō, *2, tr.*
have accustomed, cōnsuēvī, cōnsuētus, *3, tr.; w. infin.*
have become accustomed, cōnsuēvī, cōnsuētus, *3, intr.; w. infin.*
have mercy on us, miserēre nōbīs.
he, *masc. of* is, ea, id *or of* ille, illa, illud.
head, caput, capitis.
hear, audiō, *4, tr.; acc. w. infin.*
heaven, caelum, ī.
heavy, gravis, e.
help, auxilium, ī.
help, adjuvō, adjuvāre, adjūvī, adjūtus, *1, tr.*
Helvetians, Helvētiī, Helvētiōrum.
her (own), suus, a, um.
herself, suī.
high, altus, a, um.
higher, superior, ius.
highest, summus, a, um; suprēmus, a, um.
hill, collis, collis, *m.*
himself, suī.
hinder, impediō, *4, tr.*
his (own), suus, a, um.
hold, obtineō, obtinēre, obtinuī, obtentus, *2, tr.;* teneō, tenēre, tenuī, tentus, *2, tr.*
hold back, retineō, retinēre, retinuī, retentus, *2, tr.*
hold in, contineō, continēre, continuī, contentus, *2, tr.*
holy, sānctus, a, um.
hope, spēs, speī.
horseman (*pl.,* cavalry), eques, equitis.
hostage, obses, obsidis, *c.*
hour, hōra, ae.
how, quam, *interrogative adv.*
how great, quantus, a, um, *interrogative adj.*
how large, quantus, a, um, *interrogative adj.*
how many, quot, *indecl. adj.*
however, autem, *conj., postp.*

hundred, one, centum.
hurl, conjiciō, conjicere, conjēcī, conjectus, *3, tr.*

I, ego, meī.
immediately, statim, *adv.*
impede, impediō, *4, tr.*
in, in, *prep. w. abl.;* in, *prep. w. acc.*
in all (*w.* numerals), omnīnō, *adv.*
in charge of, am, praesum, praeesse, praefutūrus, *intr.; w. dat.*
in command of, am, praesum, praeesse, praefuī, praefutūrus, *intr.; w. dat.*
in front of, prō, *prep. w. abl.*
in order that, ut, *conj. (in purpose clauses);* quō, *conj. (before comparatives).* (GR., No. 546.)
in order that not, nē, *conj. (in negative purpose clauses).* (GR., No. 546.)
in the beginning, in prīncipiō.
in the front, ā fronte.
in the presence of, apud, *prep. w. acc.*
in the rear, ā tergō.
in truth, vērō, *adv., postp.*
incite, incitō, *1, tr.*
influence, auctōritās, auctōritātis; grātia, ae.
influential, am, valeō, valēre, valuī, valitūrus, *2, intr.*
inform, certiōrem (-ēs) faciō, facere, fēcī, factus, *3, tr.; acc. w. infin.; dē w. abl.;* doceō, docēre, docuī, doctus, *2, tr.; two accs.; acc. w. infin.*
inhabit, incolō, incolere, incoluī, *3, tr.*
injure, noceō, nocēre, nocuī, nocitūrus, *2, intr.; w. dat.*
injustice, injūria, ae.
into, in, *prep. w. acc.*
it, is, ea, id; ille, illa, illud.
Italy, Italia, ae.
its (own), suus, a, um.
itself, suī.

Japan, Japōnia, ae.
Japanese, Japō, Japōnis.

Jesus, Jēsūs, ū (declined: Jēsūs, Jēsū, Jēsū, Jēsum, Jēsū).
Jew, Jūdaeus, ī.
journey, iter, itineris, *n.*
judge, jūdicō, *1, tr.; acc. w. infin.*

keep, retineō, retinēre, retinuī, retentus, *2, tr.;* servō, *1, tr.*
keep in memory, memoriā teneō, tenēre, tenuī, tentus, *2, tr.*
kill, interficiō, interficere, interfēcī, interfectus, *3, tr.;* occīdō, occīdere, occīdī, occīsus, *3, tr.*
kind, genus, generis, *n.*
king, rēx, rēgis.
kingdom, rēgnum, ī.
know, sciō, *4, tr.; acc. w. infin.*

Labienus, Labiēnus, ī.
land, terra, ae.
large, magnus, a, um; **how large**, quantus, a, um, *interrogative adj.*
law, lēx, lēgis.
lay waste, vastō, *1, tr.*
lead, dūcō, dūcere, dūxī, ductus, *3, tr.;* dēdūcō, dēdūcere, dēdūxī, dēductus, *3, tr.*
lead across, trādūcō, trādūcere, trādūxī, trāductus, *3, tr.; two accs. or acc. and trāns w. acc.*
lead away, dēdūcō, dēdūcere, dēdūxī, dēductus, *3, tr.*
lead on, addūcō, addūcere, addūxī, adductus, *3, tr.*
lead to, addūcō, addūcere, addūxī, adductus, *3, tr.*
leader, dux, ducis.
leading man, prīnceps, prīncipis.
learn, cognōscō, cognōscere, cognōvī, cognitus, *3, tr.*
leave, relinquō, relinquere, relīquī, relictus, *3, tr.*
leave behind, relinquō, relinquere, relīquī, relictus, *3, tr.*
legion, legiō, legiōnis, *f.*
lest, nē, *conj.* (in negative purpose clauses).

letter *(an epistle)*, litterae, litterārum.
lieutenant, lēgātus, ī.
life, vīta, ae.
light, lūx, lūcis.
like, similis, e; *w. gen. or dat.*
Lincoln. *Use the English form unchanged in Latin.*
little, parvus, a, um.
long, longus, a, um; diū, *adv.*
long time, for a, diū, *adv.*
longer, diūtius, *comparative adv.*
Lord, Dominus, ī (in Christian Latin used of God or Christ).
love, dīligō, dīligere, dīlēxī, dīlēctus, *3, tr.*

MacArthur. *Use the English form unchanged in Latin.*
make, faciō, facere, fēcī, factus, *3, tr.*
make a plan, cōnsilium capiō, capere, cēpī, captus, *3, tr.*
man, homō, hominis; vir, virī; **band of men**, manus, ūs, *f.*
manage, administrō, *1, tr.*
manner, ratiō, ratiōnis.
many, *plural of* multus, a, um; **how many**, quot, *indecl. adj.*
march, iter, itineris, *n.;* **to march**, iter facere.
Mary, Marīa, ae.
master, dominus, ī.
meanwhile, interim, *adv.*
memory, memoria, ae; **to keep in memory**, memoriā tenēre.
mercy on us, have, miserēre nōbīs.
message, nuntius, ī.
messenger, nuntius, ī.
mile (literally, a thousand paces), mīlle passūs; **miles**, mīlia passuum.
military tribune, tribūnus (-ī) mīlitum.
mind, animus, ī; mēns, mentis.
mine, meus, a, um.
mistake, peccātum, ī.
more *(adj.)*, plūrēs, a; *(noun)*, plūs, plūris, *n.; w. gen.*
most, plūrimus, a, um.

mother, māter, mātris (mātrum).
mountain, mōns, montis, *m.*
move, moveō, movēre, mōvī, mōtus,
2, *tr.*
much, multus, a, um.
my, meus, a, um.

name, nōmen, nōminis; named (by
name), nōmine.
Napoleon. *Use the English word unchanged in Latin.*
narrow, angustus, a, um.
nation, populus, ī.
nature, nātūra, ae.
near, propinquus, a, um.
near to, draw, appropinquō, *1, intr.;
w. ad or dat.*
nearer, propior, ius.
nearest, proximus, a, um; *w. dat.*
necessary, it is, oportet, oportēre,
oportuit, *2, intr.; acc. w. infin.*
neighboring, fīnitimus, a, um; *w. dat.*
neither *(of two)*, neuter, neutra, neutrum (GR., No. 88).
neither . . . nor, neque . . . neque,
conjs.
never, numquam, *adv.*
nevertheless, tamen, *adv.*
new, novus, a, um.
next, fīnitimus, a, um; *w. dat.;* proximus, a, um; *w. dat.*
night, nox, noctis.
nine, novem.
no, nūllus, a, um (GR., No. 84).
no one, nēmō, nēminis, *m.*
noble, nōbilis, e.
none, nūllus, a, um (GR., No. 84).
nor, neque, *conj.*
not, nōn, *adv.*
nothing, nihil, *indecl. noun.*
now, nunc, *adv.;* (at that time), jam,
adv.
number, numerus, ī.

obtained, having, nactus, a, um.
occupy, obtineō, obtinēre, obtinuī, obtentus, *2, tr.*

often, saepe, *adv.*
on, in, *prep. w. abl.;* in, *prep. w. acc.*
on account of, propter, *prep. w. acc.*
on all sides, undique, *adv.*
on behalf of, prō, *prep. w. abl.*
once, at, statim, *adv.*
one, ūnus, a, um; *(of two)*, alter,
altera, alterum (GR., No. 87).
one hundred, centum.
only, sōlus, a, um (GR., No. 84).
onto, in, *prep. w. acc.*
opinion, sententia, ae.
opposite, contrā, *prep. w. acc.*
or, aut, *conj.*
order, jubeō, jubēre, jussī, jussus, *2,
tr.; acc. w. infin.*
other, alius, alia, aliud (GR., No. 85);
(of two), alter, altera, alterum (GR.,
No. 87).
ought. *See* oportet.
our (ours), noster, nostra, nostrum.
out of, ex (ē), *prep. w. abl.*
outer, exterior, ius.
outermost, extrēmus, a, um.
overcome, superō, *1, tr.*

pace, passus, ūs.
pacify, pācō, *1, tr.*
pain, dolor, dolōris.
part, pars, partis.
Paul, Paulus, ī.
peace, pāx, pācis.
people, populus, ī.
perceive, sentiō, sentīre, sēnsī, sēnsus,
4, tr.; acc. w. infin.
pertain to, pertineō, pertinēre, pertinuī, *2, intr.; ad w. acc.*
Peter, Petrus, ī.
Pilate, Pīlātus, ī.
pitch, pōnō, pōnere, posuī, positus, *3,
tr. (w. castra).*
place, locus, ī *(pl.,* loca, locōrum)*;*
from what place, unde.
place, collocō, *1, tr.;* cōnstituō, cōnstituere, cōnstituī, cōnstitūtus, *3, tr.;
w. infin.;* pōnō, pōnere, posuī, positus, *3, tr.*

plan, cōnsilium, ī; to make a plan, cōnsilium capere.

point out, dēmōnstrō, *1, tr.; acc. w. infin.*

position, take a, cōnsistō, cōnsistere, cōnstitī, *3, intr.*

power, imperium, ī.

praise, laudō, *1, tr.*

pray, ōrō, *1, tr.*

prayer, ōrātiō, ōrātiōnis.

prepare, comparō, *1, tr.;* parō, *1, tr.; w. infin.*

prepared (for), parātus, a, um; *w. ad or infin.*

presence of, in the, apud, *prep. w. acc.*

preserve, cōnservō, *1, tr.*

press, premō, premere, pressī, pressus, *3, tr.*

press hard, premō, premere, pressī, pressus, *3, tr.*

prevent, prohibeō, *2, tr.; abl. of separ.*

promise, polliceor, pollicērī, pollicitus sum, *2, tr.; acc. w. future infinitive.*

proper, it is, oportet, oportēre, oportuit, *2, intr.; acc. w. infin.*

protection, praesidium, ī.

prove, probō, *1, tr.*

province, prōvincia, ae.

put, pōnō, pōnere, posuī, positus, *3, tr.*

put to flight, in fugam dō, dare, dedī, datus, *1, tr.*

race, genus, generis, *n.*

raise (up), tollō, tollere, sustulī, sublātus, *3, tr.*

rampart, vallum, ī.

rank (of soldiers), ōrdō, ōrdinis, *m.*

ravage, vastō, *1, tr.*

ready, parātus, a, um; *w. ad or infin.;* get ready, parō, *1, tr.; w. infin.*

rear, from the, ā tergō.

rear, in the, ā tergō.

reason, ratiō, ratiōnis.

receive, accipiō, accipere, accēpī, acceptus, *3, tr.;* recipiō, recipere, recēpī, receptus, *3, tr.*

reconnoiter, explōrō, *1, tr.*

recover, recipiō, recipere, recēpī, receptus, *3, tr.*

region, regiō, regiōnis.

reinforcements, auxilia, auxiliōrum.

reliability, fidēs, fideī.

remain, maneō, manēre, mānsī, mānsūrus, *2, intr.*

remaining, reliquus, a, um.

remember, memoriā teneō, tenēre, tenuī, tentus, *2, tr.*

renowned, nōbilis, e.

report, nuntiō, *1, tr.; acc. w. infin.*

republic, rēs pūblica, reī pūblicae.

repulse, pellō, pellere, pepulī, pulsus, *3, tr.*

request, petō, petere, petīvī, petītus, *3, tr.*

rest of, the, reliquus, a, um.

restrain, contineō, continēre, continuī, contentus, *2, tr.*

return, redeō, redīre, rediī, reditum, *irreg., intr.*

reward, praemium, ī.

rise, orior, orīrī, ortus sum, *4, intr.*

river, flūmen, flūminis.

road, via, ae.

Roman *(adj.),* Rōmānus, a, um; *(noun),* Rōmānus, ī.

Rome, Rōma, ae.

rout, pellō, pellere, pepulī, pulsus, *3, tr.*

route, iter, itineris, *n.*

royal power, rēgnum, ī.

rule, regō, regere, rēxī, rēctus, *3, tr.*

safe, tūtus, a, um; *abl. of separ.*

safety, salūs, salūtis.

said, he (she, it), inquit.

sail, nāvigō, *1, intr.*

sailor, nauta, ae.

saint, sānctus, ī; sāncta, ae.

sake of, for the, causā *w. gen.*

salvation, salūs, salūtis.

save (from), ēripiō, ēripere, ēripuī, ēreptus, *3, tr.*

say, dīcō, dīcere, dīxī, dictus, *3, tr.;*

acc. w. infin.; inquit (w. direct quotations).

say . . . not, negō, 1, tr.; acc. w. infin.

says, he (she, it), inquit.

scarcity, inopia, ae.

Scipio, Scīpiō, Scīpiōnis.

sea, mare, maris (declined like gravis, grave).

second, alter, altera, alterum; secundus, a, um (GR., Nos. 87, 826).

secretly, clam, adv.

see, cernō, cernere, 3, tr.; cōnspiciō, cōnspicere, cōnspexī, cōnspectus, 3, tr.; videō, vidēre, vīdī, vīsus, 2, tr.

seek, petō, petere, petīvī, petītus, 3, tr.; quaerō, quaerere, quaesīvī, quaesītus, 3, tr.

seize, occupō, 1, tr.

senate, senātus, ūs.

send, mittō, mittere, mīsī, missus, 3, tr.

send away, dīmittō, dīmittere, dīmīsī, dīmissus, 3, tr.

serious, gravis, e.

servant, servus, ī.

set, pōnō, pōnere, posuī, positus, 3, tr.

set fire to, incendō, incendere, incendī, incēnsus, 3, tr.

set out, proficīscor, proficīscī, profectus sum, 3, intr.; ad w. acc.

set up, cōnstituō, cōnstituere, cōnstituī, cōnstitūtus, 3, tr.; w. infin.

seven, septem.

severe, gravis, e.

she, fem. of is, ea, id or of ille, illa, illud.

ship, nāvis, nāvis.

short, brevis, e.

should. See oportet.

shout, clāmor, clāmōris.

shouting, clāmor, clāmōris.

show, dēmōnstrō, 1, tr.; acc. w. infin.; ostendō, ostendere, ostendī, ostentus, 3, tr.

Sicily, Sicilia, ae.

sides, from all, undique, adv.

sides, on all, undique, adv.

sight of, catch, cōnspiciō, cōnspicere, cōnspexī, cōnspectus, 3, tr.

sign, signum, ī.

signal, signum, ī.

similar, similis, e; w. gen. or dat.

sin, peccātum, ī.

six, sex.

size, magnitūdō, magnitūdinis.

sky, caelum, ī.

slaughter, caedēs, caedis.

slave, servus, ī.

small, parvus, a, um.

smaller, minor, minus.

smallest, minimus, a, um.

so, ita, adv.; and so, itaque, conj.

soldier, mīles, mīlitis.

son, fīlius, ī.

sorrow, dolor, dolōris.

soul, animus, ī.

spare, cōnservō, 1, tr.

speak, loquor, loquī, locūtus sum, 3, tr.

speech, ōrātiō, ōrātiōnis.

spirit, spīritus, ūs.

standard, signum, ī.

state, cīvitās, cīvitātis; rēs pūblica, reī pūblicae.

station, collocō, 1, tr.

storm, expugnō, 1, tr.; oppugnō, 1, tr.

storm, take by, expugnō, 1, tr.

strengthen, cōnfirmō, 1, tr.

stretch to, pertineō, pertinēre, pertinuī, 2, intr.; ad w. acc.

strive, contendō, contendere, contendī, 3, intr.; w. infin.

strong, fortis, e.

strong, am, valeō, valēre, valuī, valitūrus, 2, intr.

strongly, fortiter, adv.

suddenly, subitō, adv.

suffer, patior, patī, passus sum, 3, tr.; acc. w. infin.

sufficiently, satis, adv.

supply, cōpia, ae.

sure, certus, a, um.

surpass, superō, 1, tr.

surrender, dēdō, dēdere, dēdidī, dēditus, *3, tr.*

sustain, sustineō, sustinēre, sustinuī,
sustentus, *2, tr.*

swiftly, celeriter, *adv.*

sword, gladius, ī.

take, capiō, capere, cēpī, captus, *3, tr.*

take a position, cōnsistō, cōnsistere,
cōnstitī, *3, intr.*

take away, ēripiō, ēripere, ēripuī,
ēreptus, *3, tr.;* tollō, tollere, sustulī,
sublātus, *3, tr.*

take by storm, expugnō, *1, tr.*

talk, loquor, loquī, locūtus sum, *3, tr.*

teach, doceō, docēre, docuī, doctus,
2, tr.; two accs.; acc. w. infin.

tell, dīcō, dīcere, dīxī, dictus, *3, tr.;
acc. w. infin.*

ten, decem.

terrify, terreō, *2, tr.*

territory, fīnēs, fīnium, *m.*

than, quam, *adv.*, or GR. 777.

thank, grātiās agō, agere, ēgī, āctus,
3, tr. (person thanked in dat.).

thanks, grātiae, grātiārum; to give
thanks, grātiās agere.

that *(conj.)*, ut; quō *(before comparatives in purpose clauses,* GR., No.
546).

that *(demon. pronoun)*, is, ea, id; ille,
illa, illud; *(relative pronoun)*, quī,
quae, quod.

that not, nē, *conj. (in negative purpose clauses,* GR., No. 546).

their (own), suus, a, um.

themselves, suī.

then, tum, *adv.*

there, ibi, *adv.*

therefore, itaque, *conj.*

thing, rēs, reī.

think, aestimō, *1, tr.; acc. w. infin.;*
arbitror, arbitrārī, arbitrātus sum,
1, tr.; acc. w. infin.; exīstimō, *1, tr.;
acc. w. infin.;* putō, *1, tr.; acc. w.
infin.;* sentiō, sentīre, sēnsī, sēnsus,
4, tr.; acc. w. infin.

third, tertius, a, um.

this, hic, haec, hoc.

thousand, mīlle, *indecl. adj.*

thousands, mīlia, mīlium, *neuter noun.*

three, trēs, tria.

through, per, *prep. w. acc.*

throw, conjiciō, conjicere, conjēcī,
conjectus, *3, tr.*

throw into flight, in fugam conjiciō,
conjicere, conjēcī, conjectus, *3, tr.*

thus, ita, *adv.*

Tiber, Tiberis, is, *m.*

time, tempus, temporis, *n.; for a long
time, diū, *adv.*

to, ad, *prep. w. acc.*

to what place, quō, *interrogative adv.*

together, come, conveniō, convenīre,
convēnī, conventum, *4, intr.*

toil, labor, labōris.

towards, adversus, a, um; *w. dat.;*
in, *prep. w. acc.*

town, oppidum, ī.

treat, agō, agere, ēgī, āctus, *3, tr.*

tribe, gēns, gentis.

tribune, tribūnus, ī; military tribune,
tribūnus (-ī) mīlitum.

troops, cōpiae, cōpiārum, *f.*

true, vērus, a, um.

truth, vēritās, vēritātis; in truth,
vērō, *adv., postp.*

try, cōnor, cōnārī, cōnātus sum, *1, tr.;
w. infin.*

two, duo, ae, o.

unable, am, nōn possum, posse, potuī,
irreg., intr.; w. infin.

unfavorable, adversus, a, um; *w. dat.;*
aliēnus, a, um.

uninjured, integer, integra, integrum.

until, ad, *prep. w. acc.*

upon, in, *prep. w. acc.*

urge, hortor, hortārī, hortātus sum,
1, tr.

useful (for), ūtilis, e; *w. ad.*

Vandals, Vandaliī, Vandaliōrum.

very, plūrimum, *adv.*

very great, summus, a, um; maximus, a, um.
very many, plūrimī, ae, a.
very much, plūrimum, adv.
victory, victōria, ae.
violently, vehementer, adv.
virtue, virtūs, virtūtis.
visit, adeō, adīre, adiī, aditus, irreg., tr.
voice, vōx, vōcis.
vote, sententia, ae.

wage, gerō, gerere, gessī, gestus, 3, tr. (w. bellum).
wait, exspectō, 1, tr.
wait for, exspectō, 1, tr.
wall, mūrus, ī; vallum, ī.
want, inopia, ae.
war, bellum, ī.
ward off (from), prohibeō, 2, tr.; abl. of separ.
warn, moneō, 2, tr.
Washington, Washingtonius, ī.
waste, lay, vastō, 1, tr.
watch, vigilia, ae.
water, aqua, ae.
way, via, ae; all the way, usque, adv.; give way, cēdō, cēdere, cessī, cessūrus, 3, intr.
we, nōs, nostrī.
wear out, cōnficiō, cōnficere, cōnfēcī, cōnfectus, 3, tr.
welfare, salūs, salūtis.
well, am, valeō, valēre, valuī, valitūrus, 2, intr.
what (interrogative adj.), quī, quae, quod; (interrogative pronoun), quis, quid.
when, cum, conj.
whence, unde, interrogative adv.
where, ubi, adv.
where . . . from, unde, interrogative adv.
where . . . to, quō, interrogative adv.

which (interrogative adj.), quī, quae, quod; (relative pronoun), quī, quae, quod.
which (of two), uter, utra, utrum (GR., No. 88).
whither, quō, interrogative adv.
who (interrogative pronoun), quis, quid; (relative pronoun), quī, quae, quod.
whole, integer, integra, integrum; tōtus, a, um (GR., No. 84).
whole of, tōtus, a, um (GR., No. 84).
why, cūr, interrogative adv.
wide, lātus, a, um.
will, voluntās, voluntātis.
wind, ventus, ī.
winter quarters, hīberna, hībernōrum.
with, cum, prep. w. abl.
withdraw, discēdō, discēdere, discessī, discessūrus, 3, intr.; mē (tē, sē) recipiō, recipere, recēpī, receptus, 3, tr.
without, sine, prep. w. abl.
withstand, sustineō, sustinēre, sustinuī, sustentus, 2, tr.
world, mundus, ī; world without end, in saecula saeculōrum.
worse, pējor, pējus.
worst, pessimus, a, um.
would that, utinam (used with the subjunctive in wishes).
wound, vulnus, vulneris, n.
wretched, miser, misera, miserum.
write, scrībō, scrībere, scrīpsī, scrīptus, 3, tr.; acc. w. infin.
wrong, injūria, ae.

year, annus, ī.
yield, cēdō, cēdere, cessī, cessūrus, 3, intr.
you (sing.), tū, tuī; (pl.), vōs, vestrī.
your (yours), tuus, a, um (when referring to one person); vester, vestra, vestrum (when referring to more than one person).

INDEX[1]

[1] Short selections, stories, and prayers are listed only under *Readings* and *Prayers* in this index.